French Politicians and Elections

1951–1969

FRENCH POLITICIANS AND ELECTIONS 1951-1969

PHILIP M. WILLIAMS
with DAVID GOLDEY
and MARTIN HARRISON

CAMBRIDGE at the University Press 1970

Published by the Syndics of the Cambridge University Press
Bentley House, 200 Euston Road, London N.W.1
American Branch: 32 East 57th Street, New York, N.Y.10022

© Cambridge University Press 1970

Library of Congress Catalogue Card Number: 73-96104

Standard Book Numbers:
521 07709 5 clothbound
521 09608 1 paperback

Printed in Great Britain
at the University Printing House, Cambridge
(Brooke Crutchley, University Printer)

Contents

Contents

MAPS

TABLES

Overseas results omitted unless otherwise specified

Introduction

These articles reproduce the results of eighteen years' study, now concluded, of French politics and elections. They are divided into four groups separated both by time and by subject: the reign of the parties before 1958, the Algerian settlement, the tribulations of the Left under 'Gaulle deux', and finally the struggle for electoral power between the General's followers and his opponents. Two short unpublished pieces (chapters 1 and 9) and the first and last pages of chapter 10 should provide sufficient continuity for the articles to be read consecutively.

The Liberation was a race between the two most effective military and politico-administrative forces, the Gaullists and the Communist Party, to establish themselves in power. The former won the race in most of the country, the latter in much of the South—but the Communists then abandoned their untenable local positions to compete for power by legal means. In that struggle their competitors were the Free French leader, as yet without organised political backing, and two big rival movements, the Socialists and MRP (Christian Democrats) who favoured neither the plebiscitary democracy of the General nor the 'people's democracy' of the Party. The electorate overwhelmingly rejected the old order in October 1945, and a constitution promoted by the Communists (and half-heartedly approved by the Socialists) went down narrowly in May 1946; in October a makeshift compromise between the three main parties was reluctantly accepted by the voters against strong opposition from de Gaulle.

The General had resigned in exasperation—and in hope of recall—in January, after eighteen months of coalition government; in April 1947 he formed his own movement, which rapidly attracted massive support. A few weeks later the Communists too were out of office. The legal government was based on an Assembly chosen in November 1946 (at an election not contested by the Gaullists). Now it found its following in the country melting before the challenge of its strong and more dynamic rivals. To survive, the moderates of the Resistance had to call on the parliamentary aid of the moderates of the old order—the Radicals, the great party of the Third Republic, and the Conservatives, among whom survivors of Vichy were soon to recover a share of influence. This dependence inhibited any attempt at reform at home or, above all, in the French Empire—where any suggestion of liberalisation was pounced upon and denounced by the Gaullists.

Introduction

The new conservative majority, without the Socialists, was entrenched by the 1951 election (see chapter 2)—though it had been foreshadowed earlier. Within nine months of the election part of the Gaullist party had succumbed to the temptations of conservatism and office (chapter 3), and the rest followed with little delay. But repression in Morocco and Tunisia and above all war in Indo-China were having catastrophic consequences on France's position in Europe and therefore raising increasing doubts on the Right (especially among Gaullists) as well as on the Left. After a narrow failure in 1953 (chapter 4) Pierre Mendès-France was brought to power in 1954 to take responsibility for ending the Far Eastern war; but the National Assembly detested him and his reluctant and disparate majority was shattered over the problem of German rearmament (chapters 1 and 5). His successors contrived—just in time—to resolve the crises in Tunisia, Morocco and Black Africa, but not the far more serious struggle in Algeria, where the sympathies of ordinary Frenchmen soon became far more engaged on the side of their 'kith and kin'. Politicians of the Left, elected on a peace platform in January 1956 (see chapter 6) were soon condoning or even encouraging the excesses of the extreme war party. They were to find that they had tied their own hands, for the settlers would permit no compromise and the army would stand by the settlers. Political and constitutional restraints, painfully re-established at the end of Hitler's war, were now breaking down under the strain of the new conflict. This is the theme of a companion volume to this one: *Wars, Plots and Scandals in Post-war France.*

In May 1958 riotous settlers and conniving colonels destroyed the regime, for which no Frenchman was willing to risk his life. This crisis brought to power the man who had renounced it—temporarily as he believed—twelve long years before. A master of silence and ambiguity, he retained to an astonishing degree the confidence of all political sides; and few people believed that the restorer of the Republic in 1945 now meant to destroy it. He was more convinced than ever that the Constitution was the root of France's ills, and his first concern was to construct and win overwhelming acceptance for his favourite system ensuring the power and autonomy of the executive. To settle Algeria, the electorate would concede him anything; and the proposals he had adumbrated at Bayeux on 18 June 1946 were at last adopted by an overwhelming vote of the French people on 28 September 1958. Yet even the General, with all his prestige and power, could move only slowly and obscurely towards the eventual outcome: the independence of Algeria. This volume shows (chapters 9–12) the stages of this process in the handling of French opinion. The obstacles in Algeria, and especially in the army, are dealt with in *Wars, Plots and Scandals.*

Free of Algeria, de Gaulle could turn to his real aim: the strengthening of French influence in the world, to which most overseas possessions had now become an encumbrance instead of an asset. But though domestic politics were always subordinate in his mind to the international struggle, he did not regard them with indifference: though 'the individual advantage of Frenchmen' counted for nothing compared to the 'higher interest of France',[1] yet the national cause could be successfully promoted only if the people united in support of it. For this he had to shatter the parties which, he believed, had been responsible for keeping the country divided and for fostering petty quarrels among compatriots (chapters 7 and 8 give some basis for appreciating the justice of these charges). In appealing to the nationalist and conservative half of the country he had obvious advantages (though in pursuing a 'Left' policy in Algeria, and in some aspects of his foreign policy, he had made some deadly enemies in this sector of opinion). But outside this natural field of attraction de Gaulle was also remarkably successful at shattering the hold on their voters of the parties of the Left. The background and tactics are discussed in chapters 13–19.

As always the General sought to make his work irreversible, impossible for his pygmy successors to undo. With this in view he changed his own Constitution in 1962 (see chapter 13) to require direct election to the presidency; stood for re-election in 1965 to give himself another seven years at the task; and dispensed in 1968 with Georges Pompidou, as he had dismissed Michel Debré six years before. But though his strategy was often as skilful as ever, his tactics left more to be desired and his style was beginning to pall. In 1965 and 1967 the Gaullist victories at the polls were ambiguous (chapters 19–22) and in May 1968 the strong Fifth Republic proved as vulnerable to working-class discontent as the weak Fourth to military conspiracy exactly ten years before (chapter 23). If de Gaulle redressed the balance and won a record victory at the election a month later, he did so only by recourse to the very means he had always hitherto repudiated: the crude (and on this occasion blatantly preposterous) denunciation of a 'Communist conspiracy' (chapter 24). It was a method which had always been open to him—as to any Laniel or Pinay—but in the past he had scorned to win temporary advantage by appealing to some Frenchmen against others. By 1968 he was still a dazzling leader of the French Right—the men he had so deeply despised in 1940 and who had so bitterly detested him in 1962. He was no longer 'the man of the nation'.

[1] Cf. Charles de Gaulle, *Le Salut* (Paris, Plon, 1959), p. 28.

Acknowledgements

Each article gives the original date and place of publication and has been reproduced exactly as it first appeared, except for the correction of misprints and the occasional amendment or omission of cross-references where appropriate. The titles, list of abbreviations and footnotes keyed by symbol are new; so are Maps 1–20 (Map 21 appeared in my *Crisis and Compromise*, Longmans, 1964). The tables of results have been reproduced from the articles; the fullest are those on pages 140 and 273. Additional tables (nos. 20–2) have been provided giving results nationally and in selected constituencies.

Chapters 10 and 12 were written in collaboration with Professor Martin Harrison of the University of Keele (the former in our *De Gaulle's Republic*, Longmans, 1960); chapters 21 and 22 with Dr David Goldey of Lincoln College, Oxford. Chapters 2, 3 and 4 appeared in *The Fortnightly*; 5, 15, 16 and 18 in *Socialist Commentary*; 6 and 8 in *Political Studies*, published by the Oxford University Press; 7 in *The American Scholar*, published by Phi Beta Kappa; 14 in *The Guardian*; and chapters 11–13, 17 and 19–24 in *Parliamentary Affairs*, published by the Hansard Society. I am grateful to them all for permission to reprint, and above all to David Goldey for allowing me to include the two pieces on the crisis of 1968, which are his alone.

I am also grateful to Jean Brotherhood and Christine Woodland for invaluable help with typing and proof-correction, and for preparing the index; to David Goldey and Frank Wright for very useful criticism and advice in the selection of material; and to my friends in all French parties. I have freely exploited their knowledge and their kindness over many years; they have, of course, no responsibility for the results.

Abbreviations

APLE   Association parlementaire pour la liberté de l'enseignement (pro-clerical pressure-group)

ARLP   Alliance republicaine pour les libertés et le progrès (Tixier-Vignancour's extreme right-wing party)

ARS   Action républicaine et sociale (Conservative deputies who left Gaullists in 1951)

CAL   Comités d'action lycéens (rebel schoolboys 1968)

CAP   Certificat d'aptitude professionnel

CD   Centre démocrate (Lecanuet's party, drawn from MRP, moderate Conservatives and right-wing Radicals, 1965)

CDR   Centre démocratique et républicaine (bogus conservative party, 1967); *also* Comités de défense de la République (Gaullist combat organisations, 1968)

CFDT   Confédération française démocratique du travail (trade union federation formed 1964 from CFTC)

CFTC   Confédération française des travailleurs chrétiens (majority changed name to CFDT 1964; minority remain as small conservative Catholic trade union federation)

CGC   Confédération générale des cadres (white-collar and supervisory staffs' union)

CGT   Confédération générale du travail (largest trade union federation, Communist dominated)

CGT-FO   See FO

CIA   Central Intelligence Agency (of the US Government)

CNPF   Confédération nationale du patronat français (main employers' organisation)

CNR   Conseil national de la Résistance (war time organisation led by Bidault, who revived the name for his pro-OAS front, 1962)

CRS   Compagnies républicaines de sécurité (riot police)

CSP   Comités de salut public (revolutionary organisations of Algerian settlers, army officers and French Gaullists, 1958)

DCF   Démocratie chrétienne de France (Bidault's right-wing breakaway from MRP, 1958)

EDC   European Defence Community (rejected in French Assembly 1954)

FEN   Fédération de l'éducation nationale (main state teachers' organisation)

FER   Fédération des étudiants révolutionnaires (Trotskyite group, important in 1968 Events)

FGDS   Fédération de la gauche démocrate et socialiste (alliance of Socialists, Radicals and political clubs born of Mitterrand's presidental campaign in 1965)

Abbreviations

FLN   Front de libération nationale (Algerian nationalists)

FNSEA   Fédération nationale des syndicats d'exploitants agricoles (main peasant pressure-group)

FO   CGT-Force-Ouvrière (trade union federation, mainly in public sector, which split from CGT 1947; vaguely Socialist in outlook)

JCML   Jeunesses communistes marxistes-leninistes (Maoist group important in 1968 Events)

JCR   Jeunesses communistes révolutionnaires (Trotskyite group important in 1968 Events)

JEC   Jeunesses étudiantes chrétiennes (Catholic students)

MRP   Mouvement républicain populaire (Catholic party, merged into CD)

NATO   North Atlantic Treaty Organisation (military)

NDP   National Democratic Party (German extreme Right)

OAS   Organisation de l'armée secrète (Algerian military and settlers' civil war organisation; attempted terrorism in France, 1962)

ORTF   Office de Radiodiffusion–Télévision française (the State broadcasting service)

PCF   Parti communiste français

PDM   Progrès et démocratie moderne (Centre party developing out of CD; Duhamel's party)

PME   Petites et moyennes entreprises (small-business pressure-group)

PR   Proportional representation

PRL   Parti républicain de la liberté (right-wing party 1946)

PSU   Parti socialiste unifié (left-wing socialist party in Vth Republic)

RGR   Rassemblement des gauches républicaines (Centre group in IVth Republic linking Radical party to its allies; became right-wing Radicals' party organisation in 1956 election)

RGRIF Rassemblement des groupes républicains et des indépendants français (bogus conservative party, 1951 and 1956)

RI   Républicains indépendants (Conservative allies of Gaullists; Giscard d'Estaing's party)

RPF   Rassemblement du peuple français (de Gaulle's party, 1947–53)

RS   Républicains sociaux (Gaullist party after de Gaulle withdrew 1953)

RTF   Radiodiffusion-Télévision française (old name of ORTF)

RTL   Radio Luxembourg

SAS   Sections administratives spécialisées (army organisation for civil affairs in Algeria)

SFIO   Section française de l'Internationale ouvrière (the Socialist party)

SMIG   Salaire minimum interprofessionnel garanti (the minimum wage)

SNESup Syndicat national de l'enseignement supérieur (Left teacher's union)

UDR   Union pour la défense de la République (the Gaullist party 1968)

UDSR   Union démocratique et socialiste de la Résistance (small centre party of IVth Republic—Pleven's and Mitterrand's party)

UDT   Union démocratique du travail (Left Gaullist party 1958–62)

UDVᵉ   Union démocratique de la Vᵉ République (the Gaullist party 1967)

UEC   Union des étudiants communistes (Communist students)

UFD   Union des forces démocratiques (small left-centre party 1958; included Mendès-France; merged into PSU)

UNEF   Union nationale des étudiants français (the French national union of students)

UNR   Union pour la nouvelle République (the Gaullist party 1958; became UNR–UDT 1962)

Principal dates

1944	AUG.	Paris liberated.
1945	FEB.	*Yalta Conference.*
	MAY	*War ends in Europe.*
	,,	Rising in E. Algeria.
	OCT.	Referendum rejects old constitution, 15·7 m to 0·6 m; limits new Assembly, 10·8 m to 5·4 m (de Gaulle wins).
		Election: CP 161, Soc. 150, MRP 150, rest 125.
1946	JAN.	De Gaulle resigns; three-party government.
	MAY	Referendum; Left's constitution loses, 9·1 m to 10·3 m.
	JUNE	Election: CP 153, Soc. 129, MRP 169, rest 135.
	,,	De Gaulle outlines *his* constitution at Bayeaux.
	OCT.	Referendum; 'three-party' constitution voted, 9 m to 7·8 m.
	NOV.	Election: CP 183, Soc. 105, MRP 167, rest 163.
	DEC.	Indo-China war begins.
1947	JAN.	Auriol (Soc) elected President on 1st ballot.
	APR.	De Gaulle founds RPF.
	MAY	CP out of office.
	OCT.	Municipal elections: RPF victory.
	NOV.	Big violent strikes led by CP; CGT splits.
1948	FEB.	*CP coup in Prague.* MAR. *Berlin blockade begins.*
1949	JULY	Assembly ratifies Atlantic Pact, 395–189.
1950	MAY	Schuman Plan for European Coal and Steel Community.
	JUNE	*Korean War begins*; US pressure for German rearmament.
	OCT.	Defeat on Indo-China's border with Communist China.
1951	JUNE	Election: RPF 120, CP 101, Soc. 107, MRP 96, rest 203.
	AUG.	Socs. out of office. SEPT. Church schools subsidised.
	DEC.	Assembly ratifies Schuman Plan, 376–240.
1952	MAR.	Pinay PM, RPF split, Socs. oppose; repression in Tunisia.
	MAY	Last big CP riot in Paris. EDC treaty signed.
1953	JAN.	*Eisenhower President of USA.* MAR. *Stalin dies.*
	JUNE	Mendès-France defeated for PM in long crisis.
	AUG.	Big public-sector strikes. Sultan of Morocco deposed.
	DEC.	Coty (Cons.) elected President on 13th ballot.
1954	MAY	Dien-Bien-Phu falls (and the government).
	JUNE	Mendès-France PM for 7 months; CP, Socs. support; MRP out.
	JULY	Peace in Indo-China; talks on Tunisia.
	AUG.	Assembly defeats EDC 264–319; MRP into opposition.
	NOV.	Small-scale fighting begins in Algeria.
	DEC.	German rearmament accepted 287–260; CP into opposition.
1955	FEB.	Mendès out by 46 (on Tunisia; his policy approved JULY, 538–44).
	AUG.	Algerian war worse; Moroccan outbreak. NOV. Sultan restored.
1956	JAN.	Election: CP 150, Soc. 99, Cons. 97, MRP 84, Pouj. 50, rest 116.
	,,	Mollet first Soc. PM for 9 years; CP at first in majority.
	FEB.	Europeans riot in Algiers; Lacoste Minister for Algeria.
	JUNE	Defferre's home rule bill for Black Africa voted 446–98.
	NOV.	*Suez war. Russian tanks in Budapest.*
1957	JAN.	Terrorism, torture and first fascist plots in Algiers.
	JULY	Assembly votes Common Market treaty, 340–236.
	SEPT.	Assembly defeats mild Algerian reform, 253–279.

1958	FEB.	Sakiet (Tunisia) bombed: US/UK mediate.
	MAR.	Paris police riot. Constitutional reform defeated.
	APR.	Government beaten 255–321 on Tunisia and US/UK mediation.
	MAY	13th: Europeans riot in Algiers; 24th: Gaullists seize Corsica.
	JUNE	De Gaulle PM (329–224), Ministers include Mollet and Pinay (Finance).
	SEPT.	Referendum approves new constitution 17·7 m to 4·6 m.
	NOV.	Election: Gaull. 206, Right 195, CP 10, Soc. 47, rest 98.
1959	JAN.	De Gaulle President, Debré PM, Socs. out of office.
	SEPT.	De Gaulle promises Algeria self-determination.
1960	JAN.	Europeans' barricades in Algiers; army does not back them.
	FEB.	Soustelle dismissed (after Pinay, JAN.).
	„	First French A-bomb.
	MAR.	Kruschev visits Paris.
	NOV.	De Gaulle promises 'the Algerian Republic...one day'.
1961	JAN.	Referendum: self-determination approved, 15·2 m to 5 m.
	„	*Kennedy President of USA.*
	APR.	Four-day army putsch in Algiers; 5 months 'emergency' in Paris.
	AUG.	*Berlin Wall* (De Gaulle anti-USSR).
	SEPT.	OAS terrorism begins in Algiers; DEC. in Paris.
1962	FEB.	Police kill 8 on anti-OAS march; ½ m. attend funeral.
	MAR.	Evian treaty with FLN; APR. referendum, 17·5 m. to 1· 8m.
	APR.	Pompidou PM. MAY MRP Ministers resign over Europe.
	JULY	Algeria independent. AUG. De Gaulle escapes assassination.
	OCT.	Government censured by 40, dissolves. *Cuban missile crisis.*
		Referendum: direct election of President, 12·8 m to 7·9 m.
	NOV.	Election: Gaull. 268, CP 41, Soc. 65, rest 108.
1963	JAN.	De Gaulle vetoes British membership of Common Market.
	„	Franco-German treaty signed.
	MAR.–APR.	Miners' strike; government defeat.
	JULY	Test-ban treaty; France and China refuse to sign.
	SEPT.	Major deflation ('stabilisation plan').
	NOV.	*Kennedy assassinated, Johnson President of US.*
1964	JAN.	De Gaulle recognises Peking.
	FEB.	Socs. nominate Defferre for Presidency.
	SEPT.	De Gaulle in Latin America.
	OCT.	*Fall of Kruschev.*
	DEC.	Assembly votes for nuclear force, 278–178.
1965	JAN.	De Gaulle attacks dollar.
	FEB.	*U.S. bombs N. Vietnam.*
	MAY	Municipal elections; Gaullists fail.
	JUNE	Soc.–MRP federation breaks down, Defferre withdraws.
	JULY	'Empty chair' at Brussels for 6 months (on farm policy).
	DEC.	De Gaulle re-elected on 2nd ballot, 12·6 m to 10·5 m.
1966	JAN.	Debré at Finance (replacing Giscard), Faure at Agriculture.
	„	Compromise over Common Market. Ben Barka scandal breaks.
	APR.	De Gaulle leaves NATO; JUNE to USSR; SEPT. attacks US in Asia.
1967	MAR.	Election: Gaull. 244, CP 73, Left Fed. 121, rest 49.
	MAY	Special economic powers; censure fails by 8.
	JUNE	*Middle East War*; de Gaulle for Arabs— and (JULY) for Quebec.
1968	MAY	Student riots, then 9 m workers strike.
	JUNE	Election: Gaull. 360, CP 34, Fed. 57, rest 36.
	JULY	Couve de Murville PM, Debré at FO, Faure at Education.
	AUG.	*Soviet tanks in Prague.*
1969	APR.	Referendum: Senate reform rejected, 10·5 m to 11·9 m. De Gaulle resigns.
	JUNE.	Pompidou President on 2nd ballot, 10·7 m to 7·9 m (CP abstain).

PART I

THE REIGN
OF THE PARTIES

1 The balance-sheet of the Fourth Republic*

Before the defeat of 1940, France's population had long been stationary; her economy, unlike that of her neighbours, had failed to recover from the slump; her political system promoted men who evaded decision and responsibility and thwarted bold and active leaders; her national unity was pulverised by class conflict and defeatism. Both her citizens and her statesmen knew that another victory as costly in resources and lives as that of 1918 would utterly exhaust their country's strength. So economic and military Maginot-mindedness—the desire to contract out from a competitive and dangerous world—found their political counterpart in reluctant resignation to junior partnership with a stronger nation: Britain or Germany.

The war brought a reaction against this defeatist mood. National self-confidence was strong in the Resistance, which was based on groups having little power in pre-war France—Gaullist junior officers and officials, Christian Democratic intellectuals, Communist workers. These forces were swept into power by a demand for domestic revolution as well as for liberation from enemy occupation. The old elites had been discredited by their record before and during the war; and the national desire for change was ratified in October 1945, when 96% of the voters preferred an entirely new constitution to retention or even revision of the old one.

But the resistance groups were too suspicious of one another to risk a concentration of authority from which adversaries might profit. The Communists were frustrated in their bids for power, which had been widely expected to succeed—and they were stopped without recourse to General de Gaulle. To Frenchmen remembering Bonaparte and Boulanger, his strong extra-parliamentary presidency seemed too easily transformed into dictatorship. By 1947 Gaullists and Communists, so recently the two most powerful forces in France, were in violent opposition to one another and to the parliamentary system. This double challenge was successfully withstood by the skill, patience and guile of the centre-party leaders. But their achievement was negative: like Sieyès in the Revolution, they survived. Whereas in other spheres the quasi-revolutionary situation of 1944–6 brought profound changes—nationalisations, comprehensive social services, important

* Written in March 1958; unpublished.

administrative reforms—the reconstruction of the political system was much less thorough.

If many of the faults of the old constitution were reproduced in the new, it was not for want of innovating zeal or experimental ingenuity. The chief architects of the Fourth Republic were MRP, a new party born from the Christian Democratic Resistance, and the Socialists, an old one from whose ranks also many Resisters had come. Both hoped to replace the old individualist parliamentary regime by a system of disciplined parties, in which personal and group responsibilities could be enforced and not evaded. But some of their proposals were defeated, others failed in practice, and many were reversed in law or in fact when the political climate changed.

The regime of organised parties which they sponsored held sway in 1946–7, years of acute economic hardship. MRP and Socialist ministers were desperately resisting infiltration and demagogy by the Communists (still nominally their colleagues), and the coalition of the three strong parties presented a sullen country with an almost unexampled spectacle of disunity, spoils-seeking and intrigue. Then the Communists joined de Gaulle in the opposition, and the parties which had made the Fourth Republic were forced to turn to the despised survivors of the Third. These groups, the Radicals and Conservatives, retained their pre-war outlook: social and economic conservatism, political individualism, resistance to colonial progress. Exploiting the dislike of France's millions of peasants and small businessmen for economic controls, encouraged by the unpopularity (among voters and deputies alike) of the dominance of rigid party machines, courted by their less experienced successors for their skill in manœuvre and their marginal parliamentary votes, the representatives of the old order rapidly regained influence. None of the six prime ministers before July 1948, but nine of the twelve since, have been drawn from their ranks. And the constitutional revision of 1954 brought, as they desired, a partial return to the pre-war system.

During these years, internal problems gave way to external. Helped by foreign aid, the early post-war governments risked loss of votes by imposing high taxes to keep up industrial investment; their policy paid delayed dividends in increased production (50 per cent above the 1929 record by 1957) and rising real wages. Prices were stabilised, except during 18 months of the Korean war. But as domestic troubles eased, overseas dangers grew, as France came into conflict with first Indo-Chinese and then North African nationalism. Till 1954 the party most responsible for both questions was MRP; and its attitude was profoundly affected by the European policy launched early in 1950 by Robert Schuman.

His proposed Coal and Steel Community was intended both to settle the ancient quarrel with Germany and to overcome the pressure-groups which in many sectors of the economy still resisted expansion and modernisation. Conceived by technicians like Jean Monnet, supported by progressive Conservatives like Paul Reynaud as well as by MRP and Socialists, the 'Schuman Plan' was comfortably ratified late in 1951, despite Gaullist, Communist and protectionist attacks. But two changes had meanwhile occurred. The Socialists quarrelled with MRP, first over economic policy and later over clericalism, and by 1952 were in the opposition. And French leaders, reluctantly accepting German rearmament under allied pressure, decided to sell it to the electorate by linking it to the popular European idea. It was very largely to save the European Army, and with it the programme of European Union, that MRP sacrificed its liberal aims at home and overseas. But by 1953 its policies were meeting hostility not only from Communists and Socialists but also among nationalist Radicals and Gaullists, who opposed the loss of French sovereignty and increasingly (like Clemenceau in 1885) saw war in Indo-China as a disastrous diversion from Europe.

In 1954 the defeat at Dien Bien Phu crystallised this strange combination, and brought to power Pierre Mendès-France, an independent and very untypical Radical. In de Gaulle's government in 1945 he had proposed drastic measures against inflation, which were rejected; he resigned, and became the chief critic of later financial policy. But as prime minister his great energies were wholly absorbed by external affairs, where all his predecessors' chickens were coming home to roost. In making peace in Indo-China, and in opening negotiations for a settlement in Tunisia, he found wide support. It was the German problem that ruined him. There was no parliamentary majority for the European Army (which was why its sponsors had delayed bringing it to a vote). Mendès-France did so (after vainly seeking a compromise) but kept his cabinet neutral. When the Assembly rejected the treaty, the prime minister with great difficulty induced it to accept a rearmed Germany into NATO. But in thus saving the Atlantic alliance he earned the bitter enmity not only of the Communists but also of the ardent 'Europeans', especially in MRP.

Mendès-France's strength and weakness resembled de Gaulle's. Though his policies met much opposition (from colonialists and pressure-group spokesmen as well as from 'Europeans' and Communists), it was for his 'style' that he was most detested—and admired. Contemptuous of his rivals, he appealed to rank and file deputies against their party leaders, to young against old, to the country against the Assembly; and he aroused a widespread response. Early in 1955 he was ousted over his Tunisian policy (which under his successor the same Assembly ratified by a 12-to-1

5

majority). But his challenge to 'the system' continued to dominate French politics.

Yet there was a contradiction in his position. He won his reputation as an advocate of clear choices, despising the mere politicians who kept office by taking no decisions and making no enemies: a premier who based his power on popular support, not parliamentary intrigue: a resister, not a defeatist, who would assert France's place in the world and not merely react to the policies of others: a leader whose favourite theme was the need for Frenchmen to recover their self-respect and national pride. Yet over the European Army he had refused to choose; and overseas his practical policy was to withdraw from untenable positions. Few cared much when this was applied to French India, Indo-China, or even Tunisia. But Algeria had been French for well over a century, had had a large European population for generations, was represented in Parliament and administered as part of France. When revolt broke out in 1954, Mendès-France himself as prime minister unequivocally announced France's determination to remain.

In the election campaign in December 1955 almost every party and national leader called for a negotiated settlement; and the conservative coalition lost ground to all the parties of the Left (as well as to the Poujadists). But the new premier, the Socialist Guy Mollet, discovered on 6 February 1956 that the many poor Frenchmen of Algiers were as fearful of Arab rule as the few rich *colons*. Opinion at home was greatly affected by this demonstration; by the conversion of the Socialist leaders and their active use of the government's means of influencing the public; by the reticence of potential left-wing critics, unwilling to break with the Socialist party or upset a ministry which favoured working-class interests at home and progressive reforms in black Africa; by the terrorism and intransigence of the FLN; above all by resentment at repeated French retreats and humiliations before great powers and small.

The public reaction did not perhaps amount to the *sursaut national* for which Mendès-France had called (it stirred few Frenchmen to demand the severe economic sacrifices which a true war effort would have required). But it did discredit the advocates of concession. Their protests against abuses of power by the authorities—in Algiers or Paris—evoked but a limited response. Their eclipse could be seen in by-elections, in opinion polls, in the defection from Mendès-France of four-fifths of the Radical deputies, in the caution even of Communist attacks on the war, in the success of pro-war demonstrations and the failure of anti-war ones. The tiny crypto-fascist groups seized their chance to assert themselves. But the true spokesmen of the new outlook were Jacques Soustelle and Robert Lacoste, both former lieutenants and ministers of de Gaulle, both recently the leading *mendésistes* in their respective parties, but both, later still, successively governors of Algeria. They expressed the mood of defiance in which articulate public opinion came to favour a policy which destroyed Mendès-France's influence, alienated the Atlantic allies, and called forth the xenophobia, ruthlessness and intolerance too familiar in wars where men feel their country's future to be at stake.

Yet on the whole the balance-sheet of the Fourth Republic is far better than that of the Third. Population is rising, not stagnating; the economy shows progress, not decline; in foreign policy political leadership has sometimes been ahead of public opinion, not behind it; national unity has often been frayed, always challenged by the Communists, but never wholly disrupted or deliberately sabotaged as in the thirties; national self-confidence and self-respect are more evident than in the gloomy pre-war years (with results which are generally healthy, though sometimes inconvenient and even deplorable). It is in the liquidation of empire that the Fourth Republic has dismally failed; and this is a hard task for a nation conscious of weakness.

Even here, liberal Frenchmen have to their credit—notably in 'black Africa'—achievements which are not the less impressive for being almost unknown outside France. But as a rule the colonies (unlike Algeria) bored the electorate, and therefore most of the deputies. They were part-time concerns of overworked ministers: Indo-China was under the Colonial Office until 1950, Tunis and Morocco under the Foreign Ministry till 1954, Algeria under the Interior Department till 1956. Cabinets were too weak, too preoccupied with immediate survival to worry much about the remote future. And so policy was constantly made on the spot, not in Paris: the start of the Indo-China war in 1946, the arrest of the Tunisian ministers in 1952, the deposition of the Sultan of Morocco in 1953, the seizure of the Algerian rebel leaders in the Tunis plane in 1956, the Sakiet bombing in 1958 were all military or proconsular decisions taken without or even against orders from home. In this sphere the weaknesses of the political system proved truly disastrous. The Foreign Minister's comment on Sakiet may yet provide the epitaph for the Fourth Republic: 'We must defend what has been done.'*

These weaknesses are all too familiar. With a third of the deputies normally hostile to the parliamentary system, a vast range of opinion must be included in every majority, so that positive action is paralysed. Governments are formed by elaborate bargaining between parties which take office to obstruct the purposes of others as much as to promote their own. The

* Sakiet-sidi-Youssef is a Tunisian border village from which the FLN had raided Algeria. After warnings, the French air force bombarded it in February 1958 on a market day, and scored a direct hit—on the school. The subsequent American and British pressure on France brought down the government—and the regime.

defection of a handful of votes can upset most cabinets; thus quite small 'veto groups' can easily frustrate policies they dislike. Premiers are worn out after six months and discredited after two terms. Decisive, uncompromising leaders are always at a disadvantage, achieving office rarely and never holding it securely. Thus brokers and conciliators come to the top, men of prudence and guile, skilled at arranging deals and compromises, at concealing differences and postponing conflicts, at confusing issues and obscuring responsibilities.

There are of course explanations and compensations. The opinions of the electorate are deeply divided, and the Assembly merely mirrors their divisions. There are good historical reasons for fearing an overmighty executive. Continuity is preserved by the civil service—and by the fact that most governments are replicas of their predecessors. Even so, ministerial crises serve a purpose: major changes in policy often require the ritual sacrifice of a cabinet to make them acceptable. The politics of compromise are not always to be despised; in 1955 Edgar Faure (whose Moroccan policy later showed them at their very worst) carried with ease the Tunisian agreements on which Mendès-France had fallen.

But by 1958 criticism was becoming insistent. Among the deputies, indeed, drastic change still found no favour; their ingrained mistrust of authority was reinforced by their direct interest in controlling it, and their remedy for the complexity and unrealism of the constitution was to vote still more complicated and less realistic amendments to it. But the long shadow of General de Gaulle fell even within the 'windowless house' of the Palais Bourbon; and outside men were asking whether France could afford a system well-enough adapted to what was once called normality, but ineffective—even occasionally disastrous—in the new world of permanent crisis.

2 De Gaulle frustrated: the 1951 election*

British politicians are often reproached with living in the 1930's, and Americans with living in the 1860's. In France the memories of 1789 are still potent. The twentieth century battle over the distribution of the national income goes on, far more bitterly than in Britain; the nineteenth century struggle for parliamentary government remains undecided. But France is essentially a peasant country, and in the countryside the really important dividing line is still the eighteenth-century quarrel between clericalism and free thought. Rarely far from the minds of politicians, it transcends in electoral importance the more familiar issues of the cost of living and the burden of rearmament, the losses of nationalized industries and the slow pace of house building, the size of the social security bill and even the prices of farm produce. The demand for subsidies to the Catholic schools estranges MRP from the Socialists, despite their common faith in parliamentary democracy and their similar attitude to most social and industrial problems. It prevents any close alliance between two groups which have almost everything else in common—the Radical party and its allies, and the right-wing Independents and Peasants, both of them economic conservatives and political individualists, owing their strength to the personal influence of small-town and rural notables rather than to the power of modern mass organizations. It causes constant friction within General de Gaulle's Rassemblement du Peuple Français, the only movement which includes supporters drawn from both camps, and it would cause far more if the General were to come to power. In some areas, especially in the west, it is the only issue that really arouses passion, and everywhere it is of first-class importance. Only the rift separating the Communists from all the rest divides Frenchmen more deeply.

   At the liberation, the political balance was distorted. The authoritarian Right was discredited by Vichy; the Radicals and the moderate Conservatives were hampered both by their recent record and by their extreme individualism. Between them, these three groups held only a quarter of the seats in the National Assembly, the Communists and MRP having rather more, the Socialists less. The lost votes of the Conservatives went to MRP, which seemed the strongest available bulwark against Communism. Yet

* Originally entitled 'The French Elections'. From *The Fortnightly*, 1017 N.S., September 1951. (A cross-reference in the second sentence has been cut.)

even before the election of the Assembly, when General de Gaulle came out against the new constitution which MRP was supporting, he was able to seduce two-thirds of the party's voters. And in the municipal elections of October 1947, after he had assumed the leadership of the RPF, he reduced MRP from over a quarter to less than a tenth of the total vote, while the new movement, with 35 per cent leapt into the first place.

The Government parties faced an alarming prospect. The form of proportional representation used in 1945–1946 favours large parties,* and might well give Communists and Gaullists together a clear majority of the new Assembly, which would make parliamentary government impossible. Yet to MRP, any electoral reform would mean suicide, especially if it included a second ballot at which their Radical and Socialist partners could make anti-clerical alliances against them. At the last moment, the prolonged deadlock was broken through the device of *apparentement*. As before, each department formed a constituency (the biggest being divided), each party ran its own list, and there was only one ballot. But lists which made a declaration of *apparentement*, or alliance, could add their votes together and count them as a whole.[1] If any list or alliance won an absolute majority of the votes cast, it took all the seats; if not, PR was retained. And in any case within an alliance, PR was used to allocate its seats to its several members. Greater Paris, where the extremes are strongest, was exempted from the new régime, but a mathematical change in the method of allocating seats was introduced there, which assisted the weaker, that is, the Government parties.[2]

It took months of pre-election wrangling before the majority parties agreed to this compromise, and meanwhile prices were rising rapidly. It was not an impressive performance, and in the circumstances it is surprising that they did so well. As in 1946, six million of the 25 million electors did not vote, or spoiled their papers; they ranged from the Calais centenarian who declared that women never voted in her day and she was not going to begin at her age, to the wine-growing village near Carcassonne which staged an electoral strike to protest against the low price of wine. The worst-hit parties were those which predominated in 1946. MRP lost 2,700,000 of their five million supporters, the Socialists 668,000 of their 3,500,000, and the Communists 450,000 of their 5,500,000. About two million votes were cast for the

---

[1] Provided they belonged to an organization presenting lists in at least 30 departments. But this provision could be evaded by running bogus lists, to bring the national total up to 30—for example, the UDSR list in Hautes-Pyrénées, which received six votes.

[2] It did so with such effect that one member was elected for Paris, although he had forfeited his deposit. This was M. Guérard, a right-wing Independent, whose list had 2·43 per cent of the votes; to save his deposit he needed five per cent.

* As explained in P. M. Williams, *Crisis and Compromise* (Longmans, 1964), Appendix VI.

Radicals and their allies, and 2,500,000 for the right-wing Independents and Peasants—a loss of 200,000 for the former and a gain of only 35,000 for the latter, though both were contesting many more departments. The RPF, in its first general election, won second place, with four million votes. Yet recalling that the MRP deserters of 1951 were already unfaithful in 1946 and 1947, the change is astonishingly small. Between the two Marxist parties on the one hand and the three mainly clerical groupings (including the RPF) on the other, the shift of votes was little more than a million, and it was most marked in the parts of France where the hold of the Church, and the importance of the clerical issue, is weakest.

In votes, the democratic Left, Socialists and MRP, barely outnumbered the five million Communists, while the moderate conservatives of the 'fourth force' held a lead of half a million over the four million Gaullists. But in seats, the moderates on each side are nearly twice as strong as the extremists. The six main groups are roughly equal.[1] The new electoral law did just what its authors intended, both by changing the way in which votes were cast, and by affecting the allocation of seats. Wherever the Government had a chance of winning an absolute majority, and so securing all the seats in the constituency, their spokesmen could and did argue effectively that a vote for General de Gaulle was a vote for the Communists. More important, however, was the second factor, which enabled the four moderate parties to win 94 extra seats, 69 of them at the expense of the Communists.[2] The Gaullists only lost 25 seats by the change, since where they chose they could usually make alliances; in seven departments, in fact, they formed part of a winning coalition which secured all the seats. But in the other 32 constituencies where the pool was scooped, only the governmental parties benefited. Among them the Socialists did the least well, for they too had difficulty in making alliances.[3] Wherever the clerical issue predominated, a combination of Socialists and MRP was likely to frighten Socialists into abstention and

[1] RPF 118: Socialists 104: Communists 103: Right 98: RGR (mostly Radicals) 94: MRP 85. There are 24 overseas independents, many of whom will associate with one of the larger groups. One colonial seat remains to be filled in September.
[2] The same voting under the previous electoral system would have returned 172 Communists and 143 Gaullists—a clear, though bare majority of the 627 members. Compared with 1946, the RPF and Right would have gained 104 seats from MRP and four from the Socialists, who would have also lost two to the Communists and six to the Radicals.

Of the 94 seats won by changing the law, nine were secured by the new method of calculation in Paris, and 37 by the mere effect of *apparentement*—the combined votes of a coalition winning more seats than they would have done separately. Only half the gains (48 seats) were due to the absolute majority rule.

Luck was rather against the Government. With an extra 0·3 % of the votes in every constituency they would have won 11 more seats; to lose the same number, they would have had to lose ten times as many votes.
[3] They obtained 16 seats more than they would have done under the old system, compared with 23 extra for the Right, 26 for the Radicals and 29 for MRP.

MRP voters into Gaullism; so in the west, along the eastern frontier and in the Cevennes, the Socialists usually fought alone.

The Government parties achieved their object, but at a high price in apparent unfairness. A party's representation might bear very little relation to its own strength; for example, in the Hérault M. Jules Moch's Socialist list won three seats for less than 39,000 votes, while 69,000 Communists secured none. It bore still less relation to success or failure since the last election. The Radical Air Minister, M. Maroselli, increased his poll by 4,000, but lost his seat to a pro-Gaullist independent with less than half as many votes as himself. The Communists lost seats in two of the three departments where they did best, and the two most successful Socialists in the country were both beaten.[1]

Consequently, but not altogether fairly, the law has had a very bad press, both in France and here. *The Times* described it as a dangerous encouragement to election-rigging by others, as if this old French custom needed any more precedents than those of 1885, 1889 and 1919—to go no further back. Supporters of the British electoral system contrived to find something shocking in the French preference for a working majority rather than abstract justice. The Communists extolled the equity of the old system which in June 1946 gave them a seat for every 36,000 votes and the Radicals one for every 59,000, and denounced the iniquity of the new one, which gives the Radicals a seat for every 28,000 votes and the Communists one for every 52,000. General de Gaulle declared that the ordinary voter was disgusted by the dishonesty of the system, although the proportion of non-voters was exactly the same as in 1946, and no lower in the twelve departments where the old system was in force (because there were no *apparentements* at all) than it was elsewhere.[2] But there is a case for the law none the less. Given the complexity of French politics, a system which allows the voter to express two choices has its advantages; over most of the country he can vote for the coalition (for parliamentary government against the extremes) and within the coalition, for the left or the right; while in the areas where nothing matters but the Church schools, he can usually vote for a clerical alliance, and within it can opt for RPF or MRP. Moreover, the gap between electoral and parliamentary politics has long been a curse of French public life, and, since the parties of the centre are obliged to combine and compromise in the

[1] One of them was M. Ramadier, the ex-Premier, who was opposed in the Aveyron by a MRP-Radical-Right *apparentement*. When the Radicals realized that they were likely to defeat their old anti-clerical ally to put in a clerical, 70 of their local leaders actually issued an appeal to their supporters to vote for Ramadier, but it was too late.

[2] There were indeed fewer abstentions in Paris, where the new system did not apply: but so there were in 1946, when there was no difference between the Parisian and provincial systems. There were also more spoiled papers, 530,000 as against 360,000 five years ago. But this was probably due to the introduction of *panachage* (see penultimate numbered footnote).

Assembly, there is a good deal to be said for a device which drives the fact home to their intransigent supporters in the country.

Among the local contests, the most interesting was that in Lyons, partly because 'Paris is the capital of France, but Lyons is the capital of the Republic', but also because of the personalities involved. The Government leader was M. Herriot, President of the Assembly (the Speaker), mayor of the town for nearly half a century (the Communists long ago christened him '*le discrédit lyonnais*'), the most determined opponent of Gaullism, and the Grand Old Man of the régime. His list was allied with the Socialists, headed by M. André Philip, with a local MRP veteran named Guérin, and with a right-wing list led by M. Montel, a former vice-president of the parliamentary Gaullists who had not taken kindly to military discipline in politics. The RPF leader was M. Soustelle, national secretary of the movement and now its chairman in the Assembly. At the head of the Communist list was the local party secretary, but its principal figure was his second, M. Pierre Cot, once a Radical Minister and now the ablest fellow-traveller in Europe, who had migrated from his unsafe former seat in Savoie. The two retiring Communist deputies had been moved down to third and fifth places to make room for this pair. Finally there was a dissident Radical, M. Chambaretaud, who waged an independent and entertaining campaign against the electoral law: '*Pour élire Guérin votez pour Herriot, pour élire Philip votez pour Montel, pour la prosperité votez pour les faillis, si vous êtes contents votez pour les sortants, mais pour du nouveau votez Chambaretaud.*' He only got 8,000 votes, but his intervention was decisive, for the Government coalition missed the absolute majority by 600. The four strongest lists, Communists, RPF, Radicals and Right, won two seats each—the RPF gaining two and the Right one at the expense of MRP, which lost 40,000 votes and both its seats, and of M. Philip, who lost nearly half his votes and was beaten. French electors prefer a deputy who performs the local chores to one who achieves an international reputation at Strasbourg.

Despite their success in Lyons, the Gaullists were profoundly disappointed with the results of the election. In 1947 they had claimed six million votes, and really seemed to have united the right under one banner for the first time since 1870. But in the Seine, their 1947 vote of 650,000 was halved. In Toulouse and Bordeaux they lost a quarter of their strength, in Marseilles and Rennes a third, in Rouen 40 per cent, in Lille, Nantes and Grenoble nearly half. In St Etienne they dropped from three-quarters of the total to one quarter. These were serious losses for a mainly urban movement. Part of the trouble was their failure to enlist the whole-hearted support of big business, scared by the Gaullist talk of associating labour and capital, and by the risk of strikes if the General should come in. In Paris the RPF's losses since 1947 were much heavier in the *bourgeois* centre than in the working-class *banlieue*. In the second Nord constituency the Government owed their absolute majority to the support of a list backed by the big textile industrialists of Lille, Roubaix and Tourcoing; it won only one seat, but it put in five Socialists (for 107,000 votes) and four MRP (for 84,000), leaving 106,000 Communists and 94,000 Gaullists unrepresented.

The more serious weakness, however, is the resistance to political discipline of the Radical and right-wing *milieux* from which the RPF draws most of its local leaders. There has been a steady trickle of resignations in protest against attempts to impose obedience either on the parliamentary or on the local level, and General de Gaulle's intransigence in refusing *apparentements* with potential allies produced another crop of defections during the campaign. It is true that alliances with every available Independent list would have only won him six more seats, at the price of diluting a parliamentary party which he would much prefer to keep pure. He will not soon forget the second chamber elections of 1948, when of 130 senators elected on the Gaullist ticket, less than 60 joined the parliamentary group. He has doubtless guarded against such a spectacular disintegration this time, but few French politicians are wholly immune to the temptations of office, and the RPF has to manœuvre on ground which is far more familiar to its opponents than to itself. Already M. Ramadier has pointed out that even if the Socialists went into opposition, only seven Gaullist votes would be needed to give the centre parties an absolute majority—and that at the price of seven ministerial posts these could no doubt be won over.

The Communist vote remains impressively stable. Of their 450,000 lost votes, nearly half were in the areas where the influence of the Church is strongest—29 north-western, eastern frontier and Cevennes departments which contain altogether only 27 per cent of the electorate. This suggests that the damage has occurred at the fringe rather than at the core of the party's support. On the other hand, whereas in 1946 they were still making substantial gains in the working-class constituencies, in 1951 this was no longer true; the main industrial departments contributed a little more than their proportionate share of the Communist losses.[1]

The Socialists, like the British Liberals, are ground between the stronger rivals on their flanks. Their 4,500,000 supporters of 1945 have dwindled almost by half. But whereas in 1945–1946 their losses were heavily concentrated in the working-class areas, the more recent losses have been much more evenly spread, being equally serious in industrial and in non-industrial,

---

[1] The Nord, Pas-de-Calais, the Rhône, the Bouches-du-Rhône, the Paris suburbs, Seine-et-Oise and Seine-Inférieure have 21 per cent of the electorate, but 24 per cent of the Communist losses occurred in these departments.

in Catholic and in non-Catholic regions. Communists and Socialists rarely lost votes to each other. There was nevertheless one important local variation in Socialist fortunes. In six of the eight departments in which they held their own or improved their position, the party was fighting alone, unencumbered (or unassisted) by Conservative or clerical associates. Shorn of most of its industrial following, the party has been thrown back upon the south as its territorial, and upon the rural schoolteachers as its social base. The election results show that it cannot afford to offend these determined enemies of clerical power, and the post-election declarations of M. Guy Mollet show that the lesson has been learnt. But the Socialists remain where they have been for five years, in a position of responsibility without power. They fear to leave office lest they precipitate the clash of the extremes, and destroy the régime; yet they cannot affect policy except by provoking an occasional cabinet crisis, the result usually being a Government a little further to the right than its predecessor. The electoral verdict will strengthen the hand of the ex-Ministers, like MM. Depreux and Philip, who have long been urging the party to seek a 'rest-cure in the opposition', against the present Ministers, like MM. Moch and Mollet, who fear that the departure of the Socialists would leave the Government dependent on Gaullist support.

The long wrangle over the electoral law harmed the prestige of all the Government parties, but MRP at least obtained compensation in the shape of a law inspired by them, and much less damaging to them than any likely alternative.[1] Their losses, though heavy, have been much smaller than seemed probable four years ago, and the party seems to have come to stay. Even for them, however, the new law has its drawbacks, for the cohesion on which they have prided themselves will be difficult to retain. Their national decline has increased the relative weight of the Catholic areas where they are most secure, and the alliance of MRP with the Socialists, which formed the basis of the old majority, will be heavily strained now that nearly half the MRP parliamentary group (37 out of 85) come from the departments where the clerical issue is decisive. Indeed, a quarter of their deputies were elected in alliance with the right and against the Socialists. A similar problem faces the right-wing Independents, 20 of whom had Gaullists among their election partners, while 34 had Socialists, and the remainder were opposed to both. Already at least a score of Independents have voted for the Gaullist who stood against M. Herriot for the Presidency of the Assembly.

The Radicals, in the old days the party which specialized in contradictory local alliances, have suffered (or benefited) less from them on this occasion;

---

[1] The law was originally proposed by two MRP back-benchers sitting for precarious south-western seats: one, M. Roques, was beaten, but the other, M. Taillade, just saved his seat by means of *apparentement.*

three-quarters of their members ran in harness with the other governmental parties. On the other hand, they and the right will suffer far more than MRP from the personal rivalries which beset loose organizations. M. Daladier's hostility to M. Herriot, his former schoolteacher, goes back long before the war, and when last year M. Daladier became president of the RGR (a loose combination of parties in which the Radicals dominate) M. Herriot forthwith resigned his honorary presidency. Though M. Daladier has failed to persuade the Radical party to sink its identity completely in the RGR, the '*guerre des deux Edouard*' is far from over. On the right the position is much more complex. PRL, which in 1946 hoped to become the Conservative party of France, has been disrupted by Gaullism, and has decided to merge into the Independent group; but the Peasant party (a splinter group from the Cevennes with large ambitions) has refused to follow its example, and the leadership of the remaining Independents is vigorously disputed between their president, M. Reynaud, their secretary, M. Duchet, and the ineligible but extremely active ex-Premier, M. Flandin. In this sector of politics electoral and parliamentary behaviour are quite unrelated. Thus M. Daladier, leader of the anti-Government Radicals, formed an alliance in Vaucluse with MRP and Socialists; but M. Antier, leader of the Peasant party and a junior Minister, fought in Haute-Loire in partnership with the RPF.[1] M. Flandin is president of the *Alliance démocratique*, which forms part of the RGR; yet he himself has a right-wing past, and the secretary of his party stood as a right-wing Independent.

Whatever semblance of organization these right-wing groups have—and it is little enough—has been forced on them by the system of party lists. This system inevitably handicaps the genuine independent even more severely than the wayward conservative. It is hard to get round. In the Allier, indeed, a list of '*Concentration républicaine*' was formed by five members of the Theuil family, and got 6,400 votes. Less successful was M. Bougrain, former right-wing deputy for Seine-et-Marne, who found only 32 supporters for his list of '*Courage civique*', which included himself, his wife, and five old age pensioners. Even among the less freakish candidates, independents and dissidents did very badly. The rebel Communists of whom so much has been made proved even weaker than the Trotskyists in 1946. The 'neutralists', mostly former Socialists standing in Paris, were equally unsuccessful. And of the 22 deputies who had deserted MRP since 1946, no less than 16 were beaten; they included Gaullist leaders like M. Michelet,

[1] The second on his list was M. Pébellier, an octogenarian retired haberdasher, who stood in place of his son—a former deputy who was ineligible because he voted for Pétain in 1940. As the oldest deputy, it fell to the father (who had never in his life been out of Le Puy) to preside at the first session. His pro-Pétain opening speech, written by the son, was an odd contrast to the opening speeches of the previous doyen, the veteran Communist Marcel Cachin.

who stood against M. Queuille in the Corrèze, and M. Terrenoire who opposed M. Pleven in Côtes-du-Nord, as well as the leftish rebels of the *Gauche indépendante*.[1]

Among the few successful Independents was M. Arthur Conte, former secretary of the Socialist party in Pyrénées-Orientales, who captured from his old party the last of the three seats which they once monopolized. The confusion of the local Socialists had some excuse; the official Socialist candidate and M. Conte were at once opposing one another and allied in the same *apparentement*, the head of the RPF list was another ex-Socialist, and a vigorous campaign was being waged by M. Jean Rous, a left-wing rebel, on behalf of his candidature at the *next* election.[*]

The general failure of independents reinforced one of the main complaints against the previous electoral system, that lists were drawn up by the party, and the elector could do nothing to affect the choice of individuals; the behaviour of the Lyons Communists illustrates its validity.[2] An effort was made to meet the point in the new law, and though it rarely worked at all, and then with perverse results it gave some interesting pointers to the standing of individual leaders, M. Pleven and M. Moch, for example, receiving thousands of votes from outside the ranks of their own parties. On the other hand, several leading figures found themselves less popular than their more obscure colleagues, among them M. Bidault and M. Pinay

---

[1] This unimportant but interesting group had three members, an abbé, a marquis and M. Boulet, President of the Association of Mayors in the wine-growing Hérault, and a prominent leader in the fight against coca-cola. Near to them stood M. Lécrivain-Servoz, deputy for the Rhône, who had passed from MRP into the RPF and thence via the Overseas Independents (*sic*) into neutralism, and M. Serre of Oran, who had been in turn MRP, Gaullist, right-wing Independent, pro-Radical Independent and neutralist, finally winding up in second place on the Communist list in the Dordogne.

[2] See p. 13. Even under the old law, the voter might strike off his chosen list the name of a candidate he disliked, and promote one he preferred. But as unaltered ballots counted as positive votes for the original list, this provision was wholly ineffective. The new law went much further, and allowed '*panachage*'; that is, while still voting for a list, the elector could give a personal vote to a candidate on a different list, to which a fraction of his vote would then be transferred. The results could be surprising; thus 7,000 votes given to M. Moch as an individual brought up the average of his list enough to give it an extra seat, but he was safely in, and the benefit went to his number three, which the voters had certainly not intended. In Bas-Rhin and Seine-Inférieure, *panachage* has led to a complicated technical dispute over how to calculate the absolute majority, in which seven seats are at stake. In Bordeaux, an ingenious 'motorists' defence candidate founded his whole campaign on *panachage*, urging everyone to '*panache*' in favour of two candidates on his list—then he would win two seats and no one would be worse off. He only managed to convince the equivalent of 2,800 whole voters. Some parties used the names of national leaders like General de Gaulle, M. Herriot or M. Pleven, though they were not candidates, to attract personal votes from other parties—they also attracted demands from their opponents that the election should be invalidated.

[*] M. Conte was soon readmitted to the Socialist party. During the Algerian war many Frenchmen from North Africa settled in the area. M. Conte became a diehard supporter of the war, and after peace was signed in 1962 he was defeated by a Communist. In 1968 he regained his seat—as a Gaullist candidate.

(the Minister responsible for housing) on the Government side,[1][*] M. Pierre de Gaulle, who was 3,000 votes behind his principal colleague, and even M. Thorez, whose name was actually struck out by 1,400 Communist voters in his Parisian stronghold.

The developments of the last 20 years have changed the political map of France remarkably little. The Government parties won an absolute majority of votes in 32 constituencies; all but four of them were in the old republican zone south of the Loire. Conversely, while the RPF reached a quarter of the votes in 22 northern departments, it did so in only four south of the river, and three of them were along the west coast—formerly a Bonapartist region. The traditional clerical areas of the north-west and north-east provided both RPF and MRP with two-thirds of their respective strongholds, though the former added the once Radical departments of the Paris basin, and the latter has established itself in a few scattered, usually mountainous parts of the south. The Socialist party comes more and more to resemble the old Radicals, as it takes over former Radical areas in inadequate compensation for its losses to the Communists. The Communists themselves are much the most widely distributed party, both geographically and socially. Weak only in the Catholic regions, they reached 40 per cent. of the total vote in three constituencies—on the one hand the north-western suburbs of Paris, and on the other two agricultural departments in the south, the Corrèze and the Creuse.[†] The peasantry of these areas are voting not for the revolution of 1917 but for that of 1789. The party names change, but beneath the surface the electorate continues to assert the same preferences and prejudices; the fundamental stability of French electoral politics is a phenomenon quite as remarkable as, though less remarked than, the kaleidoscopic changes of government. The country's tragedy is that it is a stability of equilibrium, not of harmony. In the new Assembly the parties which bid for working-class votes are almost exactly equal in number to those which appeal to a middle-class clientele. The clerical parties, relying on the curés, and their *laïque* opponents, dependent on the schoolteachers, are equally matched. No positive policy can emerge from this situation of stalemate; but that is not the fault of the politicians, it is the result of the equal division of opinions. At least the contest will still be fought with words and not with bullets.

---

[1] But despite the French loathing for taxation, the Finance Minister, M. Petsche, and his chief subordinate, M. Edgar Faure, both did very well, gaining respectively 15,000 and 6,000 votes more than in 1946. The latter was opposed by a Taxpayers' Defence list, but only 2,000 votes were cast for it; the French voter is fundamentally responsible.

[*] The unpopular housing minister was Petit, not Pinay.

[†] On Communism in Corrèze see reference below, p. 204 n.

3   Antoine Pinay and the revenge of the Right*

French governments have lived dangerously since 1947. In that spring, the Communist party went out of office, and took most of the organized workers into open opposition to the Government and to the régime. Almost at the same moment, General de Gaulle summoned all Frenchmen, and attracted millions of them (especially Conservatives) to join his Rally of the French People. Between the rival advocates of strong and dynamic government, the moderate groups waged a dogged and persistent struggle for survival. But they survived the difficult years, and when in 1949 relative economic stability was achieved, public support began gradually to swing back from the extreme to the middle parties. A general election confronted the centre groups with a new problem. It was still possible, despite their recovery, that the two oppositions would outnumber the moderates in the new Assembly. So the outgoing majority revised the electoral law, allowing allied parties to pool their votes. The Communists were unable to take advantage of this provision (since no-one would work with them) and the Gaullists were unwilling to do so. The whole benefit therefore accrued to the middle groups, which won only a bare majority of votes, but obtained two-thirds of the seats.

The election showed the country to be almost evenly divided about each of the three great cleavages in French life. Catholics and anti-clericals, parliamentary democrats and authoritarians, *bourgeois* and working-class parties, confronted each other in almost equal numbers. The permutations of these differences divide Frenchmen into six main party combinations, and these six too were equal, each having about a hundred seats. An alliance between three of them would have no safe majority—especially as the three which were nearest to agreement, clerical Conservatives, Radicals (anti-clerical conservatives) and MRP (Catholic progressives) happened to be the smallest three of the six. To add a fourth group would produce a safe majority on paper, but one so internally divided that it could hardly survive for long. Only a split in one of the other parties, the Socialists or the Gaullists, could solve the problem in parliamentary arithmetic which the French electorate had set.

* Originally entitled 'Stable Government in France?'. From *The Fortnightly*, 1032 N.S., December 1952.

The reign of the parties

For a little while the old majority remained precariously in being. The Socialists would not join M. Pleven's Government, but they continued to support it. But RPF skilfully used the clerical issue to divide the former partners. MRP, as a Catholic party, had to support the demand for subsidies to Church schools, and the Socialists had to oppose it; not to do so might, in either case, have meant political suicide. When M. Barangé's bill passed into law in September 1951, the old majority was broken. The RPF, as the largest of the six groups, believed that the game was at last in their hands, and that they would soon be able to make their own terms for entering and dominating the Government.

For a few weeks longer the Pleven ministry survived by avoiding firm commitments on controversial issues, as it had done on the clerical question. But over the budget this became impossible. To avoid tax increases which would alienate Conservative support, the Government proposed an economy programme, notably on the nationalized railways and in the social services. The Socialists, fearing to lose their few remaining working-class supporters to the Communists, voted with the opposition and turned the ministry out. The next Prime Minister, M. Edgar Faure, regained Socialist support by concessions, proposing to balance the budget by introducing new taxation instead of economies. The other wing of 'what for want of a better term was still called the majority' now revolted in its turn. Many Radical and Conservative members had pledged themselves at the election to oppose higher taxes, and at the end of February their defection overthrew M. Faure.

Expenditure, voted two months before, was already running at the next year's rates; revenue was still being collected at those of the previous year. The budget deficit mounted, and the problem grew more acute daily, but the Assembly appeared incapable of resolving the deadlock.

At the beginning of March, M. Antoine Pinay was invited to form a government. Though he had for two years been Minister of Transport, he was hardly known at all to the general public. Neither MRP nor the Radicals had any great enthusiasm for him, but both hoped for Conservative support when their own chance at the premiership came round. Since he was sure to be defeated, they would lose nothing, and gain some goodwill, by giving him their support as a friendly gesture. But when the crucial day arrived, the prophets were dumbfounded. Twenty-seven Gaullist deputies recognized in M. Pinay's speech the accents that they (or at any rate their electors) wanted to hear, and defied party discipline to vote for him. The parliamentary deadlock was broken, and a new majority was born.

The new Prime Minister followed up his popular pledge to impose no new taxes by cancelling the decision, already announced, to increase the price of electricity. With this double defiance of the trend of recent years, he acquired at a stroke an unshakable hold on public opinion. Repeatedly in the coming months he was to show the same shrewdness. Strong measures against the Communists, for example, proved a useful means of consolidating his majority. And in October, when he was faced with a dangerous right-wing attack on his Foreign Minister, the Americans came to his rescue by handing him an allegedly humiliating 'note'; by refusing to accept it he won nation-wide approval, and completely took the wind out of his opponents' sails.

This flair for judging public opinion is indeed the key to M. Pinay's success. He is not a clever parliamentarian, as he demonstrated over the 'Dorey amendment' in April. He has never enjoyed any special favour among the deputies. But he has established a strong Government by a method which no-one has been able to employ since Poincaré a quarter of a century ago; he has enlisted the force of public opinion as a means of pressure on the Assembly. Usually the demands of constituents lead members to vote against the ministry. Under M. Pinay they have been its mainstay.* His political success was striking. The Gaullist split which put him in power deepened and widened. At the end of June, a strong RPF candidate in a Paris by-election held only a third of the votes given to his predecessor a year before—and the defection was greater in the *bourgeois* than in the working-class quarters. In the Assembly, the RPF parliamentary group, which had prided itself on its discipline, began to split on crucial divisions, like the old individualist parties, into three factions—pro-Government, anti-Government, and abstainers. When the leaders tried to counter this by imposing stricter discipline, they found themselves faced by a crisis. Thirty of their members, who had in March preferred the leadership of M. Pinay to that of General de Gaulle, in July confirmed that decision by seceding from the RPF. The largest of the six parliamentary groups became, overnight, the smallest. For the first time for 20 years, there was a parliamentary majority of the Right, under a leader who appealed to the country as an avowed Conservative.

The consolidation of a Conservative majority was bound to shatter the cohesion of the RPF. Less spectacular, but more surprising, was the success of M. Pinay in weakening the other extreme movement. The Communist party admitted that the workers' illusions about the real character of the Pinay Government were enfeebling their militancy, and had led to the failure of the abortive demonstrations in the spring, for which MM. Marty and Tillon were made the principal scapegoats. Though it would be absurd to hold M. Pinay mainly responsible for the rift in the Communist party, his

---

* Apart from M. Mendès-France he was the only premier of the Fourth Republic who usually timed votes of confidence for Mondays or Tuesdays—after members had met their constituents, rather than before.

success in holding down prices and in stabilizing the Government certainly had an indirect effect, by sapping Communist strength and thus provoking dissension in their ranks.

This remarkable political success has somewhat obscured the more disquieting features of his régime. These have aroused little attention abroad, where the survival of a French government is its own justification. Yet they are not unimportant. Politically, the Pinay ministry represents an important stage in the recovery of the forces which supported Marshal Pétain and opposed the Resistance movement. Economically, its partial successes have been won largely by piling up difficulties for its successors. Abroad, colonial matters and the broad lines of French foreign policy have come under serious attack.

In domestic politics, the Pinay ministry has gone far to liquidate the revolution of 1944–1946. Effective power has passed to the groups which were then in opposition, the Radicals and Conservatives. MRP indeed remains uneasily in the Government coalition (though no one would think so from reading its press). But the other groups which made a real contribution to the Resistance movement, whether of the Right or of the Left, are all in opposition. Meanwhile the political revival of the Vichyites continues. M. Pinay himself voted for Pétain in 1940, and accepted membership of his National Council (which never met). One of his close advisers is M. Flandin, Prime Minister before the war and Foreign Minister under Vichy, to-day best remembered for his telegram congratulating Hitler over Munich. The Marshal's former *chef de cabinet* and defence counsel both sit on the Government benches.

The economic policy of the Government is also open to severe criticism. The budget was balanced, on paper, without new taxation; but this was a parliamentary rather than a fiscal triumph. It represented the abandonment of the attempt, courageously pursued by Finance Ministers since the liberation, to pay their way without borrowing and inflation. Much of the political instability of the last few years can be explained by the resistance of the public to the steady increase in the percentage of the national income taken by the State. This increase was due in part to higher expenditure, but mainly to the effort to fill by taxation a budgetary deficit previously met by inflation. The stability of the Pinay Government was achieved by a more popular policy.

M. Pinay repudiated the advice of his officials and the example of his predecessors. He reverted to the habits of the Third Republic, when politicians like his mentor M. Flandin had prejudiced the country's industrial future in the sacred cause of low taxes. He reduced expenditure by drastic cuts in the housing programme, so sorely needed to tackle the most appalling of France's social problems, and in industrial investment, indispensable if French industry was to recover from the alarming backwardness in which the war had found it.[1] His estimates of revenue were optimistically high, those of expenditure equally optimistically low. All other considerations were subordinated to the dominant point of his policy—the need to tempt hoarded capital from its hiding-place. To achieve 'confidence', a loan was offered at exorbitantly favourable terms, and M. Pinay forced through a reluctant Parliament an amnesty to those whose past defrauding of the revenue had imposed so heavy a burden on the fixed-income and wage-earning classes, who cannot evade taxation.

If 'confidence' could be restored, M. Pinay believed that all the country's economic problems could easily be solved. But the loan, for which so many sacrifices had been made, produced far less new money than had been hoped for. Industrial production declined, and the balance of payments position worsened steadily. In price policy, indeed, M. Pinay had better success. He checked the rise in the cost of living, though he did not reverse it. But this important victory was largely due to the sliding scale bill. The automatic increase of the minimum wage, when the cost of living reached a certain point, imposed both upon the Treasury and upon the *patronat* a new incentive to check the rise in prices. Commentators have described the bill as 'M. Pinay's masterstroke'. But little credit for it is due to a Government which opposed and delayed the bill as long as they dared, but were finally compelled by the opposition reluctantly to swallow it in a mutilated form.

The Prime Minister has not been well served by the interests behind him. Himself an enlightened businessman, he has preached unceasingly the need for economic liberalism to justify itself if it is to survive: to introduce real competition into the cartellised world of French industry, if necessary by opening the home market to foreign competition; to squeeze profit margins, especially in distribution; to reform the fiscal system. He has found that high-principled exhortation is not enough. The leader whose rule was to represent the return of economic freedom was soon driven to resort to the despised techniques of *dirigisme*—after the apparatus of economic control had been dismantled so completely that it could no longer be effectively used. The man who, last spring, was universally acclaimed by peasants and businessmen, found by the autumn that the shopkeepers were denouncing his fiscal proposals, the peasants were in revolt against his price policy, and the political quarters most closely connected with French industry were launching a dangerous attack on his most vulnerable point, foreign policy.

[1] M. Pinay's axe was, however, selective. It did not fall upon the huge subsidy paid to the politically powerful beet growers to encourage them, to the detriment alike of the health of the citizen and of the equilibrium of the budget, to produce quantities of alcohol for which no normal commercial market can be found.

It sounds odd to describe external affairs as the Government's weak point. For French foreign policy has shown remarkable continuity. MM. Bidault and Schuman, both of MRP, have between them occupied the Quai d'Orsay ever since the war, and their policy appeared to command general acceptance. Yet early in 1952 M. Schuman (like other Foreign Ministers in French history who had seemed stable and secure while their colleagues changed around them) discovered that his domestic political position had been dangerously undermined.

The old coalition was less united on external policy than it appeared. Its left wing, Socialists and a growing section of MRP, were keen supporters of the economic integration of Europe, but were disturbed by the Government's colonial policy. Radicals and Conservatives, more responsive to the views of industry at home and of settlers abroad, upheld the official policy in the empire, but had little desire to allow effective European competition in the protected home market. And at the end of 1951 both imperial and European policy became explosive issues.

The Tunisian crisis greatly increased the alarm of the Left over colonial developments, and it occurred in an area for which the Foreign ministry was directly responsible. German rearmament was far less acceptable to public opinion than the Schuman plan, and brought the European policy under simultaneous fire from the nationalist Right and from the Socialist Left. Consequently, when the Pinay ministry was formed, M. Schuman had already become a parliamentary liability, and he was reappointed only because MRP refused to take office without him. From within the coalition attacks have recently been launched against him by the dissident Gaullists (who had put M. Pinay into power) and by leading Radicals, M. Herriot even hinting that the sympathy of the Prime Minister was with the critics rather than with their victim. With little support outside his own party, M. Schuman's position has become dangerously insecure.* Yet, if external affairs constitute the main weakness of the existing combination, they form an even more serious obstacle to the formation of a new one.

It is not easy to find an alternative majority to M. Pinay's. Many MRP members, disliking their position of left-wing hostages in a right-wing Government, would like to return to the old alliance; but they have little hope of success, for neither Conservatives nor Socialists would make any concessions to achieve this end.

The only other possibility is to bring the 'orthodox' Gaullists into the majority. In theory this could happen in three ways: by their association with the moderate Left bloc (MRP and Socialists), with the *bourgeois* bloc

---

* In the next cabinet M. Schuman was replaced by M. Bidault, who belonged to the same party but held very different views.

(Conservatives and Radicals), or with the pro-clerical elements in each (MRP and Conservatives). The last possibility can probably be discarded—support for Church schools is an insufficient foundation for co-operation in government. Between the other two, a difficult obstacle arises; for the RPF shares the outlook of the Conservatives on external policy, and that of the Left on domestic issues.

In splitting the Gaullist movement, M. Pinay has profoundly modified its character. The departure of many of its Conservative deputies and most of its Conservative electors has shifted its centre of gravity. The Gaullist leaders were never orthodox Conservatives. They want a reformed and regenerated France, and care little what sacrifices may have to be imposed on particular groups in order to attain their objectives. They are regarded with suspicion by the leaders of French business, have no special tenderness for its interests, and are anxious to retain their popular following. They entered politics by way of the Resistance, resent the growing arrogance of the reviving Vichyites, and have reacted by a new firmness in dealing with such elements in their own ranks.[1]

At the same time the reduction of the Gaullist numbers in Parliament to 80, instead of the 200 for which they had hoped, has made the movement less dangerous in the eyes of its potential allies, as well as less aggressive in its own attitude. The shift to the Left provides a possible basis for co-operation with those Socialists who want to return to office (mostly the right-wing, 'managerial' element), with the section of MRP which is most dissatisfied with M. Pinay (generally the left-wing of the party), and perhaps also with the likeliest architect of a new economic policy, M. Mendès-France. But formidable obstacles stand in the way. Personalities are not the least of them—above all that of General de Gaulle. Past propaganda is another; each of the groups concerned has taught its followers for five years to believe the worst of the others. This distrust can more easily and quickly be overcome among the leaders, who nearly all share a common Resistance background and training and memories, than among the rank and file who often lack this common experience. In addition, the Gaullist attitude on foreign and imperial affairs, especially on the crucial problem of Indo-China, is sharply opposed to that of their potential partners.*

---

[1] One prominent Gaullist went so far as to offer asylum to a well-known Communist, with whom he had worked in the Resistance, in case the latter should be pursued by M. Pinay's police. The incident was hardly typical, but it shows the deep difference between the attitude of the authentic Gaullist and that of the ex-Vichyite Conservative.

* This attitude changed over the following year or two, as overseas commitments seemed to weaken France in Europe. Many Gaullists deplored the deposition of the Sultan of Morocco in June 1953, and in October the chairman of their parliamentary party compared the Indo-China war to the Mexican expedition (by which Napoleon III had similarly dissipated French resources outside Europe).

The *regroupement* of RPF, MRP and Socialists is thus difficult, perhaps impossible to achieve. Yet it is hard to see any other practical alternative to the coalition forged by M. Pinay. In this difficulty lies one source of his parliamentary strength. But the continuation of a given majority in the Assembly is, as previous Prime Ministers know only too well, entirely compatible with frequent changes of government. From this point of view, however, M. Pinay enjoys a much stronger position than his predecessors, because of that exceptional popularity in the country which has been so important in holding his coalition together.

M. Pinay thus presides over the strongest Government of the Fourth Republic. He has revolutionized the parliamentary situation by creating a new majority, for the most part based on a genuine community of outlook, yet still including a reluctant MRP, which remains because it can see no available alternative. He has established a personal hold on public opinion which ensures that, so long as the Conservative majority continues in being and holds the reins of power, M. Pinay himself will remain a political asset it can ill afford to discard. These are striking achievements for a politician whose name was almost unknown, even in France, only a year ago.

4 Pierre Mendès-France and the revolt against conservatism*

The British public has long been accustomed to the six-monthly changes of government in Paris. 'Crisis in France' has become a familiar headline, which makes no impression. The man in the street is convinced that our nearest neighbours are incorrigible anarchists. The specialist takes it for granted that the new cabinet will contain much the same faces, will depend upon much the same majority, and will continue much the same policies as the old. Consequently a real turning-point in French affairs is apt to pass unnoticed across the Channel.

Despite appearances, the ministerial crisis of May and June 1953 may prove to have been such a turning-point. The replacement of M. Mayer by M. Laniel indeed suggests that the issues of the crisis were unimportant, and its results negligible. But its record length and unusual difficulty—in one month the Assembly rejected as many would-be premiers as in the previous six years—deserve more serious interpretation than the customary solemn sermons on the deputies' irresponsibility and lack of contact with the people. This crisis was so difficult to solve precisely because the new Government were expected to be far stronger than their predecessors; because the basic problems of French policy were openly debated for the first time; and because the obstacle which prevents these problems being tackled lies, not in the remoteness of the deputies from public opinion, but in their over-sensitiveness to their electoral interests. Also the presidency of the Republic falls vacant in January, and the prospects of certain candidates might be affected by their showing in the crisis.

There were three grounds for expecting that the new Government would be a strong one. First, the late Mayer ministry had been defeated by an absolute majority of the deputies; its successor, if overthrown in the same way, would be constitutionally entitled to dissolve the Assembly—a power which only two of its predecessors were legally, and none practically, able to wield. Secondly, the crisis greatly increased the chance of passing the constitutional revision proposals which have been under discussion for three years. The changes are unlikely to be very drastic, and as M. Mendès-France said in his investiture speech, the real need is for new habits and attitudes

* Originally entitled 'A Real Crisis in France'. From *The Fortnightly*, 1040 N.S., August 1953.

rather than for new paper provisions. But the revision will at least give future premiers a little more authority than their predecessors have enjoyed. In the third place, the new ministry has already demanded and received special powers to act by decree, without consulting parliament. M. Mayer's request for such powers indeed proved fatal to his ministry, but this indicated, not a determination by the deputies never to grant these powers, but the ritual sacrifice of a cabinet which is their normal price for abandoning any of their authority. This is the regular function of ministerial crises in France: to bring pressure to bear on the opponents of a change, by obliging them publicly to accept responsibility for destroying a government. Everyone knew that the powers refused to M. Mayer would be granted to his successor; and this was not a ridiculous anomaly, but the normal working of the French political system.

Yet, as it turns out, the new Government are unlikely to prove a very strong one. They will have weapons denied to their predecessors—the threat of dissolution and the special powers—but not necessarily the will to use them. For M. Laniel, like M. Mayer in January, was elected by a dangerously large majority, embracing too many mutually hostile groups who agreed on nothing but the need for a temporary truce. It was difficult to prolong the crisis until real decisions had been reached, because of the impending conference at Bermuda—which, ironically enough, was nevertheless postponed on the very day of M. Laniel's election.

It is therefore arguable that this crisis, like so many others, has merely registered a shift in the parliamentary majority, without bringing about any significant change. It has completed the evolution begun in 1951, when the Socialists were driven (willingly enough) into the ranks of the opposition. The entry of the RPF into the majority then became a matter of time. When M. Pinay won over a quarter of the Gaullist deputies and most of their electors, he weakened the RPF's bargaining power, and made its adhesion possible on terms which its new partners could accept. By putting M. Mayer into power in January, the Gaullist deputies showed their willingness to join the Government; by turning him out in May, they served notice that they would require their price. 'Our continued existence is proved by our power to destroy,' as M. Diethelm remarked. M. Laniel, by giving office to some 'tame' Gaullist members,[1] has consolidated his parliamentary majority at the price of risking greater dissension within the cabinet itself.

Thus the pessimists' case appears quite plausible if attention is confined to the start and finish of the crisis. But the crucial developments occurred

[1] Among the 35 deputies who voted for every one of the six actual or prospective Prime Ministers, from the beginning to the end of the crisis, were two Gaullist members. Both obtained office under M. Laniel.

in the early stages, not at the end of it. First, President Auriol, before summoning any of the professionals who have held power for so long, sent first for two leaders who have consistently shunned it. M. Reynaud and M. Mendès-France then broke all the rules by refusing in turn to lead an impotent caretaker ministry, and insisting that they would not take office without effective power. M. Reynaud could have been elected premier, had he not declined to form a government until the constitution had been revised to permit easier dissolution of the Assembly. M. Mendès-France weakened his chances by insisting that he would choose his own ministers as individuals, without bargaining with the parties, and—unheard-of novelty—that the ministers must take a 'loyalty oath' to act as a team, by pledging themselves not to join the cabinet of his successor.*

M. Reynaud's 'bombshell' (as one paper called it) was designed to concentrate attention upon the constitutional issue. But M. Mendès-France's 'atomic explosion' was of wider significance. For he was in a far better position than his Conservative colleague to take advantage of the recent sudden change in the French political atmosphere. Six years of drift have produced their results. Power has fallen gradually into the hands of the most conservative groups, who demand an expensive military and colonial policy, but will not tax themselves to pay for it. M. Pinay's policy was based on a losing gamble on the enlightenment of his supporters; he earned great short-run popularity by reducing productive investment instead of increasing taxes, but he bequeathed to his successors a huge budget deficit, a stagnant and under-employed economy, and an alarming outbreak of social discontent. The Gaullists and the progressive Catholics of MRP soon turned against M. Pinay, for whom neither had ever had much sympathy. But the clearest sign of the change was the decision of the Radicals—the most flexible of politicians, always ready to adapt their policy to their major aim of getting and keeping power—to vote for M. Mendès-France.

The latter is himself a Radical, though his temperament and policy are quite alien to the easy-going and power-loving mentality of his party. The least disciplined of political groups, the Radicals have continued to count him as one of their recognized leaders, however vigorously he has attacked governments which other members of the party entered or even led. His own last period of office was in 1945, as General de Gaulle's Minister of Economic Affairs, when he advocated a policy of austerity—blocking of bank accounts, confiscation of war profits, strict controls against inflation, and priority for economic reconstruction over military prestige. On the last point he found himself in conflict with General de Gaulle, who (in the only

---

* He omitted this precaution a year later when he at last formed a government. When he fell, he was replaced by his own Finance Minister, M. Edgar Faure.

decision he has ever admitted to have been mistaken) rejected M. Mendès-France's vigorous policy in favour of the 'business as usual' prescription of the Finance Minister, M. Pleven. M. Mendès-France resigned, and has remained ever since in resolute independence. His annual 'Cassandra' speech on the budget, warning the country of the impasse into which it was drifting, has become a recognized institution. With unvarying consistency he reiterates his constant theme: that the future of France depends primarily upon the re-equipment of her obsolescent industries, that productive investment must have priority over consumption or military expenditure, that full employment is the key to economic policy, above all that the country must live within its means. Trying to attain too many objectives at once entails a risk of achieving none of them. Something must be renounced; and to M. Mendès-France, the war in Indo-China is the ulcer which is draining French strength, and paralysing both her economic recovery and her European policy.

Though in his investiture speech M. Mendès-France was much more cautious about Indo-China than he has sometimes seemed in the past, the suspicion of neutralist tendencies did him much harm on the Right. But if on certain aspects of policy his position has some affinity with Mr Bevan's, his fundamental outlook is wholly different. And the vigour of his mind, the austerity of his programme, a breadth of view which embraces all the country's problems in a coherent policy, and a total indifference to office for its own sake, have earned him the reputation of a French Sir Stafford Cripps. By biding his time until he could come forward on his own terms, he secured an opportunity which he used to the full. In the Assembly, with characteristic courage, he attacked the abuses of the social security system, of which the Socialists are sworn defenders, the pro-settler policy in North Africa, which has passionate adherents on the Radical, Conservative, and Gaullist benches, and the fiscal privileges of the peasantry, whose friends abound in every party. His defiance of interests before which previous governments have capitulated or succumbed, and his clear-cut and consistent policy in place of the familiar series of hand-to-mouth expedients, made a well-justified impression on the Assembly and on the public. Though the whispering campaign in the lobbies was of unprecedented virulence, he attracted more support than anyone had expected (13 short of the absolute majority he required), and less than 20 non-Communist members cast openly hostile votes.

With the failure of M. Mendès-France, the President recalled the tried and safe men. M. Bidault did indeed create the impression that he would pursue the old policies with new vigour. But his defeat was precisely calculated by the specialists in parliamentary manœuvring; the large Gaullist vote for him was cancelled by the Radical whips, who withdrew their own men's favourable ballots in the middle of the division, and left him with one vote less than the necessary 314.

In every crisis a moment comes when the deputies, conscious of the growing irritation of the electorate and of opinion abroad, decide that any solution is better than none, and accept an 'available'—which usually means a colourless—candidate. To the three men of energy there succeeded M. Marie, the professional politician *par excellence*, drowning every real conflict in a flood of sham good fellowship, relying on men's greed for jobs to overcome their scruples about policy, the negation of decision, the incarnation of drift. The dignitaries of the régime used every effort on his behalf; but to its great credit, the Assembly refused to be tempted by this false and hollow solution.

M. Pinay, who was next proposed, had one merit which his predecessor lacked—he stood for a policy, even if a bankrupt one. But most MRP and RPF[1] members refused to return to a programme which had so recently led to economic stagnation and social discontent, and to a leader whose own mild Pétainist record was improved neither by his continued friendship with M. Flandin (author of the notorious telegram congratulating Hitler after Munich) nor by the enthusiastic backing of the anti-parliamentary, pro-collaborationist press.

Neither Gaullists nor MRP, however, were unanimous in their hostility; and as M. Pinay's success in 1952 had shattered the former, many of his advisers hoped that a second candidature in 1953 could be used to split MRP. But M. Pinay himself, more broadminded than his entourage, did not yield to this temptation. By declining to stand, he left the way open to another Conservative, more modern in his outlook and with an impeccable resistance record, to succeed where he himself was bound to fail. With the Bermuda conference thought to be waiting on the Assembly's decision, the deputies were under heavier pressure than usual to provide a government quickly; having rejected two unreal solutions, they now succumbed and elected M. Laniel, knowing that he would form a cabinet too divided to act effectively.[2] They settled the ministerial crisis, but left the real crisis unresolved.

Yet some progress has been made. The Assembly has refused to swallow either M. Marie and the complete evasion of responsibility, or M. Pinay and a return to the policy of willing the ends without willing the means.

---

[1] Since General de Gaulle has broken the link with his parliamentary supporters, they should strictly be called Gaullists or RPF no longer; the new name is URAS (Union républicaine d'action sociale).

[2] This may have been the solution for which President Auriol was working; but good authorities claim that he expected M. Laniel also to fail.

There were more positive gains also, in the sphere of political authority, in that of policy, and in that of morale. Progress was less than might have been hoped, but more than might have been expected.

In terms of authority, the ministry's new advantages have already been discussed. In policy, there has recently been a marked change among the governing personnel of the country. M. Schuman, lately Foreign Minister, has declared that his own conciliatory policy in North Africa was frustrated by his nominal subordinates, the High Commissioners in Tunisia and Morocco, and has stressed the need to reassert French independence of America. M. Faure, who was Prime Minister 18 months ago, has warned the country that the Indo-Chinese war is making France directly dependent upon the United States. M. Reynaud, a high Conservative, has discussed both domestic and Indo-China policy in remarkably radical terms. In the new cabinet, M. Reynaud's friends have replaced M. Pinay's among the Conservatives, while M. Faure—dropped, like M. Laniel, when M. Pinay became premier last year—has brought back to office with him such associates as M. Mitterrand. These changes cannot but influence policy at home, abroad, and in the French Union; for they represent, not only a change in the views of the *ministrables*, but also a recognition of the new public mood.

For this mood has changed. French politics, even more than those of other countries, are fundamentally negative, moving in reaction to the previously predominant policy. After the six-year move to the Right, the pendulum seems to be swinging back. The changed views of so many leading politicians, the rise of some and the fall of others, are due not to mere parliamentary intrigue, but to domestic and foreign events and to their impact on opinion. The municipal elections and the strikes provoked fears of a new Popular Front. The quarrel over repression in Morocco, between M. Mauriac and General Juin, made the whole issue of imperial policy a question of conscience for Catholics. Events in Indo-China—the scandal of the traffic in piastres, the behaviour of the King of Cambodia—raised grave doubts about the practicability of the previous policy. The new tactics of the U.S.S.R., the Italian elections, and the riots in Berlin have all contributed to the impression of an international unfreezing; the enthusiastic welcome given to Sir Winston Churchill's initiative, and the astonishing national unanimity over the Rosenberg case, are symbolic of the new state of mind.

M. Mendès-France's candidature provided a rallying-point for all these feeling of discontent and of hope. Some political observers believe that President Auriol summoned him early in the crisis in order to minimize his chances; if so, the calculation was maladroit. For M. Mendès-France is concerned with policy, not with office, and an 'investiture through lassitude' would be an unsatisfactory introduction to a genuine régime of austerity.

He needed, not to score a nominal but hollow parliamentary success, but to acquire a platform from which to appeal to public opinion: and this the President's summons gave him. And his appeal was effective, both among the electorate and in the Assembly. Reaction cannot simply be measured by the votes: the older Radical leaders cast public ballots in his favour, but intrigued vigorously against him *en coulisse*: conversely his call for renovation and his appeal to youth found an echo (though few votes) even in circles on the extreme Right, attracted by his past record of opposition, by his personal integrity, and by the prospect of a genuine change.

For in all groups it was the younger and newer members, the rank and file deputies, who proved most responsive. The division on M. Mendès-France's investiture showed that the leaders of the different parties had all lost authority over their followers. The revolt expressed—in the Assembly and even more outside it—a repudiation not only of the policy and leadership of recent years, but above all of the political *mœurs* of the Fourth Republic. In frontally attacking the *féodalités* which have so long paralysed governmental action, M. Mendès-France found support both on the Right, traditionally sympathetic to a strong State, and on the Left, traditionally suspicious of vested interests.

From this healthy change of mood it would be easy to draw the false conclusion so cherished by the ordinary French citizen, who attributes all his country's ills to the politicians, intriguing and manœuvring in their own remote, private, and unreal world. This legend has had too long a life. For the French voter, though he will never admit it, gets the government he deserves. He clamours for the full satisfaction of his personal claims, with no concessions to the demands of his neighbours—and denounces the politicians, who have to reconcile these conflicting interests, for their failure to agree. The parties bargained stubbornly last May and June because they believed that the new Government might be able to take real decisions, perhaps injurious to their own electoral clientèle. They were, in fact, keeping in touch with public opinion—and if this process often entails giving priority to private obstruction over public interests, the man in the street is much more responsible than the politician who interprets his wishes. If opinion changes, the deputies will follow. Frustrated electors and politicians alike have long been seeking a leader, and perhaps they have found him. After six more months of stagnation and decline, the younger generation may well raise an irresistible demand for a real attempt at national regeneration, for sacrifices all round, for a leadership not associated with the 'old gang', and for the alternative policy first clearly put to the country by M. Mendès-France on June 3, 1953.

5 An old Parliament and a new majority?*

Outsiders' views of the French Parliament sway between two caricatures. One, favoured abroad, regards it as a cross between a comic opera and a bear-garden, where every month rival groups of excitable fanatics bring down a government in their passionate devotion to incomprehensible principles. The other, more popular in France itself, sees the Assembly as an exchange and mart where crafty and crooked careerists, who cultivate their constituents and sprout principles only at election times, spend the intervening years in sordid intrigues for jobs, loot, and power. Neither picture bears much relation to the truth.

The Assembly contains a fair, but not a precise cross-section of the nation. As in legislatures everywhere, the professional classes are better represented than the productive. Working-class deputies are almost all Communists, and are thus cut off from all save the purely formal aspects of parliamentary life. Even businessmen are comparatively few. There are many nominal peasants and a few real ones; this inarticulate race often seeks its spokesmen from among the innumerable doctors, schoolmasters, and lawyers. Yet though less broadly based occupationally than the House of Commons, in some ways the Assembly is more democratic. France is a less snobbish country with a less class-ridden educational system. There is no social equivalent to the old school tie, and even a title does not always win local Conservative hearts: in one constituency the son of a millionaire marquis sits as a crypto-communist, while the Conservative member is a small-town solicitor belonging to the 'Peasant' party.

Many legends about the Assembly are unfounded. Far from being 'ruled by the men of 75 because the men of 80 are dead', France chooses her ministers and M.P.s at an earlier age than Britain, while the rising young deputy does not find his progress barred—as in the U.S. Congress—by a rigid seniority rule. Nor is there any basis for the widespread belief that passionate and excitable Mediterraneans dominate political life; there are in fact more northerners sitting for southern seats than southerners for northern ones, and most post-war premiers have come from the north. Women are rather more numerous than in the Commons; most of them are

* Originally entitled 'French Politicians'. From *Socialist Commentary*, August 1954.

34

Communists. Fifty native and thirty white members represent Algeria and the colonies.

Is the cross-section as satisfactory in less tangible ways, or is there still substance in the old complaint that 'the best men keep out of politics'? This was in part a snob lament for the unpopularity and alienation from the Republic of the old ruling classes; but undoubtedly the Chamber never enjoyed the immense prestige of the nineteenth century House of Commons. And while first class brains are not the only or even the main part of the politician's equipment, it is nevertheless important that politics should attract sufficient men of high intellectual calibre. Here the Assembly will certainly bear comparison with the House of Commons to-day. Among the rank and file, the standard of debating is probably higher in France, perhaps because the deputy can still sometimes influence votes and therefore addresses his colleagues rather than the local newspaper. Moreover the French committee system, whatever its other drawbacks, gives a better training, and more scope for useful and interesting work, than anything the Mother of Parliaments can offer the back-bencher.

The complaint about the 'best men' however concerned character even more than ability; and most Frenchmen firmly believe that their public men are corrupt. There is little to support this cherished myth. There are the usual ugly rumours about other parties' funds, and doubtless some unsavoury transactions occur on the fringe of politics and business. But there has been no post-war Stavisky or Oustric scandal—though the Algerian wine affair of 1946 involved the entourage of the then prime minister. Such cases are more likely when a minister can choose his personal secretariat freely from his party, family, or friends; but even Britain is not immune from them, as the Lynskey tribunal showed. A recent case illustrates the difference between myth and reality. Last month Senator René Laniel, whose business is in difficulties, was stopped at the airport on his way to Venezuela. The incident has but reinforced the popular suspicion of politicians. Yet his party expelled the senator instead of defending him, and the police intervened although his brother was still prime minister. This surely points to the health, not to the corruption of French public life.*

Another reproach is that the deputies live in a closed world of their own. There is a grain of truth in this; many politicians relish the subtle parliamentary manœuvres which the man-in-the-street finds both incomprehensible and exasperating. But it is not the whole story. Contact between members and voters is often closer in France than here. The provincial

---

* These subjects are thoroughly discussed in *Wars, Plots and Scandals* (Cambridge University Press, 1970). For the Lynskey Tribunal see S. W. Baron, *The Contact Man* (Secker and Warburg, 1964), and John Gross's chapter in M. Sissons and P. French (ed.), *Age of Austerity 1945–1951* (Penguin Books, 1963).

deputy is often local born, and unlike the British M.P., he must spend every week-end in his constituency. And whereas the Englishman's few revolts against his party will occur only on obscure issues arousing no public interest, the Frenchman will rarely rebel unless his constituents are actively concerned.*

The French voter himself bears much responsibility for the political manœuvres which he despises. A party which wrecks a government will be bitterly reproached for doing so; but its motive is usually electoral advantage or fears. The Frenchman wants stable government and damns the politicians for not providing it; but he also requires that they keep a wary eye on his personal and group interests, which he will never sacrifice for his country. Any attempt to collect taxes from small businessmen or to impose them on peasants, to reduce the scandalous alcohol subsidy or raise above 55 the retiring age for railwaymen, meets passionate hostility from the interests affected. Yet their defenders, to whose cries the deputies are so conscientiously responsive, blame the mirror and not the original for the ugly figure their Parliament often cuts.

The parliamentary game is itself a consequence and not a cause of French political divisions and instability. When every ministry rests precariously on the support of several mutually hostile parties, there are many opportunities for the wily and adroit. But the numerous parties produce the politics of manœuvre, and not the other way round. And for the number of parties the cause must be sought in an electorate deeply divided by several distinct cleavages—between bourgeoisie and workers, between clericals and anticlericals, between authoritarians and democrats, between town and country, between nationalists and 'Europeans'. Not one of these great rifts in French unity coincides with any of the others; small wonder that no stable and coherent majority can be assembled. It is not to be found in Parliament because it does not exist in the country.

Thus French majorities are temporary combinations based on a fragile compromise between conflicting groups. The task of government falls to those men and parties best adapted to accommodation and bargaining. The Communists went into opposition in 1947 and the Socialists in 1951; the Gaullists emerged from it in 1953; all other parties have participated in every cabinet for eight years. Yet there has always been an opposition drawn from within the ministerial ranks themselves; and it is with the backing of this opposition that M. Mendès-France took power.

His weakness is that his following contains several distinct elements. Some are in revolt against feeble government and powerful pressure-groups, and are determined to override obstructive private interests in pursuit of a

---

* This last point is no longer true. On provincial ties see the later election chapters.

programme of national reconstruction; M. Mendès-France leads them, and this outlook appeals to many of the Gaullists. But there are also interest-groups which feel that recent governments have shown them too little sympathy, such as M. Antier's Peasants and the native colonial members. Others are politicians hoping to ride to power on public discontent with 'the old gang'—for example M. Daladier, who led Radical opposition to the Government both in 1949, from the Right, and in 1953, from the Left. This is a shaky base from which to launch a far-reaching appeal to all Frenchmen to sacrifice their private interests to the needs of national recovery.

M. Mendès-France has always maintained that internal reconstruction must precede the revival of French influence abroad. But he cannot succeed in it unless the deputies feel that their constituents' mood has changed, that the country has thrown off its cynical torpor and accepted the need for effort and sacrifice. He must rely upon youth and the rank and file against the suspicion and hostility of the recognised leaders of all parties. Thus his promise to resign unless peace was signed by 20th July was a clever move. Peace would win him the prestige and authority to overcome the *caciques* and carry his reforms; without that authority, better go at once than drag out a frustrated and impotent existence for six wasted months. Office without power has never appealed to Mendès-France.

Not all the leaders whom he dispossessed were unscrupulous men concerned only with clinging to their jobs. MRP, the pivot of every coalition since liberation, began as a missionary rather than a power-seeking party, though contact with practical politics has somewhat tarnished its idealism. It set out to reconcile Catholics to the Republic, workers to a reformed economic system, and France to her neighbours. In the first aim it has largely succeeded; in the second (and still more in colonial matters) it has disillusioned many of its most ardent supporters; but its concessions and compromises have been made for the sake of its European programme, on which it has staked its future—a perhaps mistaken but not ignoble cause.

The other groups of the old majority, especially the Radicals, do include many 'pure politicians' for whom policy is infinitely adjustable and only the desire for office remains constant. Yet even these 'king's friends' fulfil a useful function. British politics may turn on cabinet decision and parliamentary criticism, but in France parliamentary pressure still plays a real part in shaping (or obstructing) policy. Where day-to-day bargaining is so important there is room for professional brokers, though their price is no doubt high. The public is cynical about place-hunters who support every ministry; but in normal times they provide useful continuity and experience, and in periods of acute stress they are at least preferable to open civil war between the rival idealists. It is the 'king's friends' whose presence in every cabinet

37

makes government crises so much less disruptive than they appear, and whose bargaining skill enables them to be solved.*

Divisions among Frenchmen are many and deep. Strong and vigorous leaders would too often split the nation instead of pulling it together; and men of rigid principle are not always easily persuaded of the need for compromise. The uninspiring practical politicians perform an essential task in settling conflicts by voting and bargaining instead of fighting. Yet in the gravest crises the French nation has sometimes shown a sudden appreciation of its own unity, an angry impatience with those who prefer private interests or familiar routines to the general welfare, and an unexpected willingness to follow a strong leader of unflinching purpose. It remains to be seen whether 1954 will prove such an occasion, and Pierre Mendès-France such a man.†

* The Fifth Republic has given birth to a new type of 'king's friend' even more closely resembling the original.
† On Mendès-France's ministry and movement, see chapter 1.

6 'Throw the rascals out!': the 1956 election[1]*

By 5 December 1955, 28 groups had announced their intention to contest the election; and 18 of them succeeded in qualifying as national parties.†
Seven had been represented as separate groups in the old National Assembly
—Communists, Socialists, MRP, M. Mendès-France's Radicals and their UDSR allies, the Conservative CNI, and the formerly Gaullist RS—and two more were to be represented for the first time in the new one, M. Faure's RGR and the Poujadists.[2]‡ Five more were satellites of a 'major party'—
MRP, UDSR, and the CNI had one shadow party each, and the Poujadists had two. Four were minor parties: the *Jeune République*, an old Left Catholic group; the *Parti républicain pour le redressement économique et social*, a new body of 'Catholics for Mendès-France'; the *Rassemblement national*, an anti-parliamentary group on the far Right; and the RGRIF, a purely electoral combine formed in 1951 by a rich Lyons business man.[3]§ Only two other groups seriously attempted to obtain national status, the Left Independents who ran 21 lists, and M. Dorgères' anti-parliamentary *Parti républicain paysan*, which ran 16. Most minor parties attained the quota of 30 lists only by forming many joint lists with their parent organization, or by putting up

---

[1] Among many others I owe particular acknowledgements to Madame M. Blondel and Mr Martin Harrison. Mr Harrison also contributed the section on the national press.

[2] The CNI (Centre national des Indépendants, Paysans et ARS) is now the national headquarters of the clerical Conservatives, the hardest group in France to organize. The RS (Républicains sociaux) included about half the former Gaullist deputies. The RGR (Rassemblement des gauches républicaines) was an electoral alliance of Radicals, UDSR, and other small conservative parties. Most of the Radical representatives on it were hostile to M. Mendès-France; when he expelled them for refusing to give up these positions, they combined with the smaller groups to form a new party. Of these 9 major groups, UDSR ran 30 lists, RGR 32, RS 62, the rest at least 75.

[3] In 1951 RGRIF included candidates of very varying views; several were Vichyites. In 1956 it was almost a branch of RGR and its founder indeed stood as RGR, saying 'J'ai choisi le plus sérieux.'

* Originally entitled 'The Campaign'. From *Political Studies* (vol. 4. no. 2 June 1956). Three other articles were published in the same or the next number: on the election law, by H. G. Nicholas; on Guy Mollet's campaign, by S. Rose; and on the election in Vienne, by M. Thomas.

† I.e. the organisations described above, p. 10 n. 1.

‡ See also below, pp. 51, 57 and notes.

§ He was M. Chambaretaud (above, p. 13).

bogus lists.[1] These bogus lists were registered in constituencies (preferably near Paris or—for RGRIF—near Lyons) returning few members and having, therefore, a small deposit (£20 per candidate): the average number of bogus lists per constituency declines steadily from four in the two-member seats to one-fourth in seats with seven or more members.

The first preoccupation of a national headquarters is the endorsement of candidates. Organized parties like the Communists, Socialists, or MRP, find little difficulty with this problem. But parties in the midst of reorganization like the Radicals, or loose groups which rely on committees of local *notables*, find their *investiture* sought from every side. They may have to choose between two rival sitting members each claiming first place, between an outgoing deputy and a locally powerful rival, or between different claimants wishing to contest a new constituency; and a disappointed candidate may always decide to run a list of his own. One UDSR candidate in Paris, asked why he was splitting the Mendèsist vote, replied that he had approached the Radical member, who had offered him second place: only later did he discover that seventeen others had had the same offer. In Calvados a young protégé of General Koenig, campaigning hard against the outgoing deputies and especially the ex-premier M. Laniel, was offered and accepted second place on M. Laniel's list just before the lists closed. In Yonne a Socialist recently expelled from the party stood on the UDSR ticket: in Creuse another joined the Communist list.

The local party must pay careful attention to the rest of the list also. Sections of the department should be balanced: thus in Allier four of the six main lists included a representative each from Moulins, Montluçon, and Vichy.[2] Important religious communities like the Protestants of Bas-Rhin, or linguistic groups like the Basques of Basses-Pyrénées, expect representation. There should also be a social balance. Doctors and vets are at a premium, a peasant leader is often indispensable, a woman may be included (usually low on the list); but generals (like M. Koenig) or bearers of noble names (like M. de Broglie) may find it wise to suppress their titles. It is well to care for different shades of political allegiance. M. Pinay's

---

[1] Of the 9 minor groups, only three ran more than 32 lists: none ran 40. On the last possible evening a car-load of Lyonnais drove to the south coast, handing in a RGRIF list at every prefecture. This party reached the quota only by being allowed to count the lists it had intended to run in Algeria, where elections were postponed.

[2] In Moselle, where ex-Gaullists and Conservatives joined forces, they stated officially that, recognizing that two agricultural representatives from the same *arrondissement* could not both expect a seat, one sitting member was standing down in favour of another.

But not all lists take such pains. Thus in one Norman constituency, Le Havre and Dieppe were both represented on every list. But while Conservatives, Radicals, and Poujadists were well distributed through the area, the two big towns provided 4 out of the 6 Communists, 5 Socialists, and 5 RS. MRP had 4 candidates from the Fécamp area, and RGR 4 from Eu: all the last three lists did very badly.

secretary, in Tarn, had on his list both the Gaullist and the Vichyite candidates for the constituency in 1951. An old hand like M. Pleven, by personal influence and the judicious choice of colleagues, was able to acquire endorsements from Radicals, RGR, UDSR, and CNI.

Such a collection of *investitures* is useful in staving off or weakening rival candidates. This is most important where an alliance has a chance of winning a clear majority; here a very few votes may decide several seats, and the presence or absence, the isolation or alliance, of a petty list may have great consequences. It is occasionally alleged that the Prefect has tried to help or hinder a particular candidate by encouraging a minor list to run or retire, or by refusing to accept an *apparentement*. Such charges were made in half a dozen constituencies (out of 103), in three of which an ex-Minister of the Interior was standing: the alleged beneficiaries were not all government supporters.

When such a dispute occurs, national headquarters will be called in. But in any case it will wish to approve all local *apparentements*, for they may have repercussions elsewhere. Members fearing defeat sometimes seek support in unexpected quarters—Socialists among supporters of church schools, MRP on the far Right. Such combinations may be denounced in hostile propaganda not only in the constituency—several local alliances between Socialists and clericals were broken off later—but all over the country, as the Communists attacked Radicals and Socialists for associating with the RS. In some areas the conservative groups refrained from taking full advantage of the electoral law for fear of driving the Socialists into the arms of the Communists. There may even be inter-party bargaining: we will save M. Morice's threatened seat by an alliance at Nantes if you will do the same for M. Coste-Floret at Toulouse. Local parties may be reluctant to accept alliances made in Paris: in the south-west, Socialists and Radicals were often bitter local rivals. Or they may be split: in some western departments urban and trade union members of MRP opposed the Conservative alliance which peasants (and deputies with shaky seats) favoured. Thus an *apparentement* may affect the cohesion of a local party, its choice of candidate, its decision whether to contest the election at all. It may decide not only whether the party wins or loses, but whether it is Right or Left. Small wonder that for the first ten days of the campaign the whole interest, in Paris and in the constituencies, turns on the problem of alliances.

In the later stages the party headquarters are occupied with propaganda. They arrange for speakers and broadcasters, advise candidates, distribute literature, reply to pressure-groups, deal with the press, put out statements full of hard-headed realism skilfully blended with lofty principles, and answer the shabby and partial misrepresentations of their opponents.[1] In this rushed campaign these activities were somewhat curtailed. Few party leaders were willing to travel far. Only M. Mendès-France conducted a national tour, though MM. Mollet and Pflimlin delivered speeches outside their own constituencies, and some others crossed into a neighbouring department.

Again, less propaganda literature than usual was specially prepared. The Radicals had a well-designed series of coloured leaflets (black for the bad old days, red, white, and blue for their own proposals) setting out their various policies. The RS supplied their candidates with long and carefully drafted answers to questions; MRP sent out a model speech, together with hints on tactics ('use down-to-earth local examples'). The RGR posted a million free copies of their journal, *Unité française*, to members of the professional classes. The Socialists put out special handbills appealing to groups as varied as youth, railwaymen, Communist supporters, workers on their own account, North Africans (in Arabic), and Polish miners (in Polish). Local parties made a good deal of use of the material supplied from Paris, especially in their departmental newspapers.

These activities are performed in general by very small staffs: most non-Communist parties had from six to ten of the 'administrative class', with even fewer typists, &c.[2] A loose organization like the CNI, with hardly any full-time staff, has to recruit sympathizers for the election campaign; but in a better organized party such as MRP, more than half the regular officials may disappear at election time to stand in the provinces. The atmosphere of these headquarters varies from the tidy respectability of the centre parties, each with its *ancien des Sciences-po*, to the preoccupied bustle of the RS, the democratic camaraderie of the Socialists, and the 'boy scout' air of a group of youthful idealists like the *Jeune République*—or the barred doors and undisguised suspicion which prevail at the seat of the Communist party. Small numbers suffice because the campaign is so localized. Paris papers do not have a nation-wide circulation; radio and TV play a comparatively small part; and the local candidate has to make his own way. The assistance on which he can count varies greatly. The Communists, who alone dispose of an organization in the constituencies comparable to that of a British party, are exceptions to most generalizations, whether about methods or about aims. For them an election is merely an intensification of a permanent recruiting campaign.

[1] With the press, one object is to persuade papers not to forecast the defeat of some endangered candidate. A paper which had predicted in a constituency report the defeat of the candidate whom it favoured, found this used as a campaign argument against wasting votes on him. The journal then corrected its report and announced, on new information, the probable defeat of his rival. (Both were returned.)

[2] In Britain in 1951 Conservative headquarters had 220, Labour 100, Liberals 50: a third of each were 'administrative class'.

They have their militants everywhere, as have the Socialists in many areas, but the other groups in comparatively few. So the numbers who participate actively in running the campaign differ greatly between parties and between regions. In one typical constituency, Indre, the Communists organized a squad of sixty speakers; in another small department a Conservative ex-minister had a staff of ten; in a third an ex-premier, M. Queuille, took one story of an hotel for his headquarters—as the hotel had only one telephone, he was obliged to divide his time between politics and the letting of bed-rooms. Often the more conservative groups, since they do not seek popular membership, simply rely on the personal influence of local *notables*—mayors, local councillors, peasant leaders, and the like. They can survive in this skeleton form because they escape many of the propaganda difficulties, and all the problems of getting out the vote, which occupy a local party in Britain: no register to keep, no canvassing, election addresses sent through official channels, and a public holiday for polling day, on which neither cars nor knockers-up nor tellers are required.[1]

The recognized legal forms of propaganda are posters and election addresses. Posters must be displayed on the official sites, and there is some-times a problem in finding workers for this task. The Communists always put theirs up first, the Socialists usually second; the other parties straggle behind. One Paris candidate paid £400 to a bill-posting firm. Another hired unemployed North Africans from the labour exchange (as they were illiterate, this had its drawbacks). In Nice, indeed, it was said that the elec-tion industry was a major boon to the unemployed, who were hired to stick up *affiches* by day and to tear them down by night.[2] At the other extreme, in Colmar, the mayor, who was the MRP candidate, refused to allow one of M. Mauriac's articles to be *affiché* either on election *panneaux* (because it was not electoral propaganda) or on commercial hoardings (because it was political).

There are also easy means of evading the law. Posters can be put up before the campaign officially starts (the Communists make full use of this);

[1] Elections are normally on Sundays. But under dissolution procedure the only available Sundays were Christmas Day and New Year's Day. 2 January was therefore made a paid public holiday; the employers vainly contested this decree in the courts.

Cars were very occasionally used. A mayor in Seine-et-Marne organized transport for the aged and sick in outlying villages, M. Schneiter in Marne offered a car for any voter who requested it, and the better-organized parties may now and then supply cars to party members who ask for them.

Though there are no tellers, parties may have checkers at poll and count. On canvassing see below, p. 47.

[2] But Nice, where the mayor's party took the lead in posting *affiches* illegally on every available tree, and was joyously followed by the others, and where the Communists proclaimed that they had spent the eve of poll plastering the town with illegal posters, was hardly typical—though in this matter 'tolerated illegality' is common.

a party can sing its own praises without naming its candidate; a candidate can display his photograph and advertise his recent book, as did two unsuccessful Paris politicians; and small stickers (*papillons*) are frequently stuck on enemy posters—Communists drawing attention to the votes cast by their opponents, or Poujadists marking the posters of deputies with an imitation road sign and the words *danger—sortant*.[1]

Another important form of propaganda is the bogus newspaper or newspaper supplement, distributed free by those parties which dispose of sufficient resources to use this method (most do). Election addresses and *bulletins de vote* are distributed from the *mairies* (26 tons of them in Seine-et-Marne)[2] and there are always a few complaints that those of one list have been omitted—the Radicals suffered in this way in north-west Paris and in Moselle. These documents are not unlike their British counterparts. Some candidates write letters, others string together party slogans. As each list can send out two addresses, one often contains details about the candidates (frequently, though not always, with photographs), while the other deals with policy. Most addresses perform the customary gallop through the whole course of domestic and foreign affairs. But in Allier the Socialists contrived to mention neither foreign nor North African policy; in Marne most parties stressed local interests heavily; a *Jeune République* candidate argued that a big-party vote was a wasted vote; an independent Conservative in Paris pointed with pride to a voting record more reactionary than that of his principal rival—a device more frequently employed in the opposite sense. All Poujadists appear to have used the same addresses, which were written in a popular familiar style, and were powerful pieces of abuse.[3] MRP were, in Paris at any rate, the only party to show any imaginative technique in either posters or addresses.

The public meeting remains a major propaganda weapon. The national total was said to have averaged 2,000–3,000 a day; Marseilles had 577 during the campaign. Their number varied very greatly, both by regions and by parties: in the south many candidates visited ten villages a day, holding small meetings or receiving constituents at the *mairie*. But in the north such activity was exceptional, and in some areas two or three meetings a day was considered energetic. The campaign began in the villages and finished in the larger towns; the Communists, with their effective and permanent organiza-

---

[1] Those of new candidates in south Paris had stickers with the libellous phrase *Vendu(e) à Ulver*. Ulver was the RS member, much hated by the Poujadists.

[2] This was far from a record. And Marseilles had 23 tons of *affiches* printed.

[3] 'La trahison est partout...La tête de France est pourrie...Les politiciens vous ont trahi!... Nous vomissons la politique...Nous ne vous promettons rien sinon de nettoyer la maison... Contre les pourris, les lâches et les traîtres...Sortez les sortants!' On Poujadist posters three enormous words could be read from afar: 'Poujade...Contre...Sortants.'

Many, but not all Communists also used stereotyped election addresses.

tion, were best at reaching the 'grass roots' and penetrating to hamlets and wards. In towns they frequently organized meetings addressed to particular groups—youth, women, the ill-housed, transport workers, teachers, &c.; in one day's *Humanité*, fifteen of the fifty-five meetings announced were of this kind. Occasionally others followed this example: M. Mendès-France opened his campaign with a meeting for women in Paris, and a provincial Radical held one for his North African constituents.

Meetings were usually held in schoolrooms, cafés, cinemas, or *mairies*. There seems to have been no difficulty in finding accommodation, though in Saône-et-Loire a Socialist mayor would not allow Poujadist meetings, at Bayeux a Gaullist refused halls or poster facilities to a former Vichy minister, in Marseilles a well-known MRP enemy of alcoholism was excluded from the *bistros*—and in a tiny village in Gard the municipality refused to let the *mairie* for any election meeting, as a protest against 'the deplorable spectacle presented to the world by the National Assembly'.

In a country with big constituencies, many villages, and few large towns, candidates indeed have a hard task. Their best allies are prominent local figures—mayors or local councillors willing to lend a hand in their own bailiwicks. Some leading figures, such as MM. Pinay and Pflimlin, left local campaigning to lesser-known parliamentary colleagues while they defended the cause elsewhere; others, like MM. Faure and Pleven, were very active; one, M. de Menthon, sat silent while his political juniors answered the questions. The active candidates often travelled as a team, though some divided the department between them. And while the candidate whose re-election is at stake may work hard, the others often do not. An influential local mayor might well be more willing to lend his name than his time to his party's cause. One RS deputy even spent the election duck-shooting, so certain did his defeat appear.

All parties must pay great attention to visiting the local *notables*; but, as mentioned above, the conservative groups often conserve their own energies by concentrating on these powerful figures, and summon supporters of influence to confer in private rather than expose themselves to the turbulent citizenry. M. Pinay, for instance, held few constituency meetings, and broke them off when interrupted. One Conservative sought to win friends and influence people by inviting local mayors to lunch: his RS rival offered snacks to the *secrétaires de mairie* (the former was elected, the latter not).

The French equivalent of question-time at election meetings is the practice of *contradiction*. After the speeches, the floor (and microphone, if any) is offered to opponents or critics, who give their name and allegiance (many, of course, reply 'non-party') and ask questions or make short speeches to which the candidate replies.[1] It is very common for candidates or local leaders to attend their rivals' meetings for this purpose (a few, indeed, conduct their whole campaign in this way). Major occasions of this kind are announced in advance, and these set duels are naturally very popular. One such meeting broke the departmental attendance record in Haute-Saône; another drew 5,000 people in Compiègne; in Paris 25,000 were said to have come to hear M. Duclos debate with M. Mendès-France.

Attendances were generally reported to be higher, often much higher, than in 1951. In most smallish towns 150 to 600 (mostly men) seems to have been a normal range, descending to 15 or 20 in the hamlets and rising to several thousands on great occasions in the cities. In middle-sized places the proportion attending often reached 1 elector in 20 and even occasionally 1 in 6:[2] MM. Faure at Dôle, Mendès-France at Epernay, Mitterrand at Cosne, Poujade at Montélimar, and Schuman in a township near Metz all drew audiences of this magnitude.

Yet the utility of meetings is somewhat doubtful. As in England, sceptics claim that meetings are necessary only because their absence is resented. One MRP ex-minister, whose audiences were said to be four or five times larger than those of 1951, lost 25 per cent of his votes. An ex-Gaullist Conservative, who had served under M. Mendès-France, had excellent and attentive meetings: he lost three-fifths of his votes and his seat. M. Baylet, of the *Dépêche* of Toulouse, began his campaign a week ahead of his rivals, but gained only 1,000 votes. The Socialists in Aisne had poor attendances and put their vote up by 30 per cent. Two candidates each attracted 1,000 people in Mantes; one polled ten times the other's vote.

The spectacular reports of Poujadist activities have naturally coloured impressions of the campaign in England. They were certainly remarkable. Poujadist attempts to break up meetings were reported from about two-fifths of France's constituencies. In most they merely drowned the speakers' voices by shouts—or by cowbells, drums, loudspeakers, hunting horns, and alarm clocks. But elsewhere speakers were bombarded with eggs, fruit and vegetables, and even cream cakes. Garages were instructed not to supply one deputy with petrol; electricians were warned not to install microphones in halls; wires were cut and lights extinguished; luckless candidates were prevented from entering or leaving their own meetings. Often these demon-

---

[1] The similarities with British meetings are striking. Opponents are referred to formally, friends by their Christian names. A joke puts the meeting in a good humour: 'The only list in this constituency that stands for *real* government stability is the Témoins de Christ—you can't vote no confidence in God.' Foul hitters are not above a little discreet anti-semitism. Village audiences may need coaxing to ask questions; large towns may produce exhibitionists (in Nancy the plots of the freemasons were exposed at a Socialist meeting by a man who, next evening, appeared as a fanatical European federalist to attack the RS).

[2] Proportions of the *1951* electorate in the *canton*.

strations were more like student 'rags' than like fascist brutality. In Aveyron a member was confronted in one place by a small donkey called a *ministrous*, wearing a placard 'En 4 ans j'ai travaillé plus que toi'; in another he was politely invited to enter an empty schoolroom and then locked in by his prospective audience. But once or twice in Paris, and in half a dozen western constituencies, affairs took an uglier turn, and Poujadist 'commandos'—often imported by car from other departments, and usually led by the local candidate—resorted to physical violence in order to prove that no meetings could be held without their leave. Such behaviour is quite unusual in French electioneering, and seems to have done the Poujadists harm: in almost every case it was abandoned later in the campaign. In Nièvre the Poujadists' main enemy, M. Mitterrand, substantially increased his vote, while the Poujadists did worse than in any neighbouring department.

The Poujadist campaign was directed almost exclusively against out-going deputies, and as a rule especially against the local 'heavyweight'—often an ex-minister (so that the conservative parties suffered most), but sometimes a dominant local personality like the Socialist member in Haute-Vienne. Only in three or four cases did they interfere with the one party equipped to meet them, the Communists: much more frequently the extremists combined against some obnoxious democrat. M. Georges Bonnet, M. Tixier-Vignancour, the Alsatian autonomists, and some Poujadists encountered similar obstruction and even violence from Resistance elements, and in one or two places (notably Seine-et-Oise and Calvados) the Communists were disorderly. Police protection (strangely absent for the hard-pressed M. Mitterrand) was sometimes provided, but frequently the offer was refused. Yet, apart from the spectacular Poujadist rowdyism, this was an orderly and serious campaign.*

Few other forms of propaganda were at all widely practised. Canvassing is not well received in France: here and there a candidate toured isolated farms, but only Communists canvassed at all frequently, and even they did so only in particular regions, and usually in favourable districts and on a limited scale. Film shows made for the first time an important appearance in election propaganda, being used especially by Socialists and Radicals; in Vosges the Radical cause was represented in the villages by a film of M. Mendès-France and a number of gramophone records. Loudspeakers are generally forbidden by the local Prefect, and no exception was made for the election. Convoys of propagandist cars, organized by the Poujadists, were stopped in Paris and Lille, and disallowed in Marseilles; individual vehicles seem to have been tolerated, but were not widely used.

* For the origins of Poujadism see P. M. Williams, *Crisis and Compromise* (Longmans, 1964), pp. 162-9.

Election expenses are not legally limited. Most parties agreed that a full-scale campaign in a Paris constituency would cost between £6,000 and £12,000, and that in the provinces £3,000 to £4,000 was the most it was worth spending; much less would suffice in poor areas and small constituencies. A candidate—more concerned perhaps with the realistic and less with the ideal—estimated 6 to 8 francs per head in the larger towns (he himself had spent £5,000 in a huge Paris constituency, just below his estimate) and 10 francs per head in the country, giving about £2,500 for a typical five-member seat and about £3,500 in the large constituencies of Brittany. By no means all parties raised their expenses locally: for instance, many Conservative candidates did so, but few MRP.

Such sums were, of course, exceeded by some lavish aspirants to political honours, one of whom—M. Robert Hersant in Oise—was said to have spent £100,000 in what the French press called *une campagne à l'américaine*: publicity visits by film stars; holiday camps for schoolchildren; huge subscriptions to all local sports clubs; phosphorescent posters (with photographs) on every telegraph pole. He claimed to be a Radical (though repudiated by the local Radicals) and a Mendèsist (though never making the mistake of familiarizing the electors with any name but his own). In spite of violent attacks from Right and Left on this attempt to 'purchase a constituency', he was comfortably elected.* But the three or four other candidates who attracted attention by similar activities on a far smaller scale were all beaten.

The Paris press followed the election assiduously, but seems to have influenced it little. The campaign held the headlines throughout, despite the claims of Algeria, crime, and another election (to choose Miss France). Party papers, from *Humanité* to the Mendèsist *L'Express*, selected the news to serve the cause, and *L'Express* was diligent in unearthing (or inventing) its daily sensation. But elsewhere news items with political implications were rarely 'splashed'. Moderate Left journals featured a report on Paris housing with no undue prominence; even Algeria remained on the inside pages. Most papers confined political news to separate pages, distinct from comment. National exchanges were recorded, *apparentements* reviewed, and later on results gloomily predicted. In the news columns arithmetic was indeed more prominent than issues.

National leaders and set-piece meetings in Paris were faithfully reported, but lesser lights received very selective treatment. Most papers gave at least a page to constituency reports of varying quality but fair objectivity (except for an engaging hesitancy to prophesy the defeat of friends). Not even the most conscientious paper could give a comprehensive coverage. Party journals gave much space to features advocating the party line on the issues

* Cf. below, p. 212.

of the campaign: so did *La Croix* for Catholics. The independents, though pressing hard for constitutional reform, were more concerned to record than to initiate opinion. *Le Monde* maintained its usual high standard: it, like *Combat*, ran a *tribune libre*. *France-Soir*, *Aurore*, and *Figaro* published feature series on the various issues. But the national press played a much less central part in the campaign than in Britain.

In the provincial press one or two journals—notably *L'Est républicain* of Nancy—were outstanding for fair, informative, and intelligent reporting. But few papers gave much space to the campaign, and most preferred national agency material to local election news. Major engagements in Paris were usually recorded—the controversy between M. Mauriac and the Church over the duties of Catholics, the mass meeting at which M. Duclos challenged M. Mendès-France, *L'Express*'s eve-of-poll story about the shooting of a prisoner in Algeria. Poujadist activities received rather scant attention. Few papers showed strong bias: many gave no editorial lead, Communist meetings were announced as freely as others, rival candidates were usually treated fairly—even *Midi libre*, which went to some trouble to avoid naming the RGR candidate (a cabinet minister) throughout the campaign, still announced his meetings and gave him a (hostile) profile. When the results were known all papers, however uninterested before, devoted much space to the comments of the Parisian, and especially the foreign press.

Radio and TV seem to have played little part. Both national and local papers usually announced the parties (but more rarely the speakers) who were broadcasting that day. The Communist press gave great publicity to party broadcasts: local Socialists occasionally advertised when M. Mollet was speaking: *Combat* reported some of the main spokesmen (M. Pinay and a Communist as well as Republican Front leaders). There was no sign that this was France's first TV election: *France-Soir* was the only paper to comment on how speakers performed. The talks were far from striking, apart from the Poujadists: five or ten minutes were insufficient for coherent reasoning, ample for general recrimination. Even so, some viewers were surprised at the Poujadist peasant leader's conclusion: 'The deputies fear the States-General because they remember the guillotine. We won't need the guillotine this time, it's too expensive. A good rope is cheaper, you can use it several times, and there are plenty of lamp-posts. Vive la France!'

II

The election campaign of December 1955 was the first for nearly eighty years to be opened by a parliamentary dissolution. Normal elections were due in June 1956; the Faure cabinet, either—as it claimed—because the old

Assembly was too divided to take urgent decisions about Algeria, or—as critics alleged—to catch its opponents unorganized, introduced a bill to bring them forward six months. Rather than attack this openly, the opposition demanded a change in the highly unpopular electoral law, which many government supporters privately hoped to retain. A Cabinet crisis would prevent early elections; as it might stop electoral reform too, the Communists dropped their brief flirtation with M. Faure. But the ministry was lucky. Personal voting without proxies, recently introduced, made the wirepullers' calculations impossible; the Cabinet was defeated by an absolute majority of the house, which gave it the constitutional right to dissolve—and M. Faure seized the unexpected chance to turn defeat into victory.*

By deciding to hold the election immediately and on the existing electoral law, the prime minister defied the majority of his party and assumed the electoral leadership of the conservative coalition. Supporters of the old government expected to form alliances more easily than their opponents, and to command an absolute majority of votes, and therefore win all the seats, in many more constituencies than their rivals (though many fewer than in 1951). In this case the Communists would certainly win seats, while M. Mendès-France and his friends might lose them, even if they gained in votes. M. Faure was expelled from the Radical party, as were most well-known leaders of the moderate wing. Five of his Radical ministers resigned from the Cabinet. The opposition leader attacked the dissolution as an unfair manœuvre (the more bitter because executed by a former friend and colleague) and his paper *L'Express* pointed out that the dissolution decree appeared on the anniversary of Napoleon III's *coup d'état*. But one party, not usually slow to expose the machinations of reaction, held aloof from this clamour: the dissolution had warm Communist approval.

During the next few days the opposition parties drew together in a *Front républicain*. Four leaders—M. Mendès-France, M. Mollet, M. Mitterrand of UDSR, and M. Chaban-Delmas of the RS, signed common communiqués protesting against the dissolution, the electoral law, the inadequacy of the register, and alleged governmental misuse of the radio. But the Republican Front soon abandoned these themes. When the ministry took prompt action to remedy the radio and register grievances, this could be explained away as due to the pressure of a vigilant public. But the opposition leaders soon found not only that—as in England—politicians' grievances about other politicians' behaviour aroused no interest in the electorate, but that the dissolution was positively popular, indeed the most popular act of M. Faure's

---

* The conservative Assembly elected in 1951 (see chap. 2) had brought Pierre Mendès-France to power soon after the French defeat at Dien Bien Phu, but had overthrown him seven months later (above, p. 5). Edgar Faure, his finance minister, had then become premier, supported by the conservative coalition.

political life. The numbers hastening to register were more than double those usual in a pre-election period. It remained to be seen how the people would use this opportunity to judge their rulers.

On 6 December the Socialists made the decisive choice of the campaign, following their leaders in rejecting the proffered alliance of the Communist party, and in resolving to combine only with those men and groups who had supported the Mendès-France government to the end. This ruled out the MRP and the Conservatives but permitted alliances with some RS. Thus two blocs were in conflict with one another, one based on a Conservative–MRP alliance, the other on the Socialist and Radical parties, but both harassed on their flanks by Poujadists, minor anti-parliamentary groups, and Communists. RS might be found on either side, usually the former, and Radical federations were often divided.[1] Yet despite these complications, and the rivalries of individual candidates competing for the same clientele, the clash was much more clear-cut than in any other postwar election. Apart from the perpetual Socialist–Communist duel, each party concentrated its fire on the opposing bloc and treated with sympathy (or ignored) the political groups who under PR, or even in 1951, would have been its most dangerous and therefore most criticized competitors.

The policy of the opposition was to accentuate the cleavage between the two sides. The government parties played it down, though they naturally defended their own record and derided the prestige of the opposition leader —'Superman' as he was called in the extreme right-wing press. Mendèsists claimed to be clarifying issues which their opponents chose to obscure: government sympathizers retorted that when the need was for national unity, the opposition was dividing the nation, as M. Mendès-France had divided his own party. The contrast was seen in the fairly frequent MRP offers of *apparentement* with the Socialists, which were neither accepted nor reciprocated: in the repeated insistence of MM. Faure and Duchet that both sides had the same objectives: in MRP's proposal on 31 December for a post-election conference of all democratic parties to try to work out common solutions: and in the denunciations by MM. Mendès-France and Mollet, both of the record of the outgoing government, and of its attempts to escape

---

[1] But of 49 RS deputies who stood only 1 formed an alliance with the Republican Front (and he *faute de mieux*), while 26 joined the government side. In 8 constituencies RS candidates were *apparentés* with Radicals and Socialists (and in 2 more with Radicals alone). By this association with members (even liberal members) of a group they had denounced as authoritarian, clerical, and reactionary, the Socialists exposed themselves to Communist attack; and as RS votes brought no extra seats to the Left, the alliance seems to have been a tactical error.

The Socialists joined the Radicals in 48 constituencies, and fought alone in 48: in 6 they were allied with other Left groups, and in 1 with the Communists (see below, p. 59). MRP joined the Conservatives in 51 seats (22 with RS also), fighting on its own in 41. There were 30 in which a Conservative–MRP alliance faced a Socialist–Radical combination.

the just wrath of the people. Each side had a plausible case. It was very hard to see how the Republican Front could possibly hope to govern alone, and if it rejected Communist aid it would have to turn to the groups it was denouncing in the election. Yet the opposition had better assessed the impatience and disgust of the electorate at the reshuffling of familiar faces which avoided any genuine political change, the compromise and indecision which stultified government, the impotence of 'broad governments of national union', the repeated and open defiance of the State by 'little groups of wilful men'. It was in Jacobin intransigence that these parties saw the road to national safety and electoral success. To them the expulsion of M. Faure and his friends was an earnest that the renovation of Radicalism was to be taken seriously. By their opponents it was attacked as foreshadowing Communist purges and the perversion of justice.

Both sides made much of the divisions of their opponents. The Republican Front pointed to the allied MRP and RS candidates who, in the same journal, prided themselves on having respectively supported and opposed EDC, or to the *apparentement* of M. Bidault who deposed the Sultan of Morocco with M. Pinay who restored him. Their opponents' propaganda often echoed that of the Communists, stressing the anomalous position of the RS in the Republican Front over *laïcité* and North Africa, and challenging M. Mendès-France to say whether he would choose to govern with Communist or Conservative support. He could not avow his preference for the second alternative during the election campaign, and this enabled Conservatives to assert that the Republican Front was merely a device to bring about the Popular Front.

The menace of Communism, however, was seen in French rather than in Russian form. Fidelity to the Atlantic pact was invoked by some Conservative spokesmen, and its revision (to ensure more respect for France's extra-European interests by her partners) was demanded by the RS. German rearmament was attacked by the Communists and some RS; and MRP laid much stress on European union, blaming M. Mendès-France for the defeat of EDC. Generally, however, foreign affairs attracted little interest.

In domestic controversy there was much to make the Englishman feel at home. Both M. Mendès-France and M. Pinay offered rather unspecific hopes of a reduction in military service. The government pointed with pride to the country's prosperity: the opposition either kept silence on this theme, or complained of the better performances elsewhere, of heavy unemployment among textile workers, of desirable (if expensive) reforms not introduced— and of the size of the budget deficit. Conservatives promised to build 300,000 houses a year; the Left either criticized them for unrealistic demagogy and warned against cuts in standards, or, like the Communists, promised to build 330,000. Conservative charts showed the cost of living rising when Socialist ministers held office and stabilized by the new Poincaré, Antoine Pinay: the Left retorted that M. Pinay had prejudiced France's future by reducing investments.[1]

Other domestic themes were more peculiarly French. The government coalition put much weight on constitutional reform, praising M. Faure for the dissolution and demanding freer use of it in the future; the opposition laid more stress on a return to single-member constituencies, though both proposals found widespread support. The perennial problem of *laïcité* played a large part. It was the main burden of Communist charges of betrayal against the Republican Front, and in some areas repeal of recent pro-clerical legislation was also a principal slogan of Socialists or Radicals. Most RS and RGR candidates advocated the *status quo*. M. Mauriac, in *L'Express* and on the radio, appealed to Catholics to rate Christian charity in North Africa higher than subsidies to church schools: he was answered with some asperity by *La Croix* in France and by *Osservatore Romano* abroad—which gave rise to new charges of clerical interference. In fact, however, most of the higher clergy showed great discretion: only in the west did a bishop or two instruct the faithful to make the schools question the test of their vote.[2]

Alcoholism was a theme on which M. Mendès-France had a better hearing among his Catholic opponents than on his own side. Prudent candidates—Mendèsist or not—tempered their condemnation of this evil with an assurance that they repudiated all the specific measures proposed against it. In Paris and in Nord, which had many women voters and few or no home distillers (*bouilleurs de cru*), the latter were denounced in the most unlikely quarters; but in the east all candidates stoutly maintained that their constituents' innocent activities had nothing in common with the notorious frauds of the Normans—while in Normandy only a foolhardy (and non-political) man would venture to attack an abuse so prized by the citizens whose health it undermines. The topic was naturally much used for light relief also, the Poujadists making play with M. Mendès-France's taste for milk. Electorally, the impact of the question is hard to measure: M. Claudius Petit, who campaigned on this theme, was badly beaten—but so was the *bouilleurs'* arch-defender, the notorious M. Liautey.

In a predominantly rural country like France, local themes and interests count for more than they do in Britain. A candidate 'parachuted' into a

[1] One working-class grievance, invoked mainly but not only by the Left, was the minimum wage differential between Paris and the provinces. The RS also claimed recent collective agreements at the Renault and other works as examples of their cherished *association capital-travail*. Unlike the Left in Britain, the Communists wanted the rich excluded from social security benefits.

[2] The Poujadists tried not to commit themselves. Those who did so were divided.

constituency will clutch at the slightest local connexion—thus in Marne M. Biaggi, succeeding a deputy peculiarly indifferent to his department, pointed out that he had made his escape from the Germans on local soil. To speak Alsatian in the east or the local *patois* in the south is an important asset. An outgoing deputy and mayor will proudly recount his services to his department and city, such as his insistence that a new civic building in Rennes should be constructed with Breton granite instead of Italian materials; or he may be criticized for failing, for instance, to exclude Dutch margarine which competes with good Pyrenean butter. Paris is always a safe butt for criticism. A Conservative deputy, attacked by his own side for having served under M. Mendès-France (in itself a symptom of that leader's astonishing impact on French politics), could reply that he had already been in trouble for this with Parisian critics—*gens instables en politique*. The Poujadists have ostentatiously stressed their provincial character.

But even in Paris local considerations count. The successful Poujadist and Mendèsist candidates were indeed often unknown there—but the mayor of Vincennes saved his seat through the votes of his own suburb (half his poll, though only one-twelfth of the electorate). Elsewhere, a deputy dare not neglect his department—indeed a return to single-member seats might for this reason endanger the seats of some ex-ministers, now safe at the head of their lists.* The few members not renominated by their parties were often dropped on this account: the MRP deputy for Haut-Rhin publicly explained that he, unlike his party, thought attention to the nation's problems more important than attendance at all local ceremonies.[1] Gaullists in particular, and especially their generals, have taken this lofty attitude: no doubt it was to their credit, but it had much to do with their catastrophic defeat. Well-dug-in defences were needed to beat off the Poujadist assault.

Yet localism can be exaggerated. In one-industry regions, like the wine-growing Midi, politics will indeed naturally turn on regional problems. Elsewhere, particularism seems strongest, naturally enough, on the fringes —among Bretons, Basques, and Alsatians. Few national figures spent much time on local problems; nor did they suffer for this. M. Ramadier, the only candidate in Aveyron to campaign on national issues, resisted the Poujadist attack better than any rival. M. Pinay refused to discuss local questions at all.

National pressure groups made themselves felt rather more prominently than they do in Britain; among them the Society for the Protection of Animals, the advocates and opponents of football pools, the blind, the Commercial Travellers' Union, the friends and the enemies of church schools, and the ex-servicemen. Socialist replies to twenty-nine of these

---

[1] *L'Express* said he had been dropped for liberalism over North Africa.

* See below, p. 106, and much more fully, D. E. Butler (ed.), *Elections Abroad*, pp. 84–7.

groups, ranging from the PME (Small and Medium Enterprises) to the National Union of Students, were circulated to local parties for propaganda use. In many areas left-wing leaders of the Catholic trade unions campaigned on Socialist platforms: but there was no sign that MRP fared unusually badly in these departments.

In the constituencies the pressure-groups were said to have been more numerous and more imperious than ever before. Their interests ranged from butterfly-hunting to artificial insemination. The more serious groups questioned the candidates, and commented on their replies in the local press. But candidates do not seem to have been unduly intimidated. Of seven organizations which published voting recommendations in *L'Est républicain*, only two had had replies from more than half the lists, and some of these were unfavourable.[1] In Puy-de-Dôme the Conservative and the Peasant leaders announced that in this snap election they could not answer until after polling day. In Isère the ex-servicemen received favourable replies only from the left-wing parties; Conservatives and MRP were reserved, the Radical did not answer at all, and the Poujadist merely said 'The States-General will decide.'

Domestic problems were indeed dwarfed throughout the campaign by the dominant theme, that of the French Union and especially North Africa. The French Institute of Public Opinion (which did not cover itself with glory in this election) showed more voters concerned with Algeria than with purchasing power, wages, and housing combined. It was the main theme in the press. Every national figure except M. Bidault was anxious to proclaim his liberal attitude. The conservative parties, indeed, argued frequently that the abandonment of North Africa would mean economic disaster, general unemployment, and a collapse in the standard of living; but they equally repudiated policies of force, and blamed others for past repression. MRP leaders looked to 1951, forgot 1952 and 1953, and criticized M. Mendès-France's illiberalism in Algeria in 1954. Conservatives like M. Pinay attacked the RS as reactionary about Morocco, and (with a wonderful impertinence considering their own record) denounced M. Mendès-France for not tackling the situation in that country earlier. M. Faure pointed to his well-known opposition to the North African policy of the cabinets in which

---

[1] The seven were the Tenants' League, the Catholic railwaymen, the technical school teachers (CGT and so *laïque*), the APLE (for church schools), the European Movement, the Abbé Pierre's league to aid the homeless, and the tourist trade. The first summoned all candidates to a meeting; only the Communist went, and only two others replied, one unsatisfactorily. One successful candidate replied favourably to 6 of the 7 (not to APLE); two others (both defeated) answered 4; the Conservatives, who won three seats, replied favourably to only one.

In Ille-et-Vilaine some candidates sent personal replies—2 Poujadists to APLE, and 2 Radicals, 3 Poujadists, and 3 Dorgèrists to the local war-damage victims. The detailed results show that none of these gained any advantage in votes over his fellow candidates.

he served. The French political system offers every opportunity for 'not our fault' and 'you're another' arguments. Yet these recriminations, though undignified, implied hope for the future. Less excusable was the atrocity propaganda of *L'Express* just before polling day: partially false and unscrupulously timed, it was more effective but no more creditable than officialdom's reply, which was compounded in about equal parts of mendacity and ineptitude.

On the extreme Right there were, of course, a few French Kenneth de Courcys who discerned the authors of all France's troubles in the Kremlin, Wall Street, and the British Intelligence Service; and the Poujadists violently denounced past and future abandonments of France's empire. Otherwise, the Poujadist campaign was waged on a single and highly popular slogan: '*Sortez les Sortants!*' Others exploited this mood. Several new-comers—a Radical in Loire, a UDSR man in Paris, Conservatives in Puy-de-Dôme and Tarn—proclaimed their non-membership of the old Assembly as a reason for electing them to the new one. In Calvados the RS, to excuse his *sortant* status, pointed to his resignation from the cabinet, while the Socialist (a new man) swept aside such fine distinctions with his slogan: 'Et hop, un bon coup de balai!' The appeal was presented in its most respectable form by M. Mendès-France, pleading for national revival and stressing the claims of youth. But over most of the country the most diverse groups—Socialist and RS, Radical and Communist and Poujadist—joined in the depressingly negative cry 'Pour que ça change!'[1] Conservatives presented themselves wherever possible as 'hommes nouveaux, qui ne sont pas solidaires des erreurs du passé'. Only some MRP members met the attack head on. That party denounced the Mendès-France new deal as a reactionary reversion to the sordid individualist electoral system, the outmoded ideological quarrels, and the obsolete nationalism of the Third Republic; and one MRP candidate proudly claimed that he had never voted to turn out a government. M. Faure too made fun of the *futurs sortants*. *Canard enchaîné* had the last word in its post-election headline *Sortez les entrants!*

III

There were $2\frac{1}{2}$ million more electors registered, and $\frac{1}{4}$ million fewer abstentions than in 1951: the percentage of abstainers in the electorate fell from $20\frac{1}{2}$ to 17 per cent.[2] The Communists increased their vote from 5 million to

---

[1] Yet not long ago an American election was fought on the slogan 'Had enough? Vote Republican'. Is British election propaganda always more positive?

[2] Some 1,147,000 (or 4 per cent) of the persons of voting age were not registered (the compulsion is theoretical only). In December 1955 1,200,000 had put themselves on the list. The percentage of non-voters to persons of voting age was $27\frac{1}{2}$ in 1951, under 21 in 1956. Spoilt papers were 2 per cent in 1951, apparently slightly more this time.

5,600,000, their percentage of the poll remaining unchanged. The Republican Front parties polled $5\frac{1}{2}$ million, a gain of $1\frac{1}{2}$ million since 1951. The Socialists maintained their percentage strength for the first time since the war, and the Mendèsist Radicals doubled their votes (1 million to 2 million) and almost doubled their percentage (5 to $9\frac{1}{2}$ per cent).[1] The total vote of Conservatives, MRP and non-Mendèsist Radicals rose from 5,600,000 to 6,400,000, the gain almost wholly accruing to the Conservatives: the share of these parties was up by 1 per cent. Of over 4 million Gaullist votes in 1951, the RS held only 900,000. There were nearly $2\frac{1}{2}$ million Poujadists, reinforced by 300,000 extreme Right allies.[2] If the RPF in 1951 is considered (as its propaganda suggested) as an anti-parliamentary movement, then these forces have lost a million and a half votes to the moderate Right: if it is assessed by its later development as a conservative party, then the extremists have won $2\frac{3}{4}$ million conservative votes. But while this nation-wide shift from Gaullism to Poujadism was reproduced in many departments, it is not a sufficient explanation of Poujadist success, for the RPF never struck root south of the Loire. If M. Poujade is the poor man's de Gaulle, as M. Faure called him, he is also the de Gaulle of the Midi: and there every party suffered from his attentions.[3]

[1] Socialists up from 2,800,000 to 3,200,000, Mendèsists from 1 million to 2 million, *Divers Gauche* from 200,000 to 300,000. (*Divers Gauche* excludes dissident Communists.) I have divided Radicals, RGR, and UDSR into Mendèsists, and Faurists plus doubtfuls: deputies according to their voting record, and new-comers normally on the endorsement of *L'Express*. Candidates in 1951 have been classified, unless better information was available, in the same wing as their 1956 successors: this probably slightly exaggerates the Mendèsist strength in 1951 and therefore underestimates their gains in 1956. RS allied to both Socialists and Radicals, and/or endorsed by *L'Express*, won 200,000 votes (a fractionally better proportion of the 1951 poll in their areas than their conservative colleagues received).

Only in two constituencies was a sitting Radical deputy opposed by another member adhering to RGR: in Seine-et-Oise the former's percentage vote doubled (from $6\frac{1}{2}$ to $13\frac{1}{2}$ per cent) while the latter's increased from $9\frac{1}{2}$ to 10 per cent: and in Vienne the former gained 2,000 votes, while the latter lost nearly 6,000 (two-fifths of his 1951 poll) and his seat. In one, Sarthe, the 1951 Radical candidate stood as RGR in 1956: his vote dropped from 13,000 to below 5,000, while a Mendèsist new-comer polled nearly 19,000. M. Faure and M. Mendès-France each increased his share of the poll from about 25 to 35 per cent. But the four chief Faurists—three of whom were expelled with their leader, while the fourth remained in his cabinet—won a smaller share of the vote than in 1951, while Mendèsist rivals in their constituencies gained almost as many votes as they did.

The Ministry of the Interior was much criticized for putting Radicals and RGR together in its summary of the results. Such confusion was hard to avoid, since the Radical label was conferred on many 'conservative' lists. The Ministry's presentation was at least less misleading than that of *L'Express* itself, which (by annexing all doubtful Radicals, and 400,000 RS votes given to candidates it had refused to endorse before the poll) contrived to show the Republican Front in the lead.

[2] Conservatives up from 2,500,000 to 3,100,000; MRP from 2,200,000 to 2,300,000; RGR, &c., from 900,000 to 1 million. Vichyite candidates obtained 200,000 votes in 1951.

[3] Thus in Drôme the Communists lost 3,000, Socialists 3,000, Radicals 2,000, MRP 5,000; the Conservatives polled 16,000, as had the RPF in 1951; there were 11,000 new voters, and 24,000 Poujadists. In Isère the Poujadist vote was 55,000, 20 per cent of the poll. The Communist lost

In terms of seats the old Assembly, condemned by M. Faure as ungovernable, seemed a model of coherence compared with its successor—at least to those who forgot that it had begun life with 120 Gaullist 'wild men'. The electoral system which, according to M. Mendès-France, was designed to return a majority identical with the old one, in fact cost the former coalition and the RS 50 seats each, and the Republican Front another 9: Communists and Poujadists shared the spoils equally. Communists and the Republican Front numbered 150 each, 'Faurists' 200, and Poujadists 50: 20 RS and 20 Radicals might be expected to divide about equally between the main parties.[1]

The disparity between votes and seats is, of course, explained by the electoral law. This helped the outgoing majority less than they had hoped, for the Poujadist triumph upset all calculations, deprived the conservative allies of their majority in many departments, and so contributed largely to the Communist gains. Even so, the system worked well for M. Faure's friends: they won a seat for every 32,000 votes, compared with 47,000 for a Poujadist seat, and between 35,000 and 37,000 for each of the three Left parties. Under any alternative system they would have fared worse: normal PR would have given 35 of their seats to the Communists and 12 to the Poujadists (though none to the Republican Front): PR on the Paris system of *plus forte reste* would have bestowed 30 on their Poujadist and Republican Front rivals.[2] *Scrutin d'arrondissement* would have harmed Communists and Poujadists, and would almost certainly have helped the Republican Front more than the government coalition.[3]

M. Mendès-France's insistence that electoral reform was necessary in the interests of the régime seems, in retrospect, overwhelmingly justified. The conservative parties underestimated both M. Poujade's support and their

3,500, a Faurist Radical 7,000, MRP nearly 20,000: the Socialist gained 8,000 and the Conservative 25,000: there were 24,000 RPF in 1951, and no RS candidate in 1956. The electorate was up 28,000 (8 per cent): in the ten towns where the Poujadists did best it had risen only 5 per cent, in their ten worst it was up 24 per cent. The Communists lost votes in 9 of the first ten but in only 2 of the second ten.

[1] From France there were 146 Communists, 87 Socialists, 42 Mendèsists (as assessed above), 12 Faurists and 20 doubtfuls, 71 MRP, 95 Conservatives, 16 RS, 55 Poujadists and allies (counting independents by their political sympathies and ignoring invalidations). From overseas there were 5 Communists (a gain of 1), 8 Socialists, 14 Mendèsists (plus 3), 6 RS (minus 2), and 19 of the conservative bloc (minus 2).

[2] Though as it stood, applying only to Paris, it helped the government, saving 7 MRP and 3 other seats from the Communists.

[3] Before the election the prefects predicted that *scrutin d'arrondissement* would give the Communists 100 fewer seats than PR, the Socialists and Radicals 70 more, the government parties 30 more. *Apparentement* gave the latter 50 more and the Communists 35 fewer than PR would have done, and had no net effect on the Republican Front. Thus *scrutin d'arrondissement* might well have transferred 65–70 actual Communist seats to the Republican Front; and even if it had eliminated every Poujadist, the conservative parties could not have made up the handicap.

own unpopularity;[1] and they doubtless hoped, by rushing the election, to prevent M. Mendès-France developing his campaign. So they chose to fight under a system which did the extremists little damage and the régime much; and within limits of time which made it impossible for serious politicians to counter the propaganda which the Poujadists had been spreading, vigorously and almost unanswered, for well over twelve months.[2]

The Communists vociferously demanded a Popular Front against clerical and colonial reaction, and denounced the Socialist and Radical leaders for refusing it. They made effective use of the 1951 figures—9 million votes for the conservative parties, 5 million for the non-Communist Left, and 5 million Communists; they argued that without their aid no Left majority was possible, but that with them, enthusiasm for unity would attract new support. The Socialist leaders, however, stated publicly that they would rather sacrifice twenty seats than join the Communists, and they carried their party by a 3 to 2 majority. Socialist discipline was almost complete: the electoral law indeed prevented local parties from making *apparentements* unauthorized from Paris. This difficulty could be avoided by forming joint Socialist–Communist lists, but this was done in one constituency only, Vosges, where the textile industry was suffering from serious unemployment and short-time working. Here the Communists' claims were not borne out. Despite the local distress the combined Socialist and Communist vote rose by 8 per cent only, compared with an increase of 35 per cent in the contiguous departments; and their joint share of the poll fell by $1\frac{1}{2}$ per cent, whereas in the neighbouring constituencies it rose by $4\frac{1}{2}$ per cent.[3]

Party discipline was indeed quite effective. Eight Communists and 11 other members were renominated by their parties in lower places on the list: 2 of the Communists and 5 of the others lost their seats. Half a dozen disgraced Communists were eliminated altogether; none contested the election independently, and their constituents were unaffected. Of the 50-odd

[1] M. Pinay told journalists that the Communists would be lucky to gain 5 seats; and no one foresaw the Poujadist victory. The French Institute of Public Opinion twice concealed the Poujadists among 'others', and once allotted them 1 per cent of the votes of youth. Most constituency reporters, however reliable otherwise, underestimated their vote by half: the prefects thought at first that they would win about 5 seats, later about 10; they themselves did not seriously hope for more than 25 or 30.

The CNI would have gained seats under *scrutin d'arrondissement*: but some Conservatives seem to have preferred Communist to Mendèsist gains (as strengthening the Conservative position among the centre groups), and others to have feared the breakdown of their new-found discipline under an individualist electoral system.

[2] In Isère, for instance, their candidate held 234 meetings in 1955, only 51 of them during the election campaign. (They earned him seven appearances in court.)

[3] Socialist and Radical dissidents figured on the Communist list in Creuse, where the party did very well. It probably gained a few Socialist votes, but it succeeded mainly because Creuse was not contested by the Poujadists—because, it was said, the local prefect had persuaded them, unwisely it would seem, that their candidature would help the Communists.

non-Communist members who did not stand, a third were elderly, and half (including nearly all the ex-Gaullists) anticipated probable defeat: perhaps half a dozen were in trouble with their parties. The Socialist rebels, expelled over German rearmament and later readmitted, did neither better nor worse than their colleagues. Three recalcitrant ex-MRP members were all beaten, though in two cases their seat was lost to the party. Ex-Gaullist independents fared disastrously. Conservative voting discipline improved: Conservative lists neither endorsed by the CNI nor allied to its candidates (including the non-Poujadist extreme Right) were slightly more numerous, but their proportion of the Conservative vote was down from 20 to 15 per cent (and from 17 to 9 per cent outside the Paris area). Three Conservative deputies who stood without CNI endorsement were beaten, even though one (at Bordeaux) was supported by the local Conservative leaders. Official Radicals usually won far more votes than rival Mendèsists, even where the latter had a better claim to that title.

The party ticket is valuable to a candidate, as a guarantee that votes given him will not be wasted. But without it great names count little. M. Pinay urged Conservatives in Eure to support the young and dynamic M. de Broglie, RPF candidate in 1951 and now an independent Conservative, who could best fight *l'influence néfaste et tyrannique* of M. Mendès-France in his own department: but his vote fell by half, while the official Conservative gained 4,000. *L'Express* bestowed its own endorsement (the *bonnet phrygien*) on reliable Mendèsists in each constituency, and some candidates who were denied the *bonnet* took this seriously enough to buy up all copies of the relevant issue of the paper. But in Indre, where the RS candidate alone was approved, he received only 2,200 votes, while the bonnetless Socialist had 13,000, and the Radical 31,000. In Oise and in Seine, official Radicals disapproved (and with justice) by the paper gained seats with greatly increased votes.[1]

The faithful may have felt that the party ticket was the safest test of political virtue; many of them seem also to have agreed with M. Poujade that membership of parliament was a conclusive sign of vice.[2] Among

---

[1] The few Socialists not endorsed by *L'Express* fared worse than average; probably, however, personal reasons, or the competition of a leading Radical, caused both the paper's disapproval and the candidates' failure.

    The Conservatives denounced as especially reactionary by *L'Express* also did rather badly. But since this was not true of MRP members similarly denounced, and since the occasional Conservatives and RS who were approved by *L'Express* fared disastrously, it cannot be concluded that the paper carried great weight.

[2] Votes for individual candidates are interesting (although ineffective). They tell the same story. Even Communists may have been affected. Their member for Meurthe-et-Moselle ran 500 ahead of his second in 1951, 400 behind the same second in 1956. The Conservatives there elected three members (two outgoing deputies and a senator): their fourth man had more votes than any of these, and far more preferential signs also, but was not elected; their leader, who had more votes

M. Mendès-France's followers, sitting members (many of whom were thought to have only recently found salvation) increased the Radical vote by only 30 per cent, other candidates by over 80 per cent. A similar disparity was to be found among Conservative and MRP candidates. But with Socialists and Communists it was the other way round, and RS deputies did a trifle less badly than new candidates. Thus the discrimination seems to have told against the centre parties which had for so long shared the chief cabinet positions between them.

M. Poujade, M. Mendès-France, and the Communists, unlike the government leaders, had appreciated this mood of discontent, and all appealed to it. The outgoing coalition was thus simultaneously assaulted by three different propaganda campaigns, each reinforcing the others. The discontent was general, but its local expression varied. In Paris the Poujadists were weak; and the Radicals attracted very many former Gaullists, and nearly trebled their 1951 vote. Elsewhere, the Radical poll doubled in departments where the Poujadists won less than 10 per cent of the vote; rose by half where Poujadist strength was 10 to 15 per cent; and fell by 5 per cent where the Poujadists were strongest. This disparity was similar, though less startling, for most other parties; notably, the Communist share of the poll rose most where no Poujadist candidate stood, and fell farthest where the Poujadists did best.[1]

The Poujadist successes followed no obvious pattern. They did not correlate with the formerly Gaullist areas; nor with the departments where new voters were most numerous—rather the reverse indeed; nor yet with those where economic decline and depopulation have gone farthest.[2] The Poujadist appeal was most effective of all in the distressed and discontented southern wine-growing areas; but elsewhere it found a following, here among peasants and small business men suffering from the end of inflation, there among extreme nationalists and the anti-parliamentary Right enraged with official Conservatism by EDC, Dien Bien Phu, and concessions in Tunis and Rabat. Former royalists and members of noble families found no difficulty in voting for a movement whose very vulgarity gave promise

than any of his colleagues in 1951, fell to fourth place (3,000 votes and 2,400 preferences behind his unsuccessful follower), yet was returned. In Ille-et-Vilaine, M. Teitgen, 3,000 ahead of his fellow MRP members in 1951, was in 1956 nearly 1,000 behind his No. 3—who nevertheless lost his seat. This drop in the *téte de liste*'s personal vote was general in these constituencies, except (understandably enough) in the case of the two RS members.

[1] Out of 34 constituencies where the Poujadist vote was over 15 per cent, the Communist share of the poll fell by more than $2\frac{1}{2}$ per cent in 16, remained fairly stable in 18, and nowhere increased by over $2\frac{1}{2}$ per cent. Where the Poujadists had from 10 to 15 per cent, the Communist share fell $2\frac{1}{2}$ per cent in 5 constituencies, was stable in 22, and rose $2\frac{1}{2}$ per cent in 2. The corresponding figures were 3, 24, and 4 where the Poujadist vote was below 10 per cent, and 0, 5, and 4 where they did not stand.

[2] See below, note 1, p. 63.

of a popular appeal that more respectable enemies of the régime, whether Vichyite or Gaullist, could not hope to command. But Poujadism struck no roots in the expanding, prosperous north-east: and in the region which gave it birth it failed humiliatingly. In Lot, M. Poujade's home department, where the agitation had lasted longest, his candidate's vote was below the national average (in England he would have lost his deposit). As one journalist was told during the campaign, 'Poujade, c'est bien, évidemment — mais les élections, c'est quand même quelque chose de sérieux.'

The existence of the Poujadist movement is not in itself a wholly unhealthy sign, for it shows that France's superfluous and sheltered firms and farms are at last feeling the pinch. But the frustration and fury expressed in Poujadism do expose a grave failure of French political leadership. Alone among France's leaders, M. Mendès-France has inspired enthusiasm and hope; his capacity to do so is a national asset, and it hardly becomes those who have themselves so conspicuously failed in this task to sneer at 'Superman' or decry the 'Mendès-France myth'. Yet M. Mendès-France himself may well have contributed to the state of mind he is anxious to cure. His sweeping and bitter denunciation of his opponents must have helped to build up the very impression which M. Poujade was trying to create—that of the futility, incompetence, and even dishonesty of men in power. If the manœuvres of the government coalition played into the hands of the Communists, the opposition's exploitation of popular discontent assisted the Poujadist agitation.

The campaign had a less depressing aspect. More citizens registered, and more voted than in any postwar election.[1] Poujadist wrecking was anything but a spontaneous reaction of the electorate; and, that apart, the tone of the campaign was by general consent unusually serious. Whatever the complications of the parliamentary situation, the electorate expressed its views clearly enough. The 5 per cent increase in the Mendèsist share of the poll, while the Communists and Socialists held their own, amounted to a leftward 'swing' which would be considered remarkable in contemporary Britain. Since North Africa was unquestionably the main issue of the campaign, this amounted to a mandate—as plain as mandates can ever be—for a liberal attitude to a problem far harder to solve than Britain's in India nine years ago. Confirmation may be found in the conciliatory attitude

[1] There is not much evidence of how the new electors voted. In one (unspecified) Paris commune some *bureaux de vote* were set aside for them only: here the Mendèsist vote was 4 per cent higher than in the rest of the commune, the Communists and Socialists each 4 per cent lower, and several other candidates (MRP, RS, anti-parliamentary Right, Independent Mendèsist) slightly higher. The Poujadist proportion seems to have been unchanged. In the *Cité universitaire* the Communist vote was 26 per cent (21 per cent in 1951) and the Radical 21 per cent. A French Institute of Public Opinion poll of under 35's gave 25 per cent Republican Front, 17 per cent government coalition, 12 per cent Communist, 1 per cent Poujadist, 38 per cent Don't know.

of almost every prominent figure, and in the defeat of almost all the chief exponents of traditional colonialism.[1]

In domestic affairs the election did nothing to resolve the permanent dilemma of French democrats. Unless all supporters of the parliamentary régime stand together, its enemies can easily overthrow successive governments and so discredit the system. But if they do combine, their differences on all other questions paralyse the cabinet's capacity for decision, enforce stultifying compromises and delays, and seem to reduce democratic government to 'the shuffling of a greasy and well-marked parliamentary pack'. The demand for change here was also clearly enough expressed, in the gains of the opposition parties, but also in the outgoing coalition's call for constitutional reform, and in the popularity of the slogan '*Pour que ça change!*' or of the one word '*Assez!*' To that demand M. Mendès-France provided the only answer within the parliamentary framework. Yet the Republican Front was never within sight of an independent majority. Communists and Conservatives alike demanded to know with whose support it meant to govern. To choose the former, apart from intrinsic risks, would arouse intense suspicion at home and abroad. To choose the latter would disappoint the hope of change and perhaps discredit the one remaining leader who was believed to stand outside 'the system'. Instead of helping France to find a strong and democratic government the election of 2 January 1956, by its legal framework, its timing, and its conduct, left her farther from a solution than before.

[1] The swing was greatest in the north, and where population was growing most rapidly—

Table 1. *Left votes and Poujadist votes, 1956*

Constituencies in which:	Left % vote			Poujadist vote	
	Up				
	by more than 10%	by less than 10%	Down	Under 10%	Over 10%
North of the Loire:					
(1) Electorate up more than national average	7	9	—	15	1
(2) Electorate up less	9	18	3	22	8
Along the Loire:					
All (2)	—	3	3	2	6
South of the Loire:					
(1)	—	3	1	2	2
(2)	—	8	34	13	32

(Left includes Communists, Socialists, Radicals, and Left Independents. In one Loire and three southern constituencies independent candidates make the calculation impossible. Along the Loire the swing was *nil* in one department and small elsewhere.)

7   Political compromise on Seine and Potomac*

The tradition of Franco–American friendship is an old one. Since the days of Lafayette the two countries have more than once fought on the same side, never against each other. In both, democracy is firmly rooted, and it is the purpose of this article to suggest that, despite appearances, the French political system has much in common with that of the United States. Yet the friendly sympathy of most educated Americans for the French rarely extends to their politics.

American criticisms of French politics often echo the misunderstandings of United States institutions which prevail across the Atlantic. There it is widely considered a disadvantage that the legislature should often be controlled by the political opponents of the Chief Executive; and even the most benevolent attitude is one of admiration at the responsibility and restraint which enable American politicians to work—most of the time—a system so clearly, in European eyes, destined to deadlock. More frequently the ocean mist distorts the view, especially since the least responsible and sympathetic spokesmen are often, on both sides of the Atlantic, considered the most newsworthy. Consequently most Europeans, even well-informed and friendly ones, look on Congress very much as most Americans view the French National Assembly—as a chaotic, incoherent aggregation of small-minded and shortsighted individualists, whose incomprehensible behavior is predictable only in that, on matters of international concern, they so often seem 'like inverted Micawbers waiting for something to turn down'. That both caricatures are grotesquely unjust is beside the point. To the transatlantic onlooker the difficulties of an American administration in getting its policies (or even its budget) accepted loom almost as large as the instability of French governments in American eyes; and the politics of France and the United States often seem to bear more resemblance to each other than either shows to the British system of unchallenged executive predominance. Much admiration is lavished on the latter, not least at home; but English critics, smugly aware that their own government escapes many weaknesses which

---

* Originally entitled 'Political Compromise in France and America'. From *The American Scholar*, vol. 26, no. 3 (Summer 1957). Eight sentences are omitted at the beginning, and ten words in the fifth paragraph, which criticised a previous article in the journal by Professor Baker.

afflict the other two systems, often fail to appreciate that it lacks some of their advantages too.

I shall argue that there are some fundamental likenesses between the French and American situations that are perhaps—at least in comparison with the British—more significant than the obvious contrast. This discussion is confined to political institutions; but the behavior of men in politics depends greatly upon the social structure in which they act. In many ways France and the United States are very different societies; but in one crucial respect they are alike. Both are diversified countries, historically or geographically or ethnically too divided to give birth to two tightly disciplined parties, and deeply suspicious of great concentrations of executive power. In France these divisions give rise to several distinct parties; in the United States to two large ones, each of which contains many factions. In both, alliances are renewed at election times but rarely last long afterward; meanwhile legislative majorities are made and unmade by deals and compromises. Both in form and in substance, therefore, French and American parliamentary behavior have much in common. Even the French parties, different as they are from the American, show occasional similarities of outlook and function. For though politics in France is often considered as a kind of ideological Donnybrook Fair, this does both too much and too little justice to the practitioners. Root-and-branch enemies of the system apart, the French parliamentarian, like the American, rises to leadership, not through principled intransigence, but because he is adept at the arts of bargaining and brokerage. Of course, the shifting coalitions in the National Assembly, unlike those in Congress, immediately affect the executive branch; yet even here there is more continuity in France than is generally realized elsewhere.

It has become fashionable for Americans, seeking to explain the mysteries of their politics to uncomprehending foreigners, to use John C. Calhoun's concept of the concurrent majority as a guiding clue.[1] Every important group—farmers, labor, business and many smaller ones—has an effective veto on action which would seriously contravene its interests. But this veto, it is claimed, must not be used irresponsibly, must be suspended in time of emergency, and must for positive purposes be supplemented by parliamentary horse-trading and logrolling. This perpetual negotiating, conciliating and adjusting activity takes place at elections, in the selection of political leadership, and in the legislative process. It is contrasted—by both Mr. Fischer and Professor Baker, for example—with the presumed ideological passions of the French; and of course it is true that political extremists are

---

[1] I shall take John Fischer's article in *Harper's Magazine*, November 1948, as a lucid and comprehensive exposition of this point of view.

more numerous and more violent in France than in this country.* Yet the groups which work within the French system, and are almost lost to sight by these critics, are for all practical purposes far more important than the extremists; and they often behave surprisingly like American politicians.

In the United States a political ticket must represent all parts of the constituency and all important racial or religious groups within it. Similarly, a French party list should be balanced between localities, occupations and (in areas like Alsace) religious denominations. An American presidential aspirant is normally acceptable only if he has not offended any major interest. In exactly the same way, French deputies will (except in an emergency) elect to the premiership the most 'available' leader—namely, the one with most friends and fewest enemies. The United States Senate, as William S. White insists, is a club whose members feel a strong community spirit; so is the French Assembly, except for its Communist members (Poujadists no longer seem outside the fraternity)...Mendès-France's popularity in the country did not endear him to the deputies (although...it did win their votes for some drastic and disagreeable policy decisions). But does a President of the United States earn much credit among the Senators when he appeals over their heads to the people?

The concurrent majority principle operates in France no less than here. Just as important legislation cannot pass Congress without widespread bipartisan support, so a major bill can go through the French Assembly only with the backing of most of the moderate parties, for the opponents of the parliamentary system often command a third of the seats and generally oppose all governmental policies. The ordinary day-to-day interests of their adherents naturally suffer from this intransigence; if labor, for instance, has often been neglected in postwar France, this is because the industrial workers in effect disfranchise themselves by voting for a party hostile to the regime. But all interests willing to work within the system can exercise effective influence.

French parliamentary committees, like those in Congress, exist to allow these interests to express their views and to enable the process of legislative compromise to work smoothly. In both countries the committees, and not the administration as in Britain, have the main say in determining whether and in what form bills shall pass into law. But the French system avoids certain disadvantages of the American. The fate of a bill in France is unlikely to be predetermined by the choice of committee to which it is assigned, for any other interested committee may express an advisory view. The investigating powers of French committees are too weak for serious use—or abuse. Their chairmen enjoy much less arbitrary power than their American counterparts;

* I.e. the U.S.A.

66

nor do the deputies feel irresistibly bound to select elderly colleagues from the regions least responsive to any shift in the outlook of the national electorate. (However, the extra political weight bestowed on rural and remote parts of the United States by the seniority rule and the composition of the Senate does find some equivalent in the similar over-representation of the countryside in the much weaker French second chamber.) Even without a seniority rule, committee chairs in France are filled by men of political eminence and technical competence, who usually retain their posts for years at a time. Thus despite the supposed ideological intransigence of the French politician, the present Socialist chairman of the Assembly's Foreign Affairs Committee was first elected in a Conservative house, while the Conservative chairman of the Finance Committee has kept his place in the predominantly left-wing chamber of 1956. No French committee would limit its choice to local alternatives as grisly as those facing the Judiciary Committee of the United States Senate: a North Dakota Republican who doubts the reliability of the Chief Justice, or a Mississippi Democrat who suspects the entire Court of Communist sympathies.

Neither in France nor in the United States is every political controversy automatically absorbed in and its issue determined by the single combat between the major parties. In neither does the administration, as in Britain, not merely decide the fate of legislation but introduce all important bills itself. (British private members may not propose expenditure, and among their few puny legislative proposals almost as many are concerned with animal as with human welfare.*) In neither France nor America, therefore, is the rank-and-file parliamentary supporter of an administration party reduced to frustrated impotence as in the House of Commons (significantly, the circumlocutory phrase is needed because neither French nor American politics has a word for 'backbencher'). In neither does a politician's career and standing normally depend, as in Britain, exclusively on his status with his national party leaders; on the contrary, in Congress or the National Assembly, skill in committee negotiation and personal acceptability to colleagues of differing views are more important than the qualities of aggressive agility which earn advancement in the British parliamentary jousting ring. For in both the United States and France, the legislature remains an agency for policy decision where, consequently, members seek to persuade their colleagues; in Britain it has become a forum for propagandist appeals to the electorate for or against policies which the majority will automatically ratify. This does not mean that British politics are all conflict and no compromise; it does mean that the bargains are struck in private, in the cabinet room, the party meeting, or the Whitehall conference between

---

* This is no longer true.

civil servants and pressure groups. But in France (even more than in America) major decisions appear in the open, in electoral pacts and in the legislature.

One of the main objects of political bargaining in any country is the national budget. In Britain the government draws it up and it passes into law with only such concessions to criticism as the cabinet chooses to accept. But in Congress, it has recently been remarked, the Representatives 'patiently trim the budget here and there and then the Senate patiently pads it out again so that it is about where the President wants it.'[1] A similar process occurs in France, though there (where there is no federal system and almost all public spending is borne on the national budget) it is the house closer to the voters which usually increases expenditure and the one more removed from them which makes the cuts. In France, as in the United States, the appropriations committees often find themselves resisting the costly demands of their free-spending colleagues. Nor is the comparison merely between institutional forms; behind these lies a more important political reality. The American congressman is a constituency ambassador before he is a party man; the British M.P. is the reverse; and the French deputy is much closer to his transatlantic confrere than to his opposite number across the Channel.

Though there is no locality rule in France, half the members of the Assembly were born in the constituency they represent.[2] The localism so prominent in both French and American politics is extraordinarily absent from the British scene. Reflecting the greater diversity (both historical and geographical) of the two republics, this localism at once prevents their developing two disciplined parties, and thrives on the absence of such organizations. The well-known remark that the United States has not two parties but ninety-eight, two federal and two for each state, is a picturesque exaggeration—like too many similar comments made seriously about the French political scene, where only half a dozen parties are significant. The compromises between factions, renegotiated every four years at American conventions, are matched by the alliances made between separate parties at every French election—and are, it seems, about as lasting. A French coalition, like an American party, holds together long enough to organize the legislature, but breaks up into its heterogeneous elements once that job is done. For such diversified countries cannot be expected to produce political combinations sufficiently homogeneous to maintain unity and discipline for any length of time.

In both countries democratic parties seek to assimilate new political forces

---

[1] *New York Times*, March 9, 1957.
[2] At present France contains 103 constituencies, roughly the size of congressional districts but each represented, under a partly proportional system, by several deputies. [1957.]

to the existing body politic. MRP, for instance, has gone far to reconcile devout Catholics to the Republic which they once so bitterly opposed. The Socialists have indeed had less success in winning the working class to a 'party of government' (i.e., of compromise); but their party is no less democratic in outlook (and more so in internal organization) than either American party, or either British one for that matter. It has many impassioned ideologues in the lower ranks, but also many—some think too many—political bosses and practical administrators at the top.

The Radical party and the American Democrats, historically at least, bear a singular resemblance. Appealing mainly to provincial distrust of Paris and to the small man's suspicion of the 'special interests', the Radicals have long included the most diverse elements: northern New Dealers led by Mendès-France; southern colonial diehards and red-baiters like Martinaud-Déplat; prominent businessmen like René Mayer; old hands like Queuille, more interested in party unity and electoral success than in policy; practical politicians like Edgar Faure, forever compromising their own liberal views for the sake of immediate effectiveness. In 1955, the first of these groups captured the party machine and tried to reconstitute the old loose party as a unified body with a clear-cut program distinct from that of their rivals, a program which they would forward by means of disciplined organization, to which their members would be pledged, and for which alone they would co-operate with other parties. Mendès-France and his friends have found in the Radical parliamentary group about as warm a welcome as the Democratic Advisory Council has had from the party's leadership in Congress.

Relations between France's four main democratic groups show at least as much consensus as do those between the two American parties. On many matters, especially in foreign policy, the French Socialist and Conservative can agree more often and more easily than the liberal Democrat and the rock-ribbed Republican. In the economic field, coalition politics, no less than the two-party system, force the former to modify their program and the latter to move with the times. French Socialists, though they have introduced more public ownership than American New Dealers, have never (partly because of the Communist problem) gone so far in putting governmental influence squarely behind the labor unions. And in the public presentation of their differences, French democratic politicians use rarely, if ever, the kind of wild accusation hurled in the more rugged American campaigns, from charges of Communist associations to slogans about 'Democratic wars'.

Nor indeed should every 'extreme party' necessarily be dismissed as an enemy of democracy. The Gaullists, for example, were in many ways the Bull Moose Progressives of France. A former national leader emerged from a brief retirement to inspire a movement which drew its active supporters largely from professional men, anxious for reform, efficiency and clean government, but disgusted with ordinary politics.[1] Emotional nationalism, impatience with the power of pressure groups, and a demand for strong leadership were more conspicuous than the specific proposals put forward. A startling initial success could not be followed up within the existing political framework, and the practical politicians who had jumped on the bandwagon were soon lured off it by the traditional conservatives. Of course, General de Gaulle attracted many followers far more hostile to 'the system' than Theodore Roosevelt's supporters; yet most of them were exasperated by its weaknesses rather than bent upon its destruction. In winning over such malcontents the Gaullists were performing a function not unlike that of an American third party; as they rightly claimed, their success was to be measured not by their own accession to power but by their impact on the policies of those who held it. There were also true antiparliamentary extremists in the RPF: the movement's effect on them illustrates how both systems frustrate and minimize the influence of political wild men when they enter the democratic struggle for power. In the United States, Mr. Fischer claims, the fanatics can never get to first base. In France they can; but they can go no farther. In other words, the extremists win substantial parliamentary representation—far more than here—but can rarely, if ever, translate it into a share of governmental authority. The more numerous and aggressive they become, the greater the cohesion of the moderate parties, from Socialists to Conservatives, and the stronger their determination to keep the common enemy out.

The RPF sought first and foremost to reinforce the powers of government. But some other rebels against traditional politics, in both countries, seem to demand anarchy at the center and a strong hand at the extremities. Such movements find it harder to enter the legislature in force in the United States than they do in France, but easier to win an executive foothold. The Poujadists were, in 1956, five times as strong proportionately as the Dixiecrats in 1948, yet had no opportunity under the French system to dominate the administration of a region—or even to control a modest domain, like Huey Long or J. Bracken Lee. For the two-party system sometimes assists instead of frustrating the progress of the dangerous men. In his unscrupulous exploitation of a recent *cause célèbre* to charge his political opponents with espionage and treason, Maître Tixier-Vignancour was unpleasantly reminiscent of Senator McCarthy; but the former owed his brief opportunity for mischief-making to the complaisance of a judge, and would never have been elevated to a place of authority by the free choice of a political assembly.

The leaders of antiparliamentary movements must, if they seek to obtain

[1] I owe this point of the analogy to an American authority on Gaullism, Nicholas Wahl.

office or influence policy, make terms with the democrats as the Gaullists did. The extremists are thus frustrated by buying off their leaders: a method with drawbacks (for the exasperated rank and file may turn to still more irresponsible courses), but a highly effective one. Of all these movements, only the Communists have resisted for long the absorptive power of the parliamentary system. Enemies of democracy on the Right have never contrived at once to attain parliamentary influence and to preserve doctrinal purity. Five years ago these forces thought for a moment that they could exploit the success of a popular newcomer to the political front rank, M. Pinay. But that respectable and moderate leader has been compelled by the exigencies of parliamentary compromise and governmental responsibility to move so far in domestic, foreign and especially North African policy that today he and his Conservative colleagues are regarded by their former admirers on the extreme Right as the worst of traitors.

Both systems, then, put a useful premium on political moderation and compromise, the American proving usually but not necessarily rather more effective in this than the French. On the other side, Mr. Fischer concedes four major faults in American government: the obstacles to speedy action when so many interests wield a veto; the inordinate power of quite minor pressure groups; the handicap imposed on strong and forceful potential leaders; and the absence of any legislative spokesman for the national as against sectional interests. Precisely these charges are, of course, constantly and legitimately leveled at the French regime. But whereas the United States provides a potent corrective in the twentieth-century presidency, France suffers in addition from a further vice, the most familiar of all, governmental instability.

This is a contrast which cannot simply be explained away; yet it is less absolute than it at first appears. For if the test be continuity of executive personnel and policy, France's frequent cabinet changes give an impression worse than the reality justifies; and if it be the authority of the national leadership to win acceptance for its policies, then America's separation of powers provides a built-in instability of its own. Congress, especially but not only when controlled by the opposition, is tempted to flout the wishes of an administration which it has not created and cannot control; and the means used by the President to assert his authority are not very different from those employed by a French government in a difficult house.

Neither in administrative nor in political terms is a change of ministry in France equivalent to the same event in Britain or the United States. There are far fewer replacements in the administrative hierarchy than occur when a President is elected (or even re-elected: witness the massacre of ambassadors in 1957). A cabinet change rarely involves the ouster of all or even most of the ministers. It may be limited to the disappearance of one or two men whose credit has been exhausted or whose policies have broken down. Thus cabinets change far more frequently than the members who compose them. One 'crisis', in 1951, consisted only in the demotion of the prime minister to a vice-premiership, the appointment of a senior colleague in his stead, and the replacement of another who was gravely ill. In the ten years after liberation, with the exception of one month, France had only two foreign ministers while the United States had six secretaries of state—though lately America's quantitative record has improved.

Politically, most French cabinet changes are thus like, though usually less significant than, the replacement of Sir Anthony Eden by Mr. Macmillan; very few are like the change from a Conservative to a Labor government. In the nineteen 'crises' of the Fourth Republic, ten of the retiring premiers joined the new cabinet and thirteen of the successors were drawn from the previous ministry. But in the middle of their lives French Assemblies do sometimes undergo a real shift of orientation. In the Third Republic, chambers elected with a Left majority often ended with a rather conservative government because some center groups changed sides; conversely the right-wing Assembly of 1951 chose Mendès-France as premier in 1954 and Faure in 1955, and started Tunisia and Morocco on the road to independence. Such evolutions take account of the movements in public opinion which here find expression in mid-term elections. The French method involves more executive discontinuity, but less danger of deadlock between government and legislature, and longer respites between electoral campaigns.

Cabinet weakness is indeed a far more serious fault of French government than cabinet instability: if (as many wish) the Assembly could be compelled to accept a single ministry for the duration of its own life, it would probably choose the most colorless politician available to preside over day-to-day administration for five years. There is little point in having long ministries unless they are also strong ones. But in forcing very controversial policies through the legislature, American as well as French governments face great difficulties; and only once in recent years in either country have major social changes been made by legislation (1933–37 in the United States, 1945–46 in France). In both countries the executive possesses somewhat similar resources for overcoming parliamentary opposition; among them constituency favors and patronage are of rather greater importance here, party pressure counts for a little more in France. But in both countries the government is likely to get its way only when a sense of crisis prevails.

Mr. Fischer points out that the American President's chance of carrying his policies depends on the interests refraining from using their vetoes; and that they can be persuaded to do this only in an emergency. Consequently, he maintains that the Chief Executive finds it necessary to keep public tension at an undesirably high pitch by discovering repeated crises—for example, that over Greco-Turkish aid in 1947. The French Assembly, like Congress, accepts at crucial periods—during the 1947 strikes or the administration of Mendès-France—strong governmental action which normally it would reject. And there, too, if an emergency does not exist, it can sometimes be invented. During their early honeymoon weeks, French ministries usually secure from the deputies authority to issue sweeping decrees, subject to later parliamentary ratification, on the urgent problems of the moment—a procedure which by-passes the numerous traps and hazards lurking in the path of the ordinary legislative measure.

Normally, however, the deputy sees it as his essential function to keep an eye on the ministers. His attitude may not be very different from that of a congressional committee member grilling one of his less favorite cabinet officers; but the Frenchman's means of action are both more polite and more effective. A minister who loses the confidence of Parliament can easily be removed; this vulnerability may cause either more changes of minister or better consultation on policy. In administration, the American President checks the career bureaucracy by party appointments at the top of the agencies of government. The French politician brings into office with him a small personal secretariat (*cabinet*) drawn from his party, family, friends or civil service sympathizers; like similar groups of cronies elsewhere, this is sometimes a source of corruption. At the other end of the political scale, the French citizen suspects the deputy of betraying his interests to the powers that be—though to judge by the frequency with which he requires his representative to submit to re-election, the American voter is two and a half times more mistrustful than the French.

Yet, though far more Frenchmen than Americans use their vote at election time, and though it appears that many an American mother did not rear her boy to be a congressman, when all is said and done the French system gives less satisfaction than the American. There are both more political extremists and more discontented democrats in France than in the United States. The latter are disgruntled because of the weakness of a regime which cannot be strengthened for fear of the dangerous men. But the true extremists themselves—many fewer than the voters who support their parties—are in revolt for more fundamental causes.

The French economy has made spectacular strides in the last three years, surpassing her neighbors and even the United States; but this has only just begun to compensate for the poor performance of generations.[1] Resentment

---

[1] The immediate political effects may even be adverse, as in Poujadism—the revolt of marginal shopkeepers and farmers against economic progress, and thus an unhealthy symptom of a healthy

at the decline of France's international position and determination to check this process are fed by the feeling that her friends have sometimes failed when help was needed—as in the 1930's (to take a safely remote example), when Congress enacted 'neutralist' legislation and Chamberlain became Prime Minister of Britain. A minority of French reactionaries never accepted democracy; and when they found in the shadow of Nazi occupation an opportunity which they could never have won for themselves, they inflicted wounds whose scars will take more than a dozen years to heal. Thus the Second World War, while it posed the problem of governmental weakness even more urgently than before, at the same time made it harder to solve. It exacerbated the divisions and suspicions among Frenchmen, and so revived all their historic fears of a powerful government which might fall into the wrong hands. American politicians did not risk entrusting the executive power to a strong President during the thirty-five years which followed the Civil War.

This is the immediate answer to the obvious question which the argument of this article evokes: If the problems are so similar in the two countries, why is the same solution not acceptable? Presidential government has had distinguished advocates in France, yet has been shunned for a century by practicing politicians, for more permanent obstacles lie deeply embedded in the social structure, administrative traditions and political history of the country.

First, there is no effective driving force in France demanding a strong executive, whether of the British or American type. The industrial working class, the interest which normally expects most benefits from state action, is numerically and organizationally much weaker than in the other two great democracies, and its political weight is further reduced by its preference for the Communist party. And the groups normally most afraid of 'Big Government' and high taxes, the small businessmen and farmers, are more numerous and politically more highly regarded in France than in any other major country.

Second, French rulers have always insisted on maintaining an extremely centralized, bureaucratic and pervasive administrative structure. Federalism is too risky a device for a country in which dangerous enemies of the regime might exploit it. Consequently, France's 'state's righters'—provincials who suspect dangerous goings-on in the national capital—are protected by no autonomous institutions capable of interposing obstacles to the action of the central government. (This is why, for instance, Frenchmen take it for granted

trend. In *Le Mouvement Poujade* (p. 254 n.) Professor Stanley Hoffmann has commented on the likeness of its mentality and mythology to the aspects of American Populism portrayed by Professor Richard Hoftstadter.

that Mississippi could not treat its Negroes as it chooses if the majority of Americans, or their Administration, seriously disapproved.) But without such local defenses, the wary provincial is the more inclined to insist on checks and balances at the center—achieved in France by subordinating the government to a parliament which, it is reasonably assumed, will be too divided to be capable of oppression. Many of these recalcitrants indeed make doubly sure by voting for the extreme opponents of the regime as a further guarantee of keeping it weak. The peasant Communists of southern France are seeking to hamper, not to reinforce political authority; and though Pierre Poujade, alas, was never head of French tax administration, he has something in common with T. Coleman Andrews, nonetheless.

The third and historical obstacle derives in general from the fear that strong governments will abuse their power, and in particular from France's previous experience of a presidential constitution, in the Second Republic, when President Louis Bonaparte exploited his position and popularity to make himself Emperor. All subsequent leaders who have sought a personal plebiscitary following instead of a parliamentary majority have been accused (often justly) of similar ambitions. These fears may be out of date but they are still widely felt. If a presidential system ever were adopted they might result in eliminating any strong-minded and 'dangerous' candidate, and limiting the field to colorless and 'available' men like the German moderates who ran against Hindenburg in 1925.

Thus a vicious circle has developed. Politicians and voters, by denying to government powers which it might abuse, have made it sometimes hard for the executive to act at all. Consequently the extremist parties can recruit support not only from the tiny minorities of ideological fanatics and from the groups hostile to any political authority, but also among disgruntled democrats whose problems are not being met within the present regime or by the moderate parties. A poll taken in 1952 asked voters to say whether they preferred progress by means of reform or of revolution: 50 per cent of Communists and 85 per cent of Gaullists chose the former alternative. Yet by swelling the extremist ranks such discontented citizens keep alive the fears of the democratic groups, and so discourage that reinforcement of the executive without which effective reformist politics are impossible.

These weaknesses are certainly serious; but they too often lead to an underestimate of the strength of the Republic, which since 1875 has survived so many pessimistic predictions and so many autocratic regimes. In 1898, an acute and excellently informed British critic, J. E. C. Bodley, wrote two substantial volumes to show that France was utterly incapable of democracy and would revert to military dictatorship at the slightest disturbance. The Dreyfus affair and the syndicalist outburst provided immediate and resounding disproof; and in the crisis of the First World War, France, like England, reasserted civilian control where Germany abandoned it. Ever since Bodley wrote, French elections have been regular, fair and free; the proportion voting is almost equal to the British (more in 1956 than Britain's in 1955); and no one questions the verdict of the polls. Unpopular minorities are protected by the courts, and normally by a vigilant and liberal public opinion, against the abuse of power by political authority. In short, France, like the United States and Britain—and unlike Germany and Italy—is a country where democracy has sunk roots which are today deeper than sixty or twenty years ago. Her turbulent history makes her citizens, unlike Britons and even more than Americans, determined to keep their rulers under severe restraint, for Frenchmen believe with George Washington that 'government, like fire, is a dangerous servant and a fearful master'. A long lag in economic development, military vulnerability, and international decline have brought in France more deep-seated and lasting discontent with the system than the other great democracies have to face. Yet the similarities of outlook and of behavior should command more sympathy and understanding in the United States for the difficulties of French politicians, and in France for those of America's leaders, than either country usually displays toward its transatlantic fellow democracy.

8 Provincial, pressure-group and presidental politics*

The conflict between traditional practices and modern developments has become a familiar theme in discussions of French politics and society since the war. It is a theme with many facets. The relative power of the countryside has declined with industrialization and urbanization. The gap is steadily widening between the progressive technique and outlook of some industries, firms, and sections of the peasantry, and the antiquated equipment and mentality of others. The class struggle seems at times less significant than the clash between the regions of demographic and economic progress, impatient with *immobilisme* and eager for change, and the backward areas where a diminishing population clings tenaciously to untenable—and uncomfortable—positions; better communications have not mitigated the hostility towards Paris of the men of the declining provinces, the 'French desert'. Professional, religious, and political organizations have become stronger in the last generation, and old-style individualism has correspondingly receded. The traditional warfare of clericals and anti-clericals is overlaid if not wholly superseded by newer and deeper divisions, and the once dominant Radicals, the traditional party of the old order, have split into bitterly antagonistic fragments under the pressure of unfamiliar problems and conflicts.

The growth of Socialism and later of Communism has driven the old-fashioned Left into the arms of its former enemies. This process is well illustrated on a small scale by M. Raymond Long's painstaking study of elections in the Côte d'Or since 1870.[1] This is a rural department with a great commercial and transport centre in Dijon but no large industry. Early in the Third Republic it was firmly on the Left; Dijon had a Republican deputy in 1863 and a Socialist thirty years later. Clerical influence is weak; so was Communism until 1945. Yet today it is among the most conservative

[1] R. Long, *Les Elections législatives en Côte d'Or*; Colin, 1958. J. Kayser *et al.*, *La Presse de province sous la Troisième République*; Colin, 1958. J. Fauvet and H. Mendras, *Les Paysans et la politique*; Colin, 1958. H. W. Ehrmann, *Organised Business in France*; Princeton U.P., Princeton, N.J., 1957. C. Melnik and N. Leites, *The House without Windows*; Row, Peterson, Evanston, Ill., 1958.

* Originally entitled 'Some Recent Books on French Politics'. From *Political Studies*, vol. 7, no. 1 (February 1959).

departments in the country. Its leading figure, Senator Roger Duchet, is the most successful organizer the French parliamentary Right has ever had. Twenty years ago he was a Radical candidate in the Front Populaire election.

The political evolution of M. Duchet typifies that of the department. Its leading men have all begun their careers on the Left, as Opportunists or Radicals or Socialists, and ended as champions of moderation, supported by the minority clerical vote against newer left-wing forces. Those early Republicans who were unwilling to follow this line of action were coerced by the Catholics' ruthless *politique du pire*; throwing their votes to Radical and later Socialist extremists against moderate Republicans, the Right compelled the latter to come to terms or accept extinction. Thus a new alliance of Catholics and moderates was forged, first in senatorial elections, then (before 1914) in second ballots for Chamber seats. Both in 1919 and in 1928 the former leader of the intransigent Left entered into a combination with the Right. (But the defeated Radical candidate of 1945 took the opposite course and has since been returned by Communist votes as a *Progressiste* deputy.)

These repeated defections, and the deeper causes which account for them, have destroyed the once dominant Radical Party. By 1914 the Radicals of Dijon were driven to a choice between clerical Conservatives and collectivist Socialists which was bound to split their ranks. Between the wars their support in the country-side was similarly disrupted. Yet the older style of politics has not wholly disappeared. Rural cantons remain devoted, over extraordinarily long periods, to their local government representatives. And in 1951 the re-election of Canon Kir, the formidable octogenarian deputy and mayor of Dijon, was a striking triumph of political individualism; repudiated by his Conservative associates, he won so much Radical and Socialist support—despite his cloth—that in 1956 his former party was only too glad to reinstate him as head of its list. But even this victory of personality over organization illustrates the decline of traditional antagonisms.

A major influence in provincial politics in the Third Republic was the local press, which is described in a series of studies edited by M. Jacques Kayser. The editor contributes two careful sections on the newspapers of the Dordogne, showing *inter alia* how cheaply they could be produced, how their fortunes were bound up with those of their printers (for whom they were an important prestige asset), and how the latter could be influenced by prefectoral or municipal printing contracts, as well as by administrative seizure in the early days (a weapon recently revived in Paris itself). These provincial journals were stable, in that many departments had one of the Right and one of the Left with only ephemeral competitors; resilient in their remarkable resistance to big-city competition; and highly political. Their circulation often coincided with the limits of a constituency or department (evidence confirming that the department is now no purely artificial unit). They often played a decisive part in the committees which chose candidates, whose prospects they could make or mar. Yet a newspaper's position reflected, as well as influenced, the local political situation. Many a journal died of electoral defeat; for instance, an epic battle in Rouen in 1902, recorded in a fascinating essay by M. Mansire, wrecked the Radical paper whose candidates had all been routed by those of the conservative *Journal de Rouen*. Later in the Third Republic, as M. Kayser and other contributors (and M. Long) have shown, the provincial press declined in both seriousness and influence—in part, of course, as a consequence of urbanization.

Yet the rural sector of society remains more important in France than in most modern democracies. Its political weight, and the forces that bear upon it, are discussed in a long-awaited collection of essays edited by MM. Jacques Fauvet and Henri Mendras. The former contributes a useful introductory survey. M. Joseph Klatzmann applies an original technique to the votes of the most rural cantons in France; he argues forcefully that the peasantry, though more conservative, vote much like other Frenchmen outside the manual working class, and for very much the same reasons. Other contributions, of very varying scope and quality, deal with each party, the Catholic and Protestant churches, the Ministry of Agriculture, the press and pressure-groups (unfortunately omitting the most important of them, the FNSEA). Five local studies complete the volume; the last of these (by an ex-deputy, M. d'Aragon) suggests how these external powers look to the villager.

Here then are accounts of most of the major influences shaping the political attitudes of the French peasantry. Among the most interesting is M. Bugni-court's study of a group of villages in the Somme. He describes in detail a municipal election in 1935, which split the village into two client-groups around the two principal farmers; he analyses their composition, assesses how far politics expressed rather than caused their rivalry, and shows how matters changed as class-consciousness abruptly grew among the workers and, still more recently, among shopkeepers. In one village in 1956 almost every vote was known: nine-tenths of the shopkeepers and artisans voted for Poujade (and only one local family was Socialist—by hereditary allegiance).

Many of these essays, as well as the two books discussed earlier, bring out the importance of local economic grievances and the pressure-groups which stress them; yet established politicians seem surprisingly often to emerge unscathed from violent conflicts with enraged local interests. The past political importance of the various 'rural *élites*' is emphasized repeatedly, though changes in national politics are altering their outlook, and urbanization and better communications undermining their influence. One local study shows how Communism has gained a foothold in a part of Savoie so strongly Catholic that neither Radicals nor Socialists have ever penetrated it. In two communes industrialization offers a simple explanation, but elsewhere the main influence seems to be that of migrant workers; they leave Bonneval commune to go to sea, or Bessans to become Paris taxi-drivers, and return later in life to spread new views (though not to weaken religious observance) among their neighbours.

Where the drift from country to town is permanent, its effects naturally go deeper.[1] More and more villages, already without a resident curé, will soon be without a school-teacher too; the traditional opposition between these two loses its importance as the exodus from the village, and the improved education (and sometimes wealth) of the inhabitants, weaken the influence of both rivals. Better communications reduce the need for rural artisans and travelling salesmen, once an important channel of Republican ideas. Catholic Action is winning increasing influence on the younger and more progressive peasants; old-style Radicalism is losing its hold, and its remaining representatives today fear the Church less than the Communist Party, as their attitude to the reform of agricultural education has shown. The traditional peasant organizations, dominated by Radicals and working closely with a Radical-controlled Ministry of Agriculture, have lost much influence to newer competitors. The power of these organizations should not, however, be over-estimated; the strongest are those whose funds are not dependent on voluntary subscription, and their demagogic campaigns are often desperate devices by leaders trying to attract an undecided following away from a rival body. But if Côte d'Or is typical their advice may be followed more readily in politics than in professional matters. And though the peasant may not vote very differently from the townsman, there persists a myth of a united peasantry which can exert a potent influence in times of crisis, as M. J.-M. Royer shows in his fascinating account of the Dorgères and Poujade movements in the country-side.

This myth of peasant solidarity is, of course, consciously borrowed from the ideology and strategy of the working-class movement. The most striking feature of the business world described in Professor Henry Ehrmann's outstanding work is the absence of any corresponding social myth (though plenty of ill founded but widely believed legends persist among French businessmen). So far from vaunting their own unity and power, French businessmen seem almost morbidly aware of the suspicion and dislike with which, especially at moments of social tension, the other classes regard them.

---

[1] For the points raised in this paragraph see particularly Part II, *Organisation de l'Agriculture*, and the essay on the Radical Party.

For years, but especially in 1936 and at the Liberation, they have seen themselves as pariahs, whose outlook and problems find so little sympathy among their fellow countrymen that any appeal to public opinion is futile. Instead, organized business has concentrated on lobbying behind the scenes, in Parliament but above all with the administration. Publicity has been left to mediocre agents; both the public relations salesmen and the parliamentary spokesmen of French business arouse the author's scorn. Attempts to influence politics through money have led to trouble from the days of the old *Union des Intérêts économiques* (shown by M. Long to have played an important part in driving the Dijon Radicals to the Right) to those of the rue de Penthièvre and M. André Boutemy.*

The sense of alienation from the community, which Professor Ehrmann as an American so naturally stresses, is the odder in that—as he also points out—all quarters of French society are deeply impregnated with the bourgeois outlook, while business itself retains many traces of peasant habits of mind. There is the mania for secrecy which compels the progressive *Jeune Patron* group to campaign incessantly in the cause of 'statistical morals', and which, when a business-subsidized journal publishes American estimates of French business profits, blacks them out before copies arrive on the newsstands. There are the cult of littleness, and the related reluctance to press competition to the point of eliminating the rival and aggrandizing his bigger opponent. And there are the deep suspicions and internal divisions within the business community.

The structure and mentality of French business are indeed gradually changing as modernization, especially since the war, widens the already yawning gap between the up-to-date and the hopelessly backward firms and regions. Before the war its organization was largely a sham, and Professor Ehrmann shows the enormous importance here of the measures—and men—of Vichy, whose influence remains dominant today. Yet though the CNPF (*Conseil national du Patronat français*) is now larger, broader-based, and more impressive, it still lacks the cohesion which makes a pressure-group fully effective. Steel and metals retain their old predominance, but other industries are jealous and suspicious of them. Business managers and high civil servants are trained in the same colleges, meet in close daily contacts, often move from one sector to the other and back again. But these interpenetrating managerial elements, who form the core of modern business leadership in France, are regarded with intense fear and dislike by the small provincial manufacturers and shopkeepers who followed M. Léon Gingembre until M. Poujade showed himself a still less inhibited demagogue.

* Said to have been the distributor of the employers' political funds: see P. M. Williams, *Crisis and Compromise* (Longmans, 1964), pp. 65, 271.

The reign of the parties

The clashes between big and small, between Paris and the 'French desert', between manager-administrators and old-fashioned paternalists, are but aspects of the clash between vanguards and laggards in the French economy, with its amazing contrasts between progress and stagnation. Professor Ehrmann leaves the verdict open, but no one reading him can doubt the strength of the forces hostile to change.

Business enjoys great influence because, with no effective organization of consumers and a labour movement weak, divided and discredited by its Communist leadership, there are no strong countervailing powers. Its influence is mostly exerted behind closed doors because business is too convinced of its own unpopularity to engage in public combat on ground which it thinks unfavourable. Its political spokesmen are few and unimpressive, as Professor Ehrmann shows. Peasant deputies, as M. Dogan points out,[1] participate little in parliamentary life, rarely speaking or introducing bills except on agricultural matters. Working-class members, being nearly all Communists, are at once suspect and self-excluded. Thus parliamentary politics is left to the professionals, in both senses of the word. The fascinating game they play in the 'house without windows', cut off from the indifferent public outside, is the true theme of M. Melnik and Professor Leites, though they have chosen to illustrate its involved details, manœuvres, mentality, and myths by a minute examination of one significant episode, the presidential election of 1953.

The authors are interested in the players' psychology and attitude to 'the game', rather than in the strictly political factors which are treated as negligible. The Communists get no attention, since they are outside 'the game', and the Socialists little because it is claimed (dubiously perhaps) that they are not wholly absorbed by it and are therefore untypical. Indifference of the politicians to their electors is heavily stressed. One may wonder how far this finding emerged from empirical observation, and how far it was implicit in the authors' approach, hypotheses, and criteria of normal behaviour. Many of their conclusions are unverifiable, and some highly subjective, for example the numerous statements (not speculations) about the unconscious motives of men or parties. Confidence would be greater if there were fewer minor slips about the political record, less apparent eagerness to prefer the unfavourable explanation in case of doubt, and less reliance on gossip and rumour for material. The authors claim, of course, that they are investigating states of mind and psychological attitudes, and that the mere fact that a story seems plausible enough to publish or circulate gives it value for their purpose. But the balance of all the testimony they use is thereby loaded heavily on the discreditable side.

[1] In Fauvet and Mendras.

Though the viewpoint is thus somewhat narrow, and caution is needed in evaluating the conclusions, this is nevertheless a book full of interest. The outline of the story—Laniel's obstinate refusal to see that he could not win, the successive manœuvres and diversions of his Radical and Conservative enemies, the eventual resort to compromise candidates and the final choice between them—forms the structure rather than the substance of the work. The emphasis is on the aims, hopes, fears, calculations, assumptions, and myths by which at each stage the leaders and groups chose their own courses and evaluated those of others. The differences in psychology, not policy, between the various parties (especially between the Radicals as traditional experts at 'the game' and the new MRP and Gaullist groups which condemned it), and those between party leaders and followers, are acutely observed and described. Interesting points are made about the type of candidate attracted to the Presidency, whether as a serious contender or as an outsider, and about the self-effacing neutrality which makes success possible. Though the systematic listing and analysing of moves and attitudes in 'the game' is sometimes carried to ludicrous lengths (as in the heavy-handed treatment of the jokes current at the congress) yet much useful light is thrown on the habits of mind of closed-circle politicians.

Directly or indirectly, each of these books helps to explain the divorce between opinion and government which was decisive in the recent crisis. Several emphasize the alienation from the system of different social groups. M. Kayser and his associates deal with a once important, now largely broken link between the capital and the provinces. M. Long, with his endless parade of left-wing politicians turned conservative on achieving success, illustrates (without saying or apparently realizing it) one important cause for the disillusionment of successive generations of French workers with 'bourgeois democracy'. Many contributors to Fauvet and Mendras show how old mechanisms for manipulating peasant opinion have broken down, often without being replaced; and the introduction draws attention to peasant nostalgia for the German occupation, when the towns were utterly dependent upon the country-side. Professor Ehrmann stresses the sense of alienation felt by business despite its great influence behind the scenes.

When the citizenry feel wholly cut off from their political spokesmen, disillusionment with democracy grows, and myths of occult forces flourish. The belief that enemies are at work in the dark, that they have captured the state and are using it for their own nefarious ends, is widespread in France (not least among businessmen) and contributes to the occasional extremist outbursts which seek redress by violent, extra-constitutional agitation. Freemasons and technocrats, trusts and crypto-Communists are all equally acceptable targets for such furious and irrational movements. But, as Pro-

fessor Ehrmann rightly points out, there was less force behind these out-
breaks in the Fourth Republic than in the Third; Popular Front, war, and
liberation convinced a disillusioned people that there was no salvation in
tremendous overnight upheavals. The recent collapse of the parliamentary
régime was the result, not of the growing power of its enemies, but of the
weakened will of its protagonists.[1]* The defenders of the Republic in 1958
had neither the numbers nor the determination of their fathers twenty-four
years before.

For the sense of alienation of particular groups is reinforced by widespread
incomprehension and indeed disgust for the behaviour of the politicians.
M. Dogan emphasizes the conscious futility of much parliamentary action
by peasant members who, at election time, publish long lists of the bills
they have introduced for this sole purpose, knowing they will never pass.
M. Melnik and Professor Leites depict in remorseless detail the blinkered,
self-satisfied outlook of the politician for whom the search for place and
power is an end in itself; if they exaggerate his ubiquity, they merely reflect
what millions of Frenchmen believe. Some of the discontented are really in
revolt against the by-products of economic progress in the backward regions
and sectors, others against the consequences of the catastrophic decline in
France's international power; they call for strong government to mitigate
or, as optimists proclaim, to overcome these difficulties and reverse these
trends. Yet Professor Ehrmann in his excellent brief comments on the Vichy
episode reminds us how recently France tried an authoritarian experiment.
Alike in executive continuity and coherence, and in freeing policy from
subjection to narrow and greedy group interests, it proved not better but
much worse than the despised parliamentary democracy.

[1] This is a judgement about the state of civilian opinion, not about the determination or the
cohesion of the army.

* On it see *Wars, Plots and Scandals* (Cambridge University Press, 1970), chap. 4.

PART II

THE ALGERIAN SETTLEMENT
AND THE NEW REGIME

9 The fall of the Fourth Republic*

The outlines of the Fifth Republic are beginning to take a shape which the defenders of the defunct regime, divided and dispirited, are unlikely to be able to alter significantly. These traditional Republicans have been demoralised not only by a political defeat, but by a deeply disillusioning experience. The plot which overthrew the Fourth Republic had been far longer and more thoroughly prepared than was generally realised in May. But the two essential reasons for its success were the inability of the regime to win either obedience from its servants or active support from its citizens.

The legal government could not get its orders obeyed. It was not merely that the army in Algeria was determined to impose its will on Paris. Half the senior generals in France were openly, and the rest covertly on the side of Algiers; the air force was with the plotters, the navy doubtful; preparations for the seizure of public buildings throughout southern France, and for paratroop landings near Paris, were far advanced and would have met with no effective opposition; the police were unreliable (especially in the capital), and some even of the special riot police, the CRS, were disaffected; passive disloyalty was rife in the prefectoral corps and in the very ministries themselves. As an opposition deputy said, the government did not abandon power; power abandoned it. The state machine defied the government of the Republic.†

Other democracies, faced with the revolt of some of their subordinates and the passive disobedience of others, have called on the forces of popular resistance to rally against the menace of reaction. But when the administration of the Fourth Republic refused to obey, its citizens too proved totally unwilling to risk lives or even jobs in its defence. The great Paris Republican demonstration of the 28th was only a quarter the size of those of 1934 and 1936, and its temper seems to have been far from combative. To accept Communist support was to alienate millions of waverers; in any case Communist strike calls met with a derisory response. When Guy Mollet suggested that France was threatened with 'a Spanish war without a Republican army', he might have added that the popular enthusiasm which enabled such an army to be created was also totally lacking.

Left-wing critics may legitimately argue that the foundations of the Republic had been undermined in the two previous years. They may even

* Written in August 1958; unpublished.
† See my article on the 1958 crisis, republished in *Wars, Plots and Scandals*, chap. 4.

be right in thinking that civil war was postponed, but not finally averted, by the advent of General de Gaulle. But they are hopelessly self-deceived if they believe either that a military *coup* was not imminent in the last week in May, or that the Republic had the least hope of defeating it. M. Pflimlin could not have restored the situation by a show of firmness. M. Mollet's letter to de Gaulle did not break the resistance of a determined Republican cabinet. A Popular Front would not have revolutionised the situation, and the Communists were not (as some have ludicrously claimed) concealing immense reserves of strength for fear of alarming bourgeois democrats. These tales merely show that when things go badly wrong the Left is as prone as the Right to launch a neurotic search for scapegoats, and to console itself with easy might-have-been solutions. In fact all the cards were in the hands of Algiers. This was why the most determined and clear-sighted of the Ministers, Jules Moch, rallied to de Gaulle as the one man who could avert a patratroop invasion and a military dictatorship.

It can still be argued that de Gaulle's influence and prestige merely legitimise a *de facto* military regime and paralyse opposition to it. Neither his choice of ministers (with one important exception) nor his policy justifies this view. The cabinet is composed according to the classic *dosage* of the Fourth Republic: three seats for each big party, one for each small group, a Radical Minister of Education, a 'social' MRP Minister of Labour. Finance is in the conservative hands of Pinay because it was refused by the General's first choice, the distinguished left-wing economic civil servant Bloch-Lainé. Many key departments are held by officials or technicians, but these men are not reactionaries (indeed one of them voted for Claude Bourdet in 1951). Among the Gaullists in senior posts, Edmond Michelet has a liberal record on North African matters, while Michel Debré, who has not, has as Minister of Justice vigorously defended the political parties against attacks from Algiers, and—to the fury of *Rivarol* and *Aspects de la France*—has refused to press charges against journalists of the Left. The Paris lawyers arrested by paratroops in Algiers just after the *coup*, whose release was vainly demanded by Prime Minister Pflimlin and President Coty, were sent home the day after General de Gaulle arrived on his first visit.[1] The new government has reached an agreement with Tunisia on lines which its predecessors negotiated but could not carry through; it has put into force the Socialist proposal for giving power in overseas territories to the elected local leaders; it has won the confidence of the Moroccans and a hearing with some important FLN chiefs.

But if the General's intentions are not seriously in doubt, his power to

---

[1] This did not prevent the *New Statesman* publishing a letter of protest against their detention a week after their release, and refusing to publish a letter of correction.

fulfil them is. The administration and the army have acquired a taste for policy-making in the long years of enforcing their will on feeble governments; and a ministry which is not obeyed when it is new and popular is unlikely to acquire new strength in the succeeding months. So far de Gaulle's control over the recalcitrant state machine has been far from complete. Since he came to power the Algiers leaders have consolidated their control over their base, expelling several generals and 100 prominent civilians, forcing the resignation as mayor of Algiers of the European leader most respected by Moslems, filling prefectoral posts with soldiers, blocking the municipal elections proposed by the government, and removing some eighty SAS officers engaged on civil reconstruction in the bled, who were thought too sympathetic to the Moslem point of view. Acts of reconciliation have been announced in Paris, such as the appointment of a Moslem minister or the freeing of Lieutenant Rahmani (imprisoned for writing to President Coty to express the anguish of Moslem officers who might have to fight their countrymen). But neither of these promised gestures has yet taken place. General de Gaulle's hopes in Algeria depend on elections from which he wishes representative spokesmen to emerge; he is not himself unwilling to negotiate with those who demand independence; and he is well aware that another election faked like those of the past will ruin the last slight chance of reconciliation. But how is he to compel an army fanatically committed to integration to conduct elections which are honest—let alone believed to be honest?

It is true that Trinquier, the most dangerous of the paratroop colonels, with his regiment which controlled Algiers on 13 May, has at last been removed from the city (as has his colleague Thomazo from Corsica). These postings may be more significant than the promotion or decoration of several conspiratorial generals, including Salan, Massu, Challe (removed by the Pflimlin government for rallying the air force to Algiers), and Faure (who launched the first plot of all back in January 1957). But the habit of military intervention in politics is easily acquired; should it recur, these rewards for revolt will hardly reinforce the loyalty to the government of doubtful officers and officials. Nor will the dismissal of Périllier, the Prefect of Toulouse, who was conspicuously zealous in executing the orders of the Pflimlin government; nor the appointment as chief of the Army Staff of General Zeller, who in his recent retirement has publicly urged officers to repeat the Sakiet bombardment, denounced the *apatride* press, insisted that the army must dominate every aspect of policy, and repudiated the old-fashioned concept that soldiers owe automatic obedience to the civil power.* Key

---

* Salan, Challe and Zeller's brother formed (with Jouhaud) the quartet of generals who seized power in Algiers in April 1961. See my article on the putsch, republished in *Wars, Plots and Scandals*, chap. 10. On Sakiet, see above, p. 7 n.

89

posts in the state radio system have been given to Gaullists (following a bad example set by previous governments, especially by the Socialists). And the Ministry of Information, with greatly extended powers, has been taken from André Malraux and given to Jacques Soustelle, the chief of the plotters, who has constantly complained of the failure of France to comprehend the Algiers revolution, and of the misleading and disloyal attitude of the metropolitan press. This appointment involves a humiliating capitulation by the party leaders who, six short weeks before, refused to serve alongside Soustelle. But it is a lamentable confession of weakness by the head of the government too.

The new Minister's chief task will be to prepare for the referendum and election campaigns. He should not find it hard. All political leaders anticipate a comfortable victory for the government, and many—especially those in trouble with their own parties—are trying to exploit it to their advantage. Already several new political formations have appeared—all of course created in order to reduce the excessive number of parties. The splinters of right-wing Radicalism, shattered by Mendès-France, have drawn together again. Georges Bidault, unable to win support within MRP, has launched his 'French Christian Democracy' to attract members away from it. The rather discredited chieftains of parliamentary Gaullism have set up the 'Civic Movement for the Fifth Republic' in hopes of patenting what is now a valuable *appellation contrôlée*. Some former Gaullists turned *mendèsiste*, together with a few mavericks from other parties of the Left, are trying to mobilise left-wing support for de Gaulle through a Centre for Republican Reform. And the Socialist and Radical minorities opposed to the Algerian war have united with the neutralists of the Union of the Socialist Left, with some Catholic trade unionists, and with other non-party but left-wing groups in a Union of Democratic Forces under Daniel Mayer, Mendès-France and Mitterrand. This body, despite its common outlook on Algeria and its prominent leaders, seems likely to be paralysed by internal dissension—some seeking and some refusing co-operation with the Communists, some wanting and others fearing to create a new party, some demanding and others resisting a commitment to Socialism, some unrelentingly opposed to de Gaulle while others would prefer vigilant neutrality or even critical support.

The old parties are unlikely to make any constructive contribution. Duchet's Independents, Pflimlin's MRP, Bidault's Christian Democrats, the anti-Mendès-France Radicals, the anti-Poujade Poujadists, and the ex-RPF whom de Gaulle repudiated in 1953 will struggle furiously among themselves to obtain the newly coveted electoral label of Gaullist. But they are unlikely to break ranks so seriously as to miss this chance of annihilating the enemies on the Left. The extreme Right is electorally negligible, and the noisy attacks of *Rivarol, Jeune Nation* and even Pierre Poujade may well prove an asset for the General, reassuring moderate left-wingers that he is not a real reactionary. In the Socialist Party Guy Mollet's closest associates, Gazier, Pineau and Jaquet, have refused either to join him in supporting de Gaulle, or to combine with his critics within the party (still less with the Communists); thus the Socialists seem likely to divide (not necessarily permanently) between three large groups led respectively by Guy Mollet, Albert Gazier, and Daniel Mayer, and smaller splinters like those who are for de Gaulle but against the Algerian war. The Left opposition to the new constitution, weak and fragmented, will lie open to the charge of dependence on the Communists, who will provide the vast majority of the No votes in the referendum. But they, who have taken the most conservative line of all and insisted on defending the Fourth Republic for which no one else has a good word to say, are unlikely to attract new supporters though they will doubtless retain the old ones. It therefore seems pretty certain that de Gaulle will win easy victories in the referendum and election, and will presumably then become the first President of the Fifth Republic, reigning over a ministry (possibly under Mollet) and a constitution essentially of his own choosing.

The draft constitutional project has been much criticised, not only from the traditional Left. Responsible African leaders have expressed bitter disappointment with the French Union proposals, which some consider less generous than those of 1946. Domestic critics have fastened particularly on the unlimited emergency powers of the President; on the danger of conflict between him and the prime minister, whom he appoints but who remains responsible to the National Assembly; and on the numerous and severe restrictions on the powers of a Parliament whose past conduct, admittedly, explains the distrust with which advocates of strong government regard it. The draft has been submitted to a consultative committee composed mainly of parliamentarians, and on 7 August the minister mainly concerned, Debré, promised that all their suggestions would be most carefully considered. On the same day they voted two major amendments, one allowing ministers to sit in Parliament, the other establishing a confederal structure for the French Union, to appease African opinion. Forty-eight hours later the General himself addressed the committee and rejected both these and other proposed changes. Thus it now seems clear that no major alteration will be permitted. Less than a month has been allowed for the public debate on the draft. However, its merits and demerits are by common consent unlikely to receive much attention. The choice will be presented as—and will be—between either de Gaulle with his constitution, good or bad, or a return to the revolutionary situation of last May. It is not the most satisfactory way to endow a democratic nation with lasting political institutions.

It is too soon to draw up even a provisional balance-sheet. Certainly de Gaulle averted a *coup d'état* by the army; certainly but for him France would today be under military rule, from which Fascists in the short and Communists in the long run would probably profit. But the dangers have not been finally exorcised. If de Gaulle were to die (naturally or by assassination), to retire discouraged, or to clash violently with Algiers, the same ugly prospects would reopen. For fundamentally the new government's position is not much more secure than that of its predecessors. To survive, it too must impose its authority on angry and frightened settlers, and on determined and exasperated soldiers. Of course, de Gaulle has great advantages lacked by the Gaillards and Pflimlins. For the moment there is no Parliament to upset or frustrate him, he is enjoying a honeymoon period with public opinion, and he retains unrivalled prestige with both the Army and the Arabs. But these are wasting assets.

At home, the peasants have opened the customary chorus of protest against any suggestion of financial sacrifices. The success of Pinay's loan has brought a short breathing-space, but soon after the elections the old problems, and especially that of the balance of payments, are likely to recur. It will be an astonishing achievement if de Gaulle can persuade his countrymen to bear the cost of either winning or settling the Algerian war. Politically a strong Left, whether supporting or opposing the government, could only strengthen the liberal influences within it. But the Left is in complete disarray, its leaders divided and its followers indifferent; and when the new Assembly convenes in November, three-quarters (instead of the previous one-quarter) of its members may well be men of the Right. These blind and irresponsible men, who broke up or overthrew the last six governments of the Republic, will proclaim a belated attachment to the General during the election the better to sabotage his policies afterwards; for these are the same policies they have always opposed.

Yet the domestic difficulties are nothing to the problem he confronts in Algeria. At the risk of missing the favourable moment, he has—inevitably perhaps—chosen to temporise and make concessions to Algiers: no more than Pflimlin has he dared to hazard an assertion of authority which might drive the generals to open revolt. The army has tasted power and enjoyed the experience; it has committed itself, apparently irrevocably, to a programme of integration which most Arab nationalists seem highly unlikely to accept; yet de Gaulle, to succeed and even to survive, has to satisfy the latter—or at least enough of them to break the power of FLN—without provoking a new intervention by the former. The task seems beyond the capacity of any leader, however liberal his intentions or great his prestige. Yet de Gaulle achieved a miracle in 1940; and certainly no one else stands a chance. And if in the end he proves as impotent as the parliamentarians he has so bitterly criticised, no democrat will be able to feel any satisfaction. For French democracy will have failed with him.

10 A new political world: the 1958 referendum and election*

That de Gaulle's advent spelled the death of the Fourth Republic was never in doubt. From Bayeux in 1946 to his last press conference in 1955, his resolve to bring in a new constitution if he returned to power was unremitting...

For the General constitutional reform was more than the observance of the tradition of consecrating—and consolidating—a change of regime. It was an attack on 'the profound cause of our trials. That cause—the Assembly knows and the Nation is convinced—is the confusion and consequent impotence of the powers of government'.[1]... Not only would a new constitution bring speedy proof of the will to renovation; de Gaulle's hands would be freer to propose the constitution of his choice at a time when the old political forces were discredited, demoralized, and shattered.

It was scarcely surprising that the government concentrated its public activity during the summer on constitution-making rather than on the apparently more pressing economic and Algerian crises. Parliament's last act, before being sent off on its last recess, was to agree to the government drawing up a new constitution and submitting it directly to the nation.

It is one thing to write a constitution, another to have it ratified by the nation. While a majority was never in doubt, bare acceptance was not enough. Gaullists could never forget the 1946 referendum, with its humiliating majority on a derisory poll. The new constitution must be adopted overwhelmingly, not just to lend a prestige which the Fourth Republic had always lacked, but to show beyond all doubt the legitimacy of the regime. De Gaulle wanted to banish once for all the taunt that his power rested solely on the bayonets of the paratroops.

On paper the opposition was imposing. The hostility of the Communists, with nearly a quarter of the popular vote in 1956, was certain from the start. Throughout the summer there was always the danger that both Radicals and

---

[1] *L'Année Politique*, 1958, pp. 534, 540.

* From *De Gaulle's Republic*, by P. M. Williams *and* M. Harrison (Longmans, 1960), pp. 82–3, 88–95, 100–11, 112–13, 114–15, 116. For a fuller account see our chapter in *Elections Abroad*, ed. D. E. Butler (Macmillan, 1959), pp. 13–90, and the two provincial studies which follow it, by J. Blondel on Somme and M. Thomas on Vienne.

Socialists would also reject the government's draft. If that were to happen the theoretical strength of the opposition forces would cut the majority to an unsatisfactory level. But the probability of such a line-up diminished sharply when Gaston Defferre, who had opposed de Gaulle's investiture, talked over Algerian policy with the General and emerged to say 'I vote YES'. Thereafter the large majority at the Socialist congress in early September was inevitable. The Radicals also came into line by a narrower majority.

The non-Communist opposition was therefore reduced to the new left-wing coalition, the UFD,* and a motley crew of right-wing malcontents: Pétainists, M. Poujade, a waning star, diehard colonialists who believed Africa was being abandoned, and militant Catholics who could never accept the *laïcité* of the State. During the campaign little was heard of these right-wing opponents.

The democratic Left was not only deeply divided; it was still utterly demoralized by the discovery that no one would lift a finger for the Republic. As early as July the UFD, realizing the utter discredit into which the 1946 constitution had fallen, called for a constructive alternative to the government's proposals. At once they were denounced by the Communists for stabbing the Republic in the back. But the determination of Thorez and Duclos did not survive the discovery that their own followers would no more work for the System than fight or strike for it. When the referendum campaign got under way in September, they too were advocating a *Contrat des NON* and repudiating the defunct regime.

Communist or democratic, the opposition had some points in common. Their attack took in not only the constitution, but the manner of de Gaulle's coming to power. To vote OUI was to acquiesce in the 'murder of the Republic', and to give way to the blackmail of civil war. It was to say OUI to the hamstringing of democracy—for the new powerless Assembly would be a negation of Republican ideals. It would prepare the way for a new Prince-President who would find in the notorious Article 16 an excuse for assuming direct power.

Yet the opposition had no clear alternative. It proposed the calling of a Constituent Assembly to draft a new constitution in a month. But there was no agreement upon, and little attempt to propose, the form of institutions which might emerge. What suggestions were advanced (such as granting more powers to the Assembly, or biennial Parliaments) showed a total incomprehension of the real problems. The Gaullists' taunt that 'Voting NON is a vote for the void' was justified. Moreover, at that moment few could doubt that if the NONS prevailed the void would be filled by the paras rather than by the promised constituent assembly.

* On it see below, p. 155.

With few exceptions the democratic Left refused to campaign jointly with the Communists. It was usually dispirited, unorganized and impoverished. Prominent leaders like Mitterrand and Mendès-France announced their opposition, then retired to their departments to await the result. The burden of campaigning fell chiefly on the second-rank figures, of whom only Sartre and Bourdet were widely known. Although the UFD militants were active in the towns, vast country areas never saw a poster or had a meeting. Outside Paris the only significant press support they enjoyed was in the great Radical journal, the *Dépêche du Midi* of Toulouse, controlled by Jean Baylet, the 'Glaoui of the South-West'.*

It was evident from the most casual inspection of the posters and pamphlets that the overwhelming bulk of the opposition effort was contributed by the Communists. Their output was impressive in quantity by normal political standards, although it was clumsy and unreadable by comparison with the government's expensive professional programme. Although the Communists fought hard, they seemed at times to be seeking desperately to stem the rot in their own ranks rather than to win converts. Even in their campaign (much more in the UFD's) the signs of the forthcoming débâcle were evident. For all their sniping at the myth of the *homme providentiel*, they rarely attacked de Gaulle frontally even before their own members.

During the campaign in metropolitan France the opposition suffered little infringement of its rights. Policemen were inclined to be a little tougher than usual with bill-posting crews; some prefects ordered the removal of 'seditious inscriptions such as *Non à de Gaulle*', and posters were likely to be torn down here and there. These pin-pricks were never either serious or systematic.

The campaign for the constitution was almost wholly in Gaullist or governmental hands. In preparation for the elections some politicians of the traditional parties jumped on the bandwagon by expensively advertising their views. But scarcely any of them campaigned actively. Commending the new constitution was a job for the government, not for a political party, they declared. And so it proved. Throughout the summer the government had taken no action that might ruffle the mood of national unity. Only the offer of independence to the colonies suggested that under its new management the French State was any more capable of taking difficult decisions than before. On Algeria, de Gaulle had retired into delphic ambiguity; elsewhere decisions were temporarily shelved. The Treasury helped by giving orders

---

* El Glaoui, Pasha of Marrakesh, who dominated south-west Morocco, had urged France to depose the Sultan in 1953, and had been ruined by his return two years later. Baylet was a Radical regional boss.

that tax prosecutions should be deferred 'because of the political circumstances', and collections should be made 'with a very special tact and discern-
ment'.

Where the opposition had relied on traditional methods, particularly
public meetings, the campaign for the constitution was based almost entirely
on the mass media. In the whole of Paris there was only one public meeting
for the Oui—and that mainly for card holders. There was ample evidence
that the government was afraid of opposition activity. When de Gaulle went
to the Place de la République, to introduce his constitution from the very
citadel of working-class Republicanism, the authorities saw to it that the
square was filled with a hand-picked triple-checked bourgeois audience.
They felt it necessary to banish the opposition to the dim distance, and
surround the meeting with a thick screen of police and Gaullist militants.

Even so there were ugly scuffles, and one man was shot. Plans for the
General to tour the provinces were hurriedly trimmed. He finally spoke at
only four regional capitals at the close of the campaign. At two of them the
zeal of the thousands of police thinned and subdued the crowds. Only at
Bordeaux and Strasbourg were there impressive signs of de Gaulle's genuine
popular appeal. But meanwhile the campaign's unhappy opening had
confirmed the government's determination to take no chances.

There has probably never been such an advertising campaign in France
before. Thousands of tricolour posters with their '*Oui à la France*' slogans
assaulted the senses of the most unpolitical Frenchmen from huge sites
dominating city squares, from roadside hoardings, and from suburban walls.
Public relations experts added a cascade of tracts and pamphlets for every
audience. Cinema-goers found a cunningly-contrived Ministry of Information film tacked on to the newsreels to remind them how often France had
lacked leadership in past crises. Even the envelope sent to each elector
contained, with a ballot paper and a copy of the constitution, a copy of
de Gaulle's case for it—but no opposition statement.

The Gaullist organizations had the same preference for mass media. In
an expensive campaign one publication alone, *France-Référendum* (a carbon
copy of *France-Soir*), was believed to have been distributed free by the
million. Their posters were both numerous and professional. These organizations were granted the same official facilities for campaigning (poster panels
and radio time) as the established parties. Their claim for equality was
dubious. One or two consisted only of a small team of militants and P.R.O.s
with offices in central Paris. They were essentially front organizations for the
Social Republicans (the Gaullist party), whose established political position
on the centre-right limited its direct appeal. Their executive committees
overlapped considerably, and they freely agreed that 90 per cent of their

workers were from either the Social Republicans or the RPF. Created only a few weeks before the referendum, these mushroom organizations were merged into the Union for the New Republic only a week after the poll. But their fleeting existence enabled them to claim many times the official facilities the Social Republicans alone would have had. It was no secret that the bulk of their funds came from official sources.

The government had another useful ally in *Radiodiffusion Française.**
RTF has always echoed government policy, but it was now used even more unremittingly than usual. Since June Gaullists or sympathizers had been moved into almost every key post affecting opinion. Items which favoured the government were played up; less welcome news was glossed over. De Gaulle's tour was followed with dithyrambic enthusiasm; in skilful hands scattered cheers could be amplified into a hero's welcome. Correspondents contrived to show how French prestige was restored and her diplomatic initiatives were succeeding. M. Soustelle was allowed most of a 'news' bulletin for attacks on the motives of the opposition, and misrepresentations of their argument. It was activities like these, and subtler variations, which led Félix Gaillard (a supporter of the constitution) to suggest that the attempt to 'sell it like a shampoo' was a powerful temptation to vote NON.

Ministry of Information, Gaullist organizations, and the RTF all combined to spread the impression that the opposition was almost entirely Communist or fellow-travelling. RTF scarcely ever reported opposition comment outside *L'Humanité*. The Gaullists handed out stickers reading simply '*OUI — NYET*'. Another poster, distributed through the Ministry of Information, was cruder still: '*FLN + Communistes = Assassins.*'

The government's final weapon was the Anti-Abstention Front. Created under the nominal presidency of André Maurois, the Front flourished during the referendum, but has been comatose ever since. But for some weeks it was hard to escape its enjoiner, '*Votez OUI, Votez NON — Mais Votez.*' There were even a propaganda *bâteau-mouche* plying the Seine, and an aircraft tracing *VOTEZ* in the sky. Laudable though any campaign for civic zeal may be, would the Front have received quite such handsome subsidies if the government had not believed that a high poll was to its advantage?[1]

The press was overwhelmingly OUI. Although the new constitution was explained more or less fairly, there was no real public debate about its merits. The layman had no means of assessing the virtues or defects which polemicists found in the government's proposals. Discussions rarely progressed beyond the shouting of slogans about 'democracy', 'authority', 'stability'.

---

[1] The whole government campaign cost £3,000,000 at the lowest estimate, £8,000,000 at the highest.

* In 1958 correctly entitled Radiodiffusion et Télévision Française.

Both sides conceded that few electors actually read the document on which they voted. Most citizens probably decided on grounds irrelevant to the merits or demerits of the constitution itself. As an experiment in direct democracy it was not encouraging.

While Frenchmen were deciding whether to adopt a new Republic, the issue in Africa was between the Community and secession. The doubts of the early summer had been appeased by the final draft. Only in Niger and Guinea did the governing party opt for immediate independence, and in the end only Sekou Touré led his people into the wilderness. While Guinea voted 95 per cent NON, elsewhere the Community was adopted by majorities of 78 per cent in Niger to 99.99 per cent in Houphouet-Boigny's Ivory Coast.

The campaign in Algeria was less satisfactory. 'Ten million Frenchmen of Algeria will decide their destiny,' de Gaulle had declared on 4 June. This was a campaign without a single newspaper appearing in the vernacular of the majority of the electors. There was not one opposition broadcast from Radio Algiers. After all, Colonel Lacheroy pointed out, the FLN had all the time they wanted on Cairo Radio.* Newspapers from the mainland were seized with even greater frequency than usual. Throughout the length and breadth of the country there was no means of legally proclaiming opposition.

The army was determined to inflict a decisive moral defeat on the rebels by producing a majority which would establish beyond all doubt, in de Gaulle's phrase, 'that in the midst of their trials [the Algerians] show confidence in France and, I must add, myself'.[1] The campaign was a full-scale military operation. Polling was spread over three days so that troops could help voters safely to the polls.

A control commission from the mainland was set up to supervise the preparation of the poll. Under M. Hoppenot it laboured with obvious good faith, against some military hostility, to try to make the mechanics of the operation completely fair, and to discourage excessive official intervention. But although the sincerity of the commission was little recognized abroad, the problem was not the juggling of results—for which past Algerian elections had been notorious—but the dilemma which confronted the voters.

The FLN distributed tracts which contained direct warnings for those who voted. After so much bitter experience of what disobedience had meant to others, no Moslem could wholly disregard such a threat. On the other hand there was the French Army, massively present throughout the vote, and expecting a sign of loyalty, protecting some voters but undoubtedly putting pressure on others. Caught between such forces how could anyone make a free choice? The experiment confirmed the scepticism of those who had

---

[1] *L'Année Politique*, 1958, p. 552.

* Lacheroy was the spokesman for army HQ in Algiers.

held that after four years of war a wholly free vote was unattainable. To this judgement de Gaulle himself seems eventually to have rallied. But the referendum in Algeria could not be dismissed. For the first time Moslems and Europeans went to the polls on an equal footing. For the first time Moslem women had the vote. This step forward might well prove far more significant than the votes they cast. These showed that the army had won its struggle. On an 80 per cent poll Algeria had voted 96 per cent OUI.

In metropolitan France, if some of the campaign methods were dubious, the poll was none the less surprising. Ministers and officials publicly forecast a 65 per cent OUI—hoping for 70 per cent. Like everyone else they were taken aback at getting almost 80 per cent on an 85 per cent poll. The myth of Communist invincibility was cracked. They had won 5,450,000 votes in 1956. Now, on a higher poll, there were only 4,600,000 NONS in France. Although the non-Communist opposition appeared to be routed, the proportion of NONS in the Toulouse region and the fiefs of some other opposition leaders was above the average. When their contribution is allowed for, over the whole country at least one Communist voter in five, perhaps one in three or four, had been faithless. Ironically this revelation of the breach in the Party's ranks silenced a vocal and growing campaign for it to be outlawed.

Reservations can be made. Yet the referendum was an impressive beginning for the new Republic, and a devastating repudiation of its predecessor— which not a single organization defended during the campaign. In one of the most decisive results ever freely recorded in France, 66 per cent of the eligible electorate had assented to the Fifth Republic. Such a striking result cannot be explained away as the product of a propaganda campaign. It suggests that beneath perennial divisions the longing of the French for national unity was unquenched.

. . . .

If French democracy is precarious, it is because of the Algerian war. The threatened army 'veto' existed before the Fifth Republic and indeed brought it into being. Arbitrary interference with press criticism, especially of the army and police, began under Mollet and Bourgès-Maunoury and was checked by de Gaulle, though it has revived under Debré.[1] If intolerant politicians too often impute treasonable conduct to those who disagree with them, the fault is unhappily an old one in France, and the recent marked worsening of the temper of controversy dates from the attacks on Mendès-France in 1954, not from 1958. Bitter disputes which provoke deep emotions have had these results elsewhere; Korea evoked similar consequences in the

---

[1] But he has applied these arbitrary measures on a somewhat smaller scale, and to the fascist press as well as to that of the Left. Moreover, prosecutions have usually been announced; whether they will reach a court remains to be seen. [Few did.]

United States, and not so long ago Ireland threatened parliamentary government in Britain.

De Gaulle was well aware of the danger. Immediately the referendum was over, he set out to put his overwhelming victory to use. Salan was publicly ordered to ensure free elections in Algeria, and army officers were obliged to quit the Committees of Public Safety.* The delight of the entire Left was matched only by the dismay of Algiers, where CSP opposition collapsed in face of the army's loyalty to de Gaulle. For the first time since February 1956 Paris had imposed its will. On 23 October the General announced his offer of a cease-fire, the *paix des braves*. Two days later the FLN rejected it. It was the turn of the Right to triumph, and of the Left to be dismayed.

Successful cease-fire talks would of course have embarrassed the friends of Algiers, and encouraged the liberals. The timing of de Gaulle's offer, between the referendum and the elections, indicates how little he desired to see a new Parliament dominated by his own professed followers. But his proposed 'white flag of parley' was a mistake which enabled the Algiers press and Soustelle's radio to misrepresent his intentions. It left sufficient ambiguity about them for politicians of diametrically opposed views to fight the election as champions of de Gaulle's Algerian policy. The General made further efforts to limit the success of the Right, choosing an electoral system they disliked and opposing an alliance between the new Gaullist party, the UNR, and the old-style Right. But he failed. Entirely freely, and with no flood of official propaganda such as marked and marred the referendum campaign, the voters chose a reactionary and authoritarian-minded Assembly. They did so because of two mistakes. The first was their own: naturally enough they thought they could best help de Gaulle by voting for Gaullists. The second was the General's: the electoral system confounded all expectations by bringing about the very result it was intended to prevent.

The choice of electoral system is always important, and in a multi-party country like France it is capital. Five times in the last forty years it has been completely altered before an election. De Gaulle inherited a law designed in 1951 to damage Communists and Gaullists; no one now favoured it except politicians who owed their seats to it (and they dared not admit their preference). Everyone agreed it must be changed: but for what? The deputies were so concerned with the answer that the one restriction they put on de Gaulle's constitution-drafting powers was that the Assembly must vote the electoral law. This was evaded. The draft constitution authorized the cabinet to choose the system governing the coming election, and the people voted this provision along with the rest.

* Comités de Salut Public (CSP) on which they had sat with civilian extremists since May 1958.

The government itself was divided. The 'pure' PR of 1945–6 could be restored, unencumbered by the hotly criticized devices for pooling the votes of allied parties which had been introduced in 1951. But this would again ensure a quarter of the seats for the Communists, so that the Fifth Republic like the Fourth would never know a coherent parliamentary majority. Therefore this solution had no chance of adoption. In practice the choice lay between two systems. One would keep the existing big constituencies, usually of three to five members, in which party lists would compete. The other would restore the type of single-member system used before 1940. Given French traditions and multi-party complexities, each required two ballots. At the first only a list (or candidate) winning a clear majority of votes would be elected; at the second, a week later, a simple plurality would suffice as in Britain or the United States.

Soustelle, Debré, and most of the Right ardently advocated large constituencies.[1]* The list system was claimed to give a better chance of producing a parliamentary majority. It should give maximum scope to the tide of popular feeling, for de Gaulle and against the System, on which the Gaullist leaders counted. Moreover, the Left was split between Communists and democrats, who would not combine; and hardly a single department would give even a relative (let alone an absolute) majority to either of them separately. Thus under the list system the Right and the Gaullists might well sweep the country.

Their opponents naturally preferred single-member seats. These, they thought, should enable them to save local pockets of party or personal strength, and should favour prominent, entrenched personalities against the Gaullist political unknowns. Mendès-France and Mitterrand had been campaigning for this system for years, and even its critics (such as Mollet and the MRP leaders) reluctantly preferred it to the Right's alternative. So, in opting for the single-member system, the General was trying to check too sweeping a surge of opinion away from the traditional leaders and towards his own professed followers, the men of 13 May. But the results contradicted both his expectations and those of every practising politician and independent observer.

Choosing a single-member system did not end the matter. The pre-war constituencies could not simply be restored. Even in 1940 seats had been

---

[1] Gaullist doctrine on the electoral system has not been constant. In 1948, when the RPF was the strongest single party in the electorate, it favoured a large-constituency majority system. When its strength declined, however, PR became acceptable as an alternative, and was probably the private choice of most of the leaders. Debré, however, always favoured a single rather than a double ballot (on general and not on party grounds), and accepted the large-constituency majority system only as a transition stage to the Anglo-Saxon type of electoral law.

* Cross-references in this note have been cut.

most unfairly distributed; population had shifted since; and the number of metropolitan seats was to be reduced to give more to Algeria. New boundaries had therefore to be drawn in a hurry. The job was done by the prefects, who are often influenced by the most powerful politician in their area, and local biases were common; but these cancelled out, and only the Communists were generally (not always) discriminated against. Though rural areas gained at the expense of towns, this did not harm the Left. And de Gaulle personally made sure that there was no gerrymandering against his two chief critics, Mendès-France and Mitterrand.

The campaign was naturally dominated by the 80 per cent vote for de Gaulle only two months before. No party or politician dared ignore it. Even the open oppositions, Communist or Mendesist, spared the General and attacked only his entourage. Other NON leaders were embarrassingly sheepish: 'I voted No, but I never urged others to' protested Bourgès-Maunoury. But from the majority, who had supported the new constitution out of conviction or prudence, a deafening chorus arose. De Gaulle himself asked that his name be not exploited in the campaign. Few requests can have been so unanimously disregarded. Candidates pointed to past service under the General's banner, discreetly remaining silent about intervening periods of infidelity. A Socialist who had demonstrated against de Gaulle on 28 May, drew attention to a book he had written praising him in 1945. The astute Bernard Lafay had been one of the very first RPF politicians to discover that that movement had lost its usefulness; his opportunist changes of allegiance were so notorious that one opponent said of him 'he is not the symbol of the System, he IS the System'. Now he proudly proclaimed himself France's earliest Gaullist of all, for he had gone to school under the General's father, to whom he had been devoted.

Parties, like individuals, sought to establish titles to Gaullism. 'The General has adopted *our* policy,' was the universal cry. There were Socialist posters boasting 'De Gaulle and Mollet saved the Republic'. Conservatives proudly observed that Pinay had been the first leader to visit Colombey in May (naturally not adding that he had gone to dissuade the General from taking power). Defferre, a leading critic of the Algerian war, urged Marseilles voters to elect Socialists to help de Gaulle against the ultras who were trying to capture him; elsewhere the Right appealed for all to join de Gaulle in sweeping out the nefarious parties of the System. In the clamour and confusion it was no surprise that many voters felt the men most loyal to de Gaulle would be those who had always followed him.

In October several bodies—the remnant of the old RPF, the shadow organizations set up for the referendum, and Delbecque's newly-created Republican Convention—fused in a new Gaullist party, the UNR, Union for the New Republic. Outside it were a handful of liberal Gaullists, lacking funds, organization and leadership, and a group of militants disappointed with the old politicians' grip on the new party, who called themselves *Renouveau et Fidélité*. Neither of these splinter groups won a seat of its own at the election. The UNR had all the best-known names, Michelet on the left of the movement, Soustelle on the right, Debré for the most intransigent politicians, Chaban-Delmas for the compromisers, Delbecque for the rank and file outside Parliament.* It had the staff and militants of the old RPF. It was lavishly financed, and well advised by commercial publicity experts. It imposed itself everywhere as the authentic party of Gaullism.

The tide was not only flowing in favour of the General, it was also ebbing away from the Fourth Republic. Hostility to the established politicians of the System was familiar in French politics. It had brought votes to the Communists at every election, to the RPF in 1947 and 1951, to Poujade and Mendès-France in 1956. But this time it seemed stronger than ever. A dozen new parties tried to cash in on the demand for a change. There were the Gaullists of various hues. There were their unbending opponents of the UFD, critics both of the Algerian war and of the Fifth Republic. Then, over on the Right, there were MRP dissidents led by Bidault (DCF), ex-Radicals following Morice and Lafay (Republican Centre), and even anti-Poujade Poujadists.

The old parties, too, scented danger. Radical and MRP candidates sought shelter under other labels wherever they could. A respected MRP leader from Paris thought it wise to disguise himself as candidate for 'union for democratic reforms and the economic and social revival of the Hautes-Alpes'; indeed MRP seriously considered changing its name. That it survived the election without serious loss makes the panic all the more striking.

Both the appeal of de Gaulle and the demand for change were heard everywhere. But, being so nearly universal, they cannot really be said to have formed ingredients of a national campaign. Issues abounded—Algeria, the Common Market, relations with NATO, the future of French democracy, the alarming economic situation—but they were hardly discussed seriously. This was the result not only of general conformism, but also of the electoral system, for candidates assumed—perhaps wrongly—that they were expected to concentrate largely on parochial problems and personalities. There were 465 separate contests, but no national head-on clash.

Some order might have come into the chaos but for another decision of de Gaulle's, following his choice of electoral system. This was his intervention in a sharp dispute which nearly split the UNR as soon as it was formed. Soustelle wanted to make the new party the instrument of his old policy,

* Léon Delbecque had been the chief Gaullist organiser of the May *émeute* in Algiers.

all-out war in Algeria, for which long before 13 May he had made his parliamentary alliance with Duchet, Morice and Bidault. He wished the 'quartet' to sponsor a single candidate in each constituency; this would maximize the chance of a solid right-wing majority in the Assembly, which de Gaulle himself would find it hard to thwart. But within the UNR he found himself isolated. The other leaders insisted, with de Gaulle's approval, that they must not commit themselves to the Right. This decision deprived the Conservatives (with their satellites from the Bidault and Morice groups) of an advantageous alliance with the UNR, and instead exposed them to dangerous competition from it. Gaullist officers stood against some of M. Duchet's close friends; he attacked them as '*les colonels de division*'. Feelings were already bitter before the first ballot, and the second was to exacerbate them into hatred.

France went to the polls on 23 November. The vote was high—78 per cent. Among the thirty-nine members who were elected at once, having won over half the total vote in their district, were Pflimlin, Pinay and Soustelle—and a young newcomer, backed by the entire Right, who ousted Mendès-France. Bidault just missed. Over the whole country the traditional parties did better than they had feared. The Right continued its steady advance, Socialists and MRP held their own, and only the Radicals suffered disaster—under the very electoral system for which they had so long clamoured. They were harassed by their dissidents on Right and Left, Morice and Mendès-France; many of their orthodox leaders had voted NON; and they had no hope of holding the (largely Gaullist) votes which Mendès-France had brought them three years before.

The main victims were the previous assailants of the System. Poujadists and Mendesists, in their different geographical and political sectors, had both urged the electorate of 1956 to 'chuck out the old gang'. Now they themselves were *sortants*, and suffered the same fate; under those two labels, not one deputy survived. And the Communists, the great permanent party of protest, dropped to 3,800,000 votes. It was the first time since the war that they had fallen below the five-million mark.

The gainers were the UNR. Rival Gaullists cut little ice. Around Bordeaux the mayor, Chaban-Delmas, a UNR leader but an undoubted 'man of the System', was hotly opposed by an extreme Right group led by General Chassin (as associate of the Algiers ultra Martel, and financed, some said, by General Salan). Their slogan CHA-CHA-CHA, short for *Chassin chassera Chaban*, could just as well have been turned round; the mayor and his protégés easily beat off the challenge. Nationally the UNR won 3,700,000 votes—fewer than the RPF in 1951, but then the new movement was not fighting everywhere. Plainly a great many of them came from the Left.

Its leaders drew their conclusions. The wind was in their sails, and their appeal was not confined to the Right. There was less reason than ever to make concessions to M. Duchet's Conservative friends. UNR candidates therefore stayed in the fight, even where a rival had led on the previous ballot, unless there was danger of a Communist winning on a split vote. Where they did withdraw, it was usually in favour of the Right, but the exceptions—notably their second-ballot support of Mollet and Lacoste—were given much publicity (except in the Socialist press). The Conservatives were furious, and with good reason.

For now the bandwagon was really rolling, and on the second ballot the full force of attraction to Gaullism and revulsion from the old politicians became plain. So far, leaders of the System (other than NONs) had rarely lost supporters. But now they went down in droves. Wherever a prominent politician was standing, everyone else (occasionally even including some Communists) combined behind the candidate likeliest to throw him out. Bernard Lafay in Paris, Gaston Defferre in Marseilles each gained 400 votes between ballots. Their two unknown UNR opponents gained 10,000 each, and won both seats. Examples could be multiplied.

For Right and Left voters alike, for both clericals and anti-clericals, the UNR—which had no programme at all and claimed to be a centre party—was preferable to their traditional enemies. For those anxious to vote Gaullist but also worried about wasting their votes, the first ballot had shown that the UNR was a 'serious' party. Thus it emerged triumphant from the second round. Before the first poll it had been expected to win 80 or 90 seats at most. In the next week the shrewdest commentators gave it 120 or 130. When the second ballot votes were counted it had 188, and when unattached and overseas members had surveyed the parliamentary scene, it went above 200. Allied with the 66 Algerians, it had just half the seats. The single-member system, chosen in order to check the tide, had helped swell it instead. No other electoral law would have served the UNR so well. Like Louis XVIII in 1815, de Gaulle found himself faced with a *chambre introuvable* far more royalist than the King.

The Communists were almost wiped out; only ten were returned. Everyone had known the single-member system would do them harm, but no one had dreamed of such a holocaust. The cause was not just the sharp drop in their own poll. Even more, it was the grim determination of all non-Communists to vote for anyone, of any party, who could beat 'Moscow's candidate'. In the whole of France only six of them were allowed to slip through on a split vote. This was not a rigged result; it was what the electorate, rightly or wrongly, meant to achieve.

There were forty Socialists. The gloomiest pessimists in the party had

TABLE 2. *Results in comparable seats, 1956 and 1958*

In seats fought both in 1956 and 1958 (first ballot) the votes were (in millions):

	Com.	Soc.	Rad., etc.	Right-Rad.	MRP	Gaull.	Right	Pouj., etc.
1956	5·5	3·2	1·3	0·5	1·7	0·7	2·4	0·8
1958	3·8	3·1	1·1	0·7	2·2	2·7	3·5	0·2

expected twice as many; but the UNR had stolen the place for which they had hoped, that of the centre group attracting support from each extreme against the other. MRP did much better than they had feared, returning fifty-seven strong (a handful of Bidault's men among them). Orthodox Radicals were a bare dozen, right-wing dissidents rather more numerous. The traditional Right numbered 130. Thus, in the first National Assembly of the Fifth Republic, the Left had shrivelled into an insignificant rump. The Socialist ministers resigned, and the party went into 'constructive opposition'; the General's option for Pinay's deflationary economic policy gave them an excellent pretext for their departure. But the real parliamentary conflict, as the campaign had foreshadowed, was to be fought out within the nominal majority—between the old Conservative Right and the upstart UNR, which had robbed them of their anticipated victory.

A prime minister who reflected the outlook of this majority might prove a serious obstacle to de Gaulle's plans. Consequently, some speculated that the General might renounce the Presidency, the office designed for him, and retain the premiership where he could more effectively impose his own policy on a recalcitrant Parliament. They were wrong. In mid-December he confirmed his candidature for the Elysée, which was contested by two opponents: a respected Communist veteran, Marrane, and a distinguished scientist, Chatelet, put up by the UFD to demonstrate the existence of a non-Communist Left opposition. On 21 December the 80,000 local *notables* cast their votes. More than three-quarters supported the General, who had 62,000 to 10,000 for Marrane and 6,700 for Chatelet. Beyond the shores of France his majority was even more overwhelming. On 8 January he began his seven-year term, and chose as his Prime Minister his faithful follower Michel Debré.

· · · · · · · ·

...Most UNR members were as conservative, clerical and nationalist as their right-wing rivals, and a few were crypto-fascists (though the UNR had supported fewer open anti-democrats than the traditional Conservatives). But the new movement also took quite seriously its responsibilities as a 'party of government'. . .[e.g.] over the economic policy of the government. A team of Conservative experts had advised it and a Conservative Minister of Finance had adopted it, but the Conservative Right exploited every real hardship and demagogic grievance against the cabinet they nominally supported. Many UNR members disliked the policy itself. The new party secretary, Chalandon (who succeeded Frey when he joined the government in January), had himself been the main advocate of a more expansionist alternative. But when the cabinet decided otherwise the UNR set their teeth and accepted the disagreeable electoral consequences of a policy which was not their own.

Those consequences were serious. The electorate did not stay for long in its November mood. The UNR entered the municipal elections in March 1959 with high hopes that the wave of success which had swept them into Parliament would now carry them forward into the town halls of France. Often they were newcomers who lacked strong local roots; if they were to turn their mushroom movement into a solid party, they needed the local position and patronage which a massive irruption into municipal administration would bring them. But they were grievously disappointed, for these elections became 'the revenge of the Fourth Republic'. The Communists recovered all they had lost in November, and the UNR vote fell off, sometimes spectacularly. Lyons chose a despised Radical for the mayor's seat which Soustelle coveted; he was not even runner-up. Neuwirth, Delbecque's associate on 13 May, won 9 per cent of the vote at St Etienne—a mere quarter of his share four months before. Politicians beaten for the Assembly four months earlier—like Defferre at Marseilles or Provo at Roubaix—easily held their *mairies*, often against the same opponents. Next month the election of the new Senate underlined the change of mood. Many (twenty-five) Fourth Republican victims of November now entered the upper house—Mitterrand, Edgar Faure, Defferre, Duclos, Lafay—and at once it became the forum for serious criticism and debate which the impatient and intolerant Assembly no longer afforded.

The voters' defection from the UNR was a grave handicap to the integrationist wing in its struggle for control. For the party had become a battlefield on which the divergent forces responsible for 13 May fought for their different conceptions of their movement. The insurrection had been made in de Gaulle's name by ardent advocates of the integration of Algeria into France. What would they do if their standard-bearer decided to march in the wrong direction?

That crucial question exposed the equivocal nature of the UNR, and indeed of Gaullism. For the Gaullism of 1958 was a third phase of the movement. The first, Free France, had rallied against Vichy all types of Frenchmen, from intransigent nationalists with right-wing and even anti-republican pasts to patriotic socialists opposed to Nazism and reaction, from reforming administrators like Debré, anxious above all for effective government, to liberal Catholics who hoped that the common struggle would bring about a reconciliation of Church, workers and Republic.

When the General launched the second Gaullism, the RPF, he and other leaders wished it to retain similar characteristics: recruitment from all the French 'spiritual families', patriotic intransigence abroad and reformist policies at home. But these intentions were frustrated. Because of the cold war, the violence of the Communist opposition, the suspicions of the democratic Left, and the search by Vichyite voters and conservative politicians for a respectable patriotic covering, the RPF became a right-wing movement (with a few reforming leaders and unconventional policies). Later, as the party shed its conservative opportunists, the liberal views of some of its leaders again mingled and sometimes clashed with the nationalism of others. In 1953 the General himself publicly defended the Sultan of Morocco against the vicious personal attacks by which the Right justified his deposition. And in the Indo-Chinese, Tunisian and Moroccan controversies there were prominent Gaullists on both sides.

This remained true when Algeria came to hold the centre of the stage. In spring 1958 Mendesists were the keenest advocates of an appeal to the General; by autumn 1959 fascist stickers on the walls of Paris were proclaiming, 'De Gaulle = Mendès'. At the same time, intransigent nationalists continued to follow the liberator of 1944, in whom they saw a leader in the Bonapartist tradition, who stood for strong government and a vigorous assertion of France's position in the world. The revival of nationalist feeling over Algeria reinforced this camp with some powerful recruits (especially Soustelle) who before 1956 would have been counted as liberals.

The party leaders were well aware of the dangers of disloyalty. The common bond of personal loyalty to de Gaulle was strong, and easy to underestimate; but the fiasco of the RPF had shown that it might not be enough. Precautions were taken. Deserters from the defunct movement were not welcome in the reincarnated organisation. All UNR candidates had to sign a written oath of fidelity to the General:

Respecting the mandate conferred on me by the voters, I pledge myself for the life of the Parliament to join no other parliamentary group. I undertake to remain faithful to the objectives of the UNR; to support the action of General de Gaulle in Parliament and in my constituency; to vote according to the decision of the majority of the group on important questions...

How seriously they would take this pledge remained to be seen. Little confidence could be put in extremists like Biaggi, who had bludgeoned himself and a few friends into Parliament by threatening to run opposing candidates and split the vote, or Colonel Thomazo, who had campaigned for Chassin against Chaban-Delmas. At the other end of the spectrum, some UNR deputies were not men of the Right at all: a few ex-Socialists, a number of anti-clericals, liberals and Left Catholics like Michelet. But the Left was weaker than in the RPF days. The great majority were in between, right-wingers by background and temperament but personally loyal to de Gaulle.

Two interpretations of the party's function competed within the leadership. One group sought to use the UNR to fight for *Algérie française*, to promote integration, in short to press a positive policy upon a de Gaulle reduced to figurehead status. The other section, unconditional loyalists, wanted to make it a 'mass of manœuvre' which the General could manipulate at will. This was the thankless role Chalandon defined for UNR members:

We have to recognize things as they are. General de Gaulle is our clandestine leader. We are somewhat in the position of secret agents who owe complete obedience to their military chief, a military chief who does not hesitate to disavow them when things are going badly.[1]

The first interpretation pointed to a right-wing alliance. The second would produce a kind of rejuvenated Radical party, a 'party of government' seeking its allies on both sides and willing to support whatever policy the General and his ministers chose.

We are condemned to support governments whatever they may be, to be the pivot of the majorities which form; perhaps it will be on the Left, perhaps it will be on the Right—in any event we shall always be present.[2]

De Gaulle himself kept up a steady pressure on the party. Soustelle did not become president (none was appointed); he was denied the electoral system he wanted, which would have forced the UNR into a right-wing combination; and his colleagues in the leadership refused the pact with Bidault and Duchet. In all these decisions de Gaulle was believed to have intervened privately...

Soustelle could still hope to stimulate counter-pressure from the rank-and-file UNR members. He could exploit both their right-wing sympathies and their resentment at the sheep-like role to which Chalandon's conception of the party's task reduced them. On the other hand, loyalty to de Gaulle was the mainstay of many members' political lives. For a Debré, and for many less-known figures, to oppose the General openly would mean a real *crise de*

---

[1] UNR *Bulletin de Presse*, quoted *Le Monde*, 19 May 1959.
[2] Chalandon, loc. cit.

conscience. Past records were not always reliable pointers to future conduct: Chalandon's chief supporter was Neuwirth. Where loyalty was not enough, self-interest might tell in the same direction. The new members were well aware that they owed their seats to de Gaulle's popularity and not to their own; the municipal elections drove the lesson home. And they were soon to discover how widespread was support for any move by the General towards peace in Algeria. At the election, the (comparatively few) candidates who were liberal about Algeria without being opposed to de Gaulle had invariably polled well, even when they failed to save their seats. Now, many who might have been against him were deterred by fear that a dissolution of Parliament would smash them.

The struggle for the party's soul went on behind the scenes throughout 1959, occasionally breaking into the open. In April the parliamentary group elected an 'orthodox' chairman, Terrenoire, by 124 votes to 72 for Biaggi. 'Still two-thirds of *beni-oui-oui,*' commented Colonel Thomazo. In May, Soustelle supported Sérigny for the Senate; Neuwirth and Chalandon opposed him, and resignations were threatened on both sides.[1] In June the integrationists mounted a vigorous assault against Chalandon, whom they attacked as a rich man without any elective position or contact with the rank and file. Delbecque announced his candidature for the secretaryship, presenting himself as a parliamentarian of working-class origins and a representative of the party militants. In July the two interpretations clashed openly at the party's first *conseil national.*[2]* In September, when de Gaulle offered self-determination to Algeria, both Soustelle and Delbecque urged the party to come out for integration: the executive declined to do so, but eighteen of the sixty-seven members abstained from voting in protest. In October the party required Biaggi to resign from the new *Rassemblement pour l'Algérie française* which he had just founded, along with Bidault and Duchet, to work for the integrationist cause.

[1] [Cross-reference: cut.]
[2] From UNR *Bulletin de Presse,* no. 5, reporting the *conseil national* of 25–26 July 1959 (italics in original):

P. 8. *Chalandon:* 'There is a permanent difficulty: General de Gaulle is our creator; from him we derive our existence, our thinking, our unity. *But, if we belong to him, he does not belong to us; his position as arbitrator will always prevent him from confining himself within the bounds of a party, however faithful it may be*...Certainly there are anti-Gaullists in the country, but *more dangerous than they are those who are Gaullists on condition that General de Gaulle thinks like them, does as they wish*...there ought not to be, in the UNR's eyes, a Party policy about Algeria. There can be no policy but that of General de Gaulle.'

P. 11. *Delbecque:* 'Stop spreading stories according to which all those who disagree, sometimes with decisions which have not been studied together or decided after a majority vote, are anti-Gaullists or people who want a split in the UNR at any cost...'

P. 7 *Soustelle:* 'The party is not the Government...'

* Fuller quotations were given in the original version of this chapter in *De Gaulle's Republic.*

The Algerian settlement and the new regime

Two weeks later the Assembly's debate on de Gaulle's Algerian policy brought matters to a head. There were reports of a new 13 May in preparation: an attempt to drive Debré into resignation by demonstrations in Algiers, a split in the UNR, and private pressure by the army on de Gaulle. Chalandon and Terrenoire confirmed the reports, while Neuwirth warned that 'killer commandos' had already crossed the Spanish border. (An alleged attack on Mitterrand lent colour to the story.*) When tension was at its height, five deputies broke with the UNR, among them Arrighi, Biaggi and Thomazo. Delbecque and three others also resigned, but voted for the government and at once applied to rejoin; the Prime Minister came to a UNR political bureau meeting for the first time and successfully insisted that their applications be refused.

Both sides prepared assiduously for the party's first annual congress in mid-November. Though it was carefully held in Chaban-Delmas territory at Bordeaux, the hall was full of partisans of Soustelle, who cheered his demands for stronger action against the 'treasonous press' and for the readmission of Delbecque and his friends. Orthodox speakers were shouted down, leaders' names booed, and blows exchanged in the lobbies...

But the leaders had taken precautions. Just before the congress the Seine federation, which they controlled, swelled magically in membership—just as loyal Radical federations used to do in the bad old days of the System. The final resolution on Algeria was harmlessly non-committal; from the overwhelmingly activist congress there somehow emerged an overwhelmingly orthodox central committee. The one concession was Chalandon's voluntary retirement; but his successor was an orthodox senator, Richard. The UNR's first congress—like other party conferences in France and elsewhere—showed the difficulties facing extremist party workers who try to force the hand of moderate leaders and parliamentarians.

* On it see *Wars, Plots and Scandals* (Cambridge University Press, 1970), chap. 5.

11 Algerian self-determination: the 1961 referendum*

I

On 8th January, 1961 the French people went to the polls for a referendum. Four times since the war they had gone to vote on new constitutional proposals; this time they were to approve or reject a bill authorizing new institutions for Algeria. 'Frenchmen and Frenchwomen!', President de Gaulle asserted, 'everything is simple and clear.' But one disgruntled elector commented in her turn, 'In this vote nothing is simple but the count.'

It was the revolt of the army and settlers in Algeria which, in May 1958, had brought de Gaulle back to power. 'You will be their prisoner', he was warned; he replied, 'Prisoners escape.' On 28th September, 1958 the French people overwhelmingly approved his new constitution, by 79 per cent of the votes cast and 66 per cent of those possible. At once, to the dismay of his original sponsors, he made peace overtures to the nationalists of the FLN; they refused. A year later he tried again, proposing on 16th September, 1959 that Algeria's future be settled by a local referendum on three options—integration with France, independence, and 'association'. The FLN accepted in principle. But could the principle be applied?

There were sceptics on both Left and Right. They did not believe that an illiterate population, torn by a bitter war, could really choose in freedom, and they doubted whether any 'third force' existed to press for an intermediate solution between *Algérie française* and FLN rule. To men of the Right, these two were the sole alternatives; the Moslems wanted the former, but they would turn from it if France weakened in her determination to stay, for then they would fear to offend the FLN who might soon be their masters. So M. Bidault condemned even self-determination as contrary to 'the constitution, the penal code, military law and natural justice'; M. Soustelle accepted it (to strengthen the French case abroad) only provided the government campaigned for 'the most French' of the three solutions. To the Left, integration seemed as unreal as association; independence was inevitable, the FLN represented Moslem opinion, and only political negotiations with them could protect the European minority—though the settlement agreed

---

* Originally entitled 'The French Referendum, 1961'. From *Parliamentary Affairs*, vol. 14, no. 3 (Summer 1961).

with them might later be submitted to unanimous (and superfluous) ratification at the polls. Thus Right and Left oppositions alike wished the government to commit itself to a solution in advance of the self-determination vote.

In January, 1960, European insurgents set up barricades in Algiers, hoping to force President de Gaulle to declare for *Algérie française*. For a week that recalled May, 1958, the army wavered; but the President stood firm, the army came round, and M. Soustelle went into opposition. In June, however, de Gaulle also refused to negotiate with the FLN on the conditions which they, backed by the French Left, were demanding. Both sides were growing exasperated; and in the autumn the temperature was raised by two spectacular prosecutions. First, in September, twenty young people were charged with aiding the FLN and helping army deserters; 121 prominent intellectuals signed a manifesto defending their conduct. Then in November began the 'barricades case'—the four-month trial of the Algiers insurgent leaders of January. Opinion was becoming polarized between the 'two packs' (as de Gaulle called them); and in Parliament Right and Left were combining against the President's defence and foreign policies. On 4th November, therefore, he moved again, promising at once a new Algerian regime with 'its own government, institutions and laws' (and by implication its own foreign policy), and in the future 'the Algerian Republic'. And on the 16th he announced a referendum on the bill authorizing the new provisional institutions.

Article 11 of the Constitution of the Fifth Republic permits the President, 'on the proposal of the government', to 'submit to a referendum any government bill dealing with the organization of the public authorities' (or approving certain treaties). Three weeks after de Gaulle's announcement, the government formally proposed a referendum; then Parliament was allowed a debate, though not a vote; next the bill was published; and finally the electorate was asked, 'Do you approve the bill submitted to the French people by the President of the Republic and concerning the self-determination of the populations [*sic*] of Algeria and the organization of the public authorities in Algeria prior to self-determination?'

Right and Left alike contended that the second half of the question contradicted the first, replacing self-determination by 'pre-determination'; the new institutions would preclude integration and prejudice negotiation. The government replied that they were transitional, and the final self-determination vote could accept, or modify, or condemn them. Moreover, without them the bill would not have dealt with 'the organization of public authorities', and the referendum would not have been constitutional. This did not worry the Left, who attacked de Gaulle for not asking the one question that mattered, 'Are you for negotiations with the FLN?' And M. Bidault claimed that the referendum was unconstitutional anyway.

The cities also denounced the government's general policy, warning that a Yes to the bill would be exploited as a general vote of confidence. 'Our NON is also a NON to the monopolists,' proclaimed the Communists, and the right-wing opposition also tried to make capital out of the country's many discontents. Conversely, OUI supporters tried at once to narrow the debate to Algeria, and to widen it by stressing the indispensability of de Gaulle, without whom France would face chaos and dictatorship. The President's own speeches discussed domestic and foreign as well as Algerian affairs. But above all he appealed for a 'frank and massive OUI', and warned that a negative or uncertain response 'would prevent me pursuing my task'.

Intellectuals might dislike his personal tone, and regard his hint of resignation as unworthy blackmail. But the man in the street was impressed by the appeal, and alarmed by the threat. The critics tried to reassure him; M. Soustelle's friends put out a tract called 'The Continuity of the Republic', simply citing Article 7 of the Constitution (which provides for a new election if the Presidency falls vacant). This hardly met the charge that the opposition, being hopelessly divided, could not possibly govern. To this accusation the right-wingers replied that the Communists were secretly telling their supporters to vote OUI; thus a NON vote would be a clear verdict for *Algérie française*. For the Left, MM. Mendès-France and Claude Bourdet answered in turn that everyone knew the ultras were a tiny minority; thus a NON vote would be an obvious triumph for the Left, compelling new elections that would sweep them to power.

Both oppositions condemned the official campaign. Most of the critics denounced the referendum in principle; the familiar Communist phrase 'le référendum-plébiscite' was taken up by pillars of the reactionary Right. All of them agreed that this particular referendum was dangerous, misleading, and futile: dangerous because it might provoke disorders in Algeria; misleading because to 'the double question submitted to us by the Sphinx' (Soustelle) only one answer could be given; and futile because the new institutions were a hopeless attempt to by-pass the real nationalists by concessions to bogus ones. They would fail like the similar Bao-Dai experiment in Indo-China. M. Soustelle himself echoed the attacks on 'Bao-Daiism' by his old antagonist M. Raymond Aron; and from the far Left Professor Mandouze chimed in: 'I accept M. Soustelle's analysis' though not his conclusions.

The political climate in which the elector had to make up his mind was more thundery than ever. Early in December four defendants in the 'barricades trial', led by the deputy Lagaillarde, escaped to Spain to join General Salan (who had helped to put de Gaulle in power, but was now openly against him). It was rumoured that they were to join a military coup timed for the President's visit to Algeria later that week. On this tour, which avoided the cities, de Gaulle was met by Moslem cheers and European hatred. Serious riots by the Europeans of Algiers and Oran were quenched by massive Moslem demonstrations—the first since the war began—in favour of the FLN and its leader Ferhat Abbas. But the army (apart from the paratroops) displayed remarkable restraint and loyalty to the government, though General Valluy warned that it was 'on the edge of despair, perhaps revolt', and Marshal Juin and sixteen retired generals announced that they were voting NON.

These events had an impact on opinion. Lagaillarde's flight discredited his cause (it suffered a further blow a week before the poll when nine officers of the gendarmerie, on whom his fellow-insurgents had opened fire in the January revolt, gave evidence of this murderous attack upon them). The rumours of military plots probably helped the government—the greater the danger, the more essential de Gaulle appeared. The results of the Moslem riots were more complex and infinitely more important. By shattering the myth of Moslem enthusiasm for integration, they deterred some right-wingers from voting NON; but by destroying the chance that representative Moslems would help to work the new institutions, they made left-wingers less willing to vote OUI. Above all they gave a wholly new self-confidence to the Moslem electors in Algeria and to the FLN leaders in Tunis, and a new authority to Ferhat Abbas, a moderate. And they convinced the army, as well as the government, that an approach must be made to the FLN. Gaullist spokesmen now began to hint that a OUI vote was a vote for negotiations—although the President's own statements remained as loftily ambiguous as ever.

II

During December the parties were making up their minds. The defenders of *Algérie française* (renamed *l'Algérie dans la République* to attract left-wing support) were grouped in a Committee for the Defence of Territorial Integrity (the 'Vincennes Committee'). Among them were the Algiers integrationists, M. Soustelle's new *Regroupement National*, M. Morice's Republican Centre (ex-Radicals), M. Bidault's Christian Democrats (ex-MRP), right-wing members of the main Conservative party (the *Centre National des Indépendants*, CNI)—and a very few Radicals and Socialists. On the Left there was more confusion. The PSU (*Parti Socialiste Unifié*, the dissident Socialist party to which M. Mendès-France belongs) proposed that the entire Left should boycott the referendum;* this would give a clear result, Gaullists and centre supporters voting OUI, the ultras voting NON in isolation (which would show how few they were)—and the Left opposition claiming all the abstainers. But the Communists, who hate telling their followers to abstain, insisted (not without internal dissensions) on a NON vote.†

Three major parties, with very different attitudes, favoured voting OUI. The faithful Gaullists of the UNR gave enthusiastic support to the government's whole policy; only ten deputies out of 200 rebelled. MRP too was solid, apart from a tiny handful of *Algérie française* supporters; but they confined their support to Algerian policy. Unlike these two parties, the Socialists were in opposition; they were therefore still more explicit that theirs was a *OUI à la négotiation*, which did not affect their firm NON to the government's domestic and foreign policies and to the evolution of the regime. MM. Mollet and Defferre carried nearly two-thirds of the votes (2,191) against M. Gazier and the left wing, who favoured abstention (836 votes) and MM. Lacoste, Lejeune and their *Algérie française* supporters who were for a NON (316). The two opposition groups presented almost identical motions (save for the crucial point, 'negotiations'); and M. Lejeune won a NON majority in his own local party, Somme, only with the help of left-wing, pro-negotiation votes.

The other two major parties were still more divided. Both Radical and Conservative members of Parliament were more disposed to vote OUI than their active followers outside. The Radical party conference decided to vote NON by 1,200 to 620 for OUI and 110 for abstention; but here too the majority was made up of both *Algérie française* and peace-by-negotiation supporters. The party's campaign was thus somewhat embarrassed; its posters denounced the referendum in principle, the inopportuneness of this particular consultation, and the absence of any clear choice, while its leader's broadcasts awkwardly mingled the criticisms of both oppositions ('neither prospects of peace nor guarantees for the European minority'). In the Conservative CNI the conflict was more clear-cut. The party secretary, Senator Roger Duchet, had long been a leading *Algérie française* advocate; M. Pinay, who might have counterbalanced his influence, maintained a sphinx-like silence; and M. Duchet obtained a majority of 1,360 to 441 from a party conference in which the extreme-Right activists of Paris were well represented. But neither CNI nor Radicals wanted to risk a revolt among their parliamentarians, and neither tried to impose party discipline on their local members and branches.

---

* On the origins of the PSU, see below, pp. 157–8.
† On the Communist dissensions, see below, p. 159; cf. also below, p. 130.

Several lesser groups also took up positions. The left-wing Gaullists of the UDT (*Union démocratique du Travail*) were for OUI as a step to Algerian independence; so were the 'liberals' of Algiers. But the PSU, with the same aim, came out for NON (though the advocates of asbtention were beaten only by 413 to 353). The boycott, once vainly proposed by M. Mendès-France, was also the choice of his bitterest enemy, M. Pierre Poujade (and on 9th January that forgotten demagogue was to observe with pride that while the NON leaders had been thrashed, he had won over millions of non-voters with whom he would soon do great things). The royalist pretender, the Comte de Paris, was for OUI—his followers mostly for NON. Among Moslems, the FLN called for a boycott. So did their blood-feud enemies, the rival nationalists of MNA. But so did not their old mentor, President Bourguiba of Tunisia, whose appeal to vote OUI influenced many Frenchmen of the Left.

Every viewpoint was thus put before the public. The government's critics had access to the radio; the press was less harassed than usual; opposition leaflets were widely distributed; public meetings were freely held, and at the most popular Paris hall, the Mutualité, there were in the last week two OUI and three NON rallies. But, as in the 1958 referendum campaign, the government used a series of devices to load the dice. Petty sops were thrown to discontented groups: the shooting season was extended for a week, a bill closing superfluous bars was deferred, the angry wine-growers were privately assured that their grievances would be treated sympathetically, and a (meagre) increase in family allowances was announced. Prominent dignitaries were enlisted in a campaign stressing the civic duty of going to the polls (NON voters would go anyway). Cinemas had a Ministry of Information propaganda film, to be shown with the newsreel. The official envelope sent to each elector contained the question, ballot-papers—and a speech by President de Gaulle. Six million copies were distributed of the journal *France-Référendum*, which had not appeared since the 1958 campaign; closely modelled on the most popular evening paper, *France-Soir*, it was was again labelled 'Exceptional—free' and credited with 'Europe's largest circulation'.

The state radio and television service (RTF) has long been a government instrument. Party broadcasts were allowed between Christmas and the New Year; but the President, who opened the campaign and also made two broadcasts in the week before the poll, had almost as much time on the air as all the parties together. The Minister of Information also appeared in the last week to answer listeners' questions; the regular commentators favoured the government's case, and the selection of news was somewhat slanted.

Each authorized party had ten minutes on sound and eight on television.

On the advice of the Constitutional Council (an independent body with a Gaullist majority), those authorized had to have both a parliamentary group and a nation-wide organization of their own. This criterion admitted the six established parties, three for OUI and three for NON, but not the Algiers integrationists (who had no national organization) or the PSU, Poujadists, or M. Soustelle's *Regroupement National* (which had no parliamentary group). During the two days allowed for registration, the integrationists and M. Soustelle's movement fused—but the Ministry ruled that they had not qualified in time. M. Soustelle appealed to the Constitutional Council, which under the Constitution 'supervises the regularity of the conduct of a referendum'; it decided that it had no jurisdiction. He then applied to the busy *Conseil d'Etat*, where his case could not be heard in time.

Such tactics provoked criticism. M. Mendès-France rather oddly argued that the discrimination against the PSU was proof of the power of the 'ultras' within the state. An 'ultra' leader, M. Morice, warned democrats who tolerated discrimination against the Right that they themselves might be the next to suffer. M. Jean Baylot (who as Prefect of Police had earned a reputation for 'McCarthyism') now organized a protest by CNI deputies against abuses of governmental power. M. Soustelle himself denounced the 'restrictions on freedom of expression unheard-of since the Second Empire', the 'false slogans and techniques of psychological action', the expenditure of millions from public funds, the misuse of TV and radio and the hamstringing of the opposition. The results, he warned, would be open to doubt since 'no opinion could be put forward except that of our masters'. Yet the official campaign was far less obtrusive than in 1958—when precisely the same techniques, identical mean little devices for hampering opponents, and nearly twice as much public money were used without stint by the then Minister of Information, M. Jacques Soustelle, with no hint of protest from MM. Morice and Baylot.

Party campaigns were traditionalist, unexciting, and less energetic than in 1958. The Gaullist movements had then spent lavishly—six times as much as the UNR in 1961; the other parties were estimated to have reduced their already meagre budgets to a half or a third of the former figure. Individual politicians were often cautious, giving advice like M. Pinay's: 'Vote according to your conscience.' Among those who differed from their parties, most Socialist, UNR and PSU dissidents and many OUI supporters in CNI refrained from advertising their private views. Sometimes political rivals would avoid a clash: in Bas-Rhin and Meuse every deputy, senator and departmental councillor but one signed a common OUI statement, in Lot all three MPs favoured OUI, in Basses-Pyrénées the three right-wing leaders all came out for NON.

Orthodox UNR members were often active in canvassing the towns, visiting rural *notables*, and writing persuasive letters to the local councillors who elect senators. Small parties like the PSU or UDT welcomed the chance of publicity; aspiring politicians sometimes seized the opportunity to unhorse a dangerous rival. Thus, in Marseilles the Socialist Mayor, Senator Defferre, humiliated his detested rival, the extreme-Right leader of the local CNI, by managing a vigorous and victorious OUI campaign. In Charente-Maritime the leading figures were another CNI deputy of the far Right, and a Radical senator; the former campaigned for NON, the latter (defying his party) for OUI. In the 6th district of Paris, MRP posters attacked the CNI deputy for deserting de Gaulle. The UNR member for Amiens put up posters throughout the department, stressing that he was the only Somme deputy supporting the President; and the only meetings held in Somme (apart from 130 by the Communists) were four badly-attended rallies addressed by a former Radical candidate in his former (and future) constituency.

The Communists held many meetings, but their audiences were far smaller than usual. The PSU was active in the provinces; the older parties hardly campaigned at all. The UNR arranged large rallies in the big provincial towns, and 125 local meetings in the Paris region; they too complained of numbers that fell below normal. The most successful were certainly those of MM. Soustelle and Bidault, who drew packed and cheering crowds in Nantes, Lyons, Lille, Toulouse and elsewhere; once again, success with audiences preceded failure with the voters.

Schoolrooms for meetings and official poster-boards were available only to the six authorized parties. The law confining election posters to the official sites was disregarded as usual (the UNR printed nearly four times as many copies of its main poster as there were boards for it). But in many places the boards stood empty. There was less need for the opposition to compete with the government's display, which was far less conspicuous than in 1958. The ubiquitous OUI A LA FRANCE poster of that day was replaced, here and there, by a drawing of a friendly handshake between a Moslem and a European; unfortunately the white mechanic had in his pocket a metal ruler which had to be hastily and inelegantly retouched into a wooden one, lest it be mistaken for a parachutist's dagger.

The press, as in 1958, mostly supported the government. In the provinces the Radical *Dépêche du Midi* of Toulouse was again the principal opposition journal; in Paris the Communist *L'Humanité* and the fellow-travelling *Libération* were discreetly joined in their NON by *Le Parisien Libéré* (an extreme-Right paper read by many Communists). As usual, many journals—OUI, NON and uncommitted alike—opened their columns to different points of view (though *Libération's tribune libre* permitted only different reasons for voting NON). In most cases national party leaders were invited to contribute, though local spokesmen were sometimes preferred—the *Courrier Picard* of Amiens, more generous than the government, gave space to the PSU and Poujadists as well as the six main parties. Few provincial papers gave much news of the campaign, save for de Gaulle's speeches and developments in Algeria. Thus four days before the poll, the *Nouvelle République* of Tours devoted six full pages out of eight to the disastrous local floods; this left no space for the referendum. The largest paper outside Paris, *Ouest-France*, had until Friday in the last week less than a page of political news daily. But many politicians control small local journals, and these sometimes ran special editions (17 for the UNR in the Paris area alone, with an estimated circulation of 600,000).

The radio was not thought to have greatly helped either the parties (though their broadcasts were less abysmally bad than usual) or the government. For Frenchmen preferred to listen to the *postes périphériques*, such as Luxembourg and Europe no. 1, which gave less biased news and comment and allowed all-party discussions on the air. But in television RTF's monopoly is effective, and seems to have benefited the government greatly, especially in those rural areas which have it (sets are not numerous but each is watched by many people).

One or two novelties were tried. Officialdom distributed free gramophone records of a speech by de Gaulle (so the *Canard Enchaîné* styled the President 'Charles-Disque', after the authoritarian Charles X who provoked the 1830 revolution). The UNR tried an American technique of instructing its members in big cities each to telephone fifty persons in the directory and urge them (briefly) to vote OUI. Besides the parties, some other forces took a hand. The Catholic Church urged the faithful to vote, and often gave a clear hint that they should vote OUI (thus the Cardinal-Archbishop of Lyons, M. Soustelle's constituency, warned his flock against the partisan passions of their ordinary political leaders). Business opinion strongly favoured the government. The Catholic trade union (CFTC) and the pro-Socialist *Force Ouvrière* took no formal stand; the CGT was naturally in the opposition. Some perennially discontented peasant organizations (e.g. at Toulouse) came out for a NON vote; the Committee of Naturalized Poles were for OUI; and in the four wine-growing departments of the Midi, the local mayors advocated a mass boycott in protest against alleged governmental neglect.

Almost everywhere the campaign was orderly and rather flat. Many shrewd observers concluded that massive indifference by the general public, and irrelevant discontents among different sections of the electorate, would lead to a very low poll. As in 1958, one sign might have corrected this impression: the large numbers seeking to register after coming of age or changing address. But the ordinary Frenchman did not display his concern in public. He made up his mind in privacy, without listening to the spokesmen of the political or economic groups he normally favoured. On all sides voters were cross-pressured. Even the Communists, monolithic on the surface, were deeply divided; within a month two of their leaders were to be excommunicated for crypto-Gaullist heresies. Voters of the Right, susceptible to appeals from political generals, were also moved by the nationalist rallying-cries of M. Soustelle and his friends. The democratic Left opposition were torn between the OUI of Bourguiba and the NON of Mendès-France, between their loathing for the plebiscitary tone of the campaign and their fear of chaos if de Gaulle resigned. Some voted NON, hoping others would provide a majority of OUI; for those who thought this discreditable, 'duty' and 'honour' pointed (as one of them said) in opposite directions. But the less politically sophisticated responded *en masse* to de Gaulle's threat of resignation, and to his final broadcast appeal, two days before the poll, for a personal vote of confidence. 'I need, yes I need to know how things stand in your minds and hearts. And therefore I turn to you, over the heads of all the intermediaries...the question is one between each man and woman among you, and myself.'

III

In Algeria the atmosphere was set by the great pro-FLN demonstrations of the previous month. At last the Moslems were conscious of their strength, and now it was the Europeans who were intimidated. The plausible prophecies of disorder and disaster were not fulfilled; the Europeans feared that by rioting they would merely provoke far more formidable Moslem counter-measures, while the Moslems would not play into their enemies' hands by disorders which might renew the old alliance, now shattered, between the army and the *colons*.

The government nevertheless had reason to fear the vote in Algeria; a NON majority there would go far to destroy the effect of a OUI majority in France itself. Nor was it impossible. For most Europeans would certainly vote NON; and on the other side, the FLN was instructing its followers to abstain (here and there threatening that the first three voters in each polling-station would have their throats cut). It was doubtful whether the Moslems could be induced to defy the moral authority (or the physical menace) of the FLN—unless the army were to coerce them (or enable them to say they had been coerced). But would the army again intervene actively, as it had in the past, now that most officers were hostile or lukewarm to the policy they were to promote? Official circulars instructed them to take active steps to persuade the population to vote, and to vote OUI (never had journalists in Algiers received copies of these confidential documents from so many willing sources). The official Control Commission for Oran protested that these orders prevented them ensuring the regularity of the vote. Complaints came also from right-wingers who had fully approved of military intervention in 1958, but now claimed that it would make the results completely meaningless; the most grotesque was an attempt, based on the circulars, to prosecute the prime minister for misconduct in office—introduced by two European deputies for Algiers who had allegedly owed their own election to the support of the army. Arrested ultras complained bitterly about conditions in the internment camps—in the past, when the camps were occupied only by Moslems, they regarded identical complaints as *prima facie* evidence of treason. M. Soustelle and his friends of the Vincennes Committee contrived simultaneously to insist that the army must take over full powers in Algeria, and that it was dangerous and criminal to involve it in politics.

Friendly and critical journalists agreed that the army was less active than in any of the previous votes (though not necessarily less effective, since so many hill villagers had been moved—by choice or constraint—to the plains where they could be better protected and controlled). Over most of the country the FLN made no serious attempt to stop people voting. The expected disorders did not occur. In the countryside polling was quite heavy (68 per cent) and so was the OUI majority. But in the towns nearly all Moslems stayed away from the polls and left the Europeans to return a large NON majority (72 per cent of votes cast at Algiers, 86 per cent at Oran). Over the whole of Algeria (excluding the Sahara which voted heavily OUI) there were 4,414,000 electors, of whom 1,748,000 voted OUI and 782,000 NON, while 1,800,000 did not go to the poll. Most of the 340,000 soldiers entitled to vote in Algeria were probably among the OUI supporters; nevertheless among the less advanced rural Moslems there was a substantial vote in favour of de Gaulle as the man to make peace. This cannot be wholly explained by the efforts of the army. It partly offset the bitter hostility of the Europeans, and the clear demonstration of pro-FLN loyalties (again, by choice or constraint) of the Moslems of the towns.

The results in France were more favourable than the government had dared to hope. The electorate had since 1958 increased by 600,000 to 27 million. There were 15 million OUI votes (down 2½ million; 75·25 per cent of *valid votes cast*, against 79·25 per cent in 1958); 5 million NONs (up 370,000; 24·75 per cent against 20·75 per cent); and 6,400,000 non-voters (up 2,400,000).

As usual, the turnout was highest in the north. It was 8 per cent below

TABLE 3. *Referendum results, 1958 and 1961*

| | Thousands | | % of electorate | |
	1958	1961	1958	1961
OUI	17,669	15,197	66·4	55·9
NON	4,625	4,996	17·4	18·4
Spoiled Papers	304	604	1·1	2·2
Non-voters	4,007	6,389	15·1	23·5
Electorate	26,603	27,186	—	—
Population of voting age (estimated)	27,800	—	—	—

1958, falling furthest in the south-east quarter of France. But weather rather than politics may account for this, for the pattern was very like that of the last January vote (1956, when 83 per cent turned out)—except for a relatively high poll in Normandy, Brittany and Alsace, and a low one in the wine-growing Midi where the mayors were leading a boycott. Frenchwomen—to judge by four Lyons polling-stations where their votes were counted separately—were a little less likely to vote than men (though the difference was smaller than usual) but much more likely to vote OUI (women 77 per cent, men 66 per cent). Of 400,000 Moslem Algerians in France, only 500 voted.

The distribution of the NON vote was very like 1958 (Table 4). The largest increases probably reflect changes of population, not of opinion, for they occurred in the regions favoured by immigrants from Morocco and Tunisia; of the eleven departments where the NON share increased 3 per cent or more, eight were in the south-west or on the Mediterranean coast. (It was also in the south-west that most ballot-papers were spoiled.)

TABLE 4. *Departmental distribution of NONs, 1958 and 1961*

| 1958 (by departments) | 1961 % of electorate | | | | |
	Over 20	17·5–20	15–17·5	10–15	Under 10
Top 30	25	5	—	—	—
Middle 30	4	11	11	4	—
Bottom 30	—	—	3	19	8

NON leaders of the Right, like those of the Left in 1958, all failed to carry their home towns. But most took some of their followers with them, and doubtless they deterred others from voting OUI. An estimate of the right-wing opposition total must allow for four components: the half-hearted who finally abstained (whose number cannot be determined); the few extremists who had already voted NON in 1958 (perhaps over 100,000); the 370,000 who went to swell the NON total; and those who, within that total, silently replaced the left-wing defectors who this time voted OUI or stayed at home, rather than join the same camp as MM. Soustelle and Lagaillarde.

How large were these transfers? If they were heavy, the NON vote would fall in the left-wing areas where it had been strong, and rise in the right-wing areas where it had been weak. The discrepancy between different types of area should thus reflect the size of the transfers. For example, in the most right-wing polling stations in Toulouse the NONs' share of the electorate rose by 4·6 per cent, in the most left-wing it fell by 2·7 per cent. In the city of Lyons it was up 4 per cent; but it rose 7 per cent in the most conservative district and fell 4 per cent in the main working-class suburb. Such big gaps suggest large in-and-out transfers and a right opposition vote of 8 to 10 per cent of the electorate, i.e. over two million. But they are not representative; the gap elsewhere was much smaller. In the whole Toulouse region, the median change in the most right-wing towns was +3·0, in the most left-wing +0·2. In the south-east it was +0·3 and −3·1; in Normandy and Brittany, +1·0 and −0·9; in the north, +1·3 and −1·2; in Champagne, +1·9 and −0·3; in the centre, +1·6 and −2·0; in Lorraine, +1·4 and −1·3; on the south-west coast, +4·5 and +0·6; on the coast of Provence, +3·7 and +1·5; around Paris, +5·1 and +3·8.

Thus the NON share increased in Left strongholds in two regions only: the Midi with its *colon* newcomers, and the Paris 'red belt', where alone more Communists voted NON than in 1958. In the 45 departments with a low NON vote in 1958, the NON share was up this time by 1·5 per cent; in the 45 with a high NON vote, it was up only 0·4 per cent. From these figures it can be calculated that the right-wing NONs, though much more numerous in some areas than in others, probably numbered about 1,200,000 over the whole country. The Left were therefore justified in contending that the great majority of NON, as well as OUI votes were cast in favour of peace in Algeria.[1]

The precise significance of these results may be hard to assess. But their general importance is clear enough. First, the referendum showed that the French electorate accepted self-determination and would not fight on to keep Algeria French. The Left had taken for granted, on this as on many other matters, that the public agreed with their views; they argued that the

[1] Similar conclusions, based on other evidence, are reached by F. Goguel in *Revue française de Science politique*, XI. 1, pp. 5–28 (particularly for Paris and Haute-Vienne) and by J. M. Royer in *Esprit*, no. 293, pp. 472–80.

referendum was superfluous, since 'everybody' accepted self-determination. Yet it had been official French policy for only fifteen months and was still bitterly contested; in office, neither M. Mendès-France nor M. Mollet had ventured to propose it. Thus the demonstration of feeling was useful, especially for the army. The *Algérie française* party had paralyzed French policy for years and had destroyed one Republic; now its weakness was at last displayed. M. Soustelle denounced cowardly war-weariness, the indifference of 'northern Frenchmen' to the fate of their 'southern compatriots', one-sided official propaganda and the silencing of the opposition. General Salan condemned the 'Munich spirit' of his countrymen. They could still hope that this outlook would change if the price of peace proved too high, and if a mass emigration of the *colons* evoked public sympathy for the victims of Arab nationalism. But they could no longer misrepresent the present mood of the people. The army noted that mood, and any risk of a military coup against the regime disappeared—at least for a time.[1]

The referendum had a second result. Two days after it, the FLN publicly abandoned its six-month-old contention that negotiations with France were impossible, and that they must therefore rely on Communist aid to fight the war and on UN intervention to end it. Overnight they again began calling for the direct talks which, according to the French Left, the referendum had obstructed. Of course they also condemned any new institutions from which they were excluded; consequently, the first result of de Gaulle's triumph was the shelving of the bill he had asked the voters to approve. 'Everything' was perhaps not quite as 'simple and clear' as he had maintained. But the provisional institutions which were not to be set up as yet might later—if the delay allowed time for the war to be settled—offer a framework for bringing the FLN into the government of Algeria. At any rate, both sides made repeated and unprecedented gestures of goodwill to prepare the climate for negotiations.

There was a third result. As in 1958, and to hardly less striking a degree, the electorate had confirmed their confidence in the President. The 'intermediaries'—parties, pressure-groups, army, intellectuals—who agreed only in disliking the regime and disapproving most of its policies, had been humiliated again. For the coming negotiations, General de Gaulle had the free hand he had sought. But how long would his credit last? And how long can democracy survive without intermediaries?

[1] Written in February 1961. [A coup was tried in Algiers in April.]

12 Algerian independence: the April 1962 referendum*

'Prescribed by the constitution, the referendum thus enters into our habits.' Calling on his countrymen to vote on 8th April, 1962, in the third referendum since he took power, President de Gaulle went out of his way to emphasize that their vote would have repercussions far beyond the Algerian problem with which it was formally concerned. It would 'definitely consecrate the practice of the referendum' he told them. 'Henceforth, on a subject which is vital for the country, every citizen may be called upon, as now, to judge for himself and assume his responsibilities. No one can doubt that the character and operation of the institutions of the Republic will be profoundly marked by it.'

For the President the referendum is 'the clearest, the frankest, the most democratic of procedures'. He has used—and plainly intends to use—it for a treble purpose: to settle major decisions in an irreversible way; to renew, at frequent intervals, the 'current of confidence' between the people and the Chief Executive which earlier Republics so conspicuously lacked; to embarrass and dislocate the political parties, whose audience in the country, though feeble, might prove an obstacle to his plans.

In the 1958 referendum 85 per cent of the electorate voted and only 20 per cent of these—Communists and a handful of dissident Socialists and Radicals—refused to approve the constitution of the Fifth Republic. In January 1961 the voters were called on to give a single answer to a double question; a bill endorsing both the principle of self-determination for Algeria and the establishment of an autonomous executive there.[1] The keen supporters of *Algérie française* joined the left-wing opposition, but together they could still muster only a quarter of the voters—though 22 per cent stayed away from the polls.

The provisional executive was no sooner approved by the nation than it was shelved by the President, for the referendum led to the reopening of the negotiations with the nationalists. These, continuing intermittently for a full year, were finally concluded successfully with the signing of an agreement

---

[1] [See chap. 11.]

* Originally entitled 'The French Referendum of April 1962'. Written with *Martin Harrison*. From *Parliamentary Affairs* vol. 15, no. 3 (Summer 1962).

and a declaration of a cease fire at Evian on 19th March 1962. The referendum of 8th April asked French voters to support a bill simultaneously approving the Evian agreements and authorizing the President to take all measures he deemed necessary to implement them by ordinance. For the first time opposition came essentially from the Right.

Weak in numbers in metropolitan France, the partisans of *Algérie française* held two strong cards: the sympathy of many army officers and the passionate support of Europeans in Algeria. Out of the collapse of the Algiers putsch of April 1961 the Secret Army Organisation (OAS) had emerged there, led by the extremist survivors.* By autumn, helped by accomplices in the local administration and ruthless terrorism, they controlled the Europeans and vied with Paris for dominance in the major cities. At the end of the year they began blowing up the homes of their opponents in France itself. This campaign aroused intense popular indignation. The apparent impotence of the police in the early weeks fanned left-wing suspicions that the *plastiqueurs* enjoyed complicities in high places (had not the Gaullists come to power in 1958 as conspirators willing to use force to keep Algeria French, in compromising company with many of their present opponents?). Fearing to alienate the army by seeming to accept left-wing support, the government banned demonstrations against OAS, and those held in defiance of the bans were repressed by the police with a savagery which was bitterly condemned by the main police union itself. Two months before the referendum the government's callousness and ineptitude had left it isolated and friendless.

Then the atmosphere suddenly changed. On 13th February the government, with belated wisdom, authorized a funeral procession for demonstrators killed by police action the previous week; half a million people turned out in the largest gathering France had seen for almost thirty years to give an impressive warning to the OAS—and to the authorities. Government spokesmen attacked OAS with unambiguous vigour; the slow police infiltration of OAS networks began to bear impressive fruit, as arrests multiplied even in Algeria. In Paris plastic-bomb attacks almost ceased from early March. And on the 19th the Evian agreements were signed; the seven-year war against the nationalists was over.

The government naturally seized its chance. A massive vote in favour of the agreements would make them irrevocable in the eyes of history and world opinion, and would impress the FLN and the army—if not the OAS extremists. But the referendum was to mean more than this. De Gaulle himself saw it as a means of renewing his mystic monarchical communion with the people—the provincial tours by which he normally communed with the masses had been suspended for months. For many leaders of the Gaullist

* On the putsch see *Wars, Plots and Scandals* (Cambridge University Press, 1970), chap. 10.

UNR this seemed the most favourable moment to go to the electorate with hopes of maintaining their inflated parliamentary strength of 1958. Government and parties therefore treated the referendum as the overture to an election campaign, and adjusted their tactics accordingly. Not until a week after the vote was it learned that no election was to be held.

Under the constitution a proposal to submit a bill to referendum must be made by the government during a parliamentary session. (In fact, it was announced by the President and subsequently proposed to him by the government, whereupon he agreed. Parliament was recalled for a two-day special session to debate the Evian agreement—but was not allowed to vote on it.) A referendum bill must either affect the 'organization of the *pouvoirs publics*' or ratify either a treaty with a foreign power or an accord with a member-state of the Community. The Evian agreement was clearly not a treaty—Algeria was not yet a sovereign state; nor was she a member of the (now defunct) Community. Possibly article 2 of the bill, giving the President full powers to implement the agreement, might be counted as 'organization of the *pouvoirs publics*', but its constitutionality was still dubious. The constitution permits Parliament to grant the *government* the right to legislate by ordinance (Article 38), but it neither authorizes nor forbids a grant of power to the President by referendum. It does permit him to take supreme powers under article 16 to meet the gravest national crises, but the situation scarcely warranted this—and for the President it also had the major disadvantage of suspending his normal power of dissolution.

Consulted on the drafting of the bill, the appropriate independent juridical authority—the Conseil d'Etat—is reported to have given an adverse opinion by a two-thirds majority. (During the Fourth Republic it was cabinet proceedings that leaked; now it is those of the Conseil d'Etat. One member, who is detached as an opposition deputy, alleged that the Conseil had proposed amendments clearly limiting the President's extended powers to Algerian matters but these were rejected by the government.) Some critics maintained that the cession of Algeria would be unconstitutional, since article 2 categorically proclaims the Republic 'indivisible'. Yet article 53 (proposed, ironically enough, by M. Ferhat Abbas when he was a deputy in 1946) allows territory to be ceded if the inhabitants consent—which the subsequent self-determination vote in Algeria would show. What *was* clearly unconstitutional, though practically unavoidable, was the exclusion of Algeria—still part of the Republic—from the April referendum (on which even overseas departments like Réunion and Martinique were consulted). But political judgments had changed and legal purism seemed anachronistic; if constitutional or procedural irregularities there were, the verdict of the sovereign people would grant absolution on April 8th.

Some critics argued that the referendum was unnecessary; the 1961 referendum had already given de Gaulle full authority to carry through self-determination and establish provisional Algerian institutions. But the primary purpose of the bill's drafting was, of course, political. Technically it might be redundant, but de Gaulle meant both to demonstrate that the nation approved the settlement and to gain the maximum advantage from their approval. He and the government also saw that the Algerian settlement could be put to further advantage. In his first broadcast he told the voters that their OUI would not only ratify the Evian settlement but also demonstrate confidence in his person, and 'grant me the right to do what is necessary to achieve the end; in short, that in the arduous task which falls to me, and of which Algeria is one part amid others, I have their confidence with me for today and for tomorrow'. As M. Debré succinctly put it, 'the referendum is not only a judgment; it is an engagement'.

This calculated mingling of peace in Algeria with blanket approval of the President naturally embarrassed the politicians. The government clearly intended to exploit the OUI they could not avoid—for with an election believed imminent, politicians dared not risk apparently saying NON to peace. For de Gaulle this embarrassment was a major asset of 'the clearest, the frankest, the most democratic of procedures'.

The Communists in particular faced a difficult problem. Both in 1958 and in 1961 the party had ordered its followers to vote NON, but many had refused its lead. In 1958 massive defections at the referendum were followed by the loss of a third of their vote at the subsequent elections—yet then they had said NON only to the Gaullist régime and to its military backers who were determined to continue the war. In 1962, if elections again followed a referendum, the party might suffer a catastrophe instead of realising its rising hopes of regaining lost ground.

Refusing to fall into the trap, the Communists resolved on their OUI even before publication of the bill, and maintained it despite terms which may have been designed deliberately to drive them into opposition. Their energetic propaganda campaign explained that they were approving a peace settlement which public opinion, under their leadership, had forced on a reluctant de Gaulle. This prudent decision escaped disaster at the cost of softening the party's opposition to the régime, weakening the combativity of its troops and exasperating some party workers who resented opportunist behaviour by a revolutionary vanguard. Whichever reply the Communists advocated, the referendum was bound to do them some harm.

The other parties were affected similarly—though less dramatically. Only the Gaullists gave whole-hearted approval. MRP (which formed part of the government's majority) and the Socialists and Radicals (who were both in opposition) gave similar 'Yes—But' responses. They made it clear that their support was limited to Algeria and unrelated to the rest of Gaullist policy. The Conservative CNI, also represented in the government and including both loyal Gaullist supporters and bitter opponents of the régime, was so torn by dissension that it told its followers to vote according to their consciences and let its parliamentarians campaign for either OUI, NON or Abstention.

These were the six traditional parties which alone, in the last referendum, had been allotted poster sites and broadcasting time. The qualification imposed in 1961 was that a 'party' must have both a national organization and a parliamentary group. Last time Soustelle attempted to qualify a seventh party by fusing the Algerian integrationist group in Parliament with his National Rally outside, but the government thwarted him by declaring he had not fulfilled the conditions in time.[1] However, in 1961 the political situation had changed; the old qualification would have embarrassed the government by barring the opposition from all propaganda facilities. But the National Rally had recently been dissolved as a blow against OAS apologists and sympathizers. The government therefore altered the criterion to admit the Algerian integrationists by qualifying any party with a parliamentary group in either house.

Even so, it had difficulty in finding political spokesmen who would advocate an outright NON on the supposed brink of a general election. In the end Poujade and Bidault were the only prominent public figures to do so; most opponents prudently counselled their followers not to vote OUI. Some favoured abstention, or even the spoiling of ballot papers, either because they were hostile to the Algerian settlement (like the right-wing ex-Radicals of the Republican Centre) or because they objected to the President's double question (like the Unified Socialists—left-wing opponents of the war and the régime whose best known member was Mendès-France).* Others denounced the referendum as unconstitutional and illegitimate and called on conscientious citizens to boycott it. This was the position of the Algerian integrationists early in the campaign, though later they moved toward an implied NON.

As usual the campaign was brief and dominated by the government. Meetings were few even, unusually, among the Communists. Many politicians contented themselves with a communiqué in the local press or even total silence. Only in the last few days did poster panels finally fill, and there was

---

[1] See P. M. Williams 'The French Referendum, 1961' [reprinted as chap. 11, above]. Soustelle's appeal to the Conseil d'Etat was heard ten months after the referendum and dismissed on the ground that the electorate's OUI had automatically purged any official irregularities.

* The PSU, who had largely absorbed the UFD of 1958 (above, pp. 90, 117, below, p. 155).

TABLE 5. *Referendum results, 1958, 1961, April 1962*

	Thousands			Percentage of electorate		
	1958	1961	1962	1958	1961	1962
Electors[1]	26,603	27,184	26,983	—	—	—
OUI	17,669	15,200	17,505	66·4	55·9	64·9
NON	4,625	4,996	1,795	17·4	18·4	6·6
Spoiled papers	304	595	1,102	1·1	2·2	4·1
Non-voters	4,007	6,393	6,581	15·1	23·5	24·4

little of the fly-posting and graffiti which usually enliven a political campaign. Party propaganda plainly had an eye to the elections as much as to April 8th —notably in the referendum broadcasts, two ten-minute periods on radio and eight minutes on television for each party. These were probably the chief means of communication between parties and electors. They were chiefly remarkable for a curious decision by the Algerian integrationists who divided each of their broadcasts between a moderate speaker who skilfully appealed to the uneasy conscience of the Right, and an extremist whose violence must have alienated all the sympathy won by his predecessor; and for the astonishing skill with which M. Motte made CNI's inability to agree on an answer seem the only possible course for a conscientious and responsible party.

There was a generous poster campaign for OUI, organized by the Ministry of Information and as usual paid for by the taxpayer; cinema programmes contained the usual carefully-doctored 'newsreels'. On radio and television political debate was almost non-existent and news-bulletins highly suceptible to ministerial pressure. Nevertheless, the government freely commandeered prime broadcasting time; the President spoke twice, M. Debré and other ministers followed. Despite the universal forecasts of a massive victory the government was leaving nothing to chance.

On 8th April, 17,505,000 Frenchmen voted OUI (90·7 per cent of valid votes cast). The President's policy won the support of 64·9 per cent of the electorate, compared with 55·9 per cent in the previous year and 66·4 per cent at the high tide of Gaullism in 1958. In every department but Corsica— as ever an eccentric exception because of its many non-resident voters—the OUI rallied an absolute majority of the electorate; everywhere it had at least 75 per cent of the votes cast. Yet this was a success rather than a triumph.

The turnout was 75·6 per cent, the lowest at any postwar national consul-

---

[1] In 1958 the unregistered population of voting age was estimated at an additional 1,200,000; comparable estimates are not available for later years.

tation except the referendum of October 1946. It was 9·3 per cent less than at the 1958 referendum, though only 0·9 per cent below 1961. But then the January weather and widespread peasant discontent—there was an electoral boycott among the Midi winegrowers—had brought the poll unusually low. Now the weather was a lesser disincentive though late snows lingered in the mountains, particularly in the Centre, and some snowbound ballot boxes had to be ferried by helicopter. Government-sponsored 'front organizations' campaigning against abstention had not the extravagant finance of earlier referenda, and, despite the President's appeals, many electors may have felt their vote was not needed since the outcome was never in doubt. The bulk of the Communist supporters who had broken discipline to abstain in earlier referenda probably followed the party's more congenial OUI. How far the abstainers who took their places were politically motivated is not clear. Some were members of the democratic Left protesting at the exploitation of the double referendum question. Others were uneasy and unconvinced members of the Right—though a correlation between strong NON forces and high abstention was far from general.

Where turnout was unusually low in 1961, it now tended to rise against the trend—as much as 5·6 per cent in Aude in the wine-growing Midi. Outside the south a decline of up to 3 per cent in turnout was general and reasonably uniform. Abstention in France is as much a matter of local tradition as a response to a particular referendum; the general pattern of turnout was therefore remarkably stable. Voting was highest in the North, Alsace and most of Normandy and Brittany, lower in the South, and lowest in the rural Centre; 60 per cent of the voters of Creuse went to the polls compared with 84 per cent in the industrial Nord.

As in previous referenda, the massively loyal backbone of the OUI was Brittany and Alsace, joined by the frontier departments of the North and East and most of the South-Centre. Here only one in twenty or even one in thirty electors voted NON and smaller *communes* rolled up OUIs on a positively Eastern European scale. The NON drew its greatest support on the Riviera and the Midi, around Marseilles and Bordeaux and through much of the south-west—areas where right-wing activism put down its roots even under the Fourth Republic. Commercial and personal ties with Algeria are often strong and settlement of immigrants from North Africa has been unusually heavy. A subsidiary region of support for the NON lay in a North-Central group of departments around the Paris basin, an area of large-scale agriculture and a solid core of rock-ribbed conservatism.

Only in Gironde (which includes Bordeaux) did the NON attain 10 per cent of the electorate, but in towns like Marseilles, Bordeaux, Lyons and Montpellier polling stations with NON votes of 20 per cent were not uncommon. With the exception of M. Pascal Arrighi at Vico in Corsica, right-wing leaders found, like dissidents in the two earlier referenda, that they could not carry their home towns.* But most took an honourable proportion of their followers into opposition.

The switch in the Communist line produced some striking changes in the geography of the OUIs and NONs. In Creuse and Corrèze, the heartland of peasant communism, the 23 per cent and 30 per cent NONs of 1958 fell in 1962 to 4·4 per cent and 4·8 per cent respectively. The swing in the Paris 'red belt', contrasted with the evolution of the bourgeois districts, was even more impressive. Though a few Communists spoiled their ballots or stayed at home, more followed the party line than at any time since de Gaulle's return.

TABLE 6. *Communists and Conservatives in Paris and suburbs*

	Percentage of Electorate			
	1956 Communist vote	1958 NONs	1961 NONs	1962 NONs
Communist strongholds				
Bagnolet	49·0	48·2	41·4	5·5
Gennevilliers	49·0	40·6	42·9	4·6
Pierrefitte	46·5	35·4	40·1	5·3
Saint-Denis	48·2	39·8	41·5	5·8
Stains	49·8	40·6	43·2	4·8
Conservative strongholds				
6th Arrondissement	13·5	13·3	17·3	12·3
7th	10·6	10·3	15·8	23·7
8th	8·8	9·2	15·7	15·2
16th	9·4	9·6	15·2	15·3
17th	14·8	13·6	16·4	11·3
Whole Seine Department	26·6	22·8	23·5	8·3

Of those electors who did vote, a larger number spoiled their ballots than in 1961 in every department except Somme, though the national rise was modest—from 2·2 per cent of the electorate to 4·1 per cent. The PSU was jubilant: it alone had campaigned consistently for a NUL vote, distributing ready-spoiled ballots reading 'Yes to peace—No to Gaullist power'. But outside the south-west there were only seven departments where NULs were over 5 per cent of the electorate, none where they were more than 7 per cent. The sharpest rise came in those south-western areas where NULs had been a relatively common form of protest in 1958 and 1961, reaching 9·5 per cent

* Arrighi, a Radical deputy, had seized Corsica for the army in May 1958. This broke the government's will to resist and ensured de Gaulle's return.

in Tarn-et-Garonne. This area is the fief of the great Radical regional daily *La Dépêche du Midi*, now campaigning for the NUL after two successive NONs, but NULs of a very different kind may have come from the many one-time inhabitants of North Africa now resettled in the region. The PSU claimed some modest local successes. The NUL was above average at Louviers (former stronghold of Mendès-France), Belfort-Ville and Decazeville (two of the rare towns with PSU mayors)—but often the rise was unimpressive even where they were locally strong. Certainly not all NULs were of PSU inspiration; reasons for spoiling ballots varied locally, and tradition may have had an important influence. Sometimes the correlation between NULs and a powerful current of NONs (as in Lyon and Marseilles) indicated the NULs were coming from the Right; elsewhere (notably some Communist bastions in Paris) above-average NULs suggested rather that not all Communist militants followed their leaders all the way to an opportunist OUI.

The striking decline in NONs conceals a notable gain in support for the Right. In 1958 there were fewer than 200,000 extremist opponents of the régime; in 1961 rightist NONs were about 1,200,000. Now there were 1,800,000 (NONs from other quarters were almost certainly negligible). Immigration from North Africa is only a fraction of the increase; as in Paris, right-wing opposition gained limited ground fairly generally from former OUIs or abstainers. Considering the bitter intensity with which France had fought for Algeria, it was, even so, a remarkable achievement to carry the Evian agreement with only 6·65 per cent of the electorate registering total disagreement. But while many of the dissenters may still be loyal to the Republic, they formed an ominously large potential nucleus for extremist movements, which the régime would disregard at its peril.

Despite the apparent referendum triumph the elections did not take place. Instead, de Gaulle overruled their most enthusiastic advocate, M. Debré, and sent for M. Pompidou to form a new government. Supporters of elections had argued that Gaullist chances were at their zenith, but de Gaulle preferred his bird in the hand. By holding elections he would temporarily deprive himself of that most useful weapon against unruly parliamentarians— the dissolution. (For when the President dissolves the Assembly prematurely he cannot again dissolve it for a further year; when the legislature runs its full course the President's dissolution power is unimpaired.)

The President realized that the referendum was not as encouraging as the crude figures suggest. The tactics adopted by all but the Gaullist UNR were the clearest warning of the kind of election that would follow. At any election the UNR would lose some of its exaggerated gains of 1958; the opposition would be fortified. With the Algerian problem on the way to a settlement, politicians would not so readily treat de Gaulle as indispensable (and therefore invulnerable). And in the Fifth Republic both massive UNR loyalty and general deference to de Gaulle have played an important part in maintaining the Assembly in its minor role. Electoral prospects for 1963 certainly appeared even less bright—but that situation could be met when it came. Meanwhile, in the sharpening of parliamentary attitudes de Gaulle must have recalled the impatient manœuvring with which the politicians of 1945 prepared the departure of the Liberator of 1944.

The referendum of 8th April opens a new phase in the evolution of the Fifth Republic with characteristic ambiguity. To refuse elections and appoint a prime minister from outside Parliament were moves in the direction of a more presidental régime; so M. Pompidou was careful to flatter the politicians and choose nearly all his ministers from their ranks. Whether these attentions would prevent a concerted offensive to recover their lost prerogatives remained to be seen; the early omens were unfavourable, for the new premier's majority was unexpectedly slim and was at once endangered by the resignation of the MRP ministers on the issue most propitious for the opposition, European unity. But the parliamentarians might still be deterred from exploiting their opportunities and venting their irritations by the same factor that had restrained them for so long; their need of de Gaulle to deal with Algeria. The war was over. But peace had still to be restored.

13 The General triumphs: the autumn 1962 referendum and election*

The first National Assembly of the Fifth Republic was dissolved by President de Gaulle in October 1962. It was born almost four years earlier in November 1958, two months after 79 per cent of the voters and 66 per cent of the registered electors had approved his new constitution against some left-wing opposition, mainly Communist. The electorate used the new electoral law (single-member seats and two ballots, as before 1940) to eliminate not only Communists and anti-Gaullists but many leading politicians of the old order. Of 465 seats, nearly 200 went to the Gaullist party, the UNR, and over 100 to the Conservative CNI, which had both campaigned hard for de Gaulle and *Algérie française*.

Before long the two causes proved incompatible, and at the referendum of January 1961 the right-wing followers of Jacques Soustelle and Georges Bidault contributed, with the Communists and the left-wing PSU, to the NON vote of five million. The old parties—Socialists, Radicals, MRP and the moderate wing of CNI—continued to support de Gaulle (though not always his policies or his government) as long as the war kept alive such threats as the generals' *putsch* of April 1961 or the OAS terrorism of 1962. But once Algeria was settled they were likely to rally an opposition majority, exasperated by the President's methods of governing, to thwart his foreign policy, oust his ministers, and perhaps revive the old overweening Parliament to which many of them were still attached.

De Gaulle therefore faced a strategic problem. A quick settlement in Algeria was essential to him, but it would destroy his usefulness to the politicians; and at a general election (due by April 1963) gratitude for peace in Algeria might be outweighed by accumulated resentments at home, especially if the popular President remained above the battle while the parties, the press, the interest-groups and the local politicians mobilised opposition to his followers. An alarmed UNR wanted the President to exploit the coming Algerian settlement by an immediate election. But although in April 1962 the electorate overwhelmingly approved the March agreement with the FLN (even the Communists prudently voting Yes), de Gaulle did

* Originally entitled 'The French Referendum and Election of October–November 1962'. From *Parliamentary Affairs*, vol. 16, no. 2 (Spring 1963).

not dissolve Parliament. Instead he replaced Michel Debré as prime minister by Georges Pompidou and tried to conciliate the most Gaullist of the old parties, MRP. But within a month his bitter attack on MRP's cherished conception of a federal Europe reopened and indeed widened the gap between the President and the parties; the MRP ministers resigned, and the politicians were reminded that co-operation, to de Gaulle, meant submission. The OAS danger still kept them in check: but for how long?

When the terrorists narrowly failed to assassinate the President in August, he saw his opportunity. Another attempt might succeed, he warned the country, and that would mean chaos—unless all Frenchmen were able to go to the polls to choose a successor by direct popular election. Whatever effect this surprising remedy had on the OAS, it faced the parties with two disagreeable alternatives. If they accepted, future Assemblies would confront a chief executive enjoying both a democratic mandate and enormous constitutional powers; and de Gaulle himself, if they ever thwarted him, could threaten to resign and seek re-election by the people. But if they refused they would face an immediate referendum campaign against him on most unfavourable ground: a purely negative opposition to letting the people choose the head of their government.

De Gaulle meant to make sure they would refuse. He sent his bill to an immediate referendum without first submitting it to Parliament as his own constitution (Article 89) required in the case of amendments to it. The government argued that it could use an alternative procedure (Article 11), but found hardly any reputable jurist to argue that the abolition of the old presidential electoral college (of some 80,000 *notables*) was not a constitutional amendment. Its action was officially condemned by the *Conseil d'Etat*, the highest administrative court, and even (unofficially) by the docile *Conseil Constitutionnel* (who, however, did not forbid the bill being promulgated after it was voted). Even Michel Debré, who was the constitution's main author, claimed not that the procedure was legal but only that 'practical necessity' must prevail. But the dangers of allowing the umpire-captain to break his own rules were plainer to the opposing team than to the spectators. To the political class it was both a natural instinct to condemn an act which humiliated Parliament and threatened to weaken it further and (therefore?) an imperative duty to oppose a blatant breach of the constitution. But to the electorate this reaction seemed, and was presented, as either the familiar incomprehensible quibbling of professors of law or the politicians' self-interested defence of their claim to decide issues behind the ordinary voter's back.

The leadership of the opposition was taken by Gaston Monnerville, President of the Senate, who had helped to smooth de Gaulle's path to power in May 1958, but now feared that the Senate—a stronghold of the opposition—would be the victim of the next referendum. His violent attack on the bill set off a chorus in which all but the Gaullists joined; for even the few others who approved the bill condemned the procedure. Parliament met, and on 5th October carried a motion of censure by 280 votes, 40 more than were needed. The opposition fully anticipated defeat at the referendum, but they looked for their revenge to the general election. When de Gaulle met their challenge by dissolving Parliament, the press began to speculate whether the UNR could hold even a hundred of its 173 seats.

As usual the authorities employed every weapon at their disposal in the dual campaign. There was the customary distribution of minor benefits to various categories of voters which Gaullists had scorned so bitterly in the Fourth Republic and used so assiduously in the Fifth—though in a new and ingenious variant the prime minister refused to commit himself to favour the church schools in a forthcoming administrative decision, lest this be thought an election manœuvre. Radio and television were thoroughly exploited, provoking protest strikes among their staffs; with almost no press support the government needed outlets for its view, but it lost many listeners to the independent stations outside the French frontiers, whose debates and panel discussions were the outstanding success of the campaign. The parties' share of broadcasting time was more derisory than ever, ten minutes each for the referendum, and for the election only seven minutes, simultaneously on both media and concentrated for all parties into two evenings. As usual they made poor use of these poor facilities, except for Jacques Chaban-Delmas of UNR, who skilfully appealed to the women and the young men who were so numerous in the electorate and so few in the old presidential electoral college. The Minister of Information surprisingly commended the direct popular election of the chief executive as a system which worked well in the United States, Britain and West Germany. But the supreme governmental weapon was, as always, de Gaulle's own broadcast, in which on 18th October he added a refinement to his customary threat of resignation: it was to apply not merely if the referendum vote was negative but even if the majority was '*faible, médiocre ou aléatoire*'. Hitherto it had always been supposed that the confidence the President needed was that of a majority of registered voters. In 1962 this interpretation was denied in advance—unofficially.

The precaution was prudent, for while on 28th October there was a OUI majority of votes cast, it was only 46 per cent of the electorate. The OUIs were 4,850,000 fewer, but the NONs only 3,300,000 more than in 1958 when few but Communists had voted no. All the party leaders together had swayed far fewer votes than the President alone. But they could still hope that many

TABLE 7. *Results of four referendums, 1958–1962*

	Thousands				Percentage of electorate			
	1958	1961	1962 Apr.	1962 Oct.	1958	1961	1962 Apr.	1962 Oct.
Electors[a]	26,603	27,184	26,983	27,579				
OUI	17,669	15,200	17,505	12,808	66·4	55·9	64·9	46·4
NON	4,625	4,996	1,795	7,932	17·4	18·4	6·6	28·8
Spoiled	304	595	1,102	565	1·1	2·2	4·1	2·0
Non-voters	4,007	6,393	6,581	6,273	15·1	23·5	24·4	22·7

[a] Usually about a million persons of voting age fail to register.

who had stayed at home or voted for de Gaulle personally would return to their old allegiance when they had to choose their deputy.

To the Gaullists, however, the referendum had been a preliminary ballot in the election, and they waged the election campaign proper as a second referendum to confirm the first. The same arguments, inducements and threats were freely employed, but there were now frequent assurances that there was no intention of crushing the parties and every desire to work constructively with them. For although most Gaullist strategists hoped to hold more seats than their opponents conceded them, and then to win over some moderate Conservative deputies, they still expected to need MRP support in the new Assembly. Conciliation, therefore, might bear fruit when the next government came to be formed; and meanwhile it minimised the danger of a hostile coalition. For the UNR had learned in 1958 from its victories over better-placed rivals that a candidate with most votes on the first round (when a clear majority was needed to win) could still be defeated on the second (when a plurality was enough) if his opponents concentrated their votes against him.

The parties' preoccupations were different, for there were not many constituencies where they could hope to lead on the first ballot. Wherever the Communists led, other voters (even some Socialists) might well turn at the second ballot to a UNR candidate to beat him, and indeed, as 1958 had shown, many Conservative and Socialist voters preferred a Gaullist candidate to one from the rival party. Thus, if the four parties fought one another, the UNR would benefit. But if they made an electoral pact it could be plausibly represented as a conspiracy to remove de Gaulle and return to the crises and intrigues of the Fourth Republic.

The parties made the worst of both worlds, failing to agree on any positive constitutional alternative to de Gaulle's proposal, and drafting a joint policy statement which, except on foreign affairs, was totally devoid of content.

Both the failure and the pseudo-success were damaging reminders of the unattractive features of what de Gaulle, in a bitter broadcast on 7th November, called 'the régime of woe' and 'the parties of old'. (The UNR asserted its intellectual independence by promptly denouncing, not *les partis de jadis*, but *les partis d'autrefois*.) While the Gaullist alliance of the UNR, the small Left Gaullist UDT and Malraux's 'Fifth Republican' candidates worked almost without a hitch, the *Cartel des Non* was a disaster for its members. It left them vulnerable both to the charge of selfish conspiracy against de Gaulle and to that of querulous inability to work together—and gave them no electoral compensation, for constituency pacts were rare and ineffective except between traditional allies (such as the Socialists and Radicals). In Gironde and Seine-et-Oise, where the *Cartel* parties ran a single candidate for each constituency, Right and Left rarely succeeded in joining more than a part of their forces. Symbolically, the two Conservative leaders officially supported by the Socialist party, Paul Reynaud and Bertrand Motte, drew no Socialist votes and went down to overwhelming defeat.

Nor could the Socialist leaders ignore the ardent wooing of their voters and local parties from another quarter. The Communists, reduced to ten seats in 1958, could hope to retrieve some of their losses only by a deal with the Socialists—who themselves would lose heavily if Communist candidates opposed them on the second ballot, but might well gain some seats from a pact and save others that were in danger (including that of the party leader, Guy Mollet). Shortly before the poll Mollet advised his followers to vote Communist in the ten or twelve constituencies where their only choice on the second ballot would be between 'an unconditional follower of de Gaulle and an unconditional follower of Khrushchev'. He repeated the advice after the first ballot, arguing that the Communist problem was left untouched by reducing the party's parliamentary representation, that even forty Communist deputies would be far fewer than proportional representation would have given them, and that they could exercise no real influence in the Assembly—whereas forty extra Gaullists might give the 'spineless' party a clear majority. But the Gaullists, solemnly warning that the politician returned by Communist votes was their prisoner ever after, could now rejoice that Mollet had dealt a mortal blow to what was left of the *Cartel des Non*, and yet still hope to win over Conservative or MRP supporters horrified by the company their ally was keeping.

As the first ballot approached, the Gaullists became more optimistic and their opponents less. The government's hopes soared when a poll privately taken showed the UNR far ahead of all rivals with nearly 30 per cent of the votes; the last few days had brought heavy gains to the Gaullists and heavy losses to the Socialists. The poll stayed private, for UNR strategists

TABLE 8. *General election results, 1958 and 1962*

	Opposition				Gaullist			
	Com.	Soc.	Rad and Ent. D.	MRP	Cons. and C. Rep.	UNR and UDT	V. Rep. (Cons.)	Not voting
Votes (millions)								
1958 (1)	3·9	3·2	1·7	2·4	4·5	3·6	—	6·2
(2)	3·7	2·5	1·1	1·7	3·9	5·2	—	6·1
1962 (1)	4·0	2·3	1·4	1·6	1·7	5·8	0·8	8·6
(2)	3·2	2·3	1·1	0·8	1·2	6·2	0·2	6·1
	Of valid votes							Of all electors
Percentages								
1958 (1)	19	15½	8	12	22	17½	—	23
(2)	20½	14	6	9	20	28	—	25
1962 (1)	22	13	7½	9	9½	32	4	31
(2)	21	15	7	5	8	40½	1½	28
Seats (465)								
1958	10	40	25	57	146	187	—	—
1962	41	65	41	36	28	229	20	—

1958 Rad. incl. RGR; MRP incl. DC; Cons. incl. C.Rep.; UNR strictly defined.

1962 Rad. incl. Ent. Dem.; MRP incl. its V. Rep.; Cons. incl. C. Rep.; UNR incl. UDT; V. Rep. excl. MRP and mainly Cons.

Smallest groups and isolated independents omitted.

welcomed the general expectation that they would do badly, believing this would bring them voters afraid of de Gaulle's departure. But the opposition was already beginning to realise its weakness. Monnerville was politely asked by the two well-entrenched Radical deputies for his department to give up his idea of campaigning there. And the Socialists interspersed their denunciations of the President for violating the constitution with protests against his threat to resign.

The first ballot, on 18th November, confirmed the parties' worst fears. The Gaullists, with 6½ million votes (31 per cent of those cast), had attracted half the OUI voters and gained a long lead. The parties which had been for NON in October had 11 million votes now; but without the 4 million Communists they were barely stronger than the Gaullists alone. Their 3 million gains since the referendum fell far short of the drop in the pro-Gaullist vote. The politicians had rightly assumed that many more people would support the President in a referendum than his party in an election, but had not foreseen that nearly half of the uncertain voters would refuse to oppose him either.

The UNR contested more seats and most other parties fewer than in 1958;

but Gaullist candidates also gained votes while others lost them. CNI (Conservatives) suffered most, especially those in the Paris area who were particularly reactionary and had flirted with the OAS. MRP, instead of making its expected gains, lost heavily; its progressive young newcomers of 1958 had voted No in the referendum, and were now wiped out. The Socialists also lost, though Radical candidates did slightly better. The 'two packs' once denounced by the President both fared disastrously, the ex-Gaullist campaigners for *Algérie française* polling even fewer than the 340,000 votes of the PSU. Generally, de Gaulle's opponents on the Right suffered in 1962 the fate of those on the Left four years before.

The Communists, who had lost 1,600,000 votes in 1958, regained only 200,000 of them in conditions which could hardly have been more favourable. But the second ballot was to modify this picture, for even where they gained nothing from other parties' withdrawals, their vote rose between ballots by about 20 per cent. If this increase happened everywhere, some 800,000 people—half the defectors of 1958—were willing to vote for the party when a seat might be at stake, but would not come out to 'show the flag' on the first ballot. This 'concealed' Communist vote (which had been far smaller in 1958) was offset by no similar concealed anti-Communist vote. It has to be taken into account in estimating the willingness of voters of the Left to support the Communist when their own man withdrew; and while comment based on the crude figures suggested that their vote was delivered almost intact, a calculation allowing for the concealed Communist vote indicates that many defaulted: 25 per cent even of the PSU voters, 40 per cent of the provincial Radicals and Socialists and almost two-thirds of the Paris Socialists refused to support a Communist. But in parliamentary terms the Left alliance paid large dividends: the Communists increased their representation from ten to forty, the Socialists made up for losing a quarter of their votes by gaining twenty seats, and the Radicals too returned ten stronger than in 1958. Half the deputies of these parties owed their election to Communist support, and so did two MRP members and three Conservatives. The 'barrage' did not avert a Gaullist majority in the Assembly, but did prevent it becoming overwhelming; and it defeated the UNR's prospective leader, Michel Debré.

The voters themselves did not rush to the winning bandwagon as they had in 1958. Then the UNR's real success had come on the second ballot, when it gained $1\frac{1}{2}$ million votes even though thirty-nine constituencies did not poll, having elected a member on the first round. This time, with ninety-six fewer seats polling, the Gaullist national total (counting those Conservatives with UNR support) was slightly down between the ballots. In 1958 the bandwagon had given the UNR far more surprise wins and fewer surprise

TABLE 9. *Party fortunes and surprises, 1958 and 1962*[a]

	Com.	Soc.	Rad., etc.	MRP	CNI	UNR (and UDT)	V. Rep.
			First ballot				
1958: no. candidates	461	421	149	214	241	343	—
% who poll:							
over 50% ⎫	0·1	0·5	—	$3\frac{1}{2}$	$6\frac{1}{2}$	2	—
30–50 ⎪ of valid voters	10	13	7	14	24	27	—
10–30 ⎬	73	59	51	53	61	62	—
0–10 ⎭	17	28	42	29	8	9	—
1962: no. candidates	463	330	128	189	204	400	30
% who poll:							
over 50% ⎫	2	0·3	2	7	$2\frac{1}{2}$	11	57
30–50 ⎪ of valid voters	$16\frac{1}{2}$	14	21	14	$19\frac{1}{2}$	52	23
10–30 ⎬	68	55	54	39	48	36	20
0–10 ⎭	14	31	22	39	30	0·5	—
			Second ballot: surprise wins and losses				
% of *winners* among candidates with 10–30%:							
1958	—	3	5	19	23	42	—
1962	$2\frac{1}{2}$	$15\frac{1}{2}$	13	11	5	13	17
% of *losers* among candidates with 30–50%:							
1958	79	44	20	48	12	8	—
1962	66	17	19	28	44	19	—

[a] The 1958 figures were calculated by Dr B. D. Graham.

losses than any other party; in 1962 its candidates enjoyed no such advantage. (The Communists remained the party most discriminated against, though slightly less so than in 1958; the Socialists had a slight advantage; the Conservatives, who had gained most after the UNR in 1958, lost most after the Communists in 1962.)

Indeed, the Gaullist victory, though sensational in returning a clear majority for the first time in a French Parliament, and striking in first ballot votes, was not quite so impressive in comparison with the second ballot in 1958, which had shown the Gaullists' real strength at that time. In the few comparable cases UNR candidates fared rather worse at the second ballot (compared with 1958) in straight fights with a Socialist than did MRP candidates in the same circumstances. Where a Gaullist had a straight fight with a Communist both times, the Communist vote was up by one-fifth in 1962 compared to 1958 (a little less in the Paris area) and the UNR vote down by a quarter (more in Paris). Where these two parties also had a Socialist opponent in 1958 but not in 1962, the results were significantly different;

the Communist increase was much greater (especially outside Paris) and the UNR loss much less, only 10 per cent in the capital and only 4 per cent in the provinces. Plainly some Socialists were voting for each side; in the provinces most of them seem to have gone Communist, in Paris UNR.

In fact the UNR, assisted by its alliance with and later absorption of the UDT, consolidated its claim to be a centre party. It failed to hold many of the votes it had taken from the Communists as a party of protest in 1958, but more than made up for them at the expense of the parties which had then supported de Gaulle but now opposed him. Nothing could be more misleading than the common suggestion that France voted extremist: on the contrary, the far Left utterly failed to repair its disaster of 1958 and the far Right went down to a most humiliating defeat. Indeed, it was precisely because the Gaullists stood so successfully as a centre party that their rivals faced such difficulties. The President drew part of every party's vote to build the strongest electoral force in French history, both in votes and seats and so lamed all the others that their independent survival (except for the Communists) became doubtful. Yet a single political movement could not extend from right-wing Conservatives to democratic Socialists. So long as the UNR sought to become a modern form of French Radicalism, its rivals would find difficulty in differentiating themselves from it (as the first vote in the new Parliament showed) except on foreign policy. If the Gaullists decided to organise as a (badly needed) modern and responsible Conservative party, there would be a natural vacancy for a left-centre party to dispute the succession with it and the Communists. But few UNR leaders wished to abandon the equivocal position which had served them so well and embarrassed their opponents so seriously. If (which was doubtful) they could continue to maintain it after de Gaulle's departure, they might still attract many MRP and Conservative voters and the anti-Communist moderate left; the Radicals and Socialists might be doomed to disaster in the short run unless they made pacts with the Communists, and in the long run if they did. The clash between one combination dominated by the extreme Left and another which in time would absorb the votes of a solid Right, though it did not occur in 1962, was not impossible in the future.

For in 1962 de Gaulle again performed an astonishing feat. Under an electoral system devised to express local grievances, favour well-known personalities and shatter waves of popular emotion, he transferred his popularity to unknown candidates and won a working majority; and the referendum result showed that many who voted for parties other than the UNR were not hostile to the President. Thus for the first time in history the French electorate voted to approve a government's record. The election of

1958 had registered no confidence in the Fourth Republic; that of 1962 recorded approval of the Fifth; the referendum was designed to prevent a return to the old system. For, even if the Gaullist party does not survive its leader, France will choose her future chief executives by direct election and not through an omnipotent Parliament or a college of conservative village politicians. The effect on political habits is already apparent and will be profound.

PART III

THE TRIBULATIONS
OF THE LEFT

14   Cautionary tale for Socialists*

The Party Conference was going badly for the leader.

As I listened to the speeches last night and this morning [he said] I realised that something in the proposed new constitution, especially in the new statement of aims which I drafted, had bruised and irritated and shocked the feelings of many of our comrades, above all the older party workers...But remember the time when the old statement was approved...After all, there have been some crucial changes in the last forty years in the life, the conscience, the ideas of socialists nationally and internationally...

I have heard it suggested in this discussion that we are turning middle-class, losing our essential contact with the mass of the country's workers. But I believe there is no worse mistake than to think that when we gain among one section of the people, we are bound to lose in another...

We must remain true to the principles and essential doctrines of socialism, renewing our tactics and intellectual methods of presentation and penetration, as our predecessors did when life and circumstances changed...A tradition is an attachment, not to mere words, but to a living idea.

From the floor, the protests mounted. One delegate called for a revision of the rules to keep the parliamentary party under stricter control. 'These proposals', another complained, 'water down the party's doctrine.' A third paid perfunctory tribute to the leader, then protested that he had no right to engage his reputation in the debate. 'These changes mean a shift to the Right.'

The date was 12 August 1945. The occasion was the 37th annual congress of the French Socialist Party. The leader was Léon Blum.

French Socialism is very different in structure from the British model. The trade unions did not create the party. Though a few of them view it with wary and non-committal sympathy, most are hostile, being allied instead to a strong Communist party—which poses problems unknown to the British Labour Movement. Again, across the Channel the whole political struggle is transformed by the existence of numerous parties; the nation-wide campaign to win the floating vote disintegrates into local and regional skirmishes, most of the party leader's national prestige vanishes with it, and even among his colleagues he no longer has the power to make or break a career.

* From *The Guardian*, 3 October 1960, the opening day of the Labour Party's Scarborough conference at which the unilateralists defeated Hugh Gaitskell's policies (the decision was reversed a year later). He had recently been beaten on 'clause 4'.

Thus in dealing with the activists in the constituencies, Blum had few of Attlee's assets: no trade union block vote, no electoral pressure towards prudence, strong competition on the left, less standing for the leadership. The French Socialists were indeed the party of the Labour militants' dreams, for the active members could really impose their will—at the price of frequent clashes with the parliamentary party. In 1920 they had voted overwhelmingly to enter the Communist party—against the great majority of the Socialist deputies (and voters). In 1938 they had mainly favoured Munich—again unlike most of the deputies. And now, in 1945–6, they refused to adapt the party, as Blum wished, to the new world born of the war.

Blum hoped to attract new blood from the Resistance, whose national and local leaders often called themselves democratic socialists. But these men were suspect in the eyes of the old parties, which they despised, and they would never join an organisation which was as vociferous in proclaiming the class struggle as it was lax in pursuing it. Could the Socialists rejuvenate themselves sufficiently to win over these idealistic, radical sympathisers who were merely bored by the traditional party game?

They could not. Passionately conservative, the militants eyed leaders and parliamentarians with jealous suspicion. They resented Blum's interest in new men, often from the middle class, who had not worked their passage with the party. They resented any open tampering with the hallowed class-war creed, though they hardly even pretended to take it seriously—for notoriously the Socialists were 'herbivorous Marxists', quite unlike the Communist carnivores. Above all, perhaps, the militants resented the challenge to look beyond the closed circle of the party, the uncomfortable suggestion that their familiar habits and traditions, machinery and outlook might need any adaptation to the changing world outside.

The 1945 congress deferred a decision on Blum's proposals till after the coming general election. The Socialists entered the campaign with high hopes, fully expecting to emerge as the strongest force in Parliament, dominating governments and imposing policies. Instead they were third, inexorably squeezed between Communists and MRP. The Socialist right and left wings began a bitter tactical dispute. The two most powerful—and most proletarian—local federations, Nord and Pas-de-Calais, took opposite sides. By their numbers and their tradition of disciplined block-voting, they enjoyed (when combined) an influence over conference decisions somewhat like that of the two great general unions in Britain. Now, Nord's leader was as solid as Sir Tom Williamson;* but the new man from Pas-de-Calais meant to take a line of his own.

* Now Lord Williamson; then general secretary of the National Union of General and Municipal Workers.

At a special conference in February 1946, held in private, Blum's proposals were rejected. Members of parliament were to hold no more than a third of the seats on the executive; the leadership was to be checked by a national council, representing the local parties and meeting quarterly; above all, on the motion of the Pas-de-Calais leader, the key phrases in the old statement of aims were reaffirmed, intact.

The leftward move brought disaster. When Socialists and Communists combined to put forward a new draft constitution, it was rejected at the polls. The Democratic and Socialist Resistance Union denounced its electoral alliance with the Socialist party. Hastily and clumsily, the latter swung back to the right; amid the recriminations which followed, the Socialists went down to another general election defeat.

This was the end of Revisionist control of the party. At the annual congress in August 1946 the general secretary, Daniel Mayer, came under fire for bad organisation and false doctrine. The opposition won a narrow majority on the executive, threw out the Revisionist officers, and brought in new men, intransigent enemies of any tactical or ideological compromise. The new general secretary was that militant leader from Pas-de-Calais who had insisted on reaffirming the party's commitment to the class struggle. His name was Guy Mollet.

Still the Socialists' fortunes declined. Yet another general election, in November, brought yet another reverse. Over the years, membership fell to barely a quarter of the 1946 figure. Many Resisters dropped out of politics, and with no infusion of new blood the Socialists became an ageing party, less and less attractive to youth. By 1949 the former Revisionist leaders—Daniel Mayer, André Philip, Edouard Depreux—were demanding an end to the coalition with the Right, while Mollet in reply prudently warned them that by provoking a political crisis without a solution, they took the terrible risk of opening the way to power to General de Gaulle.

The years passed. In 1951 the Socialists were driven into opposition; in 1956 a vigorous campaign against the Algerian war brought them back to power. Mollet became premier; faced with riots in Algiers, he changed his policy. But he had not been a militant for nothing; he could still command the Marxist language needed to induce party audiences to endorse his actions in Algeria and Suez. One old Revisionist, André Philip, was expelled from the party for a bitter attack on the leader. Another, Daniel Mayer, was forced out of Parliament because, as President of the League for the Rights of Man, he refused to vote for setting up internment camps in France. In May 1958 Algiers exploded again; this time it was not a policy but a regime that collapsed. General de Gaulle did come to power—but now with Guy Mollet as midwife. When the Socialists decided to support the General's proposed constitution, the old Revisionists finally left 'the old home' and set up their own new party.

Fourteen years after defeating the Revisionists, Mollet is still in solid control of the Socialist party. There is a minority which criticises him for opportunism; its principal figures were already against him in 1946. A much smaller minority opposes him from the far Right, preferring the policies of Soustelle and Bidault; two of its three leaders were in the anti-Revisionist camp fourteen years ago. One of the chief Revisionist spokesmen is a Mollet man today; all the other Revisionist leaders are active in the new Unified Socialist party.* Mollet had no regrets at their departure. As he reminded his docile followers, '*They were never real socialists anyway.*'

* Most later left the PSU in its most sectarian period, but a few leaders have stayed in it.

15   The Republican collapse*

Not for twenty years has the French Left been in such a state of disintegration. The Chamber of 1936, dominated by a powerful Popular Front majority, abdicated its powers to a military saviour four years later. The weaker Republican Front of 1956 took half the time to arrive at the same result; and the Left again finds itself divided and dispirited by the experience. To the last century's conflict over socialism and the last generation's quarrel over communism there have been added in recent years a bitter division over the problem of the day, Algeria, and in recent months an acute difference over the man of the hour, General de Gaulle.

The conflict over communism is fundamental. In quiet times illusions over communist policy always revive; invariably some new act of barbarity, like the murder of Nagy, reveals the unchanging reality. There is especially little excuse for self-deception in France, where the Communist Party has disillusioned its own supporters by its bureaucratic, uncompromising, and rigid Stalinism. Yet the problem is a genuine one. Five million voters are excluded from the political balance by the intransigence of their leaders and the repugnance of the rest of the Left for their policies; their untouchability confers excessive weight upon the parties of the Right. When these behave unusually disastrously, or the situation becomes truly desperate, some elements on the Left will always feel that co-operation with the Communists, though distasteful and dangerous, is nevertheless a lesser evil. Last May, facing the threat of a military coup, some Socialists reacted in this traditional way; but they were far fewer than in any comparable previous crisis.

The division over socialism is older but less fundamental. It has never prevented temporary co-operation between socialists and non-socialists on the Left, though that co-operation has rarely been wholehearted. Socialists liked to condemn their Radical rivals as at heart conservatives, out of touch with the present century, on whom no one could rely to support a bold social programme. Yet though many of these criticisms were valid, no political group in France was more thoroughly wedded to the slogans, the reflexes and the traditions of 1900 than the Socialists themselves. Léon Blum and Daniel Mayer tried in 1945 to induce the party to renounce the Marxist doctrines it had long ceased to believe, abandon the sterile battle against a defunct

* Originally entitled 'The French Left Disintegrates'. From *Socialist Commentary*, August 1958.

clerical danger, and appeal to the new Left which was emerging in the Resistance movements and among the younger generation. They were frustrated by the determined opposition of the older militants, who in 1946 ousted Daniel Mayer from the leadership and replaced him by their own nominee. His name was Guy Mollet.

Yet the division between Socialists and Radicals by no means corresponds to a division between a true and a false Left. The first effective opponent of the Indo-China war (long accepted by the Socialists) was a Radical, Pierre Mendès-France. He became the chief advocate of conciliating North African nationalism, and the one leader of the Left who found a genuine echo in public opinion—especially among that younger generation which the orthodox Socialist Party seemed quite unable to reach. He and Guy Mollet fought the 1956 election in alliance, concentrating on the theme of peace in Algeria. But a week after becoming prime minister, Mollet reversed his policy under the shock of the Algiers riots of February 6. It proved a popular change, and one which enabled the Socialist leader to consolidate his hold on his party while it destroyed the Radical chief's influence over his. As the consequences of the new course emerged—the arrest of Ben Bella in a Moroccan plane, the Suez expedition, and the bombardment of Sakhiet—they alarmed prudent conservatives like Paul Reynaud and Edgar Faure. But critics on the Left were few: only a dozen Radical and two dozen Socialist deputies, and these latter hamstrung by a rigid party discipline—André Philip expelled from the party, Daniel Mayer driven to resign from the Assembly, Madame Brossolette ousted from her senatorial seat. In private most political leaders admitted a compromise in Algeria to be necessary; but more and more opponents of official policy came to feel that General de Gaulle was the only man who enjoyed sufficient prestige with Arabs, French civilians and soldiers alike to make it possible.

The means by which the General came to power dealt a shattering blow to this nascent Gaullism of the Left. Men like Mèndes-France (strongly predisposed in de Gaulle's favour and himself a victim of 'the system') could not accept a government installed under the threat of a military coup. But at the same time public opinion reacted strongly – and indiscriminately—against the men and the régime which had brought France to this desperate state. Politicians of all opinions foresaw that the autumn elections would produce a tidal wave in favour of the national saviour and against the old political formations; and many of them—especially those at odds with their parties—began actively to exploit the situation. A dozen new organizations were formed—of course in the name of reducing the number of parties. The splintered fragments of right-wing Radicalism drew together; Georges Bidault launched a new Christian Democratic movement to shatter the party he had been unable to convert;* the surviving Gaullist *caciques* patented their newly valuable *appellation contrôlée* in a new movement with which, they hoped, politicians seeking their label would have to make terms.

Similar activity was not lacking on the Left. Few of the *mendésistes*—apart from their leader—felt any allegiance to the Radical Party, in which they were now a small minority. In the new situation they saw a third opportunity, after those lost at the Liberation and during the Mendès-France government, to create the new *Parti travailliste* of which Blum, Mayer, and so many others had dreamed. They have therefore joined with minority Socialists, Left Catholics, and the neutralists and fellow-travellers of the *Union de la Gauche socialiste* in a new combination, under Mayer's chairmanship, of all the minorities which have been drawn together by their common opposition to the Algerian war. This *Union des Forces démocratiques* has attracted some support from left-wing organizations without strong party allegiance—the Teachers' Union, the League of the Rights of Man, the left wing of the Catholic unions. But few of the partners are willing to form a new united party embracing non-socialists like Mendès-France and Mitterrand. Many, especially in the *Union de la Gauche socialiste*, insist on an understanding with the Communists which others refuse; and while most are hostile to the de Gaulle government, some (including Mendès-France) seem to hope for a reconciliation. With so many divisions in its ranks it is hard to see how the *Union des Forces démocratiques* can organize an effective campaign for a cause which, this autumn, seems in any case doomed to defeat.

This belief that de Gaulle is sure to win the referendum and the elections, that if opposed by the Left he will be driven against his will to rely on the Right, and also that he alone offers any effective hope of a peaceful solution in Algeria, has led a number of left-wingers—many of them reconverted Gaullists, though they are drawn from all parties—to set up a new movement, the *Centre de la Réforme Républicaine*, to campaign in favour of de Gaulle. But this group has won over no major figure, not even Jules Moch who shares many of their views (he opposed Mollet's Algerian policy but voted for de Gaulle because, as Minister of the Interior in May, he discovered how totally the Republican government had lost all authority over the army and the administration, and therefore decided that de Gaulle offered the sole alternative to military dictatorship). Without a prominent leader, without a basis for constituency organization, and without much encouragement from the government—Soustelle's appointment dealt them a heavy blow—the Left Gaullists' hopes and prospects are meagre indeed.†

* Bidault had been a leader of MRP.
† The evolution of de Gaulle's Algerian policy satisfied the Left Gaullists, who mostly rejoined the main body of the movement in 1962: above, pp. 118, 141.

The new movements seem unlikely to weaken seriously the historic and bureaucratic, but still powerful parties against which they are in revolt. Both the Socialists and the Communists remain deeply traditionalist in their thinking and in their policies. Alone among all the tendencies and factions, the Communists refuse to envisage any constitutional change whatsoever, insisting on campaigning in the referendum for a simple negative vote in defence of the régime for which their followers have shown themselves so conspicuously unwilling to fight.* They even denounce their perpetually disappointed but persistent suitors of the *Union de la Gauche Socialiste* for futilely seeking a 'constructive alternative'.

The May crisis had a greater impact on the Socialist Party, but its leaders have exerted every effort to minimize the shock. Though Guy Mollet's entry into the de Gaulle government exasperated many of his former followers, he did not lose control of the party machine. It was only his old enemies who turned to the *Union des Forces démocratiques*, and few even of these were willing to desert the *vieille maison*; the old friends who opposed their leader during the crisis, including his closest associates, Gazier, Pineau and Jaquet, were most anxious not to widen the breach. When at the critical moment Mollet found himself in the minority, they willingly agreed to suspend party discipline and allow him to vote for and join the new government; they refused to work with the old critical minority, still less with the Communists. It is this centre group, unshakably attached to the traditions—good and bad —of the party and the Republic, which seems to hold in its hands the future of French Socialism.

Thus the prospects are gloomy. A united non-Communist Left supporting de Gaulle might have powerfully influenced his policies; in the opposition, but strong enough to be independent of the Communists (whether or not tactically associated with them) it might equally have exerted effective pressure on the government. But a Left shattered into fragments, some for de Gaulle, some with (and dependent on) the Communists, and some opposing both, can influence no one. In May the Left, including the Communists, demonstrated their impotence in a revolutionary situation. The referendum and election campaigns of the autumn seem only too likely to confirm their bankruptcy.

* This attitude changed: above, p. 95.

16   First signs of recovery*

In the last few years the democratic Left in France have suffered a series of shattering blows. They came to power in January 1956 after an electoral campaign against the Algerian war; yet their own leaders promptly took responsibility for waging it, and public opinion followed them. Two years later the army vetoed a change of policy and imposed a government on Paris; the people would not lift a finger to save the Fourth Republic, and the left-wing Parliament capitulated to a military saviour as another left-wing Parliament had done eighteen years before. The minority which consistently fought these developments now suffered another shock—for General de Gaulle defied the men who had brought him to power and (slowly in Algeria, but at breathtaking speed in the rest of Africa) pursued the very liberal policies *they* had been advocating so long and so vainly. The Left Opposition have found it hard to adjust themselves to seeing measures they favour carried out by a regime they detest.

Back in 1946, when Guy Mollet became general secretary of the Socialist Party, he was the scourge of the revisionists. At the head of the intransigent Left, he overthrew Daniel Mayer and André Philip for tampering with the party's constitution and Marxist traditions. Ten years later Mollet became Prime Minister. Right-wing politicians who disliked most of his policies supported him because of his conduct in Algeria (and so for a long time did the Communist Party). There was a Left Opposition around Mendès-France which included a few Socialists (mostly former revisionists led by Mayer and Philip) and had some sympathizers in the government, notably Mitterrand and the progressive Colonial Minister, Defferre. Further Left the UGS (Union of the Socialist Left) grouped neutralists and fellow-travellers led by Sartre and Bourdet.

In May 1958 the Algiers Europeans rioted in the hope of keeping out a supposedly liberal Prime Minister. This time the army sympathized, joined their Committee of Public Safety, and threatened to impose General de Gaulle's return to power by force. Public opinion was passive, and strike calls by both Communists and democrats found a derisory response. Most leaders of the democratic Left feared dependence on Communist aid, and dreaded a civil war they were bound to lose. Reluctantly they decided that de Gaulle was the lesser evil (and half the Socialists cast the votes for him

* Originally entitled 'New Mood on the French Left'. From *Socialist Commentary*, May 1961.

which they had just sworn, by 112 to 3, never to give). The opposition groups condemned this capitulation, and they were joined by some 'orthodox' Socialists (led by Gazier) and Radicals (notably the illiberal ex-Premier Bourgès-Maunoury)—while of course the Communists also opposed de Gaulle. In the autumn the Socialist Party decided to support the General's new constitution, for Defferre (an anti-Gaullist in May) had become convinced of his liberal intentions in Algeria; he and Mollet easily defeated the critics. Gazier stayed in the party, but the old opposition leaders now formed a new one which in 1959 was joined by Mendès-France and his friends, and in 1960 merged with the UGS as the Unified Socialist Party, PSU. Here at last the opponents of both the Algerian war and the Fifth Republic found a common political home.

But to which were they more hostile? Had de Gaulle been the 'prisoner of the ultras' as they believed, the question would be meaningless. But in January 1960 the General refused to make any concessions to another insurrection by the Algiers Europeans, and his original sponsors—notably Soustelle and Massu—went into opposition. Nevertheless the war continued, and the Left Opposition blamed de Gaulle, especially when truce talks with the FLN failed at Melun in June. Meanwhile the reports of French atrocities were causing grave problems of conscience among young men due for military service. In September 1960, twenty young people were charged with assisting the FLN and helping conscripts to escape the call-up; a manifesto by 121 (later 200) leading intellectuals defended their conduct. In October the National Students' Union organized a demonstration of the entire Left in favour of peace talks; it was boycotted by the Communists and savaged by the police. In November the Algiers insurgent leaders of January 1960 were put on trial, and used the case to denounce the government for betraying the Europeans. De Gaulle was alarmed at the growing bitterness of both sides, and he acted quickly to redress the situation. He promised to set up new institutions, precursors of a future Algerian Republic, and announced a referendum (held on January 8, 1961) to approve both these measures and also his policy of self-determination for Algeria.

What was to be the attitude of the Left Opposition, which favoured self-determination but not the new institutions? Many (including Mendès-France) wanted the entire Left to boycott the referendum, refusing either to support the regime by voting Yes or to join with Soustelle's right-wing opposition in voting No; in isolation the latter's weakness would be revealed. But the Communists rejected this proposal. In the Socialist Party it was taken up by Gazier, but he (and the tiny *Algérie française* group which wanted to vote No) were easily defeated by Mollet and Defferre. Among the Radicals, the Right and Left oppositions combined to produce a No majority. The

PSU decided narrowly against a boycott, and then plumped heavily for a No vote. As in 1958, therefore, the Left Opposition chose a course rejected by three-quarters of the country, disliked by their own supporters (the left-wing No vote was smaller than in 1958), and even contrary to their own aims. For throughout the campaign they argued that the referendum would prevent peace talks. Instead, within forty-eight hours of de Gaulle's victory, the FLN was again calling for the direct negotiations it had been opposing for months.

So the parties of the Left have earned little glory in recent years. The orthodox Socialists were discredited, on the whole deservedly by their conduct in office under the Fourth Republic, less justifiably by their acceptance of the Fifth. But their critics were no less vulnerable. What in 1956–57 was a courageous stand for justice had by 1958–59 become a noble but futile rejection of unwelcome reality; and by 1961 it looked disagreeably like a grudging repudiation of their own policies because they hated to admit they had misjudged the man who was succeeding where they had failed.

The state of the parties, then, gives little ground for optimism. True, the Communists are in disarray. Their hold over their fellow-travellers was shaken by Hungary and has never been regained. Their hold on their voters was loosened by de Gaulle in 1958 for the first time since the war; a third of their $5\frac{1}{2}$ million supporters deserted, and have not returned (local by-elections even suggest that in some areas their vote has been halved). And their hold on their members is weakening too, as the excommunication of Servin and Casanova shows. These dissidents sought to work with the democratic Left (they favoured joining in the October 27 demonstration) and to give peace in Algeria priority over the struggle against Gaullism (they wanted the Left to boycott the referendum). Plainly they found support inside the party; in no previous internal dispute have so many deviationists been unmasked, such elaborate explanations been required of the leaders, such defiance been shown by the rebels. Casanova even wrote that he preferred his self-respect to his place in the *Bureau politique*; 'unheard-of language', exploded Thorez. Perhaps something is at last changing in the most Stalinist of Communist parties. But for the moment it is at its lowest ebb for twenty years.

The Socialists are not in much better case. When the minority resigned in 1958, the bitterness went out of their internal quarrels—and some life went out of the party. The secession may have taken few Socialist votes (though these have fallen off badly lately) but it removed many active members, and accentuated an already dangerous trend: for the Socialist Party to become an aging, bureaucratic body strong in local government and among civil servants but (outside one or two regions) lacking contact with the working class. However, the hopes placed in the PSU are unlikely to be fulfilled. Electorally it has had little success. And internally its first congress, in March, heard complaints of failure to attract youth, workers, peasants, and Catholics; regrets that party workers seemed inactive; and heated arguments between the reformist minority and the extreme Left. Power is plainly passing to the latter, and their sectarian outlook seems as unlikely to improve the PSU's independent fortunes as it is fatal to any eventual reunion with the older party.

Perhaps then it is fortunate that in the Fifth Republic the parties are less important than ever before. But as they decline the pressure-groups rise; and happily, under the impact of a lively younger generation, these are beginning to fill the void, and are taking more interest in politics, and broader views of France's problems, than ever in the past.

The students' role has been particularly encouraging. Before the war they were mostly on the Right and against the Republic, and in the Fourth Republic they were usually contemptuous of politics. But lately things have changed. Conscription for Algeria faces them, like other young Frenchmen, with a crisis of conscience (whose seriousness is attested by the churches). Some have helped the FLN, encouraged call-up evasion, or joined civil disobedience through the Non-Violent Movement. (Active student leaders of the last generation, still on the far Left but opposed to actions so offensive to the public, find it strange 'to be thought old-hat at twenty-nine'.) Despite pressure from below, the present Students' Union leaders have refused to encourage illegal action. But they have renewed the relations with the banned pro-FLN Algerian Students' Union which were broken four years ago— losing their government subsidy in consequence. They have worked hard to unite the rival organizations of the Left for joint actions against the war (such as the October 27 rally). And they have routed the opposition of right-wing students campaigning against any political commitment by the Union.

There are also signs of a trade union revival. A new militancy is suggested by the recent CGT successes in works council elections (while the Communist Party itself is losing votes). It is reflected in a sudden interest in working-class grievances by the Gaullist Party, the UNR, which has become suddenly critical of its own government. It burst out in the token strike in March in gas and electricity and among the highly-organized teachers and civil servants; all displayed an unprecedented solidarity which has amazed their own leaders. For the first time since 1953 this year may see major industrial disputes.

Thirdly, there are new stirrings in agriculture. As recently as February 1960 the main peasant union was giving aid and comfort to de Gaulle's right-wing opponents. In 1961 it abandoned this activity, and even changed its agricultural policy to satisfy its younger and more progressive elements (who want modernization and reform of distribution rather than the demagogic pressure for high guaranteed prices which the rich reactionaries favour). It was these young peasant leaders, mostly active Catholics, who helped to save MRP in the 1958 election and in the long run may transform that party. It was their absence which the reformists lamented at the PSU congress. So far their impact has been mainly local and professional, for instance in organizing growers to fight and defeat the distributive monopolists. The spectacle of Socialist civil servants and their wives volunteering to help sell artichokes in the Paris streets has its ludicrous side. But over the next decade there are real grounds for hope in the rise of these young farm leaders, eager to overcome the antagonism of peasant and worker, country and town, which the Right has exploited so skilfully for so long.

In day-to-day politics, and over Algeria, the peasants play little part. But the trade unions do. The teachers and the students have taken the lead, and the manual workers have followed. The Socialists of Force-Ouvrière and the CFTC (Catholic) unions joined in the October 27 demonstrations in Paris and the provinces; they were among the eleven organizations which jointly demanded negotiations to ensure peace, self-determination, and protection for the minority (there would have been twelve, but the Socialist Party kept MRP out); and they have renewed their broken links with the banned Algerian workers' union.

On one level even the parties have been affected by the new mood. Last July a number of prominent lawyers, intellectuals and politicians of the Left held a 'colloquium' at Royaumont, near Paris, to discuss self-determination in Algeria and civil liberties in France. Another followed at Aix in October; here and at the third (in March at Grenoble) the participants included front-rank leaders officially representing the parties of the Left. Mendès-France and Mitterrand, the Left Gaullists and the PSU, were now joined by Defferre and Pineau as Socialist Party delegates as well as the Communists Billoux and Guyot (who here, contrary to their attitude elsewhere, were most conciliatory). For the first time for many years, therefore, the rival political groups of the Left have participated in common discussions and—despite their differences over the referendum—have reached a wide measure of agreement about the crucial Algerian problem. As long as the war continues, and for some time afterwards, French politics will remain turbulent and dangerous. But at last there are some quite hopeful signs for the long run.

17 De Gaulle's challenger, Gaston Defferre*

In October 1962 President de Gaulle sent to referendum a bill providing that future Presidents should be elected by direct popular vote; if no candidate had a clear majority the top two alone would meet in a decisive second ballot a week later. Except for the Gaullists themselves, all the political parties denounced the procedure as a blatant breach of the Constitution, since Parliament was not allowed to debate the bill; and all criticised the measure itself for giving excessive authority to a President, elected for seven years, entitled to select the prime minister, and able at will to dissolve the Assembly or by-pass it by referendum. This devaluation of Parliament, and this dominance of a President chosen by the people, would utterly undermine the power of parties which already, except for the Communists, carried hardly more weight than the British Liberals. Indeed this was de Gaulle's object: the parties had to oppose a proposal which the people were sure to approve. At the referendum 62 per cent voted for the bill, and at the November election the Communists stagnated, the other parties all lost votes, and for the first time in French history a disciplined majority was returned to Parliament to support the government.

The old parties faced a dual threat. In time, unless they adapted themselves to the new political conditions, they were doomed to decline. Immediately, the next battle would be fought on bad terrain for them. For a presidential election was due by December 1965, and could be precipitated at any moment by de Gaulle's resignation. Then, if each party presented a candidate, the second ballot would be fought out between a Communist and a Gaullist (who would win). If all the centre parties chose a joint candidate they would seem to be conspiring to bring back the old order. But if any of them allied with the Communist party, they would frighten moderate voters into the Gaullists' arms.

The strategic decision depended on SFIO, the Socialist party, for no strong anti-Gaullist combination of either the Left or the Centre was possible without it. But the Socialist leadership was non-committal. Conservatives, Radicals and MRP had proved unsatisfactory allies in 1962, failing to wean

* Originally entitled 'De Gaulle's Challenger'. From *Parliamentary Affairs*, vol. 17, no. 3 (Summer 1964).

their followers away from de Gaulle when they did not succumb to his attractions themselves. Despite losing a quarter of its vote, SFIO by its bargains with the Communists had gained twenty seats and saved ten more, including that of its leader M. Guy Mollet. Such deals might prove equally profitable in the local elections of 1964 and 1965. But they would make the Socialist party increasingly dependent on an ally which most Frenchmen and many Socialists deeply distrusted, and within two weeks of the election M. Maurice Thorez had gleefully predicted that 'The Socialist party and its members will never again be just exactly what they were a month ago.'

Some voices within SFIO maintained that the choice went far beyond electoral tactics, and hoped to use the coming presidential election to enforce a thorough reconsideration of the party's doctrine, appeal and leadership. But the leaders persuaded the 1963 party conference to postpone decision to a subsequent meeting at which four questions would be posed: should SFIO advocate a presidential or a parliamentary constitution? with what allies should it fight? should it nominate a presidential candidate? and if so, whom? M. Mollet did, however, indicate his preference for a small coherent party, *pur et dur*, rather than a broad amalgam of left-wing forces; for restoring a parliamentary system; and against concentrating attention on the presidential battle. He announced that he would never stand for the presidency, and privately hoped no Socialist would do so. To oppose de Gaulle, he preferred a person of high moral stature 'like Albert Schweitzer'.

The unanimous decision of the party's extraordinary conference at Clichy on 2nd February 1964, endorsing M. Gaston Defferre's candidature for the Presidency of the Republic, was thus a dramatic change of tactics by SFIO. But it was much more: even, to one very distinguished political commentator, the most important event in the domestic policy of the Fifth Republic, and indeed in the history of the French Left in the twentieth century. For the first time the opposition was taking the initiative instead of waiting for de Gaulle. And perhaps a first tentative step had been taken towards the creation of a strong democratic Left in France.

Once before, in 1945, the revisionist leaders of SFIO had seen a great opportunity to broaden the base of reformist Socialism in France. The War and Resistance had thrown up a new political generation, and proved at last that a Catholic could be a loyal democrat. By admitting young newcomers to an active rôle, by abandoning the faded Marxist vocabulary which no one had taken seriously for forty years, and by gestures of goodwill towards the progressive Catholics, SFIO could become the nucleus of a great French Labour party. But even the prestige of Léon Blum could not impose such drastic changes of habit and tradition. Although the SFIO militants accepted an electoral alliance with UDSR (a new party of Gaullists and reformers, born in the Resistance), they treated these new friends so ungenerously that a major source of potential recruits dried up. In a debate not unlike that on Clause Four in the Labour Party, M. Guy Mollet led a revolt which appealed to the verbal heritage of the past, and reaffirmed both SFIO's bogus Marxism and its real anti-clericalism. In 1946, after two election defeats, Blum's revisionist friends lost control of the party to M. Mollet. Not until Clichy, eighteen years later, was he in turn to suffer a setback in a party conference.

The post-war victory of the Left had not prevented a sharp shift to the Right, as the new general secretary led SFIO into conservative coalitions in order to keep de Gaulle from power. But in time that threat receded, conservatism lost credit, and M. Mendès-France briefly attracted support for his own new version of the 'Labour party' dream. The Socialist leaders viewed him with suspicion and their uneasy alliance with him broke down when in 1956, after a joint election campaign against the Algerian war, M. Mollet's government postponed reforms in Algeria till after military victory. Friction within SFIO intensified in May 1958 when M. Mollet played the decisive rôle in bringing de Gaulle to power, and in September he was denounced by old enemies and deserted by many close friends when he urged Socialists to support de Gaulle's new constitution. But he was re-established in his control of the party by the unexpected support of his most powerful but most moderate critic, M. Gaston Defferre. The general secretary's old opponents (including some leading revisionists of 1945) now left SFIO and drifted into a dissident socialist party, PSU. There the 'Labour party' wing was soon swamped by the Left extremists, who found in PSU a new if tiny battleground for their endless internecine warfare.

Socialist support for de Gaulle was short-lived. By 1959 SFIO was in opposition, and by 1962 peace in Algeria allowed it to express its mounting antagonism to the General's policies and style. M. Mollet, for years a violent enemy of the Communists, now urged his followers to vote for them to keep a Gaullist out. Many Socialists were attracted by tactics which conjured more seats out of fewer votes, and the Communists played on the new mood of proletarian solidarity. They called for joint discussions on a common programme, vowed that unity was more essential than any policy proposal, and praised even the timid reforming plans of the Radical party. For to M. Thorez and his colleagues talks were an end in themselves, breaking their long isolation, promoting a new Popular Front which they would dominate by weight of numbers, and helping them to silence the growing opposition within their own ranks.

The divided Socialists gained time by a press debate on the long-term issues separating them from those M. Mollet now called 'our Communist pals'. But both supporters and opponents of the Communist alliance agreed that SFIO must first strengthen its hand by recruiting any democratic socialists who would enter the fold. Discussions (*colloques socialistes*) were opened in December 1963 with the lost sheep who had strayed into (and sometimes out of) PSU, and also with representatives of independent Left groups, often Catholic, which flourished among the younger peasants, students, Christian trade unionists, and would-be Fabian societies like the Club Jean Moulin. Friendly journalists had christened them the 'living forces' in contrast to the 'moribund parties'. To these fringe groups the crisis of the old organisations and especially the Socialists offered another opportunity, perhaps the last, to realise the old dream of a 'Labour party' embracing both Catholics and anticlericals, enjoying some trade union support, and frankly reformist instead of hypocritically revolutionary. While they regarded SFIO as tainted by doctrinal sectarianism and electoral opportunism, they knew they had allies within the party and later tried to strengthen these through the *colloques socialistes*. But the catalytic agent on which they mainly relied was the coming presidential election. For here the deals and bargains of a parliamentary election would not work. The voter, choosing between national leaders rather than among ideological preferences, would behave in a different way. And the Communists, if a democratic Left candidate could out-distance them on the first ballot, would have to come into line on the second when their own man had been eliminated. Indeed, even on the first round many of their supporters might vote for a left-winger with a chance of victory instead of a party nominee with none; and if this mood spread, would the Communist leaders put forward a candidate at all?

This strategy offered good prospects against any opponent but de Gaulle (and its most optimistic advocates hoped even the General himself would fall short of an absolute majority, and might then refuse the humiliation of a mere second-ballot victory).[1] Even in a losing fight against de Gaulle, a good showing by the Left's standard-bearer would crystallise the demand for change and might lay the foundation of the progressive coalition of the future. But in the short as well as the long run, these men believed, the condition of any advance was independence of the old party machines. The candidate, therefore, would have to be imposed on the parties from outside.

The independents had no weapon but publicity, but they used that brilliantly. After the holidays in 1963 an extraordinary campaign opened in *L'Express*—once the weekly organ of Mendès-France's extreme sympathisers, later veering towards a Popular Front in its virulent anti-Gaullism, but always restless and publicity-conscious. A series of eulogistic articles described de Gaulle's unnamed opponent-to-be: 'Monsieur X'. The publicity stunt

[1] A candidate of the extreme Right, Maître Tixier-Vignancour, came forward in April. He will no doubt take votes from de Gaulle rather than Defferre, and so would any likely Centre candidate.

attracted much attention, but it had a major political consequence too. Other papers speculated about the identity of Monsieur X, and Gaston Defferre's name was repeatedly mentioned. Probably the purpose and certainly the consequence of the *Express* campaign was to drive him to brave party disapproval and declare his candidature.

Born in 1910 into a Protestant family, a prosperous lawyer who became an active Socialist in the 1930s, M. Defferre rose to prominence through the Resistance. He had sat in Parliament for Marseilles since 1945, and had been mayor since 1953 (after a brief earlier term at the Liberation). By general consent he had given this turbulent and formerly corrupt city the best administration it had ever had. In 1945 the left-wing local party in Marseilles revolted against the Socialist alliance with UDSR, was disaffiliated by headquarters, and won only 6 per cent of the vote to 25 per cent for M. Defferre. In 1954 M. Mendès-France offered M. Defferre office, though party disapproval foiled what an opponent at Clichy ten years later recalled as 'a first attempt at bribing us'. In 1956 M. Defferre as Mollet's Minister of Colonies carried a great colonial reform, thanks to which Black Africa was the only overseas domain of the Fourth Republic where nationalist demands were satisfied in time to avert violence; but in 1957 he was dropped as an opponent of the government's Algerian policy. In May 1958 he voted against de Gaulle, but after talking to the General in the summer, he annnounced his conviction that the Fifth Republic would pursue a liberal policy in Algeria and his intention of voting for the new constitution. His conversion determined that of his party and saved M. Mollet from defeat. At the November election, under a new electoral system, M. Defferre lost very narrowly to a Gaullist (the decisive votes may have come from Communists) although he increased his own vote by 40 per cent. He was promptly returned to the Senate, regained his Assembly seat in 1962, and became chairman of the Socialist deputies.

As a candidate he had many advantages. Ailing in the rest of France, SFIO was flourishing at Marseilles. In the 1950s its membership trebled locally while nationally it dropped 30 per cent, and under the Fifth Republic it rose by a sixth at Marseilles although it was still falling elsewhere. Outside the party M. Defferre was a strong vote-getter, doubling its poll at the expense of Centre and Communists alike between 1946 and 1958 (in the country SFIO lost 25 per cent). Even he, however, could not stop large defections in 1962. The climate of the new régime made his municipal record a very valuable asset, for ideology was at a discount as against constructive reform, and the low repute of parliamentarians gave greater eminence to the successful mayor of a great metropolis. Indeed in a régime which scorned intermediaries between the State and the citizen, and was accused of dark designs against the power of local authorities, the civic head of France's second city was a natural champion of the worried municipalities and of the other despised intermediaries.

In national politics M. Defferre suffered none of the discredit which attached to so many Fourth Republican politicians. But outside the south he was not well known, and he aroused respect rather than enthusiasm. (An opinion poll on a dozen potential presidents found that while almost all had more opponents than supporters, M. Defferre, not yet a candidate, evoked a record 'no opinion' response of 61 per cent.) Although he opposed de Gaulle's policies he had, like 80 per cent of his countrymen, supported the 1958 constitution—which, to PSU, disqualified him as an opposition candidate. In the tangled politics of Marseilles he was on fairly friendly terms with the local Gaullists, who could not stomach his bitter enemies on the extreme Right. An outspoken enemy of the fascist OAS, as mayor he worked devotedly to help the thousands of refugees from Algeria who descended upon Marseilles determined to vote against him. As a revisionist socialist he stood with the progressive wing of his party on Algeria but with the moderates on domestic issues, and in 1962 he was the chief critic of the Communist alliance which locally would have paid him large electoral dividends. When first asked if he were a candidate, Defferre modestly said what many observers felt: 'I can claim to be a good mayor and I think I was a decent minister—but the Presidency of the Republic, that's in a different class.'

The machines reacted violently to the campaign on his behalf. A non-party candidate of the Left would endanger their freedom of manœuvre, their hold over their own followers, and their leadership of left-wing opinion. With one accord the Socialist and Communist leaders and party papers replied by minimising the importance of the presidential election. M. Claude Fuzier, secretary of the Paris Socialists and editor of *Le Populaire*, called it 'only one moment of our struggle'; 'only a stage in the struggle', *L'Humanité* echoed. To choose a candidate before there was an agreed policy, warned M. Fuzier, was putting the cart before the horse; his Communist opposite number delightedly expressed 'complete agreement'. M. Mollet condemned a broad democratic party as a *grande nébuleuse*; *L'Humanité* applied the phrase to Monsieur X. M. Fuzier warned against playing de Gaulle's game by fighting on his terms, and the Communists enthusiastically took up the theme.

M. Defferre's admirers among the 'living forces' kept up their pressure. In mid-December a manifesto, inspired by the Club Jean Moulin, called for a new style of leadership independent of the established parties. It appealed for a candidate of the Left who would break with the old organisation, traditions and terminology; would work for a democratised system of presidential government enabling the ordinary citizen to participate in political life, as he could not in the Fourth or Fifth Republics; would pledge his government to associate the trade unions and other popular organisations with its work; and would reconcile Catholic democrats with democratic socialists. But as it was being drafted M. Defferre was already asking the SFIO executive for leave to declare himself a candidate. This was a gesture to the party, but a response to the rebels; a handful of journalists and publicists had engineered an operation which confronted the recognised leaders of the Left with a *fait accompli*. The public announcement to the Marseilles local party followed a month later. In the Paris press it had wide publicity; but RTF, the state television network, managed to photograph the candidate only from afar or from behind, and *Le Populaire* omitted it altogether.

M. Defferre stated his terms clearly. He meant to draw up his own pro-gramme, neither bargaining with the parties nor submitting it for approval, and he refused to deal with the Communist bosses. He told one critic that while programmes were important, it was character that determined a politi-cal leader's reaction to an unexpected or dangerous situation (a tacit reminder that the last French Socialist premier had reversed his Algerian policy under pressure from rioting settlers). And when asked about the perennial church schools dispute, he replied publicly that 'a Socialist's first characteristic is tolerance' (not printed in *Le Populaire*)—and added privately that he was not bound by SFIO policy and meant to seek an end to the old quarrel.

The reactions came quickly. Comments from the centre parties varied from the open sympathy of the Radical leader M. Maurice Faure to the cautious reserve of MRP (whose voters leaned to de Gaulle even more markedly than their militants clung to the Left). Genuinely or maliciously liberal Gaullists greeted the opposition challenge as the Left's belated accep-tance of a strong executive and welcome recognition of the legitimacy of the Fifth Republic. The Communists denounced M. Defferre for compromising with the régime, boycotting its chief opponents (themselves), and refusing a common programme of the Left. But these were opening moves, and if the candidate's campaign enjoyed real success the rival parties would have to adjust their positions accordingly. Only one organisation—his own—could make or mar his prospects from the start. It was at Clichy that the real decision would be made.

There was no doubt that the party would endorse M. Defferre's candida-ture, but much about its terms. Critics like M. Fuzier could still hope to transform the candidate Gaston Defferre, a member of SFIO, into Gaston Defferre the candidate of SFIO. They insisted on proclaiming his close collaboration with the party leaders, while he wanted to emphasise his inde-pendent choice of tactics. Although approving his policy—for a united Europe, for economic planning, for educational expansion, against the French bomb—they meant to stress that it was SFIO's while he preferred to present it as his own. On the constitutional problem there was disagreement, M. Defferre envisaging a strong presidency with new safeguards against abuse, M. Mollet advocating an improved model of the traditional parliamentary régime. Lastly, the candidate would not base himself openly on a specific political alliance, and hoped the momentum of his campaign would bring him support on his own terms. But the 1962 election had shown politicians with seats at stake that the old traditional coalition of the anticlerical Left could still work wonders; and with local elections only six weeks away many of them were reluctant to offend a potential ally—or opponent—as weighty as the Communist party.

The doubters used all these themes. They expressed their resentful suspicion of the Mendèsist journalists and intellectuals who had stolen a march on them. M. Mollet cited an earlier socialist rebel (Marcel Déat) who began by appealing to the 'living forces' against the moribund parties and ended as a Nazi. They asked M. Defferre how he could hope for a parliamentary majority if he ignored the Communists in his presidential campaign. They reminded the conference that it had never endorsed the presidential system, detected signs of crypto-Gaullism in the candidate's outlook, appealed to the militant's pride in SFIO's traditions and to his loyalty to its established leaders, and—like M. Mollet—warned him against submerging its identity in a soulless electoral cooperative with no more ideological foundation than the American Democratic Party. The force of such arguments might depend on the length of the hearer's memory. M. Defferre's friends could reply, without contradiction, that a presidential campaign behind a popular party leader was the way to revive SFIO's flagging organisation. And they could convincingly ridicule the idea of a presidential candidate condemning the direct election of the President: was his slogan to be 'Vote for me and lose your vote'?

The factional clash was sharp and at times bitter, but neither side could carry it too far. M. Defferre's candidature had attracted enough interest in the party to ensure him a narrow majority, and the bastions of M. Mollet's power were beginning to crumble. For years the general secretary had enjoyed steady support from two dominant local parties, his own (Pas-de-Calais) and his neighbours (Nord). But now M. Defferre's local party was bigger than either, and Nord was alarmed at the threat to party unity. Even at head office many younger men (and one or two seniors) were turning to the rising sun. So, if the issue were pressed, M. Mollet would lose the vote and control of the party. But M. Defferre could not afford such a Pyrrhic victory, for a narrow endorsement from his own political friends would start his campaign under a fatal handicap. Although various ingenious procedural manœuvres were tried to evade the issue, it had really been settled in advance: the balance of forces within the party made each side prefer a compromise resolution to an open clash, but gave M. Defferre much the stronger bargaining position. The final motion therefore gave him virtually all he wanted. Unable to win, M. Mollet would have been wiser to support M. Defferre from the start; but he retreated from his untenable position in time to keep his hold on the machine. And while the party chose M. Defferre, it showed its reluctance to choose *between* him and M. Mollet; the average militant fervently wanted his two leaders to agree. His mood was one of gradual modernisation without repudiation of the past, not of revolutionary transformation of the party's base and outlook.

M. Defferre had surmounted his first obstacle; many more remained. Communist opposition hardened by February into open hostility—'Defferre can be stopped'—accompanied by renewed demands for discussion of a common programme. A majority of PSU was also hostile, its leaders arguing characteristically that 'Gaullism without de Gaulle is more dangerous than Gaullism with de Gaulle', and replying to M. Defferre's appeal for the long view ('the horizon of 1980') by proudly proclaiming that PSU's horizon was bounded by 1964. But one reaction was not expected: General de Gaulle devoted twenty minutes of his press conference to rebutting M. Defferre's constitutional views (though never pronouncing his name). Politicians had attacked the General before, but he had never deigned to reply. The Fifth Republic's first dialogue had begun.

M. Defferre's candidature might have long-term significance as well. His movement attracted some younger peasant and trade union leaders away from their traditional suspicion of party political activity (and it was doubtless no coincidence that in February the Communist press virulently denounced the best-known of these, M. Michel Debatisse of the Young Peasants). Moreover, the candidate broke with a 150-year-old tradition of French oppositions in proposing to make the existing constitution work better instead of trying to upset it; and, repudiating an ancient prejudice that had paralysed the French Left for years, he recognised the need for a strong executive power in the twentieth century. To his admirers, therefore, the campaign offered an exciting prospect: breaking the moribund parties and regrouping the democratic Left on a more modern, more dynamic and less hidebound basis; settling the ancient dispute between progressive Catholics and freethinkers; and in the long run winning over enough Communist votes to revitalise the democratic Left and confer on France the blessings of the two-party system. But all this was a lot to expect from an election campaign, and the candidate was multiplying his difficulties by challenging simultaneously the party machines, the non-political traditions of the unions, the anticlericalism which was still the main cohesive (though no longer the driving) force on the Left, and the distinctive ideological heritage of the party militants. If his campaign failed, might he not leave the reformers worse off than he found them?

If, however, the reformers accomplish some of the changes they advocate, the institutions of the Fifth Republic will be entitled to a large share of the credit; if not, the supporters of the same Fifth Republic will deserve some, at least, of the blame. For by creating a new mould and forcing political action into it, by obliging men and parties to adjust to majority election of the chief executive, the new political framework will have played a big part in bringing about any readjustment of party lines that may occur. Indeed by accepting and exploiting this transformation of political habits, M. Defferre has gone far to justify—in constitutional outlook if not in substantive policy—the far Left's charge of crypto-Gaullist deviations. The Gaullists have, of course, always claimed that their constitutional reforms were designed to organise political activity more effectively and democratically than under the old closed-circle parliamentary régimes. They have appealed for a modern and vigorous opposition, providing a real alternative; and they should take some pride in having obliged their opponents, against much internal resistance, to reconsider their methods of action and even thought.

Many individual Gaullists did indeed greet Defferre's candidature in this way. But the official reaction was different. RTF gave three minutes to the Clichy conference and thirty seconds to M. Defferre himself. Almost as soon as his candidature was announced the authorities, abruptly ending a year's procrastination, announced the detailed regulations for the presidential election. The official campaign would last two weeks. Each candidate would have equal time (two hours) on television, which he could share with members of his own party but with no one else; no limit was placed on the appearances of ministers in this period. During the twenty months before the campaign opened, the opposition candidate would be kept off the screen —while the incumbent President will no doubt be seen frequently. Not for the first time the Gaullists were discrediting their own cherished institutions, and demonstrating that the pursuit of grandeur abroad does not preclude the practice of pettiness at home.

18   The Communist riposte*

Before 1962, no western Communist Party was as rigidly Stalinist as the French. Two years ago a thaw seemed to be setting in, but now the ice has frozen again. Last November the Party killed its fellow-travelling daily *Libération*, which was showing signs of independence, by suddenly cutting off its subsidy. In March the rebellious communist students were finally subdued, and a hundred Party intellectuals who defended them were disciplined. At the same time communist electoral strategy altered abruptly.

In the general election of 1962 the Party demanded anti-Gaullist unity, supported leading Conservative capitalist opponents of the General, appealed for 'no worker's vote to fail Comrade Guy Mollet'; they withdrew their own men in favour of rivals, who had fewer votes on the first ballot but better prospects on the second. These tactics, which won the Left many seats, were continued till early 1964. But then the change began. Eighteen months earlier branches were rebuked because they had not withdrawn in favour of 'good Conservatives', after March 1964 because they had.

A year later the change was complete. At the municipal elections of March 1965 the 'reactionaries' included many of yesterday's allies—not just Conservatives but MRP anti-Gaullists (so lately 'progressive Catholics') and moderate Radicals ('staunch Republicans')—and to associate with any of them was once more to betray the workers. In theory the Party still called for unity with the socialists, but in practice it risked frightening off moderate voters and potential partners by demanding a majority of seats and the mayoralty wherever it was strong—hardly the technique of communists a-wooing. When local socialist parties chose coalitions with the Centre instead, as most did, they were warned to expect no communist help at the second ballot, even to avert a Gaullist victory. A few, indeed, were split by lavish communist offers to dissident left-wing minorities.

The chief victim of splitting tactics was the main opposition candidate for the Presidency, Gaston Defferre, mayor of Marseilles. The Gaullists hoped to destroy his presidential chances by ousting him from his *mairie*, and rigged their new municipal electoral law against him. The communists had the same aim; for while Defferre appealed for their votes he would not consult them about policy—to do so, of course, would have driven Catholic floaters into the Gaullist camp. When by 9 to 1 the Marseilles socialists decided to

* Originally entitled 'Communists in France'. From *Socialist Commentary*, May 1965.

maintain their old Centre alliance, the communists offered several winnable seats and the mayoralty to the minority (a group of anti-clerical freemasons). It was a tactical triumph, for though Defferre won, he had to fight the CP for his political life in Marseilles and so was bound to alienate its voters from his presidential ticket. But the strategic cost was high, for every French socialist was reminded of the 'salami tactics' by which communists prefer to slice up and swallow their rivals.*

Similarly, in the Paris area the Party had a regional pact with the local socialist bosses (who—unlike Defferre—had been ferocious supporters of the Algerian war). It had elected one of them, Georges Dardel, as president of the departmental council—but now alienated even him by abruptly demanding that he throw over his anti-Gaullist MRP allies. (He won easily.) Old friends were treated no better. The first advocates of unity, the Left Socialist PSU, were deliberately almost frozen out of the Paris unity pact. De Gaulle's most consistent opponent, François Mitterrand, might once have led a Popular Front; now he supported Defferre but urged him to work with the Party. Yet Mitterrand's local communists broke a seven-year-old pact and stood against him in collusion with a socialist who had Gaullist inclinations and support. (Mitterrand, too, won easily.)

Many CP activists had resented working for their local enemies, and preferred the new tough line. No contender for Maurice Thorez's succession wanted to flout their wishes. But the cause of the change probably lies deeper than this, for the CP now clearly sees de Gaulle as the best President it has got. In Parliament communists and Gaullists sometimes vote together against the rest, or sit silent while others cheer an attack on the General's foreign policy—which the Party frequently praises. It may not like his domestic measures but it can exploit the discontent they provoke. So today it works to split, not to unite the opposition. Gaullists often claim that 'every Frenchman is, has been or will be a Gaullist'. Who's next? The Communist Party?†

* For a fuller account, see below, p. 183.
† This comment looked worse six months later than it did three years later.

PART IV

THE STRUGGLE FOR
THE SUCCESSION

19 Party, presidency and parish pump: the 1965 municipal elections*

The town halls of France have always been a prize for politicians. They offer a platform for leadership, a source of patronage, a headquarters for a clientele and a base for a career. In the Third and Fourth Republics with their short-lived coalition governments, the mayor's chair was one of the few places where a political leader enjoyed sufficient tenure and authority to display his capacity for executive leadership. In the Fifth, with Parliament strictly subordinate and ministers overshadowed by General de Gaulle, the political eminence of the successful mayor is further enhanced by the flatness of the surrounding landscape.

The Gaullists have therefore twice tried to use the municipal elections in their drive to reshape the party system. In 1959 they replaced proportional representation in the towns (except in major cities with over 120,000 inhabitants) with the majority system already used in the villages. Votes were cast for a party list, though names could be deleted or written in; if one list had a clear majority it won, taking all the seats; if not, a second ballot was held a week later at which the list with most votes won. Between the rounds lists could be altered, and coalitions with a chance of victory were built up by hasty and frantic bargaining. But in 1964 the Gaullists changed the law again, in all the 159 large towns with over 30,000 inhabitants. Lists could still be withdrawn, and had to be if they polled under 10 per cent of the vote, but they could no longer be altered in any way at the second ballot. All negotiations therefore had to take place before nominations closed. Those Gaullists who favoured a British-type 'first-past-the-post' system had moved a long way towards their objective.

As in 1959 the Gaullists hoped to profit from new rules simplifying the political conflict; and as in 1959 they were disappointed. Then they expected further gains from the popular reaction against both the Communists and the old Fourth Republican parties, which had brought them many victories in the general election six months before. Instead, many a mayor beat off in March 1959 the Gaullist challenger who had captured his parliamentary seat in November 1958. Some observers concluded that the Gaullist move-

* Originally entitled 'Party, Presidency and Parish Pump in France'. From *Parliamentary Affairs*, vol. 18, no. 3 (Summer 1965).

ment was finished—and discovered their error in 1962. Now the same sequence has been repeated: a Gaullist parliamentary success engendering excessive optimism about their municipal prospects, a municipal setback causing a spate of premature obituaries.

This time the Gaullist strategists apparently hoped the new law would polarise politics. Parties too weak to stand alone, and unable to bargain between ballots, would have to make terms quickly with their stronger neighbours; when the Socialists succumbed to the welcoming Communist embrace, the rest would have to rally in self-defence to the UNR. At the last parliamentary election in 1962 the centre parties, from Conservatives to Socialists, had found it hard to pool their resources even for self-preservation; and even where they did, they looked like a purely negative electoral co-operative, united only in order to restore the divided, unstable and unpopular coalitions of the Fourth Republic. But at a municipal election the Centre is much more cohesive. Most French towns have been ruled for years by a centre coalition, usually including and often led by the Socialists. Instead of a bitter conflict about the content of a joint programme—all the harder to agree on because it affirms principles which are unlikely to be realised—there is a common record of civic achievement to defend. Instead of a sordid squabble about the choice of candidates there is a recognised leader, the existing mayor, often with a team used to working together. The pressure to polarise is much weaker.

Another obstacle to polarisation was the new tactics of the Communist party. From 1962 the Communists had tried desperately to escape from political isolation, and had made sweeping concessions to anyone who was willing to ally with them. In 1965 all that had changed. They would have no truck with 'reactionaries' like the Christian Democrats of MRP and the conservative Radicals; they bargained ruthlessly with the Socialists; and they warned any politician who rejected their alliance at the first ballot that they would not withdraw in his favour at the second. Their new line transformed the situation inside the Socialist party, which holds the balance of power in many municipal elections and councils, plays a greater role there than anywhere else in French political life, and draws much of its support from the personal influence of its many successful mayors.[1]

In 1963 the Socialists had seemed to be moving irresistibly towards a Popular Front with the Communists. The trend was slower in 1964, and the municipal election law reversed it instead of reviving it. Almost all the Socialist mayors chose Centre alliances instead – even some who had had Commun-

[1] Only one voter and one deputy in seven was a Socialist, but 47 mayors in the 159 large towns (to only 25 Communists and 26 Gaullists) and 11 in 31 major cities. Municipal defeat could shatter the party, as at Tourcoing where it lost the *mairie* in 1959 and 40 per cent of its vote in 1965.

ist support in 1959, even the few who had belonged to (but were repudiated by) the left-wing socialist party, the PSU. Where they were too weak to elect a mayor the Socialists often inclined to a Popular Front, for fear of being crushed between the Gaullist and Communist steamrollers, but most of them later switched over to the Centre because of Communist intransigence. Only in three regions did the Popular Front tactic prevail: the Catholic west and Alsace-Lorraine, where the entire Left is so weak that all anti-clerical groups usually stand together, and the Paris area, where no centre party commands any strength. (In 1962 the UNR won all thirty-one parliamentary seats in Paris, wiping out its reactionary Conservative rivals, and another twenty-five out of forty-two in the suburbs, where the Communists took all but three of the rest.) The Socialist bosses of the Seine department negotiated a Popular Front pact early on, though the strongest of them repudiated it later rather than accede to new Communist demands.* MRP candidates in Paris were thus driven to ally with the Conservatives, whose 'Centrist' label was made only slightly more plausible by the appearance of rivals on the extreme Right.

In the provinces, however, the Communists failed to impose their terms. There are thirty-one major cities with over 100,000 inhabitants; Popular Fronts were formed in one which is a Paris suburb, in seven where both Communists and Socialists are very weak, and in three of the other twenty-three. The choice split the Socialists in four of the eleven cities which had a Popular Front and two of the twenty which did not; similarly, Conservatives often divided between Gaullist and Centre alliances in places where the Right as a whole was strong. MRP joined coalitions with the UNR in about a third of the larger towns, and with the Socialists in rather more. The Communists usually found partners in the PSU, so that the UNR, which had no allies in nearly half the larger towns, was the most isolated party of all.

With few Popular Fronts and the centre parties unusually united, there were three-cornered contests nearly everywhere instead of the expected polarisation.[1] The uncertainty of Gaullist tactics reflected this failure of their calculations as well as the dissensions in their own ranks (for some UNR leaders see their future as a centre party rather than as the core of an anti-communist Right). First they raised the municipal stakes by their first-past-the-post law, which ensured that they, with or without allies, would either monopolise every seat on a council or be eliminated altogether. Then they feared that this blunderbuss they had so cheerfully taken from their political arsenal might—as in 1959—prove after all to be a boomerang. Anticipating defeat, some Gaullists sought shelter (usually vainly) on centre lists and

[1] Of the 31 major cities, 3 had only two lists competing, 17 had three, 9 had four, and 2 had five.

* Georges Dardel. See above, p. 173.

others prudently stood as 'non-political' administrators—though still promising governmental favours if the town voted right. A month before the election, however, a startling change took place. President de Gaulle, who had discouraged his ministers from standing, now urged them to do so. Generals, admirals and former prefects were hastily mobilised to represent the cause in towns where they were thought to carry weight. The Minister of the Interior, M. Frey, spoke of the municipal elections as an opportunity for the Gaullists to broaden their appeal and organise a nationwide majority, and two days before the poll, the Prime Minister on television (a medium virtually denied to the opposition) urged the voters to follow 'the spirit of the Fifth Republic' by 'eliminating party politics from all levels of public life'.

Despite this appeal, on Sunday, March 14th, 70 per cent of the electorate in the 159 large towns and 80 per cent elsewhere went to the polls to vote for stability. Where there was a second round on March 21st, it usually told the same story. In the 159 towns no party except the Communists captured or was ousted from more than four *mairies*, and only seventeen outgoing mayors were beaten. Indeed, of the thirty-one major cities only ten have had more than two mayors since 1947, even including this year's changes, which hardly suggests that the new electoral law was as necessary to stable municipal administration as the Prime Minister and other Gaullists claimed.

Local circumstances accounted for the few defeats. Failure to cope with the problems of rapid growth explained the UNR's loss of Grenoble to the Left and of Le Mans to MRP—and its gains from a right-wing Radical at Poitiers and from MRP at Cholet (won by M. Frey's *chef de cabinet*). But success in organising expansion brought rich political rewards to M. Fréville (MRP) at Rennes, M. Royer (independent Gaullist) at Tours, and M. Mandle (a close associate of M. Mendès-France) at Evreux. At Caen, the second-fastest growing town in France, a popular former sub-prefect who had once worked with the MRP mayor now stood against him and claimed all the credit for the UNR; he increased the Gaullist poll but the mayor gained more. Thus Gaullist candidates could not always translate governmental sympathy into votes, and some suffered from trying too blatantly to do so. At Lyons a junior minister warned that the politics of the next council would affect the flow of subsidies from Paris; his poll was barely half that of M. Soustelle in the last municipal election, and 70 per cent of the votes cast went to the vaguely Radical mayor, who had carefully associated local business and professional men with his administration. This defeat, however, was exceptional. Generally the Gaullists did as well as in 1959 in the Paris area and much better in the provinces. Even so, they were still well below their peak and the opposition well above its low point, both reached at the parliamentary election of 1962.[1]

The Popular Front alliances had a few successes. They gave the Communists half a dozen victories in the Paris suburbs, mostly from the UNR, and the Socialists two in provincial towns, Lorient and Montauban, where the Left had failed through disunity in 1959. But they attracted fewer votes than the total polled by the left-wing parties separately in 1959.[2] Even where all the supporters of these parties turned out, more of their opponents generally did so. Without Socialist allies the Communists usually did no better than in 1962 and less well than in 1959. Among their worst results were Grenoble and Aix-en-Provence, where their intransigence had alienated even the PSU, but they did capture three provincial *mairies* from divided Socialist parties which had rejected their overtures: Nîmes and Alès in the Midi, and Le Havre, a depressed port in prosperous Normandy.

Of all the parties it was the Socialists who were most embarrassed by the new electoral law. Since any nationwide alliance would have split them, they allowed local parties to decide. Most chose MRP or Conservative partners, whose voters were often vulnerable to Gaullist appeals. Some stood alone or with much weaker allies, losing votes (but not the *mairie*) at Limoges, but winning them at Montpellier, at Tours, and in the industrial north where they are strongest—and are still a working-class party.[3] Even in the Paris area where they are weak, several of their mayors refused the Communist alliance; one or two were beaten but most—at Clichy, Issy-les-Moulineaux, Puteaux—held both their following and their *mairies*. Indeed the mayors of Amiens and St Quentin won easily against their own local parties.

Others were divided too. MRP and Conservatives were in opposition nationally but allied to the Gaullists in many towns (though far fewer than in 1959). Radicals, as always, participated in combinations ranging from far Left to far Right—and sometimes in both in the same place. Even Gaullists

---

[1] Where comparable lists competed both times at either ballot in any of the 159 towns, I calculated the party's gain or loss in its share of the electorate 1959–65 as a percentage of its 1959 share (thus, with 20 per cent in 1959 and 30 per cent in 1965 it gains 50 per cent). The median Gaullist gain 1959–65 was 3 per cent around Paris and 13 per cent in the provinces. But compared with 1962 their vote was down by a quarter.

[2] In 28 such towns the median drop was 11 per cent and the Left's total was up in only 6. In 13 others, where there had also been a Popular Front in 1959, its percentage rose in 5 (usually slightly) and fell in 8 (usually heavily); Communists led its list in 1 of the 5 and 6 of the 8; again the median was − 11 per cent. In 22 towns, mainly Paris suburbs, the Communists gained (median + 10 per cent) from an alliance with Socialists too weak to fight on their own in either election; in the rest of the Paris area they held their own; but elsewhere in the provinces they lost (median − 10 per cent).

[3] Here, their median gain was 15 per cent and the Communists' median loss 8 per cent. Over all the towns where the two fought one another in comparable conditions, the Socialist share was up in over two-thirds (median + 11 per cent) and the Communist up in under one-third (median − 9 per cent).

occasionally defied their party to save their seats. But the Socialist divisions were the most apparent because they had both a nationwide organisation and a tradition of discipline. Members risked expulsion if they defied instructions to join the Communists in Paris or to oppose them at Marseilles—though the wind was tempered to M. Dardel, mayor of Puteaux (no lamb). In fact Socialist indiscipline was rarer than usual, but much more public because it occurred before the election, instead of being crowded into the brief bargaining period between the ballots. Indeed the whole process of negotiation between the parties over seats and alliances received far more publicity than ever before. M. Frey even claimed it as an aim and a virtue of his electoral law to disgust the voters by displaying this sordid spectacle of political intrigue. Yet his own prefects used far cruder and more widespread pressure to help the government's friends than in the Fourth Republic, when Gaullists had accused the old parties of exploiting the state for factional ends.

Few voters were impressed. Old political patterns survived and in general won popular approval. The law did not force painful national realignments on the parties, which were able to escape its pressure by varying their tactics by city and by region. It did something to simplify but little to clarify the political scene. Locally it enforced choices, reducing the average number of lists in large towns from six and a half to three and a half. But in the process it divided many parties and confused many voters: a warning of the complications which a first-past-the-post parliamentary election might produce.

Those who wished to reform the party system always put their main hope in the coming presidential election campaign—as unfavourable ground for traditional politics as the municipal contests were favourable. Each of these contests, however, had repercussions on the other. President de Gaulle has bitter enemies on the far Right, who once looked to him to save French Algeria and destroy French democracy, and now support Maître Tixier-Vignancour for the presidency. In the city of Paris, a conservative stronghold, they fought the municipal election in order to frustrate the Gaullist bid for control. They won nearly 10 per cent of the vote at the first ballot, and a good many of them then seem to have voted Communist to beat the UNR. The reactionary Parisian Conservatives also recovered slightly from their 1962 disaster to win two of the fourteen districts, and robbed the UNR of victory in another by staying in on the second ballot. Thus the Gaullists, who hold every parliamentary constituency, won only thirty-nine municipal seats to thirty-eight for the Popular Front and thirteen 'Centrists' who held the balance of power.

On the Left the chief presidential candidate was the Socialist mayor of Marseilles, Gaston Defferre. His supporters hoped he would both attract support in the Centre and moderate Left, and appeal to Communist sympathisers eager to vote usefully against the regime; no one ever thought that he could beat de Gaulle, but he could challenge any other Gaullist when the General retired. One aim of the municipal election law was therefore to embarrass him and his party by forcing the pivotal groups into a definite choice; if Defferre allied openly with the Communists he would offend moderate voters, if he fought the Party he would alienate its followers. In addition, one clause of the law chopped up Marseilles into electoral districts (with boundaries drawn to his disadvantage) so that he could not lead his own ticket throughout the city like other mayors.[1]

Defferre's strength lay in his success as administrator and party leader in his tough and turbulent port; if he lost his *mairie* he was finished as presidential candidate. The Gaullists were not alone in using the municipal election against him. For the Communist Party feared either to fight him nationally and risk a humiliating loss of prestige and support, or to endorse a candidate who would not negotiate with it about his programme. The municipal campaign allowed the Party to escape from its dilemma by playing the Gaullist game. Either Defferre would accept a coalition with the Communists in Marseilles, remaining mayor but marking himself as their ally on the national scene, or they would break him. The Gaullists had done their best to ensure that he would be beaten if he refused; but by a nine to one vote the Marseilles Socialists decided to maintain their existing alliance with the Centre. To split them the Communists then offered glittering prizes—including the *mairie* in case of victory—to the tiny dissident minority of anti-clerical freemasons.

Defferre now had to fight the Communists for his political life. Shrewdly, they ran their new Socialist allies in districts where Defferre's Conservative supporters were standing, and won over perhaps 20 per cent of the Socialist voters. But his defiance of the Communists helped Defferre win bourgeois voters away from his Gaullist rival. At the first ballot he and the Communists had 36 per cent of the vote each, with 18 per cent for the UNR and eight for the anti-Gaullist extreme Right. This last group openly applauded the OAS terrorists, whom Defferre had once wanted 'hanged or shot'. But their voters were mainly refugees from Algeria, on whose behalf the mayor had worked hard. At the second ballot they tacitly supported him, calling him 'a political adversary' and his two rivals 'our sworn enemies'. The local Gaullist leader, too, received well-publicised instructions to withdraw in Defferre's favour from the UNR managers in Paris (who could not afford to offend centre voters elsewhere by openly playing the Communist game in

---

[1] Lyons was also divided, and Paris had been for years. The Marseilles Socialists had favoured division long ago, but in 1965 it contradicted the professed Gaullist aim of ensuring that cities would be governed by united councils, and was plainly aimed at Defferre.

Marseilles). But he refused to withdraw. He was then in turn defied by his own ward leader (once an ally of Defferre's) in the key district, where four of the nine Gaullist candidates wanted to stand down. Legally five were needed. Protected and persuaded by each side in turn, the fifth man finally signed; it is said the prefect phoned the Elysée for an hour before registering the withdrawal. The courts rejected sensational charges and counter-charges of blackmail, intimidation and kidnapping which recalled Marseilles' old reputation (almost eliminated under Defferre) as the Chicago of France.[1] At the second round Defferre's coalition won forty-one seats, nine of them in the key ward. The Communists and their allies had twenty-two, and the Gaullists none.

For the man in the street Defferre, beating off two powerful opponents, emerged from the campaign stronger than he entered it. But the alliance with the Marseilles conservatives, his only possible means of self-defence, was a political combination of the old style and a disappointment to progressives who yearned for a united French Left, that would rely on new methods and mobilise new energies among hitherto non-political people. These hopeful reformers now concentrated their enthusiasm on Grenoble, rather than Marseilles. There the strongest opposition party were the Communists, who had called for a Popular Front but demanded both the mayoralty and a majority of places on the list. Both Socialist parties, PSU as well as SFIO, refused and chose instead to ally with a non-political municipal action group formed in 1962 to press for better government. (Grenoble was the fastest-growing city in France, and its population, increasing by half in 10 years, had overwhelmed the Gaullist municipal administration; in particular the water supply failed in the winter in apartments above the second floor.) The group's leader, M. Dubedout, an engineer in a local nuclear plant and a devout Catholic, had negotiated with the UNR before agreeing to lead the opposition. To everyone's astonishment, his list doubled the previous Socialist vote and far outstripped the Communists on the first ballot. Under strong pressure from many of their local supporters, and against both their own categorical statements and the wishes of party headquarters, the Grenoble Communists withdrew their list and on the second ballot their votes easily put Dubedout in.

Le Monde headed its analysis of the municipal results 'M. Dubedout's elections'. But it was wishful thinking. Dubedout attracted the participation and the votes of non-political citizens, not because he had found a magic

---

[1] The city may owe this reputation to its many Corsicans, whose electoral traditions are colourful. In the island itself in 1965 court cases were brought after half the contested elections, including all those in the main towns, usually because of alleged fraud in dealing with postal votes. In Ajaccio the main party, the Bonapartists, ran extra lists so as to have a majority of checkers during the poll and at the count. It easily routed its chief opponents, the Bonapartist Workers.

formula to use against the regime, but because his town had acute local problems and a huge rootless population of newcomers. As we have seen, such discontents might help Gaullists no less than their opponents, and indeed Dubedout himself might easily have become a Gaullist candidate.

Indeed surprisingly few French voters were discontented. Most preferred stability, which usually meant the centre parties. The Gaullist offensive failed; they were unable to drive out the 'parties of yesterday', and lost their seats where they were weak. But if already installed they held their own, and they increased their vote in most places, often substantially. Their relative defeat was thus less significant than a victory would have been. This is difficult ground for Gaullists to fight on; few of them have put down local roots, and they cannot count on the appeal of nationalism or the prestige of the General to pull them through. At a presidential and even at a parliamentary election they get the credit for providing stable and successful government. But in most French cities exactly the same factors work to the advantage of the opposition. It is dangerous to draw conclusions from one type of contest and apply them to the other, for the French voter has learned to practise his own form of ticket-splitting. The opposition parties thought they had buried Gaullism in 1959, and in their turn were interred with indecent haste by government spokesmen in 1962. *Il est des morts qu'il faut qu'on tue.*

20 The rivals emerge: the 1965 presidential election*

I. THE CANDIDATES

'It won't be boring in 1965.' General de Gaulle was the chief victim of his own rather ominous prediction, for in six short weeks of autumn electioneering his opinion-poll rating dropped by 20 per cent. On December 5th he had only 44 per cent of the vote instead of the comfortable overall majority he and everyone else (including the author) had initially expected. At the second ballot on December 19th he was re-elected with 55 per cent of the vote, still a successful political leader but no longer the incarnation of national unity.[1]

Direct popular election of the President was instituted by de Gaulle—and opposed by every party but his own—in the referendum of October 1962, six months after the Algerian war ended. Within eighteen months there were three candidates in the field. On the Left Centre Gaston Defferre, Mayor of Marseilles and a leading Socialist, hoped to use the leverage of his campaign to create out of the debris of Socialists, Radicals and MRP (Christian Democrats) a new party to compete with Gaullists and Communists. As no leader on the Right Centre wanted to stand against competition from both de Gaulle and Defferre, the Extreme Right could hope to garner a harvest of anti-Gaullist bourgeois votes. A brilliant McCarthy-like political lawyer, Maître J. L. Tixier-Vignancour, defence counsel for many OAS leaders and killers, stepped confidently into the vacant place; but at first he was hardly taken more seriously than the third contender, André Cornu, an obscure Breton senator.

On the extreme Left the Communists disliked Defferre for his support of united Europe and NATO, his acceptance of the Fifth Republic, his appeal to the Centre, and above all his refusal to negotiate with the political parties, of whose unpopularity he was well aware. With Gaullist connivance they mounted a violent attack on him in Marseilles at the local elections of March 1965.

---

[1] [For the presidential campaign see also D. B. Goldey, 'Organization and Results' in *Political Studies*, vol. 14, no. 2 (June 1966).]

* Originally entitled 'The French Presidential Election of 1965'. From *Parliamentary Affairs*, vol. 19, no. 2, Spring 1966. This article was not proof-read before its appearance in the journal, and four trivial corrections have been made to it (single words on pp. 187, 192, 203, and a phrase on p. 199.)

Forced to fight them for his political life, Defferre moved further Right, proposing a federation of parties including MRP as well as Socialists, Radicals and small progressive groups. Younger MRP members welcomed the proposal but the leaders (who feared the Gaullism of their voters) probably endorsed it only because they hoped the Socialists would refuse. When they too agreed to the plan, it had to be jointly scuttled by the party bosses in two long June nights of fruitless negotiation.*

After the federation collapsed, Defferre refused to launch a 'Gaullist or fascist' campaign against the parties and withdrew his candidature, leaving the machines securely in control of their dwindling forces and the Left opposition without a candidate for the presidency. Cornu fell off a horse and withdrew; but another senator, Pierre Marcilhacy, became the respectable if uninspiring choice of a self-appointed right-wing convention managed by J. P. David, a minor political boss who ran a bogus party of 'European Liberals'. During the summer only Tixier-Vignancour was working hard, touring the beaches and spas with a political circus and earning plenty of publicity. When political business resumed in the autumn there would be just three months to the election.

With the breakdown of Defferre's move towards the Centre the way seemed open to push the Socialist Party to the Left. Having met Defferre's attack with the help of those who favoured alliance with the Communists, Mollet could no longer revert to his original choice—Maurice Faure, President of the Radical Party and leader of its most moderate wing. But left-wingers hoped they, not Mollet, would direct the leftward move. The PSU (largely Left Socialists who had rebelled against Mollet's leadership) now belatedly—and privately—urged Pierre Mendès-France to stand; but he was against the presidential system, and declined. They then put forward the president of the League of the Rights of Man, Daniel Mayer (whom Mollet, then a militant left-winger, had ousted as general secretary of the Socialist Party twenty years before).† But neither Communists nor Socialists meant to allow the tiny and tiresome PSU to bring about left-wing unity.

To stop Mayer an alternative candidate was needed—and available. François Mitterrand led a small bogus party, UDSR, vaguely allied with the Radicals. Originally a rather conservative independent, he had moved steadily leftwards and from 1957 had been on good terms with the Communists (until he gave loyal support to Defferre). But now they, like Mollet, urgently needed a presidential candidate—and not one from their own party, who would risk a conspicuous loss of votes both to de Gaulle and to a left-winger with broader support. Mitterrand announced his candidature early in September. Like Defferre he would not negotiate with the parties, but

---

* For Defferre see above, chaps. 17, 18 and 19. † See above, p. 151.

called on them to make up their minds about the policies he put forward on his own responsibility. He too supported united Europe and NATO and his domestic proposals were (except over Church schools) indistinguishable from Defferre's. But with the election now only twelve weeks away, the Socialists rallied to him cheerfully within one week, and within two the Communist Party, forgetting all about the programme freely negotiated together in their eagerness to escape from their political ghetto, endorsed as an 'acceptable platform' policies which in March they had called a capitulation to reaction.

The decision of the Left had immediate repercussions in the Centre, where the obvious choice had been Maurice Faure: a leading member of the Committee of Democrats which grouped Conservatives, MRP and Radicals, and one who could count on Mollet's good will. His candidature was to be launched at the European Movement's conference at Cannes in early October. But the Socialist defection killed it, giving Mitterrand enough momentum to win over first the Communists and then most of the Radicals, who still felt the pull of left-wing unity; and it was Mitterrand, not Maurice Faure, who came to Cannes to proclaim his European convictions.

Now the moderate Right was in serious disarray. The Committee of Democrats had been cool towards Defferre, and its Conservative members had not appreciated the gestures of their MRP partners in favour of a federation which excluded them. An MRP candidate was therefore unlikely, and a Radical was badly placed to oppose Mitterrand. But now the Conservatives (like the PSU) noticed that their ranks included that rarity, a popular ex-premier: Antoine Pinay. In an absurd comedy which played throughout September, the Committee of Democrats sought (with unexpected aid from Guy Mollet) to persuade Pinay to do his duty. But not for nothing had he been running a slow race with the General for the last two years. Very late in the day he finally refused, and after frantic efforts to draft a non-political figure or even a former Gaullist minister, the Democrats turned at last to Jean Lecanuet, the president of MRP, who accepted the candidature and resigned his presidency. His party and its allies could hardly have offered a new and unknown candidate a less impressive launching-pad.

Four of the six final contenders were now in the field. At the very last minute Marcel Barbu, an organiser of housing co-operatives, stood as an enemy of bureaucracy and spokesman of 'France's bottom-dogs'.[1] A few days before, on November 4th, General de Gaulle had at last confirmed what

---

[1] A seventh candidate, the peasant demagogue Paul Antier, sponsored by Pierre Poujade, was also nominated but withdrew in favour of Lecanuet, to whom his extreme Right backers also transferred their support. Barbu had trouble finding the hundred local councillors from ten departments whom the law requires as nominators. Curiously, their names are not published—so he could be accused by both the Left and the Gaullists of being the others' stooge.

most Frenchmen had expected all along. The timing and manner of his decision to stand did his cause great harm.

Yet his over-confidence was not surprising. For six months the parties, on Left and Right alike, had been busy with manœuvres conducted in slow motion within a close circle of politicians, and reminding the bored or disgusted man in the street of the hated ministerial crises of the past. When Defferre had sparked some public interest, the machines had destroyed him. So with better-known figures keeping well away from the field, the opposition was represented by a left-wing opportunist who inspired confidence in no one; the unknown young leader of a party which had spent the year facing Left and Right in turn; a political adventurer with a fascist record; an obscure senator and a bizarre crank, both without serious backing. The parties had learned nothing and forgotten nothing; no wonder the result seemed a foregone conclusion.

2. THE CAMPAIGN

Yet the General was wrong to believe his opponents would again do his work for him. In 1962 the Algerian War had only just ended. But in 1965 France had been at peace for three years, and Frenchmen were preoccupied with the domestic problems which had never seemed to command the great man's attention. After seven years, and at 75, their benevolent monarch was seeking re-election for seven years more. But he could not last for ever, and increasingly they were worried about 'afterwards'; *l'après-gaullisme*.

If the parties had done nothing right before the campaign opened, the President did nothing right once it had begun. Confirming the contemptuous impression given by his long delay, his brief announcement of his candidature showed all the old hallmarks: before de Gaulle—nothing; under de Gaulle—perfection; if not de Gaulle—catastrophe. Indeed he acted as if he believed the critics who had charged him with reducing the French people to a state of civil slumber broken only by automatic reaffirmations of confidence in his leadership. Yet where was 'depoliticisation' when local elections in March brought out masses of voters, Defferre's federation aroused great interest, and Tixier drew huge crowds to his meetings at the resorts? When the campaign opened in earnest even normally non-political citizens followed it with intense attention.

The usual methods of French electioneering were all brought into use: posters official and illegal, small local meetings (mostly for Mitterrand or Tixier), big rallies in the main towns at which—as in Britain in 1959—television unexpectedly stimulated interest and large and eager crowds attended. While Mitterrand's campaign was wholly traditional, except for the helicopter in which he flew about, his rivals employed some techniques less familiar in France. Tixier's summer 'circus' and his propaganda film 'Sept ans de malheur' were successful publicity stunts. Lecanuet also showed a film at some meetings, and at his final Paris rally a huge audience saw de Gaulle's television address and then heard the candidate reply to it. Lecanuet buttons, scarves and handkerchiefs were an innovation, and his campaign, financed by a few large companies, organised by a public relations firm—the same that managed James Bond—and advised by a market research organisation, provoked opponents to complain that he was being sold like a toothpaste.

Far more important were radio and television. The State radio gave the candidates two hours each, and on the private stations (which have a bigger audience) there were several debates between their leading supporters: the UNR and Socialist general secretaries; Tixier's campaign manager Le Pen and a Gaullist deputy, who almost came to blows; Pierre Mendès-France and Michel Debré, whose two two-hour debates aroused so much interest that a third was arranged on the spot. During the final fortnight each candidate had two hours on television, and it was the medium in which de Gaulle had so long been the unchallenged champion that did most to provoke—or at least crystallise—the opposition to him.

For years the government had systematically exploited ORTF (state radio and television). Clearly, it did not think two weeks of equal time for opposing candidates was a dangerous concession; its main concern was to give no handle to opposition criticism. The administrative arrangements were made not by the Constitutional Council (which should supervise election campaigns, but had been criticised as a Gaullist tool) but by an *ad hoc* Control Commission of senior civil servants;* and for the two weeks' campaign ministers were formally instructed by the premier not to make public appearances except in case of 'necessity'. The Gaullists' confident expectations broke down by the second week, when 'necessity' obliged the ministers to appear with unheard-of frequency; and when the controllers of features and news bulletins blandly ignored the Control Commission, which was punctiliously regulating the candidates' broadcasts. These infringements of impartiality (which were corrected for the second round) did not offset the impact of five speakers who came on television to say what they thought even if it was not what the authorities wanted. Few if any Frenchmen were unaware how the medium had been manipulated; and every opposition candidate reminded them, promising that if he were elected he would naturally allow his opponents access to this public service. Yet the critics made all the greater impact (as a few intelligent Gaullists had foreseen) because opinion had not been 'vaccinated' in advance against argument on

* On it see D. B. Goldey's article in *Political Studies*, loc. cit., pp. 210–12.

the screen. But they were also far more skilful than the older politicians, who in previous referendum and election campaigns had regularly read in monotonous tones their dreary and platitudinous election addresses. Now for the first time two youngish and personable political leaders, who seemed quite capable of managing national affairs responsibly, were using the medium properly.

De Gaulle did not adjust at once his style or strategy to face this competition. Not being a candidate like the others he would neither campaign himself nor encourage his followers to do so. If ministers were told to observe discretion while the battle was on, the UNR was to be neither seen nor heard. Such activity as was permitted was directed by a 'non-partisan' Civic Action Committee managed by one of his former secretaries. The President renounced his two hours of television time, except for a brief final broadcast; the one he made on November 30th was a belated admission of the opposition's success.

In announcing his decision on November 4th he sounded no new note, but repeated the old appeal against 'the State abandoned to the parties and sinking into chaos...but this time without hope of redress'. Every Gaullist spokesman took up the theme, which critics summarised in a phrase he never used as '*Moi ou le chaos*'. It was a poor advertisement for Gaullist stability, but the General thought 'the five oppositions, five candidates...who agree only in wanting me to go' would reinforce it by exposing 'their mutual contradictions, their irreconcilable clienteles, their divergent combinations'.[1] Instead they left their lesser rivals severely alone, concentrated their fire on the President and, to an astonishing extent, all exploited similar lines of attack.

They devoted much of their time to contesting the vaunted stability which had served the Gaullists so well. Mitterrand and especially Lecanuet stressed their youth, and referred discreetly to de Gaulle's age and 'the moment of decision which must come eventually'. There were warnings that the General might not serve out his term, but might try to choose a successor unknown to the voters.[2] His decision to stand again, and his reasons, were called an open vote of no confidence in the UNR. All his opponents accused him of flouting his own constitution and promised to work it correctly, accepting—despite their initial hostility—that the President must be a national leader with a policy, and not a mere figurehead. All dissociated themselves from existing party organisations and discipline and stressed

[1] From his 'extra' broadcast on 30 November. Tixier was the only candidate to attack another—Lecanuet, who was attracting all the moderate votes he had hoped to win.

[2] By a referendum allowing the prime minister (whom he appointed) to succeed to a casual presidential vacancy. A more popular variant on this theme was the sticker, 'If Grandpa is only 75, hurry up and put him in charge of your affairs'.

their personal independence, but none repudiated parties as such. Marcilhacy claimed (correctly) to be the only candidate not selected by himself. Tixier-Vignancour, Mitterrand and Lecanuet each said his personal campaign was only a beginning from which a new party should arise—on the Right, Left Centre or Centre—better adapted to the new world than the old decaying machines. Indeed the last two linked their own political futures to the success of party realignment, and Lecanuet made it the central note of his final television broadcast.

Even on policy issues there was agreement on the criticisms and sometimes on the alternatives proposed. All the oppositions called for an expanding instead of a stagnant economy and complained that France was lagging behind the rest of the Six. They all denounced the lamentable shortage of schools and cheap housing (the Gaullists had done much to meet the former, nothing for the latter). They all discovered (as the Gaullists had always known) that women had votes, and delivered appeals specifically addressed to them.[1] The convergence even extended to foreign policy. Tixier's Atlantic loyalty was uncompromising, and his zeal for the United States startled those who recalled his previous vitriolic anti-Americanism. Mitterrand and Lecanuet both declared their support of NATO, but Lecanuet promised he would not be subservient to the US, and Mitterrand agreed with de Gaulle in favouring modifications of the alliance terms though not with the President's method of seeking these. All the critics attacked the President's changing foreign policies (Mitterrand claimed there had been fourteen), accused him of sabotaging European union, and condemned France's nuclear deterrent. Tixier, the old ultra-nationalist, even used one television appearance for a brief lesson in strategy illustrated by a carefully chosen map of the world reducing France to the smallest possible space.

This similarity of approach enabled the oppositions to capture one of the most telling Gaullist themes. The unity of the nation above the petty divisions of region or class or political faction had been a note which the General struck successfully in every appeal he made. But now his opponents, too, professed non-partisanship. Strident anti-communism seemed at last to have disappeared from the French political vocabulary; even Tixier hardly denounced the red peril and positively appealed for Socialist and Radical votes. Mitterrand hoped to conciliate Catholics by seldom referring to his orthodox left-wing position over the Church schools. Lecanuet made the abolition of 'internal frontiers' (between Catholics and anti-clericals) as well as external ones (among the Six) the main grounds of his call for a new party. Every

[1] A strange by-product of the campaign was the success of 'the pill'. Early on, Mitterrand casually proposed repeal of the 1920 law against selling or advertising contraceptives. Suddenly finding it an immensely popular theme among women, he gave it a prominent place in his own speeches; all his competitors took it up, and the government set up a committee of enquiry.

candidate endorsed the demand for an amnesty for those in prison for Algerian war offences, and Tixier, calling for the release of generals who had plotted against de Gaulle or of students who left bombs outside left-wingers' homes, was unexpectedly echoed by pleas for national reconciliation from the Centre and Left.

The most conspicuous feature of the whole campaign was this interchangeability of topics by which everyone, seeking to win away their rivals' supporters, was drawn towards the centre. Subjects and attitudes peculiar to one candidate were remarkably few. Lecanuet appealed primarily to former Gaullist voters and claimed to be the heir of Defferre (whose federation he had helped to scuttle). Mitterrand made the most of the unwonted left-wing solidarity behind his candidature and stressed—notably in his final broadcast—the historical fears and glories of the French Left in the rhetorical tradition of sixty years before. Neither was above an occasional word calculated to please the critics of foreign aid or the supporters of *Algérie française*. But only Tixier thoroughly exploited the Algerian amnesty and the strong popular aversion to foreign aid, calling for the money to be spent at home and not on 'nigger kings'. He committed himself to the farmers' cherished demand for price parity, and to cutting taxation by 11 % (10 % would not have sounded sufficiently serious), cheered South Vietnam, and championed free enterprise. Lecanuet also attacked 'collectivism and Marxism' and praised individual initiative—while the candidate of the Left said that some denationalisation was perhaps desirable. Lecanuet tried to tempt UNR politicians, many of them worried about 'afterwards', by promising to work if possible with the existing parliamentary majority, but concentrated mainly on the need for a new 'democratic, social, European' party of the Centre.

The old parties, after their feverish activity in choosing and endorsing candidates, took back seats for the campaign itself. None was asked to speak officially for a candidate on the radio or television, as the law allowed. Each candidate had an *ad hoc* committee of supporters running his campaign, and on these there was not much love lost between members of different political loyalties. The parties played little part at public meetings, though at Lecanuet's a Conservative and a Radical leader, Bertrand Motte and Maurice Faure, were prominent speakers. Mitterrand, in contrast, was somewhat embarrassed by Communist support, and appeared entirely alone, except in towns where the Socialist or Radical mayor introduced him (if the mayor was a Communist, he stayed well away).

Among other organisations, the Algerian refugee societies were the backbone of Tixier's campaign and the leading advocates of united Europe virtually formed Lecanuet's general staff. Trade union and professional organisations preferred not to endorse any candidate, so that only the

Communist-dominated CGT and the anti-clerical teachers came out for Mitterrand; but the influential Peasants' League (FNSEA) urged its members to vote against de Gaulle and so in effect did the CFDT, no longer officially a Catholic trade union.*

The press gave good coverage to the campaign, including the television broadcasts. Editorially the principal provincial dailies were divided fairly evenly between de Gaulle, Mitterrand, Lecanuet and complete neutrality; but few were heavily committed like the *Dépêche* at Toulouse, and most avoided offence to their broad local clientele by not blatantly taking sides. Most Paris papers leaned to the opposition, but *France-Soir* was actively Gaullist and so in the end was *Le Figaro*. As the Communists were now subordinating foreign to domestic policy, *L'Humanité* did not publish a Tass communiqué which sounded too friendly to de Gaulle, and corrected 'tendentious interpretations' of the party line in the 'French and foreign' press—i.e. *Pravda*. *Le Monde*, while as usual giving space to everyone, at last ended years of editorial balancing by coming out (cryptically) for the opposition. The intellectuals' vote was treated as important news even by *Paris-Match*. Their extreme-Right minority divided between Tixier and Lecanuet, and the Left majority was thoroughly unhappy with Mitterrand and the party bosses behind him. A good many came out for de Gaulle, while *L'Express* gave half its endorsement to Lecanuet, arguing that if he came close behind Mitterrand the Socialist Party would swing back to Defferre. On the same grounds J. P. Sartre switched his advice at the last minute from abstention to voting for Mitterrand.

Such tactical assessments of the campaign's progress played a part in more influential quarters also, and were helped for the first time in France by regular opinion polls. These showed, as politicians sensed, that the battle was going badly for the General and well for Lecanuet (everybody underestimated Mitterrand). Soon the prospect of a second ballot appalled the Gaullists. Early in the last week meetings were multiplied, ministers and deputies mobilised, and a new and bitter note struck. Along with the familiar claims of constructive reform at home and assertive independence abroad, and warnings against the Fourth Republic's past impotence and the opposition's present divisions, there were now personal and violent attacks on the rival candidates—most vitriolically against Mitterrand but most intensively against Lecanuet. Radio and television (apart from the candidates' broadcasts) also reverted to their normal partisanship.

De Gaulle himself, though naturally never stooping to the excesses of his supporters, at last adopted a new tone. In his unexpectedly defensive

---

* In 1964 the old CFTC had changed its name and abandoned its Catholic commitment, which were both preserved by a right-wing dissident minority (mostly miners).

'extra' broadcast of November 30th, his reminders of social reforms and nationalisations by his Liberation government seemed aimed at the Communist voter. His final appeal, instead of threatening 'chaos', spoke warmly of his ministers as 'a team of action and success'. Lecanuet did not modify his tactics to meet the Gaullist attack; he had throughout stood more in the centre in his broadcasts than in his addresses to right-wing audiences in the provinces. But Mitterrand did change, suddenly announcing himself a few days before the poll no longer as 'the one and only candidate of the Left', but as 'the candidate of the Left and Left Centre'.

The results of the first ballot on December 5th exceeded the worst Gaullist fears: the President had fewer than 44 per cent of the votes cast. A second ballot was needed at which the law allowed only the top two candidates to stand (unless one chose to withdraw). So Mitterrand was now the sole opponent, and Gaullist spokesmen at once denounced him as the prisoner of the Communists—and Lecanuet as the man who had split the 'national' vote (the Minister of the Interior even implying that he had been unpatriotic to stand at all). But this bitter outburst was quickly stopped. The Gaullists were firmly instructed that there was to be no demagogic anti-Communist campaign, that the second ballot was not to be fought as a contest between Left and Right, and that Lecanuet and his supporters were to be ignored, not denounced. For the General would not give up his claim to stand above factions and represent the whole nation, while the shrewder Gaullists feared to alienate potential votes—and the Control Commission now kept an eye on the news bulletins. The last two weeks of the campaign thus regained the seriousness and dignity from which it had momentarily departed.

Now the Gaullists mobilised for a serious contest. The most sensational change was in the General himself, who revolutionised both his approach and his style. Interviewed by an ORTF journalist, he answered questions not only on foreign policy but on the mundane problems of motorways and telephones with easy command of the subject and jovial familiarity. The historic de Gaulle having failed to win his customary electoral triumph, for the first time in his life and to the delight of most of his countrymen *le Grand Charles* became a candidate—and an appealing one.

His supporters followed their instructions, sometimes with bizarre results. Left-wing Gaullists were encouraged to claim that the General represented France's finest progressive traditions, and Malraux asked where Mitterrand had been when Republican Spain was fighting for its life—to loud applause from his elderly, bourgeois, Catholic Parisian audience. A Gaullist weekly of limited circulation printed eight million copies of a 'supplement', *France Avenir* (successor to the old *France Référendum*)—but at least one provincial

UNR deputy did not send it out, since its references to Mitterrand as a young Catholic would have done him good not harm. In a Paris suburb voters found in one envelope three leaflets attacking him as an enemy of the Church, a threat to the bourgeoisie—and a bogus progressive who never supported real left-wing causes.

The opposition was no less eager to steal the enemy's clothes. Mitterrand now called himself 'the candidate of all democrats' (*républicains*) and, without changing his policies, specifically 'welcomed' all votes coming over from his eliminated competitors.[1] Most of them gave him cautious support. Barbu did so 'without enthusiasm' and Marcilhacy only by implication: he agreed to Mitterrand's request to watch for electoral fraud in the overseas territories, where the General had won some majorities of Eastern European dimensions. Many of Lecanuet's voters would not support a man of the Left; knowing this, their leader advised them either to spoil their ballots or cast them for Mitterrand—but not for the General. Wholehearted endorsement of the candidate of the Left came only from the champions of the Extreme Right: Tixier and his whole campaign committee, the Algerian refugee organisations, the exiled Soustelle and Bidault, and every former advocate of all-out war in Algeria or fascism in France.

Hatred of de Gaulle in these quarters had been plain for years. But it also affected responsible and moderate Conservatives—especially their most politically conscious and active representatives, among whom the Gaullist contempt for 'intermediaries' was taking its toll. Jean Monnet and the European lobby led the way to the left-wing camp, followed by many bankers, generals and clerics astonished by the company they were keeping and the discovery that so many of their friends were doing the same. Thus while a good many left-wing spokesmen and some voters still preferred de Gaulle, a large fraction of the Right saw in him an enemy far more dangerous than Mitterrand.

3. THE RESULTS*

The parties, on both Left and Right, were already opposing de Gaulle together in the referendum of October 1962, when he had won 12,800,000 OUI votes—though at the election a month later Gaullist candidates had only 6,600,000. But many of the six million defectors did not vote for the opposition parties, for between referendum and election 2,400,000 fewer valid votes were cast. Now, in 1965, in two record polls of 24,000,000

---

[1] Later, when the votes were safely in, he thanked 'all the democrats and only the democrats' who had supported him. For his last three rallies he chose conservative Nantes and Nice, as well as his 'capital' Toulouse.

* For a fuller account see D. B. Goldey's article in *Political Studies*, vol. 14, no. 2 (June 1966).

TABLE 10. *Presidential election results, 1965*

	Thousands		% of vote		% of electorate	
	1st	2nd	1st	2nd	1st	2nd
Registered	28,235	28,240	—	—		
Not voting	4,233	4,375	—	—	15·0	15·5
Spoiled	244	662	—	—	0·9	2·3
Valid	23,758	23,203	—	—	84·1	82·2
De Gaulle	10,387	12,645	43·7	54·5	36·8	44·8
Mitterrand	7,659	10,557	32·2	45·5	27·1	37·3
Lecanuet	3,767	—	15·8	—	13·3	—
Tixier-V	1,254	—	5·3	—	4·4	—
Marcilhacy	413	—	1·7	—	1·5	—
Barbu	278	—	1·2	—	1·0	—

TABLE 11. *France at the polls, 1956–1965 (millions of votes)*

	1956	1958	1958(1)	1961	1962 April	1962 Oct.	1962(1) Nov.	1965 (1)	1965 (2)
Parliament	1956	—	1958(1)	—	—	—	1962(1)		
Presidency	—	—	—	—	—	—	—	1965	
Referendum	—	1958	—	1961	1962 April	1962 Oct.	Nov.	(1)	(2)
Electorate	26½	26½	—	27	—	—	27½	28	—
Not voting, spoiled	5	4	7	7	8	7	9	4½	5
Gaullists	1	—	4	—	—	—	6½	—	—
de Gaulle	—	—	—	—	—	—	—	10½	—
OUI	—	17½	—	15	17½	13	—	—	12½
NON	—	4½	—	5	2	8	—	—	10½
Communists	5½	a	4	a	—	a	4	{ 7½	—
Soc. & Rad.	5½	—	4½	—	—	a	3½		—
Right & Cent.	9½	—	8	—	—	a	4	6	—

a Parties favouring NON.

de Gaulle had 10,400,000 on the first ballot and 12,600,000 on the second (when 600,000 papers were spoiled). Broadly it seems he lost a fifth of the 1962 OUI voters at the first ballot and regained them at the second, while the extra voters helped swell Mitterrand's final poll to 10,500,000—far more than the NONs of the referendum and not far below the opposition's total at the election of 1962.[1]

The 1965 results reproduced familiar geographical patterns. De Gaulle and

[1] No doubt this is too simple: some voters changed their minds; non-voters were not always the same people; NONs as well as OUIs may have stayed home at the 1962 election; not all the newly-registered voters were Algerian refugees. It merely suggests the trend.

Lecanuet were both strongest in the traditional heartlands of French conservatism, though Lecanuet penetrated more deeply in the north-west and in the few Catholic departments of southern France than he did in the east. Mitterrand did best south of the Loire, in areas which had voted for the Left ever since manhood suffrage in 1849, but he failed to carry the whole working-class vote in the northern industrial areas, where with clear majorities in towns like Lille and Roubaix de Gaulle continued to poll far better than the parties of the Right and Centre had ever done. Even in those Paris suburbs where the Communist Party commands half the entire electorate, Mitterrand failed to poll all the left-wing vote—though the shortfall was much greater in districts where the Socialist Party competes with the Communists on fairly even terms. In the provinces both the leading opposition candidates frequently ran more strongly in the countryside than in the towns, and those industrial areas which voted most heavily for Mitterrand were not usually the most modern or the most prosperous. Tixier-Vignancour reached 10 per cent of the vote only in southern departments, usually coastal and urban, where the bulk of the Algerian refugees had settled in a traditionally left-wing region. In the north generally and the industrial areas in particular, he failed to poll half the votes cast against de Gaulle's Algerian peace settlement in the referendum of *April* 1962—and in Mitterrand's home department, alone in France, Tixier fell below 40 per cent of that figure.

Regional voting patterns could for the first time be supplemented by data from two major polling organisations, which reported similar findings. De Gaulle owed his final majority to women, and was much stronger among the elderly than with those too young to remember 1944. His support among workers was lower than in other classes but still quite substantial, though among them alone a majority favoured Mitterrand. Lecanuet's support, its regional distribution apart, was unlike that of right-wing candidates, for he appealed to the young rather than the old, men more than women, managers rather than shopkeepers. Detailed local investigations confirm this impression: in one small western town he polled best among the young workers of the housing estate; in the ultra-Conservative Paris suburb of Neuilly his best result (and de Gaulle's worst) was in a polling station where senior civil servants are concentrated.

At the second ballot the number voting hardly fell at all, though there were 2 per cent spoiled papers—near average for French elections. More voters went to the poll in the hilly areas with bad communications where fewest had done so two weeks before. Within single towns, within regions and over France as a whole, the second turnout stayed high or even rose where the Left was strongest. Poll data, regional patterns and local breakdowns within towns all indicate that Tixier's voters went overwhelmingly against de Gaulle, especially in the south where the refugees were numerous, poor, and absorbed into a society with predominantly left-wing traditions. The turnout fell most and the spoiled ballots were commonest in the most right-wing of Lecanuet's strongholds. For his voters, especially the more conservative of them, were much more hesitant than Tixier's; Mitterrand took from 30–60 per cent of them according to regions, and over the whole country not many fewer than de Gaulle. This was far more than anyone had expected, and he took most where Lecanuet's vote was least traditional and conservative (in the East rather than the West, among the officials rather than the bourgeoisie of Neuilly, in progressive Eure and Seine-Maritime rather than conservative Vendée and Maine-et-Loire).

France's first direct presidential election showed many factors familiar in the United States. Mitterrand's department (Nièvre) regarded him as a favourite son and gave him far more of its votes than the Left had ever won (at the expense of de Gaulle and Tixier rather than Lecanuet). Even Marcilhacy polled 10 per cent of the vote in his home area, and Tixier and Lecanuet also did well in theirs. But if politicians could command support in their own right they could not always transfer it to others. Mollet could not carry Arras for Mitterrand; Pflimlin did not deliver the MRP vote in Alsace to Lecanuet, or Maurice Schumann that of Nord to de Gaulle. Marcilhacy had only 500 votes in Nantes where his sponsor J. P. David was mayor. Other notables made a better showing. Lecanuet did best of all in Mayenne and Maine-et-Loire where influential MRP leaders campaigned hard for him, but poorly in Lozère where de Gaulle triumphed with the support of both deputies (MRP and Conservative) in defiance of their parties. At Dijon Mitterrand had the backing of the eccentric Conservative mayor, the 89-year-old Canon Kir, and greatly improved on the usual Left vote. Maurice Faure worked for Lecanuet on the first round and for Mitterrand on the second, and in his south-western department most of Lecanuet's voters went Left. But in none of these decisions (except Kir's) were the officers clearly leading their troops rather than following them. Lecanuet's own cautious advice to his voters showed that he recognised the limits of his influence.

Nor did the political parties play a decisive role. De Gaulle ran far ahead of the UNR (though in a very few towns he fell behind a popular Gaullist mayor's vote in the recent local elections). Poll data and election results agree that the Communist Party kept its faithful voters behind Mitterrand, but did not retrieve those lost to de Gaulle in 1958. Socialists and especially Radicals were more likely to desert the candidate of the Left. MRP voters were still tempted by Gaullism, though probably less than before. Compared to the last parliamentary elections it was in their strongholds that the parties failed to hold their voters: MRP in Alsace, Socialists and perhaps Communists in the northern industrial towns where they are best organised. Both Mitterrand and Lecanuet ran most ahead of expectations in areas where the parties sponsoring them were too weak ever to win a parliamentary seat, since voters who had then stayed at home or fallen back on a second-choice candidate could now usefully express their real views.

Parties were thus not decisive as an organisational base, for the men they sponsored did relatively worst where they were strongest and best where they were weakest. But they were useful for sending literature and arranging meetings, and indispensable to confer on a candidate the stamp of seriousness. Marcilhacy, who did not campaign in the country and was less impressive on television than Lecanuet, still made a good impression among viewers. One had ten times the other's vote mainly because he had the substantial backing his rival lacked: and it came essentially from political parties.

Other organisations which seem to have influenced the voters may, like the politicians, have merely expressed their constituents' views: Algerian refugee organisations which supported first Tixier and then Mitterrand; farmers' leagues opposing de Gaulle because of his agricultural policy; trade unions trying to lead forces mobilised in industrial struggles on to the electoral battlefield. It was argued that Mitterrand did best where the workers had been most militant—Decazeville, Hennebont, Montbéliard. Yet in the mining areas where in 1963 the government had suffered its one great industrial defeat, de Gaulle polled heaviest (in the east) or took most votes from the Left (in the north). Religion seems not to have been a major factor, and the Church was at its most discreet—and divided. But its historic influence remains, and in the Cévennes, where the religious wars had their greatest impact 250 years ago, de Gaulle had 65 per cent in Catholic villages only and under 20 per cent in Protestant ones only. Indeed political tradition was the strongest single factor in the election, though the Gaullists were partly justified in claiming that they breached it in the most modern parts of France—at Mitterrand's expense in the North, Lecanuet's in the East.

The most novel factor of all was television, operating for the first time with good nation-wide coverage and as a medium used freely and equitably by all comers. Interest was intense (in the northern coalfield miners had their pithead bus timetables changed so that they could watch the candidates). But the evidence about its political impact is not clear-cut. Opinion polls found 20 per cent of viewers saying it had changed their minds, and de Gaulle losing more ground among viewers than among others—mainly to Lecanuet on the first round, but also slightly to Mitterrand on the second. But by the second week of the campaign many voters had had a surfeit of television politics (though they came back for the last night when all candidates broadcast); and in the second round the polls found minds made up and people refusing to watch, or to be influenced by, the candidate they opposed. While direct questions to viewers showed Lecanuet gaining most and Mitterrand much less, in the end the latter did far better and the former less well than forecast; and indeed Lecanuet's very best results came from areas with a low density of television sets. Indirect evidence is also inconclusive. Both the main opinion polls found de Gaulle's support melting fast in the two weeks of television campaigning. But one of them had detected the movement starting when the candidates were nominated, and accelerating after the General's poor opening broadcast.

Television was therefore not the only factor, but it was important in three respects at least. It rapidly made unknown men into national figures. It exposed the electorate to critics who brought out skilfully and effectively the worries of average Frenchmen. And it kept the tone of the campaign on a responsible and serious level: Tixier, who had made his reputation by sensational scandalmongering and outrageous verbal violence, was dull and ineffective when he could not use his favourite weapons.

France's first presidential election was, then, a great success. The institution, so contested by the parties three years before, was warmly welcomed by the nation. In a record poll, after a healthy and vigorous campaign, the voters discriminated intelligently between serious, dangerous and insubstantial candidates. Moreover, the campaign contributed to national unity. For the politicians tried hard to conciliate their opponents—both democratic, to win votes from their rivals, and even extremist, to win them from de Gaulle. Once welcomed as allies, can the Communist worker or the Algerian refugee ever be pushed back behind the already crumbling walls of their political ghettoes?

For Frenchmen of the Right and Centre the election revealed a strong competitor for the succession in a young politician whose appeal was largely on Gaullist lines and to emotions hitherto touched almost exclusively by the General. Though he was launched by two old parties and advocated the creation of a new one, Jean Lecanuet won far more votes than he or anyone else had originally expected because he personally was an attractive candidate. François Mitterrand also enhanced his stature and influence by the tactical skill with which he recruited and held together his difficult team and the vigour with which he presented his case. But while other opposition voters chose a man, his showed loyalty to a party or a tradition represented by 'the one and only candidate of the Left'.[1] He did best where

---

[1] At the second ballot a poll found 51 % of de Gaulle's voters and 20 % of Mitterrand's choosing their man from confidence in him; 18 and 52 % from approval of his ideas; 26 and 24 % from distrust of his opponent.

the Left's appeal is essentially historical and traditional, and less well (relative to the normal Left parties) in 'modern France' than in 'static France'.

With de Gaulle personally in the field the influence of specific issues and policies is not easy to detect, probably because it was small. Agricultural policies no doubt lost him votes among the farmers and 'stabilisation' in the declining industrial areas. Some commentators have maintained that three-quarters of the voters (de Gaulle's and Mitterrand's) were ratifying the General's foreign policy. But few Frenchmen (or others) vote about foreign policy, which deeply divided Mitterrand's following and did little to recruit de Gaulle's—though his assertion of an independent French role in the world was unquestionably popular.[1] European unity no doubt appeals to specific minority groups (farmers, *cadres*, the young) rather than to average Frenchmen, but is now a domestic as well as a foreign issue; and though the most European of the candidates won only 15 per cent of the vote, every opposition spokesman clearly judged de Gaulle's European policy one of his most vulnerable points.

Above all, the campaign's underlying theme was 'afterwards'—*l'après-gaullisme*. Here the General played into his critics' hands. No longer afraid of an imminent catastrophe, Frenchmen wanted to know how their government meant to conduct their affairs in the normal times which seemed to lie ahead. Until December de Gaulle failed to sense their mood. Having paid them a compliment they appreciated by allowing them to choose their leader, he then withdrew it by treating their choice as a mere ratification. He left it till almost the last minute to announce that he sought a new term which he would begin at 75 and end at 82, gave no new reason for his decision, refused to behave as a candidate, and showed no awareness of 'the moment of decision which must eventually come'. Like Churchill's in 1945, his campaign reminded the voters of all they found least attractive in him—satisfaction with his own achievements, contempt for criticism, unconcern with their humdrum daily worries, perhaps even a secret feeling that if the deluge came after him it would at least improve his historical image. Of all people, it was Marcel Barbu, the usually inarticulate 'bottom dog', who best caught the mood of those ordinary non-political Frenchmen for whom de Gaulle had spoken so often, but with whom he seemed now to have lost touch—'We shall re-elect de Gaulle but we want to humanise him, so that he thinks a bit less about France and more about Frenchmen. Vote for me, the harmless candidate, to make sure of a second round.' Just before the first ballot an opinion poll found only 38 per cent wanting the President defeated.

[1] One poll found 76% approving it. De Gaulle's television broadcast was jeered almost continuously at Lecanuet's Paris meeting—except the reference to ending France's 'unworthy subordination' to her major ally.

But while 26 per cent hoped he would win easily on the first ballot, 10 per cent hoped he would do so only narrowly and 10 per cent cent more only on the second round—so that nearly half his own supporters felt like Barbu that he needed to be brought down from his Elysian heights to the earth where other Frenchmen dwell.

A result which would have been a triumph for any other Gaullist was rightly regarded, for him, as a severe setback. But it was de Gaulle's strategic and tactical errors which dominated the campaign, and it would be rash to conclude that any other Gaullist would inevitably have been routed—still less that the opposition is sure to capture the Assembly in 1967. Everything depends on the next sixteen months: whether Mitterrand and Lecanuet can at last make the political leaders act rather than talk about the party reorganisation that has been debated for seven years; whether the Gaullist politicians keep their nerve and unity or start a *sauve qui peut*; whether the President can regain the initiative as he has so often done in the past, and if so what use he makes of it. Recalling de Gaulle's first words to the cheering crowds in the Algiers forum in June 1958, *L'Est Républicain* of Nancy headed its editorial the morning after his re-election '*Nous a-t-il compris ?*'

21 A precarious majority: the 1967 election*

The French general election of 5th and 12th March 1967 was, of course, a routine choice of a new National Assembly in which a majority had to be found to keep a government in power. But for the first time in forty years this normal political operation was taking place in normal conditions. The country was at peace with no domestic or international crises to face; thus the President's personal appeal was less compelling. At last, therefore, a general election would test the popularity of the new institutions and the Gaullist majority, and show the political impact of the social changes which have transformed French society since 1945.

Traditionally general elections have resolved themselves into hundreds of separate constituency battles. They had always worried Gaullists more than a referendum or a presidential campaign where the President could appeal to his countrymen from a national platform. On this occasion their anxieties were the greater because there was no crisis on the horizon; whereas in times of danger de Gaulle was a tested asset to them, they would now have to stress an argument of unknown potency—the claim that the Fifth Republic could provide stable government for France in a normal period. For this reason, the election marked a new stage in President de Gaulle's long campaign to uproot the old political system and replace it irrevocably with the new regime. The contest thus provides an opportunity to assess the surviving influence of the old order and to evaluate three new trends, produced by Gaullism or modernization or both. These developments are the rejuvenation of organizations and personnel as the post-war generation makes its political debut; the nationalization of campaign techniques, of issues and of leader-

* Originally entitled 'The French General Election of March 1967'. Written with *David B. Goldey*; from *Parliamentary Affairs*, vol. 20, no. 3 (Summer 1967). This account of the national campaign was supplemented by four articles describing the special characteristics of the election as seen from different points of the geographical compass and of the social and political spectrum. These articles—respectively, by R. E. M. Irving and A. Macleod, S. Rose, R. W. Johnson and A. M. Summers, P. M. Williams and D. B. Goldey (below, pp. 222–5)—dealt in some detail with a Marseilles constituency and, more briefly, with the Socialists in the northern industrial area, Communists in a Paris suburb and Catholics and conservatives in the rural and clerical inner west. An account of the election in a left-wing rural department, Corrèze—by L. A. Whitehead, J. H. G. Lord and A. J. Petrie—appeared in *Political Studies*, vol. 16, no. 2 (June 1968).

ship; and the polarization of political forces at the expense of the centre groups which have usually dominated the country's government ever since France became a democracy—and indeed before.

The normality of the election itself marked a change. Not only was there no immediate crisis; for the first time since the war a Parliament had run to the end of its legal term; and for the first time in French history, as Gaullists frequently pointed out, a single government, that of Georges Pompidou, had stayed in office throughout a Parliament's life. Only one tradition was faithfully maintained: as usual the dying Assembly altered the electoral law shortly before the election was due. But the amendments were minor and did not change the existing system of single-member constituencies, in which two ballots are held a week apart; to be returned at the first, a candidate needs a clear majority of the votes cast, while at the second he merely needs more votes than any rival. Of the changes, one added five new seats to the expanding Paris region, bringing the total to 487 (470 in France and 17 overseas). Another debarred a candidate from the second ballot unless his vote at the first had exceeded 10% of the registered electorate:[1] in 1958 and 1962 the hurdle had been much lower (5% of votes cast) and this remained the limit above which a candidate saved his deposit and had some basic expenses (petrol and election addresses) reimbursed by the State. Finally, broadcasting and television time were divided equally between the parliamentary majority and opposition, which had 90 minutes each for each ballot.[2]

Yet another unusual element in this normal campaign was its duration, for the politicians—if not the general public—had been suffering from election fever ever since the Presidential contest got under way in September 1965.[3] At the first ballot on December 5th, President de Gaulle had only 44% of the vote to 32% for François Mitterrand, the candidate of the Left, 15% for Jean Lecanuet, a leader of the Christian Democratic MRP who enjoyed Conservative and some Radical support, and 5% for Tixier-Vignancour of the extreme Right. At the second ballot on the 19th, with only two candidates allowed, de Gaulle won by 55% to 45% for Mitterrand.

The successful projection of the presidential candidates during that campaign gave both Mitterrand and Lecanuet crucial positions in the subsequent attempts at party realignment, while the unexpectedly close result filled the opposition parties with new hope, and inspired changes in the composition

---

[1] He had always needed 25% of the electorate to be returned at the first ballot.

[2] The allotment to individual parties was made (without difficulty) by mutual agreement. In addition, a party which ran 75 candidates, but had no parliamentary group, was granted 7 minutes before each ballot. These broadcasting rules were vigorously attacked by the opposition, but the new Paris region seats and the new second-ballot rules went through Parliament unopposed.

[3] [See chap. 20.]

of Pompidou's government and in the tactics of the Gaullists. Giscard d'Estaing, the leader of thirty Conservative deputies who had taken the Gaullist side when their colleagues went into opposition in 1962, was replaced at the vital finance ministry by Michel Debré—who favoured a more expansionist economic policy, but soon discovered that the situation gave little room for manœuvre. A much more effective electoral operation was the promotion of the energetic and progressive but monumentally tactless minister of agriculture, Edgard Pisani, and the appointment instead of Edgar Faure, a conciliatory wizard of long Fourth Republican experience, with the mission of regaining peasant votes lost at the presidential election. Tactically, there was an attempt to capitalize on the remarkable range of political views—from moderate Right to extreme Left—revealed among the public figures who had favoured the General's candidature. Left-wing Gaullist deputies like René Capitant and Louis Vallon were encouraged to express their criticisms of the government's social and economic policies; the two Edgars, Faure and Pisani, presented themselves as leaders independent of the main Gaullist party, the UNR; Giscard d'Estaing, freed from the constraints of office, bid for the Conservative vote by differentiating himself ostentatiously from his recent colleagues. At one point it seemed that, as he and others wished, there might be rival Gaullist candidates competing at the first ballot, reuniting only at the second round behind the strongest among them.

The UNR party leaders, however, saw no reason to allow these newcomers to profit from the loyalty and discipline shown by orthodox Gaullists during and since the Algerian war. More important, the spectacle of Gaullists fighting one another at the first ballot risked the loss of their major asset, the belief that they were the only movement sufficiently united to give France strong and stable government. Pompidou therefore insisted that each constituency must have only one Gaullist candidate and that allies outside the UNR must negotiate in his 'Committee of the Majority' for their allotment of seats within the coalition, renamed 'Fifth Republic'. He got his way, and so on the whole did the UNR. Sitting deputies from other parties who had generally supported his government were treated with generosity, twenty of them receiving the Fifth Republican ticket. Giscard won a few concessions, but far less than he had hoped. The newer and more progressive Gaullist groups were rarely allotted winnable seats. But the distribution of the party endorsement, to which the success of 1962 had given a greatly enhanced value, was no longer decided by UNR headquarters but essentially by the prime minister. He used it to centralize a Gaullist movement which had once seemed on the verge of licensed fragmentation.

This was the crucial decision of the campaign, for the discipline successfully imposed on the majority threatened the opposition parties with disaster and obliged them to make a similar effort. In that effort, the former presidential candidates played a crucial role. They tried to use their new national reputations to build new parties under their own leadership and based on their presidential supporters. Lecanuet brought his MRP and Conservative following together in a new organization, the Democratic Centre (CD)—a fragile construction ill-adapted to survive the strain of the serious defeat it was to sustain. Mitterrand succeeded in setting up a Federation of the Democratic and Socialist Left (FGDS) embracing the Socialist and Radical parties, minus some right-wing Radical dissidents, but plus some of the predominantly intellectual left-wing clubs on the margin of normal politics, which had combined for the purpose in a 'Convention for Republican Institutions'; he failed to bring in the PSU (the Left Socialist party) or the Left Catholic clubs, among whom he was distrusted. His Federation was to emerge in fairly healthy shape from the election. But the principal beneficiary of the operation was its formidable partner, the Communist Party.

At the previous election, in 1962, the Communists had given top priority to the defeat of Gaullism and made some striking sacrifices of their own electoral interests in order to ensure the defeat of UNR members by Socialists, Christian Democrats or even 'good republican' Conservatives. Two years later their tactics changed, and at and after the municipal elections of March 1965 they refused to support Conservatives, MRP or right-wing Radical candidates, and insisted that Socialists or Radicals who sought their support must cut themselves off from dealings with such 'notorious reactionaries'.[1]* Understandably, they were reluctant to help elect Socialists or other allies who would promptly abandon them to deal with Lecanuet; equally understandably they preferred helpless partners who had no alternative course open to them; and at this stage they may also have wished, for reasons of foreign policy, to ensure the safe return of a Gaullist majority. Uncertain of their motives, the leaders of the non-Communist Left disagreed on the attitude to take towards their overtures. Moderate Radicals like Maurice Faure favoured Lecanuet and opposed any transactions with the Communists. Other Radicals and some Socialists, like Gaston Defferre, feared that a Communist alliance would alienate some of their voters and that a breach with the Centre would destroy all their bargaining power. But over half the Socialist deputies and nearly half the Radicals owed their election in 1962 to Communist support at the second ballot. The Socialist leader Guy Mollet joined Mitterrand and his friends of the Convention in encouraging the trend towards a Popular Front.

[1] [See chap. 18.]
* Above, pp. 178–9.

The Federation reacted to harsh Communist pressure with long hesitations and open dissensions which did its prestige no good. But an agreement was finally signed on 18 October 1966; each partner would fight the first ballot independently but at the second would support 'the best-placed candidate of the Left' wherever a Left victory was possible; elsewhere the Federation reserved the right to stand down for a CD candidate against the Gaullist. The PSU was later fitted into this accord, and acquired first-ballot Federation support for thirty of its candidates (notably Mendès-France) in return for withdrawing its own men in neighbouring seats; in regions where negotiations failed, the PSU fought (disastrously) on its own. This national pact between the Communists and the Federation went far beyond the hasty, localised and restricted deals of 1962. But revolts against the Federation's decisions on persons and policy were surprisingly few, and the small number of dissident candidates on the first ballot foreshadowed the discipline (unprecedented even in 1936) which the politicians of the non-Communist Left were to display on the second.

The Federation thus renounced the traditional Socialist and Radical tactics of seeking different alliances in different areas, winning Centre support against the Communists in some regions and Communist support against the clerical Right in others. This decision denied to Lecanuet's followers any opportunity to play a similar game, manœuvring according to regional circumstances between the Federation and the Gaullists. Already the CD had lost a third of its parliamentary following—Conservatives and especially MRP members who, recognizing their electors' wishes, had endorsed de Gaulle for the Presidency and were offered in return the Fifth Republican ticket for Parliament. Then one of Lecanuet's chief supporters, Maurice Faure, refused to break completely with his Radical friends by joining the CD. Lecanuet could not even find himself a winnable seat. With his options restricted by the Federation's choice, he began to change his tone as election day approached. He denounced the Communists with increasing insistence; allowed his party to leave unopposed such spokesmen of the far Right as Jacques Soustelle; and muted his vigorous attacks on Gaullist policy into appeals for a change of course which would permit him to support the government. These decisions divided the CD. The concessions to the Gaullists, and even more to the extreme Right, offended his progressive young MRP followers who had sympathized with Defferre.* At the same time his overtures to the majority exasperated extreme right-wingers whose main political driving force was now their hatred of de Gaulle; on polling day many of them seem to have preferred the more progressive but more anti-Gaullist Federation.

* Above, pp. 165, 170, 187.

Among the smaller groups, the extreme Right had two incongruously named outlets of its own: Tixier-Vignancour's Republican Alliance for Liberties and Progress (AR), and the European Liberty Rally (REL), comprising the most openly fascist element in Tixier's old following, which now found him deplorably moderate. There were a Democratic and Republican Centre (CDR), with its title and slogans calculated to confuse potential Lecanuet voters to the advantage of the Gaullists; and a dissident Gaullist party—which for a time worried the official leaders—of would-be candidates denied the party ticket, among them one or two sitting members and rather more former deputies. Most of these non-parliamentary groups ran fewer than 35 candidates. Only the PSU, with 104, obtained television time, which it sensibly used to give a platform to Mendès-France. In addition to the usual motley crew of cranks, there were also a few politicians—mostly sitting members or mayors, but also a few newcomers like the ex-minister Pierre Sudreau—who thought their local position so strong that they could do better without a party label.

Though the details were as complex as ever, the main lines of the contest were much clearer than usual. Gaullists and Communists contested all 470 French seats, the Federation or its PSU allies all but two dozen, and CD 351. Only five deputies from small parties were elected (four PSU men, all with Federation support on the first ballot, and a dissident Gaullist) and only 21 altogether—including the overseas members and the locally entrenched independents—who had not the endorsement of one of the big four.

This simplification of the political struggle was accompanied by a fairly extensive rejuvenation of the country's parliamentary personnel. All parties made an effort to bring forward younger men—and even a few women. The most centralized parties, Communists and Gaullists, did most to promote new candidates. The projected purge of the older UNR deputies indeed turned out to be quite limited in the end, though thirty (out of 230) were persuaded to retire voluntarily and two stood as dissidents when they were refused endorsement. But many able young Gaullists, often civil servants and usually members of a minister's *cabinet*, were sent out to attempt a breakthrough in areas where they had some local ties and where the government could hope for successes—in Brittany and above all west-central and south-western France.

Less solidly established and more hampered by the problems of coalition organizations, the Federation and the CD found it harder than their rivals to unleash their 'young wolves'—still less to discourage the 'old crabs'. Both finally decided to endorse all sitting members from their component parties and many ex-members beaten in 1962; their claim to be rejuvenating French public life was hardly strengthened by their commitment to all too familiar figures from the old regime and the struggles over Algeria, Indo-china and even Munich: Frédéric-Dupont and Bernard Lafay (CD), Robert Lacoste and Georges Bonnet (Federation). To compensate for a decision they doubtless thought inevitable, Lecanuet and Mitterrand both tried to bring forward new candidates: young progressives from MRP in the one case, from the Convention and clubs in the other. Each leader tried to establish his authority and link his prestige with the promotion of a new generation and a new type of candidate loyal to himself, in a party organization domi-nated by the men and machines of the past.[1] Local ties were not neglected, but youth and energy could now be successfully invoked as qualifications alternative to the long traditional *cursus honorum* in local government. Among these political forces and their predecessors (though less so among the more centralized Communists and Gaullists) a personal position, an administrative reputation and a regional attachment had hitherto been assets almost as important in a parliamentary as in a municipal election. Now the changes which had already affected the centralized parties began to influence the looser ones also. In modern, urbanized France, rapidly being transformed by the Common Market, the parochial local worthy seems as out-of-date as the priest-eating demagogue. To defend his constituency the individual politician is coming to need the education and training to argue with planners and organization men in Paris or on his regional development committee; and on the national scene his party is expected to show by its cohesion and discipline that it is capable of giving France an effective government.

The campaign emphasized the increased importance attached to a national label by candidates and voters, and the growing predominance in the parties of their 'presidential' rather than their organizational leaders. Jean Lecanuet, in an open-necked shirt, presented 'his' candidates from both official and commercial billboards. In Paris particularly, posters of Federation and PSU candidates also carried large photographs of Mitterrand and Mendès-France respectively. The Communists had most attractively produced literature for students and cadres, and a poster of mother and child looking hopefully upward to the heavens. The Gaullist campaign was run by the prime minister's office, not by party headquarters, and the genuineness of orthodox candidates, like that of certain brands of proprietary whisky, was vouched for by the signatures of Pompidou and Giscard on their posters and handouts. Gaullist propaganda emphasized the stability of the regime not the personality

---

[1] The Centre's failure and the Federation's relative success meant that the operation benefited François Mitterrand far more than Jean Lecanuet, who, moreover, was not in the new Assembly to rally his troops.

of the President, who stared down larger than life from commercial hoardings. These innovations were more important for the trend they symbolized than for their effect on the indifferent public. Before 1962 posters served to tell the voter about a candidate's views; now they remind him of an election in progress. His information comes from radio and television, which emphasize the party leader and programme rather than the virtues of individual candidates.

On television, old party chieftains were seen only the first night and the screen was dominated by Mitterrand, Lecanuet, Pompidou and Giscard— and by assorted Communists, speaking for the only party not to succumb to the cult of personality. The television speeches, always predictable and often dull, had far less impact than in the presidential campaign; rental services complained that business was poor. But the radio debates, interviews and listeners' questions on the two commercial networks found a ready audience, especially in the towns. Competing with each other for listeners (and advertisers), Europe No. 1 and Radio Luxembourg saturated the airwaves with political programmes. The high point of the radio campaign was the debate between Mendès-France and Pompidou, broadcast from Grenoble by both the ORTF and the private stations late at night on the final Monday. After that, politicians sensed that voters 'already informed up to their ears' were losing interest in a campaign which had lasted for eighteen months. The announcement of General de Gaulle's eve-of-poll broadcast for the Saturday aroused much more CD anxiety than Gaullist enthusiasm. The breach of an established convention shocked the politically-minded; in the towns the speech was heard with indifference, but it may have swayed rural voters.

If news media are increasingly national, party organizations (except for the Communists and Gaullists) are still local in character. National headquarters distribute posters and information, but the candidate utilizes only what he thinks best. Nominees of the same party more obviously than before recommended the same line to their electors in their campaign publications; nonetheless candidates with strong personal positions played down their party in order not to offend potential support. But almost all serious candidates were clearly either identified with or hostile to the majority. Most candidates held constituency meetings before the first ballot, a few before the second; they were generally well-attended, but rarely exciting. Some candidates in Paris played a pre-recorded message over a well-publicized telephone number. The first brochure issued by *Services et Méthodes* urged Gaullists to throw out the ball at football matches as the best way of appearing in regional television broadcasts; this was probably the only hope for opposition candidates to reach the screen.

Broadcasting time is free in France, but professional services on a national scale from Paris are expensive; CD and the Gaullists probably spent most at this level. Estimates of national spending by the majority (or the government) started at over a million pounds and ranged far upward. CD, Gaullists and Communists spent heavily in some marginal seats, as did a few well-connected Federation candidates—and Mendès-France, for whom the *Nouvel Observateur* did a special (and not universally appreciated) Grenoble edition. In one or two Oise constituencies more money was probably spent on the electorate than on the election, but Oise is notoriously a special case in (metropolitan) France.* Estimates of constituency expenses ranged from a few hundred pounds for the sitting member in a safe rural seat to over £2,000 for a newcomer in a hotly contested urban district.[1] The majority automatically produced £400 for any candidate who requested it, as well as the campaign information and advice provided by *Services et Méthodes*, who also offered campaign key rings and other gimmicks—at an extra charge.

Political leaders, however, were sometimes as impervious to the expensive advice of their publicity agencies, as were their voters to the lure of key rings. Bought by the Gaullists from Lecanuet after the 1965 presidentials, *Services et Méthodes* were said to have urged Pompidou to campaign on the slogan: 'With and After de Gaulle: Stability, Security, Efficiency—the Fifth Republic!' Only the second half survived the presidential veto. They also distributed a *Dossier du Candidat*, some of which (e.g. on agriculture) was very well done, and constituency statistics for each candidate, with a list of notables and cafés. One CD agency produced a smaller *1001 Conseils du Candidat*, which was generally thought superior; but Lecanuet apparently rejected the slogans and campaign strategy provided by other market researchers. Unable to afford these luxuries, the Federation ridiculed candidates sold like soap powder, and repudiated reactionary devices like opinion polls. But the Communists, in their new and more flexible mood, began consulting pollsters well before the elections and even allowed some of the results to be published.

All the surveys agreed that the majority's weakest card was social policy, especially housing and (regional) unemployment; its strongest, the stability of the régime. Nevertheless, left-wing spokesmen plunged eagerly into a constitutional debate which could only help their opponents. Only after the first ballot seemed to remove any threat to the régime did attention turn to other issues. The Left attacked on housing, where the Gaullists promised more, and on unemployment, claiming it was deliberately planned to help

[1] Excluding petrol and election addresses: see above, p. 205.

* Above, p. 48. It has had this reputation since the Third Republic (when a Rothschild represented the department).

control inflation—which the majority hotly denied. PSU's alternative economic plan was an impressive opposition effort, but its circulation was limited; Mendès-France, however, was often treated by both the majority and the media as the real spokesman of the Left (though the Communists attacked him vigorously). Some left-wingers spread confusion by approving the substance of the General's foreign policy while deploring its motives; the Communists contented themselves with noting its positive aspects, while loudly condemning the *force de frappe*, which the whole Left opposed. CD concentrated its fire on European policy, but this debate was confused by the majority's claim to be equally good Europeans, citing the agricultural settlement as a victory for Europe as well as France. CD and Gaullists hedged on the Pill, which was favoured by the Left.

All these specific issues were overshadowed by the general concern for stable government. All the important parties stressed that they were ready to translate an electoral majority into a disciplined parliamentary one. But CD could not convincingly expect to form a majority. Instead, therefore, CD stressed that it alone could save the country from division into two hostile blocs—a division felt acutely within CD itself, for its MRP militants were attracted by the Federation, its Conservative voters by the Gaullists (and its senators by Giscard). CD's increasingly strident anti-communism did it little apparent good now that the prospect of Communists in the majority, and even in office, no longer traumatized opinion. It was positively harmed by its suspiciously Fourth Republican promise to support the government, but only under certain circumstances.

Like CD on the Right, PSU on the Left, which had only 104 candidates, seemed a dissident party for which it was useless to vote. Both Federation and Communists insisted that their second ballot pact, based on common objectives, showed they were capable of governing together during five years; Mitterrand even claimed the Federation alone could get a majority. The Communists—who (pollsters found) were thought by many voters to belong to the Federation—used the effective slogan 'To vote usefully, vote Communist from the first ballot!'

It was an appeal which has acquired a new meaning in the Fifth Republic, and not only for voters of the Left, now that Frenchmen seem more ready to elect a government and less determined to select a constituency ambassador than before. Since no disciplined majority can emerge from second ballot alliances arranged on a departmental basis, a party which wants to be taken seriously must look like a potential majority even before the first ballot. Opposing candidates of the same tendency, such as Federation and PSU, are thus no longer welcomed as offering the elector a choice but condemned as presenting him with a dilemma, and tend to discredit one another. Disregarding differences within tendencies, then, the electorate now prefers to confine its choice to the major party of either government or opposition. If the run-off is to offer this clear choice, the first round must be used to eliminate 'dissident' factions. This reverses the old rule: choose (your favourite) on the first ballot, eliminate (your enemy) on the second.

Although the final election results were to confirm this tendency to polarization, the figures of the first ballot gave an impression of unexpected stability. In an electorate increased by 760,000, four million more people (12%) cast valid votes than in 1962; yet the proportions of votes cast for the Gaullists, Communists and non-Communist Left all altered by less than 2%. Only the CD lost seriously—4% down.[1] But this stability was misleading, for in the past five years both politicians and voters had changed. Twenty former MRP and conservative deputies had turned Gaullist; a few Radical candidates did the same, and more (including a dozen deputies) preferred the endorsement of the Centre, or none at all, to that of the Federation. Among the electorate, those who stayed at home in 1962 were probably mostly admirers of de Gaulle who had in the past voted for the old Fourth Republican parties. Neither UNR supporters who approved of direct election of the President in the October 1962 referendum, nor Communists who opposed it, would have faced similar difficulties in choosing between President and party at the election a month later. In 1967, therefore, even if the Gaullists and Communists kept all their former voters, their percentage of votes cast could have dropped sharply as the temporary defectors flocked back to the polls—and to their old allegiance. Instead they held their own, a false stability which concealed a real gain. For the returning voters were not flowing back to the Centre and the Federation, from whose component elements de Gaulle had detached them in 1962. The higher total poll masked a transfer to the Gaullist party of a section of the General's personal vote; and a recovery by the Communists of half the support they had lost in 1958.[2]

Changes in party support are better measured by comparing the percentage of the electorate supporting the four major groups (or their old components) in the 78 seats contested by them all both in 1962 and in 1967. In these constituencies the CD failed to maintain its share of the electorate while the other three, thanks to the higher poll, all increased theirs by at least 3%. However, where the Centre in 1967 inherited from an MRP candidate in 1962, they held their own; their losses came either among mainly CNI voters

[1] Partly because the ministry of the interior invented a new 'miscellaneous' category of candidates whose predecessors would often have been classed with the right-wing parties in 1962.
[2] There were signs that this recovery was already in progress at the second ballot in 1962, though not at the first [see above, p. 143].

TABLE 12 *Four General Elections, 1956–1967*

		Comm.	Other Left	MRP, Cons.	Gaull.	Extr. Right	Don't vote	Elector-ate
			Votes (millions) at first ballot					
1956	—	5·5	6·5[b]	5·4	0·9	2·9	4·6	26·8
1958	(1)	3·9	4·5	7·8	3·6	0·7	6·2	17·2
1962	(1)	4·0	4·1	3·1	6·9	0·2	8·6	27·5
1965	(1)	—	7·7[a]	4·2[a]	10·5[a]	1·3[a]	4·3[a]	28·4
1967	(1)	5·0	4·7	2·9[c]	8·5	0·2	5·4	28·3
			In seats fought at second ballot					
1958	(2)	3·8	3·3	6·1	5·2	0·2		
1962	(2)	3·2	3·4	2·0	6·4	—		
1967	(2)	4·0	4·7	1·3[c]	8·0	—		
Seats								
1956	(544)	145	162[b]	166	16	55		
1958	(465)	10	65	203	187	—		
1962	(465)	41	106	64	249	—		
1967	(470)	72	120	27[c]	234	—		

[a] For presidential candidates.
[b] Including right-wing Radicals; 1 m. votes, 32 deputies.
[c] Excluding 'miscellaneous'; 1 m. votes, 17 deputies.

TABLE 13 *Increase in Party Shares of the Electorate, 1962–1967*
(first ballots) in comparable seats

		No. of seats	Comm.	Fed.	CD	Gaull.
4-cornered		78	3·6	4·6	− 0·5	5·3
„	(i)	39	3·7	4·5	0·3	5·6
„	(ii)	39	3·5	4·7	− 1·2	5·0
3-cornered		8	2·8		4·9	4·3

(i) CD represented 1962 by MRP, (ii) by another party or by rival candidates.

who turned to the Gaullists, or where progressive MRP supporters switched to the Federation: Roubaix, Pontoise, Cholet, St Malô, Paris 29.

The Left made substantial progress, particularly in the Greater Paris area and in the northern and eastern half of France. But its gains varied from one region to another, and were differently distributed between the Communists and the Federation. Both advanced spectacularly in industrial Lorraine—the centre of the miners' strike in 1963, still suffering from textile and mining unemployment. In some constituencies—Bordeaux, Nantes, Montbéliard—big recent strikes also helped both sections of the Left. Elsewhere its new voters often turned overwhelmingly, and almost indifferently, to the party which had most chance—behaving at the first ballot as if it were already the second.[1] In general the Communists made gains in most regions, except the city of Paris where they lost votes, and some poor rural areas where they stagnated.[2] Nationally, they gained a million votes. In many areas the Federation outstripped them, but its net gain was only half a million because of its very heavy losses in south-western and west-central France. There, many conservative Radical politicians had defected to the Right rather than combine with their old Socialist enemies in an alliance with the Communists; while Radical voters deserted in droves, hoping that deputies from the party in power might channel economic benefits to these depressed regions.

Such Gaullist advances in the rural areas were possible only because the traditionalist policies and style of Edgar Faure had appeased the discontented farmers. The Centre thus lost the only asset which might have helped it resist the pressure polarizing votes behind the big political battalions—those which looked capable of keeping a stable government in office. The MRP and CNI leaders thought they had touched rock-bottom in 1962, when they lost half their support; in 1965 Lecanuet's good showing against the President himself had raised their hopes of recovery; but in 1967 the Centre candidates (absent from 100 seats) polled a million fewer than Lecanuet, and even fell behind their dismal 1962 performance.

The pressure towards parties capable of providing a government told heavily against small groups and independents alike. A few of the latter surmounted it where they enjoyed exceptional personal support, but little formations were fatally handicapped. Even though the 10% rule proved less murderous than expected, because of the higher poll, it eliminated from the second ballot 613 candidates who failed to attain the required figure: only two Gaullists, few Federation or Communist candidates, but nearly half Lecanuet's men, four-fifths of the PSU, and almost all the Gaullist and extreme-Right dissidents. Only six rebels took even a quarter of the Gaullist vote, and the two sitting members who stood as dissidents when they were denied renomination polled only 7 and 8% of the votes cast.[3] The two far-Right groups—Tixier's and his even wilder rivals—attracted between them only a sixth of his presidential following. Among the rebels against the

---

[1] In one Sarthe seat a sitting Communist gained 8,000 votes, the Socialist nothing; next door the Federation deputy gained 6,500, his Communist opponent 2,000. In the northern mining area, three Communist deputies gained 12,000 between them and their Socialist rivals under 1,000; three Socialist members for neighbouring seats together gained 12,000 and their Communist opponents 4,000.

[2] See the article on Corrèze by L. A. Whitehead, J. H. G. Lord and A. J. Petrie in *Political Studies*, vol. 16, no. 2 (June 1968).

[3] Partly because the few members denied renomination were those thought to have lost local support. One dissident was elected—in a safe Norman seat where the whole opposition vote swung to him at the second ballot to oust the regular Gaullist deputy.

parties of the Left, Maurice Faure, the chief Radical opponent of the Federation, lost nearly two-fifths of his vote and saved his seat only by a most humiliating capitulation (at the expense of his closest political ally) before the second ballot. A Socialist who refused the Federation ticket fared disastrously at Perpignan. Socialist parties which had split over municipal alliances with the Communists paid a heavy price in 1967—at Le Mans, Douai, Boulogne-Billancourt. Yet the pro-Communist rebels against Defferre were slaughtered by the voters of Marseilles;[1] and the PSU failed catastrophically wherever it challenged the Federation. The electorate showed no aversion to a left-wing alignment, but their positive preference was for political discipline and efficacity.

The results certainly helped to polarize and rationalize the political scene; they also did something to rejuvenate political personnel. Both Gaullist *jeunes loups* in central and south-western France, and Convention candidates from the non-Communist Left, scored some spectacular increases in their party's vote. But youth alone was neither necessary nor sufficient; in both these groups there were notable failures, while the new candidates of the older parties rarely did well, and Lecanuet's bright young men (with only one exception) quite failed to stem the tide flowing against them. Moreover, sitting members, against whom the electorate had often discriminated in recent years (especially in 1958) usually did better than other types of candidate in 1967. The big gains among the party men were often achieved by *sortants* or celebrated figures.[2] Deputies who had won in 1962 only because of divided opposition, and had now been given up for lost by their parties, often gained thousands of votes even when they went down in the end. There was a marked difference between party performance in different constituencies, but it was not caused by a tidal wave sweeping new men to the front.

The false stability of the first ballot was to be matched by the false surprise of the second. The first round had assured a choice between two potential majorities. On the Right the Gaullists became the one alternative, for the CD failed to lead in enough seats to negotiate a high price for withdrawing elsewhere. This failure doomed Lecanuet's strategy of influencing the government from outside, while the success of Giscard's candidates seemed to show

---

[1] Above, pp. 172–3, 183. Defferre's ally Leenhardt did poorly against the Communist whose offer to stand down for him he had declined in 1962. Conversely, Montalat at Tulle kept safely ahead of the Communist for whom he was notoriously unwilling to withdraw [see p. 216 n. 2]. In each case it was the incumbent who did well.

[2] Of the Communist *sortants* 14 (over a third) gained over 5,000 votes; of the Federation, 23 (a quarter); of the Gaullists, 42, and even of the CD, 5. The prime minister added 10,000 to the Gaullist vote in Cantal, and M. Billotte 13,000 at St Maur; a former Gaullist minister, M. Boulloche, gained 14,000 to win Montbéliard for the Federation, and M. Mendès-France did the same at Grenoble for the PSU; but members whose fame was purely local, like M. Philibert (Socialist, Aix) or M. Richard (Gaullist, Pornic) also gained 12,000 each.

that conservative voters approved his slogan 'Oui mais' and his strategy of pressure from within.[1] The defeat of CD also had repercussions on the Left, impelling the Federation to apply its agreement with the Communists throughout the country. The second ballot, then, offered a choice between a coherent government party and a single opposition, allied if not united.

But this clear choice was less of a foregone conclusion than the press—and the authorities—assumed. They foresaw that Right and Left would not polarize perfectly, but mistakenly thought this would help the Gaullists. Official spokesmen seem to have misled themselves by their own ingenious arrangement of the figures to minimize the opposition vote, and other commentators—not least the pollsters—by the assumption that all CD voters would again go Gaullist while many Federation supporters would again refuse to go Communist. These predictions were hazardous, for the presidential election had shown the decline in anti-Communist and the strength of anti-Gaullist feeling: nearly all Tixier's followers and a large minority of Lecanuet's—both from the extreme Right and Left Centre—had chosen Mitterrand rather than de Gaulle. Now, once again, many anti-Gaullists rallied to the Left as the most effective opposition force. In 50 seats where a CD candidate had contested the second ballot in 1962, but allowed the Left and the Gaullists to fight it out in 1967, it seems that most of his vote went Left to Federation candidates and a third even to Communists. In the 15 seats fought at the second ballot by Gaullists, Communists and Centre in 1962, but by Gaullists and Federation only in 1967, the Left's share of the electorate rose from 18 to 37%.

Discipline within the Left was more effective than ever before. The Communists were less generous than in 1962, but made some concessions, withdrawing in fifteen 'special cases' in favour of Federation candidates with fewer votes than themselves but more chance of victory: in most of these seats the gap in votes was tiny, but one or two beneficiaries, close associates of Mitterrand, were as much as 3,000 behind their Communist rivals. In return, the Federation hardly ever invoked its 'escape clause' for seats which no left-winger could win, and only a very few CD candidates (a Radical deputy at Bayonne, a Conservative mayor at Brest) were enabled to defeat a Gaullist by its help. The alliance therefore applied almost everywhere, and it was honoured—partly because those Federation politicians unwilling to withdraw for a Communist had usually declined to stand rather than promise to do so. Even sitting Socialist members obediently gave up their seats to a rival they had failed to outpace. Only four Federation candidates broke

---

[1] But the President of the Republic did not; his government's prompt demand for special powers to reform the economy was clearly designed to show that what Giscard called 'the modern form of political action' was just as ineffective as the traditional.

TABLE 14 *Party shares of the Electorate; increase 1962–1967*
(second ballots)

Contest: Gaull. vs.		No. of seats	Left (Com, Fed)	Right (Gaull, CD)	Gaull. only
'62	'67				
Com	Com	66	7·4	0·5	—
Fed	Fed	66	7·4	2·3	—
Com	Fed	17	16·1	− 6·5	—
Com, CD	Com, CD	10	3·5	3·9	3·6
Com, CD	Com	18	11·2	− 6·9	10·4
Fed, CD	Fed	17	14·2	− 5·8	7·7
Com, CD	Fed	15	19·8	− 11·0	6·6
Fed vs. CD only		14	6·2	2·5	—

discipline and stayed in against a Communist with more votes; they were disavowed by the Federation, expelled from the Socialist party, and abandoned by between a fifth and a half of their first-ballot voters. Elsewhere, the pact was usually observed by the great bulk of Federation voters, but the defections were often heavy in Communist strongholds. Over the whole country it was clear that Federation candidates could garner votes which a Communist could not: over five-sixths of the Communists who fought at the second ballot polled fewer votes than Mitterrand had taken in their constituencies (many of the exceptions being sitting members), while half the PSU and Convention candidates, 70% of the Socialists and 75% of the Radicals ran ahead of him. Suspicion of the Communist Party was certainly weaker than ever in the past.[1] But it had not disappeared, and in marginal seats Communists still lost to Gaullists where a Federation man could have won. Had the Party made more concessions in 'special cases', there would have been no Gaullist majority in the Assembly.

The changes in second-ballot voting patterns brought a harvest of sixty seats to the Left: 32 to the Communist Party and 28 to its rivals. The Gaullists lost forty and the CD and miscellaneous groups, seventeen.[2] But these national totals were the result of more complex movements. The Gaullists won four of the five new constituencies around Paris (but lost a seat in each area affected, so that their success need not imply gerrymandering). Their lost seats in the capital, the north and east, Brittany and the Rhône Valley were somewhat offset by gains from the CD in the conservative west and in the Alps, and by a few gains from the Left, mostly in southern France

---

[1] The evidence suggests that defections did not only occur among non-Communists, and that in a few seats both in 1962 and in 1967 many Communist voters refused to obey instructions to vote for a particularly obnoxious Socialist.

[2] Outside metropolitan France the majority took 12 seats (instead of 7).

and usually where the Right had split its vote in 1962. Some further changes took place within the left-wing camp; the Communists took seven seats from Socialists or Radicals who had won on the second ballot with right-wing support in 1962, but now had to withdraw when they ran behind the Communist at the first ballot. However, the general pattern was clear enough. In the most industrialized areas the Gaullists lost 38 seats and captured only 5; in the mountainous regions—Alps, Pyrenees, Massif Central—they gained 12 and lost 3. Brittany was the only rural area where they suffered seriously. The party of modernization thus saved its majority by trimming its programme to satisfy the backward areas; and though its successes there were won by the promise to modernize, they are bound to increase the political weight of the decaying zones within the Gaullist movement. The price of victory may, therefore, be to weaken in the future some of the assets which have served the Gaullists so well in the past. And, while the party has consolidated its position, the personal appeal of the President plays a steadily diminishing role in its success.

Between 1958 and 1967 the French electorate was called eight times to the polls. Of all these eight occasions the 1967 election was certainly the one in which President de Gaulle played—by his own choice and that of the politicians—the least prominent part. His broadcast seems to have displeased his advisers, had little impact, and was not repeated a week later. His name was used far more sparingly by Gaullist candidates and propagandists than ever before—indeed the *Services et Méthodes* handbook for candidates referred to him only once. The 1967 results confirmed the hypothesis that the presidential vote for de Gaulle had shown a consolidation as well as a shrinking of Gaullist strength, and that the gap between the General's electoral support and that of his followers had sharply diminished as the former fell and the latter rose. The Fifth Republic candidates won 8,450,000 votes at the first ballot—1,500,000 more than in 1962 and only 2,000,000 fewer than de Gaulle on 5 December 1965. Although the numbers voting dropped somewhat between the two contests, no less than 60 Gaullist candidates won more votes than the General had gained in their constituencies.[1] In choosing the Fifth Republic's standard-bearers, managing their strategy and dominating the public campaign it was Pompidou, not de Gaulle, who appeared as the effective leader and, after the first ballot when

---

[1] Of the 60, 36 had a CD opponent, 24 had none. Among them were 16 of Giscard's men, 8 other Gaullists identified as non-UNR, and half the ministers who stood (12, not counting Giscard). Most were in the west, the Alps or the Massif Central, hardly any around Paris or in big cities, none in the industrial north. More than half were elected at the first ballot; of the 27 who fought the second, 9 again ran ahead of the General and so did 7 others (though 5 of the 10 and 3 of the 7 were nevertheless beaten).

victory was thought to be assured, was given most of the credit for it. Experienced Gaullist campaigners found their loyalty to the President was a diminishing asset—largely compensated by growing support for a regime which had given France the stable government she had never known before. Their impressions were confirmed by the opinion poll of April 1966, which found 35% saying they would be more inclined to vote for a candidate endorsed by the President and 34% less likely to do so; for a candidate favouring the institutions of the Fifth Republic, the corresponding figures were 41 and 23%. It was shrewd judgment to choose 'Fifth Republic' as the Gaullist party label, and to concentrate on the institutional debate into which the opposition parties were so obligingly eager to follow.

Yet while stability served the Gaullists better as a theme than ever before, it did not work exclusively to their advantage. Just as in municipal elections, well-known incumbents sometimes benefited from the voters' satisfaction and registered a sharp increase in their personal following. Still more strikingly, the Gaullists were not this time the only beneficiaries of the demand for stability. The Left also profited from the unity and discipline which made it look for the first time like a future alternative government, while the CD suffered from their failure to create the same impression.

The Gaullists' advantages remain, therefore, but their importance is likely to diminish. The decline in the President's personal appeal will be accentuated as the elderly voters who have always been most favourable to him cease to predominate among the electorate; in five years the oldest register in French history will have become the youngest. Nor is it certain that the appeal of the Fifth Republic will remain the Gaullists' monopoly in the future. The younger generation may find them less attractive if the backward areas come to acquire more influence within a party which has hitherto claimed with some justification to represent 'modern France'. Even their corner in stable government may be broken if, the day after tomorrow, their rivals on the Left begin at last to look capable of providing a real alternative.

Yet while they cannot count on repeating the victory of March 1967, there should be no doubt that a victory it was. Only in relation to the artificially inflated expectations of the first ballot could it be interpreted as a disappointment for the regime. The Gaullists have persuaded their countrymen to treat a general election as an occasion for choosing a government: a remarkable feat in France. At a bad moment for the economy, they have persuaded the electorate to return them to power for the third time running: a remarkable feat anywhere. After the presidential election, few people would have expected them to do as well. And whether they win or lose next time, they have gone far towards their long-term aim: to transform the French party system so that the old order cannot be brought back.

22 Change in the conservative west: the 1967 election in a region*

Under the Third Republic, the rural departments of Maine-et-Loire, Sarthe and Mayenne were among the most conservative in France. Their politics were dominated by local dignitaries and the traditional ferocious battle over clericalism. In 1945 the Socialists inherited anti-clerical Sarthe, the MRP Catholic Maine-et-Loire and Mayenne. Since 1958 the Gaullists have conquered the region by appealing to its conservative political ethos and to its dawning desire for economic progress. The majority now hold 11 of the 14 seats, but in local politics MRP and Socialists preserve some strength. While the return to single member constituencies in 1958 reinforced some political traditions, General de Gaulle himself and now the new institutions of the Fifth Republic have at last provided a national focus for politics; the stability of the regime is appreciated in this conservative area. The erosion of the ancient clerical controversy is particularly important, for the Catholic west is no longer morally isolated, while migration to the towns and the introduction of local industry have reduced its economic and social isolation.

In all three departments newer forces and organizations jostle entrenched habits and structures. Anxiety for the future makes a member of the majority —and a fortiori a minister—more attractive as a channel for the necessary state subsidies. But it is still important to have local roots. One of the few UNR deputies who has built a strong personal position, Joël Le Theule, mayor of Sablé, comes from an old Sarthe family; Michael d'Aillières (Republican Independent), hereditary deputy (and mayor of D'Aillières), tutoies his rural electors who call him M. Michel—'for after all we have known each other for over a century!'

In the countryside, notables and the administration still retain some of their traditional power. A Prefect can promote good candidates or suppléants or discourage them from standing; he may also attempt to pressure mayors who need his services, but he must do so prudently. Mayors too probably have more influence on candidates than electors; in this suspicious country, criticism is more likely to hurt a candidate than praise is to help him. But mud-slinging is likely to discredit the thrower as well as the target, and may finally benefit a third party.

* Originally entitled 'Change in the Conservative West'. Written with D. B. Goldey; see above, p. 204 n.

Similarly, potential deputies may be discouraged from standing against a member who has a Bishop's—or Abbot's—benevolent neutrality. Religious attitudes, therefore, still affect the selection of candidates. The influence of the Abbey of Solesmes is said to extend over some 800 (registered) souls in Sarthe, but the political activities of the clergy are now generally very discreet; only some of the older parish priests still publicly fight the wars of the Vendée at election time. Bishops urge the faithful to vote but avoid endorsing any party. The old parochial battle between *curé* and *instituteur* being much appeased, electors now worry more about economic problems than doctrinal disputes, and look to the Region, the National Plan and the Common Market to help resolve their difficultues.

Rural horizons have been further extended with the spread of radio and television to the remotest hamlets and the replacement of partisan local papers by the great (and politically neutral) regional dailies. It may cost a candidate a million francs to mail a special constituency newspaper to all electors. In the countryside television is probably the chief medium, especially in the evening. It seems to have been less important in this campaign than in 1965; but radio, particularly the debates on the two private networks, had considerable lunchtime audiences in the towns.

Despite manifest changes, rural campaigns are still largely carried on in the traditional manner, at least by candidates with a local base.[1] For a 'parachuted' Gaullist, information on the local scene from *Services et Méthodes* can be usefully completed by the Prefecture. Mayors and farmers' leaders must be cultivated, and each tiny commune visited, by all serious candidates. In the village café, the candidate stands a round, an earnest of his interest in the inhabitants, whose problems he will then discuss. Saturday market day (eve of poll), candidate and *suppléant* may go through the square shaking hands, buying (and being offered) a round in the local, visiting supporters (champagne) and the Maison d'Agriculture (whisky nowadays).

If local problems and personalities are still prominent in the countryside, national political issues and themes are more important in the towns, and the style of campaigning is different too. At Le Mans both Gaullists and Communists spent vast amounts on posters, tracts and rallies, and invited visiting luminaries to their big public meetings.[2] The most original campaign was run by Edgard Pisani (Minister of Equipment), who was suspected of trying to turn his natural brusqueness to electoral advantage. Greeted by animal noises at a meeting in Mayenne, he remarked on the number of cows in the audience; that meeting had to be abandoned. Mooing, sabot-shod

---

[1] Outsiders may have to stress national issues; the Federation candidate in Sablé hardly mentioned local questions.

[2] The candidate did strikingly well, despite the fears of one shrewd Gaullist campaigner that massive expenditure might shock local opinion.

hecklers followed him back to Angers where he exceeded their fondest expectations: 'You really have to be primitive to come to a Minister's meeting dressed like that to ask your stupid questions!'

Pisani's tactlessness was a heaven-sent excuse for criticism by clerical, conservative Angevins, offended by his divorce and his agnosticism, but unwilling to say so publicly (certainly a change). Nonetheless they reluctantly voted for him in the end: the Minister had trumps in the promise of investment credits. The rousing of the region from its secular stagnation was in fact the major long-term issue of the campaign. Generally this aided the technocratically oriented Gaullists who hold the purse strings (although the area has been losing ground since 1958). Joël Le Theule was made to promise in one village to report to them every Christmas, as someone they could trust, on their future economic prospects. In a hamlet near Mamers, Michel d'Aillières explained how it could get credits to improve its failing water supply and develop communal land for commuters from the town.

This new interest in economic development owes much to the modernizing administration, but also to the politicians: Charles Barangé, MRP patriarch in Maine-et-Loire; Robert Buron, its leader in Mayenne; Joël Le Theule (Gaullist) in Sarthe; all members (Barangé is president) of the Pays de la Loire Regional Expansion Committee. Representing three generations, their initiatives appeal mainly to those under forty. But whatever the electoral results, men like Barangé and Buron who founded MRP to replace charity with justice, and to reconcile Catholics and the Republic, have won a permanent victory.

The decline of the chateau and state subsidies to parochial schools have freed the Church from its sterile battle with the Republic. Only the Communists mentioned the church-schools issue in their posters—and then only in small type. Young working class priests (unlike their bourgeois brothers) now share the political and social attitudes of their poorer parishioners, and are drawn to the PSU if not the Federation.[1] The traditional paternalism of chatelain and mill owner is increasingly resented by farm tenant and factory worker. In Anjou the CFDT, led by militants formed in the *Jeunesses Ouvrières Chrétiennes*, alone has labour leaders capable of arguing with the Prefect.[2] A new generation of peasant leaders from the *Jeunesses Agricoles Chrétiennes* see their future in modernization and Europe rather than tariffs and moonshining.

Indeed, most of the usually outrageous religious and economic pressure groups, like the *bouilleurs de cru*, were remarkably reticent during the

---

[1] Some conservative parents even feel that state schools are less subversive of the social order than some of the younger parochial-school masters!

[2] Though still not ready to break with French working class tradition and sit on the official Regional Expansion Committee.

campaign. Only the small shopkeepers and stall-holders clamoured in the traditional way for abrogation of the TVA (value-added tax), largely because it was unfamiliar and involved bookkeeping. Gaullist members were anxious to explain that they were in favour of exemptions and simplifications, while at the same time extending a technocratic hand to the younger business and professional men who found in Pisani the sort of no-nonsense candidate dear to them.

Its young *patronat* tempted by Gaullist 'efficacity' and its labour and peasant activists demoralized by the defeat of Defferre's 'grand federation', MRP found it difficult to produce attractive young candidates for *Centre Démocrate*. Even where it did, CD's conservative cast repelled left-wing MRP militants (and some local leaders too) without attracting back its traditional, Catholic clientèle from the Gaullists; once a party bastion, the region now returns only one MRP, from Mayenne. Even there, the majority took MRP's other seat and held the third. It is also dominant in Sarthe, where Le Theule and d'Aillières won easy victories on the first ballot. The Gaullist ex-mayor of Le Mans narrowly survived a challenge from his MRP successor*—who garnered some Socialist votes. Le Mans Socialists, divided over municipal cooperation with the Communists, were deserted by many voters who helped triumphantly re-elect the department's one Communist incumbent next door. But in its last stronghold in rural Sarthe, the Federation comfortably returned its sitting member. Here Socialist collaboration with the 'new left' in Mitterrand's Federation (and 'republican discipline' with the Communists) was perhaps facilitated by the rallying of their hereditary enemies, chateau and abbey, to the majority. In Maine-et-Loire too, the right—having finally forgiven the regime for Algeria—now votes solidly Gaullist; they crushed a young rebel mayor† to hold five seats on the first ballot, and Pisani's on the second. Of the region's 14 constituencies, the majority won 8 on the first round, 3 more on the run-off; Communists, Federation and MRP held one seat each, on the second ballot.

For all the ferment, the elections in this conservative area favoured sitting members, 12 of whom were returned, 9 of them Gaullist. Pisani's difficult victory indicates that religion no longer bars the way to the pork barrel; the inner west is coming into the national circuit. The majority, playing successfully (for the moment) on both stability and change, has still to implant itself and permanently conquer the new voters. 'In three years it will all have changed, though God knows exactly how,' remarked an intelligent young sub-prefect. 'Unless the notables keep up they've had it. But they're past it. A new generation is coming!'

* Above, p. 180.   † Of Cholet; above, p. 180.

23 A precarious regime: the Events of May 1968*

by DAVID B. GOLDEY

'Their election begins. Our struggle continues' read the posters of the *atelier populaire* of the *ex-Ecole des Beaux Arts*. The real campaign for the June election took place in the streets of Paris in May; the voting returns simply confirmed the last great popular demonstration of 'The Events', the massive turnout on the Champs Elysées after de Gaulle's speech on the 30th May. For this was no ordinary election to confirm or replace a majority. It was the last and only peaceful way left to reaffirm the authority of the state and the legitimacy of the regime, shaken by student riots in Paris, a nation-wide general strike, and a middle-class crisis of conscience and confidence in itself. The other alternative was civil war.

The general election of March 1967, which returned a narrow and uncertain Gaullist majority, was the first to have taken place in thoroughly normal conditions since World War 1. That of June 1968, which returned a massive Gaullist majority followed a period of quite abnormal and sustained chaos. The dissolved Assembly had voted its confidence in Prime Minister Pompidou's government on May 22nd, in the midst of public disorder, and despite the silence of the Elysée, the paralysis of the state and the disarray of the majority. The students, whose lack of confidence in the system had pre-cipitated the crisis, boycotted the elections to the slogan of '*élections trahison*'.

Perhaps one ought not to be startled that French students challenged their government in a year when Berlin students forced the resignation of a mayor and American students help convince President Johnson to retire. Nor be astounded—after Berkeley had helped elect Governor Reagan and Berlin had contributed to the progress of the NDP—that riots in Paris led to the liberation of ex-general Salan (leader of the fascist OAS) and the election of a vast conservative Gaullist majority. Nor be surprised by the brutal reaction of the police in Paris, Berlin or Chicago. Perhaps one ought to settle for *The Times*'s analysis of 'student troubles in the western world—a combin-ation of educational grievances, political disillusion, moral concern, frustra-

---

* Originally entitled 'The Events of May and the French General Election of June 1968'. From *Parliamentary Affairs*, vol. 21, no. 4 (Autumn 1968). The second part, reprinted as chap. 24, is from vol. 22, no. 2 (Spring 1969).

tion, boredom, enthusiasm, and a certain amount of imitativeness'. Nonetheless, although student unrest is now endemic throughout the world, it took a particularly dramatic turn in France. How does one explain these inchoate events, foreseen neither by the authorities nor by the revolutionary activists?

THE BACKGROUND

The first element is demographic. After almost a century of stagnant population, there was a marked rise in the French birth rate at the Liberation. The First World War gave a peculiar skew to the French population curve: the generation that came of age from 1935 to 1945 is very thin on the ground. A relatively small active population supports both the great new wave of the not yet productive young and the growing numbers of longer-lived unproductive old people. This reduced generation rules and runs the country: in the civil service, business, the university, political parties and trade unions. Because of the peculiarly hierarchical structure of much of French life, in the Communist party and trades unions almost as much as in the university, the secular war between successive generations is perhaps particularly acute. Moreover, for the Resistance generation which has a practical monopoly of the French Establishment, and which has known depression, defeat, occupation, and the disappointed hopes of the Liberation, the abstract student complaints of the oppressive and repressive nature of French society and the evils of more widespread prosperity, seem even more incredible, incomprehensible and insane than they do to the middle-aged in countries with less tortured histories. And as in other countries, the confrontation between mutually uncomprehending generations takes place most acutely where they meet most directly: at the universities. In France, for want of intelligent forward planning, the old structures of the university have been submerged by the great increase in the number of students, a result of the baby boom plus easier access to university studies—but not for the children of the working class of whom there are few in French universities. The crisis has been particularly acute in Paris, where there are now well over 100,000 students, more than in all of France in 1945.

But Paris is not only congested with students—and traffic. Difficulties of housing and transport in all the great towns of the world make life in them nasty and brutal for the poor; the progressive destruction of urban amenities by the invading automobile is perhaps the most striking sign of societies which spend too much on individual consumption and not enough on social investment; what French students came to denounce as the *société de consommation*. Paris has these problems, plus the State as well. It has been commonplace, since Tocqueville, to remark that authority and activity are excessively concentrated in the capital by a centralized, bureaucratic state,

227

constructed under the ancien régime, and completed by Napoleon on the ruins of the Revolution. This centralization means also that relatively limited problems of public order in central Paris may threaten the government of all France, as in 1830 and 1848. It also helps explain that permanent feature of French political life, the divorce between the state and the citizen (sometimes dressed up as alienation), and a style of authority brilliantly described by Michel Crozier, which encourages autocracy at the top and anarchy at the bottom at one and the same time.[1]

The effects of the traditional French style of authority and centralization have been more apparent since 1958 with the decline of Parliament and the political parties, and the monarchical government of General de Gaulle. The collapse of any effective Opposition and the special role of the Elysée have turned most ministers of the Republic into something like the secretaries of state of the old monarchy, half way between courtiers and quasi-permanent under-secretaries. Increasingly recruited from the upper ranks of the civil service, ministers (with a few notable exceptions) became insulated from public opinion and the daily problems of reconciling opposing political priorities, and grew excessively concerned with administrative convenience, fixing favoured interest groups, and avoiding initiatives and responsibilities which might compromise them with the Elysée. Mediocre ministers often satisfied themselves with the complacent manipulation of public opinion, echoing the self-satisfaction of the General at his press conferences. The government's misuse of the news services of the state broadcasting system, the ORTF, was but one example of a style of authority erected into a system of government. Far-seeing Gaullists saw the disadvantages of this method but General de Gaulle himself felt televised adulation was necessary to combat an occasionally critical press. Controls that were acceptable during the Algerian war were maintained when a prosperous nation was at peace; the French were treated by their government as 'perpetual minors'. One reaction to this attitude was the initial public sympathy for the explosion of May.

But centralization also had consequences for the workings of government and the universities, the trades unions and the political parties. French government in the first fortnight of May was a classic example of how not to manage a crisis, of dithering, crossed lines of authority, flights from responsibility and of too little and too late. The difficulties began when the Prime Minister, alone capable of moving the government machine, was away in Afghanistan, and the Elysée was too distant from the conflict and the President of the Republic too tired to make the necessary decisions. The inherited centralization of the state, the increasing bureaucratization of politics, the

---

[1] Cf. *The Bureaucratic Phenomenon* (London, 1964).

reluctance to act without a nod from the Elysée, meant that when anarchy challenged authority in Paris, paralysis struck the provinces.

At Paris the problems of centralization and bureaucratization in the University were compounded by intolerable overcrowding and under-administration. The Ministry of National Education managed to combine all the faults of the Fourth Republic with most of the Fifth; traditionally the preserve of the profession it supposedly controlled, it was nearly impervious to reform since the political radicalism of French teachers is equalled only by their professional conservatism. An attempt was made under the Fifth by giving the Ministry a Secretary General, not quite the equivalent of a British Permanent Undersecretary. But Ministers changed frequently and were not always noted for their reforming zeal or administrative capacity, and the secretary-general was the Elysée's man in the Ministry. An internecine war pitted the permanent services, the secretary-general and the minister's *cabinet* in a war of all against all, Leviathan in the Elysée intervening only occasionally. The result was the Fouchet reforms, left incomplete, too rigid and always underfinanced, when Alain Peyrefitte became Minister of Education in 1967. Peyrefitte, a young man with a distinguished career to make, sought to protect himself by packing his inflated *cabinet* with personal cronies. Centralization meant that when the students took on the university authorities they directly challenged the authority of the State. It meant that the university authorities could make no real concessions without consulting the Minister, a man who in May 1968 had been sitting for 15 months on a file full of incomplete reforms for fear of controversy which might upset the General and compromise his own political future.

Centralization also meant that when workers went on strike, they aimed to wring concessions from the state, which they held responsible for mounting unemployment, and to force the state to wring from the employers concessions which the unions were usually took weak to wrest for themselves. For another permanent characteristic of French public life, a counterpart to the centralized organized state, has been the weak organization and the fear of central direction in political parties and trade unions. French unions claim to represent something like 20% of the labour force; the claim is certainly exaggerated. Out of 2,000,000 claimed members, perhaps half are up to date in the payment of their dues, which are in any case wholly inadequate. Moreover the unions are divided among five central bodies; half the total membership is split between the CGC (office staff and technicians), the (mildly socialist) FO, the CFDT, of Catholic inspiration and the most militant of all the centrals, and the CFTC which remains Catholic and conservative. The other half is in the CGT, under Communist domination since 1945. But even the CGT retains its original confederal structure and part of its old anarcho-syndicalist tradition, shared also with the breakaway FO and even the CFDT. This indigenous tradition of the French labour movement, particularly strong for example among the Paris engineers, glorifies action and spontaneity; it denies organization and negotiation; its myth is the *grand soir* not the long pull; it is a reflection of the historic weakness of French labour rather than a source of strength to it.

Like the trade unions, French parties are stuck with doctrines and old quarrels which no longer correspond to their situation. The traditional form of a French party has been that of a loose alliance of local potentates in a national electoral cooperative. The organizational backbone of the Gaullist parties since 1958 has been the state machine in Paris and the provinces. Only the Communist party has an organization in any way comparable even to the British Liberals, and of all the major western Communist parties, the PCF has suffered most from the problems of destalinization.

THE PCF

The most stalinist of the major western parties and the most firmly locked in its ghetto, the party has had to cope all at once with destalinization, the Algerian war, de Gaulle, and the increasing prosperity and decreasing militancy of its aging base. It suffered not only from a dramatic loss of votes in 1958 but also from a crisis of recruitment at a time when its polar star, the Moscow dominated international communist movement, was breaking up. The disaggregation of the international movement, and the challenge to Soviet primacy in it, posed a special problem for the PCF. A mass party in a democratic country, with a revolutionary doctrine but supremely opportunistic tactics, the PCF made faith in the Soviet Union the surrogate for faith in the revolution which never occurred in France, and seemed increasingly improbable as the French working class began to taste the delights of consumer durables.

This dilemma also presented the party with its opportunity to escape from its ghetto. As the prospect of Russian invasion and Communist insurrection receded, the PCF became less frightening as a political ally. In this operation it was helped by the Gaullists' strangely assorted policies. Domestically the Gaullists were trying to polarize political life, internationally to depolarize it—hoping to capitalize exclusively both on the latent, if waning, anti-communism and the latent, if anodine, anti-Americanism of the majority of the electorate. The General's assault on American hegemony gratified the Soviet Union and its French friends and, in a sense, legitimized the foreign orientation of the PCF (although occasionally embarrassing it locally). The party was further helped to reintegrate itself into normal French political life by apparent destalinization in Russia, ideological concessions by the PCF, and the desperate need of Socialist deputies for Communist votes on the second ballot of general elections. In the short run, the General's foreign policy was far more agreeable than anything to be expected from the Communists' left-wing electoral allies; in the long term, the party might profit from the government's conservative social and economic policy, which involved squeezing domestic reforms for foreign priorities. The longer the General stayed in power the further polarized French politics would become, to the ultimate benefit of the PCF: for the General's plebiscitary appeal would die with him but by then the democratic parties might be permanently weakened. Moreover, for their own immediate advantage the Gaullists and Communists had helped the old party bosses wreck the one possibility of a strong left-centre coalition, Gaston Defferre's attempt to reform and enlarge the Socialist party (SFIO). The General's rule thus gave the party certain immediate gratification while promising substantial long-term advantages.

The PCF therefore voted with the Gaullists on most foreign policy issues in the Assembly, while at elections it bartered the votes of its obedient followers to pay its passage back into a left coalition of which it was by far the strongest partner. It was ready to make a certain number of electoral and ideological concessions to its allies to make sure they were not tempted back toward the Centre, and to increase their dependence on the party. But the concessions would not be sufficient to elect a left-wing majority which the PCF did not dominate: otherwise the Communists rightly feared their sometime partners would abandon them after the election to govern with the Centre.

However uneasy its alliance with the left, however embarrassing its foreign policy options, the great difficulty of the PCF was internal. It was trying, in a polycentric world, to accommodate destalinization and to escape from its isolation; but all these three changes threatened what it was most determined not to surrender: the special organization and discipline, role and claims of any communist party. Verbal gymnastics could modify the claims in order to satisfy the SFIO; its own municipal practice and its electoral propaganda made it look more and more like another social democratic party; the party's own militants were increasingly lacking in combativity (though its *permanents* were still available for breaking up meetings of the new Maoist party). But those attracted to more thorough-going reform could now look to Italy, and those already repelled by it to Peking: both fractions received moral and material support from these two powerful *partis frères* while the leadership continued to look to Moscow. The one major western party in a position to try and put the Italian theories into practice, the PCF feared for its apparatus if it did. No longer really a party of structural opposition, it sought to root out Chinese sympathisers for fear they would develop a base in the party and then split it, as the Communists themselves had done with the Socialists in

1920. The party thus refused to choose between its domestic interests and mass electorate, and its primary foreign loyalties and bolshevik organization. But despite the denunciation of Israel in June 1967, it seemed that in the long run it would find itself in a situation where it would finally abandon the USSR and with it the revolutionary myth.

Of the two great areas of French life where the writ of the Communist party ran—the intellectual and working class communities—the moral and organizational authority of the party was sapped in the former and disputed in the latter; the PCF had therefore lost much of its moral hegemony and some of its organizational clout. But the habits of mind it had nurtured and maintained for a generation both in the university and among the workers survived: a theoretical utopianism combined in practice with intellectual mendacity, extreme verbal violence, and unscrupulous opportunism, all redeemed by the revolutionary myth.

The tensions in the party between the Italian and Chinese alternatives were felt most acutely among intellectuals and the students of the Union des Etudiants Communistes (UEC), which had also been penetrated by Trotskyites. Finally, in order to destroy the base of the Italian faction and to avoid the risk of infection, the party decided to break the UEC; the largest fraction reformed under the leadership of Alain Krivine in the Trotskyite Jeunesse Communiste Révolutionnaire (JCR). Instead of cutting the ground out from under the heretics, the party had cut itself off from the students, as it had previously alienated many intellectuals. Released from the rigid discipline of the party by the destruction of the UEC, its student members naturally gravitated to the JCR and the FER, another smaller Trotskyite organization, and to various Maoist groups, the most important of which is the Jeunesse Communiste Marxiste Léniniste (JCML).

Action was one way for a '*groupuscule*' (a mini-sect or grouplet) to increase its audience. Examples of student activism elsewhere (especially Germany) served as a goad; the JCR had already made a name for itself in the winter riots in Berlin. With memories only of the PCF's ambiguous position over Algeria, its electoral opportunism, and its hesitations over Vietnam, the students looked for where the action was, and found it incarnated in the colonial wars of the Third World. If the European working classes, like the American before them, had sold out for refrigerators and jalopies, the historical mission of the working class to liberate all mankind by liberating itself would have to be transferred to the *pays prolétaires* of Asia, Africa and Latin America.

Moreover UNEF, the French National Union of Students, was also prey to attempted takeovers by the groupuscules, also in an attempt to enlarge their audience. The crisis within UNEF resulted from the breakup of the two well-disciplined groups that had formerly disputed the leadership of the once representative body: the Communists and the left Catholics. Student organization was weak anyhow, especially in the newly built faculties. UNEF had been systematically discriminated against by the government, to punish it for its independent (and courageous) stand on the Algerian war. It had already lost ground in several faculties, with the predictable result: it was pushed towards extremism in an attempt to recoup its losses, since it no longer had anything to lose on the other side. As the groupuscules struggled, sometimes physically at UNEF congresses, to take over the organization for their own political ends, more moderate or apolitical students decided their interests would be better preserved by leaving UNEF, or having their faculties represented within UNEF by 'autonomous' unions. Such was the case, for example, at 'Science Po', the Paris Institute of Political Science, where potential civil servants frequently prepared for their exams. The battle of tendencies was so severe that in July 1967 the UNEF conference rejected the report of its President; unable to compose their differences, willing to break the organization if they could not control it, the groupuscules further discredited UNEF. In May 1968, the President of UNEF had recently resigned and the organization was led by its vice-president, Jacques Sauvageot. Having helped torpedo the one representative student organization because it wasn't tame enough, the government found itself in the midst of half-completed and ill-conceived educational reforms with the University of Paris submerged in a flood of discontented students, and without representative student spokesmen. It was to find that disorganization was more dangerous than organized opposition. Whereas UNEF had lost its subsidy for criticizing government policy as it affected students, the new generation of student activists wanted to mobilize students for an attack on the state. But with the dilapidation of UNEF, mobilization of students on university questions was not easy.

Along with the decline of UNEF and the PCF, the other force in the student community, the Catholic Church and the JEC (Jeunesse Etudiante Chrétienne), was also being shaken. For less obvious than the developments on the marxist left have been the organizational problems and doctrinal disarray of the French Catholic Church, the other great exception with the PCF to the organizational poverty of French public life and the only other great national institution with a solid base and a self-confident world view. The fixation on Cuba, Algeria, North Vietnam or China as the last best hope of mankind also found an echo among left Catholics. The missionary tradition of the French Church had sensitized it to the problems of decolonization through its experience in Asia and Africa, and then to the awful economic and social problems of the underdeveloped countries in that last great

233

reservoir of popular Catholicism, South America. Difficulties in some of the women's orders, the radical example of the Dominicans, the influence of Teilhard de Chardin, PSU curates in the West, the revival in a modified form of the worker priest movement all testified to this ferment. Thus, the Church like the PCF was going through an intellectual crisis, and was finding its moral authority questioned from the left by its own members. The rejection of capitalism on grounds of Catholic social theory, the interest in South America and Asia, buttressed hostility to the United States and provided a further bridge across to the new left; and Vietnam was probably the keystone of the main arch. Several Catholic student militants were among the first to be arrested in May.

Vietnam was crucial in other respects too. It pressed especially on French sensibility since France had fought her own '*sale guerre*' there from 1946 to 1954. It seemed to show that if the most powerful nation in the world could be beaten by a small but determined people, revolution elsewhere, anywhere, was possible. 'Vietnam is the Stalingrad of Imperialism' was a favourite thought of the Maoists. Vietnam provided the Trotskyite and Chinese factions with a common platform, an argument against the official Communists, and a reservoir of sympathy and support which they otherwise would not have had, or risked forfeiting by their arid and endless doctrinal battles. It provided the occasion for confrontations with the university and the police; it encouraged a running battle on the left bank and at Nanterre between the extreme left and the extreme right, organized in the proto-fascist league, *Occident*. Remembering the services *Occident* supporters had formerly rendered beating up opponents of the Algerian war, the police tended to treat them with kid gloves; the same moderation was not often shown with left wing demonstrators. All this activity maintained a febrile atmosphere in the Faculties. And this excitement permitted those students who were dismayed by the dismal theoretical arguments of the groupuscules to be salvaged and utilized by the extremists in various front organizations. The *Comités Viet-Nam de base* which organized meetings; the '*quête d'un milliard*' set up to collect a milliard francs to buy hospital ships for Ho; and various Viet-Nam Solidarity Committees, in which the PSU (the small left Socialist party) and the Catholics were also active, all participated in the same work. The *quête* was at first violently denounced by the Communists who rallied to it only late in the day. The committees, therefore, also served as engines of war against the PCF, and during the Events they served as the base for the 400-odd Comités d'Action Populaire formed in Paris and the provinces, the Comités d'Action Lycéens (CAL) formed in the grammar schools, and sometimes as the base for the *comités d'occupation* in the Faculties.

Former Communists and left Catholics also shared a systematic training in apologetics, and their intellectual reflexes were often similar; furthermore, the pattern of French instruction rewards the well-finished theoretical exposition of abstract categories. The intellectual traditions of both organizations and the entire bent of French lycée training produced activists ready to argue furiously—and without reference to mere fact—over the correct interpretation of Frantz Fanon, or Régis Debray or Chairman Mao. But even expert casuistry can become tiresome and JCR and JCML enthusiasm tended to be dulled by dreary cell arguments on the proper line. Vietnam provided an opportunity to escape interminable discussions for real *engagement*, while still dreaming perhaps of a French cultural revolution. And there was the old and honoured tradition of the French *engagé* intellectual, found in Sartre's books and Camus's life, daring all on an existential choice in a hostile universe, like Ho or Guevara or Debray; of action against great odds and an opportunity to outrage the bourgeoisie. Finally, the utopian desperation and romantic revolutionary myths now common to students throughout Europe and America had a special resonance in a country with a revolutionary tradition. That tradition was shared as well by some of the teachers who had most contact with the students, the 25 to 35 year old *assistants* and *maître-assistants* who had already been embittered by what they saw as Socialist treason, Communist duplicity and Gaullist repression during the Algerian war. They were also the slaveys of the French university system; students and *assistants* thus had a further common interest in university reform.

Nonetheless, if alienation in and from the University was more widespread than was understood, no one, including the most committed revolutionaries, expected the May events. The various police and special services knew of most of the activists and their organizations; but the very disorganization of the system of higher education made it difficult to estimate the relative importance of these groups and their potential audience. Trouble had been confidently predicted at the beginning of every recent academic year because of the pitiable state of the University of Paris. But catastrophe on this front had been inevitable for too long and always avoided, or at least postponed, at the last minute by patchwork improvisations, *le système D*. The usual explosion predicted for autumn 1967 did not occur, just as the trades unions had been unable to mobilize against the decrees raising social security contributions, and Edgar Faure had managed to buy off the peasants before the elections of 1967. The students' sympathy for the General's anti-American foreign policy seemed to mitigate their hostility to the dominant French caste, and their 'revulsion from the full-bellied consumer's society'. Every poll showed general approval for the President's foreign options, even if different groups were dissatisfied with the domestic consequences of that policy: unemployment and the economic stabilization plan were the price for a

235

mounting gold hoard. The power elite thus enjoyed the protective coloration of *grandeur*, and the prestige of the President offered some compensation for the widespread if apparently aimless resentment at the domination of everyday life by the Establishment.[1]

France was rapidly modernizing and urbanizing, though the political system might not properly echo the dislocations and dissatisfactions caused by the simultaneous effects of an industrial and a managerial-technological revolution; their challenge to traditional French values, not least bourgeois ones, had been discussed by various scholars, French and foreign. But it could be argued that the coming generation was self-confident, flexible and numerous enough to cope. The university, which had once prepared a small number of the sons of the bourgeoisie for the leisurely life of the liberal professions, was now responsible for the numerous sons and daughters of the middle classes destined to end as *cadres moyens*.

The marriage of France with her century was perhaps more of a shotgun wedding than was apparent or admitted and the strain of getting French industry ready for the opening of the frontiers under the new accelerated Common Market timetable was considerable. But the Gaullists continued to win elections and the prestige of the General seemed only occasionally tarnished; and the regime itself seemed less and less dependent on this prestige, and appeared to be gaining acceptance in its own right. It was conceivable that Gaullism would render reform of the party system inevitable if only by so thoroughly undermining the old parties. Prosperity seemed to have drained the revolutionary zeal of the Communist party's working class reservoir. May Day parades before the First World War had provoked the middle classes to stock up and fill bathtubs with water, their instinctive reaction to the threat of siege. In the 1950s the parades had been banned for fear the party faithful might riot. The May Day march of 1968, the first permitted in 15 years, was as orderly and prosperous as a Labour Day march in New York. In the long run, it was reasonable to suppose that the PCF itself might be absorbed into the system and that France would be without a party of structural opposition for the first time since the Great Revolution, with a consequent stabilization of her political life. The old revolutionary tradition, which had passed from the pre-1914 syndicalists to the post-1917 bolsheviks, now threatened to be snatched from the PCF by the cultural revolutionaries of the Latin Quarter. That might not be an unmixed blessing. As Annie Kriegel noted in August 1966,

it remains to be seen what will happen in a country like France, for so long used mercilessly to rending itself, if a party of real structural opposition is no longer

[1] A. Grosser, 'The French Power Elite', *Encounter*, xxx, 6 (June 1968), p. 56; F. Bourricaud, 'The French Student Revolt', *Survey* 68 (July 1968), pp. 30–1.

available. Ought one to consider that contemporary society is endowed with an exceptional power of assimilation, an invincible taste for homogeniety and a tranquil indifference to Utopia? Or ought not one to think that revolutionary protest, bereft of political expression, will take novel and not necessarily less costly courses?[1]

But did it really matter if the students, traditionally anarcho-surrealist by temperament anyway, had a new cause? It did. For the progressive disintegration of the University of Paris meant that a minor accident might have irreversible consequences. The accident was the conjunction of the campaign against the Vietnam war with the campaign against the new university campus on the north-western edge of Paris, Nanterre.

The government's attitude to the early phase of the Vietnam agitation was ambiguous. *Occident* was allowed to raid opponents of the war, and demonstrators were often roughly treated. All demonstrations, even innocent if rowdy celebrations of the end of exams, had been severely repressed in the Latin Quarter ever since the Algerian War. The editor of the *New Statesman* has recounted how the experience of one of these incidents converted him to socialism. Paddy wagons could regularly be seen in the square before the Sorbonne, and not only students, but clients of side-walk cafes, visitors, and inhabitants of the neighbourhood, were all accustomed to being pushed about by the police at the first hint of any trouble. But in the spring of 1968, a mammoth anti-war demonstration in the Boulevard St-Michel was not only tolerated but encouraged by the authorities. There were well-informed whispers that among the welter of pro-Ho groups, many of which discussed the theory of urban guerilla warfare, one was a front organization for the French secret service, run out of the Elysée. The government encouraged this harmless (it thought) agitation when it suited its own foreign policy aims, and perhaps also to embarrass the PCF; in sharp contrast, it systematically used the police to discourage and repress demonstrations on domestic or educational matters.

In the Latin Quarter the animation was confined to the streets; but at Nanterre it invaded the university buildings. Nanterre was the setting of the duplicate Arts, Social Studies and Law Faculties, an attempt to take some of the pressure off the Sorbonne. It provided some residential accommodation, mostly for poorer and foreign students; otherwise it recruited from the western quarters of the capital, the wealthy residential districts. It opened with a car park but no library, surrounded by a shanty-town for immigrant workers, and in four years grew from 2,000 to 11,000 students. Appropriately enough, the rail link from Paris stopped at '*Nanterre La*

---

[1] 'Les Communistes Français et le Pouvoir', *Le Socialisme Français et le Pouvoir* (Paris 1966), p. 217. [On the Gaullists see above, p. 221.]

Folie—Complexe Universitaire'. In this half-completed university complex with no social amenities, set in a reeking slum with neither cafes nor cinemas, the only private distraction available was sex, and the only communal activity, politics. The groupuscules had some success in the vastly overcrowded sociology department where they found a certain number of sympathetic professors. But all the organized groups, including UNEF, were weak at Nanterre.

The first sit-in at Nanterre, in March 1967, was in the women's dormitories as a protest against restricted visiting hours. Agitation continued and the police were called in. Instead of a student union, a swimming pool was built (more, it ought to be added, than is provided in most French universities) and opened in January 1968 by the Minister for Youth and Sports, M. Missoffe (whose daughter was at Nanterre). But the inauguration did not pass without an incident provoked by Daniel Cohn-Bendit, who now emerged into public prominence as a new student leader. But the Minister emerged with some credit from the encounter, and Cohn-Bendit wrote to apologize. The situation continued to degenerate however in much the same way as it had at Berkeley or Columbia, where student dissatisfaction had become linked with wider political issues. And as in America, action was seen as the best way to rally the amorphous mass of dissatisfied students; the more outrageous the better, since retaliation by the authorities would bring fresh converts out of a sense of solidarity. The occasion came with the Tet offensive; to celebrate, militants of the Comité Viet-Nam National broke the windows of the American Express Company. One of those arrested was a JCR student from Nanterre; to retaliate the Nanterre JCR and the anarchists (with whom Cohn-Bendit was linked) occupied during the night of the 22 March the holy of holies, the room where the University Senate met. Thus born, the Movement of 22 March then proceeded to a more or less systematic disruption of the university. Lectures were interrupted with demands for discussions on Vietnam; when this was refused, the Movement would simply move in and take over the hall; the walls of the Faculty were covered with slogans. Confrontation was inevitable; the Dean had already closed the Faculties at the end of March. Student radicals planned an Anti-Imperialist Day for the 2nd and 3rd of May. Word of an attack by *Occident* inspired them to block most of the entrances to the buildings and arm themselves for battle; inside, professors were prevented from lecturing in halls arrogated by the militants to their seminars and films. After an inspection by the Rector of the University of Paris himself, the Dean of Nanterre again closed the Faculties the evening of 2 May, and Cohn-Bendit and five others were charged before the disciplinary committee of the University of Paris, which had not seriously inconvenienced anyone in living memory— and which sits at the Sorbonne.

THE EVENTS

The arena was thus moved to the middle of Paris, and Cohn-Bendit, certainly the most acute of all the various student leaders, brought his troops to the Sorbonne, where they massed in the courtyard on the afternoon of Friday, 3 May. The Rector of the University of Paris and the Dean of the Sorbonne knew what had been going on at Nanterre, and were concerned for the proper preparation of a grammar examination for teachers. Moreover, *Occident* threatened to invade the courtyard too and fight it out with the JCR, the FER, and the 22 March Movement, whose leaders and *services d'ordre* were all there. Students in the courtyard may have started breaking up chairs in order to be ready to defend themselves. In any case, the Rector and Dean had the building cleared, thereby increasing the numbers in the courtyard and after consulting the Minister called on the police, who had already steered the *Occident* commando away from the Sorbonne, to evacuate the Sorbonne. The Prefect of Police, Maurice Grimaud insisted on being given a written order, but the police seem to have decided that if they were going to have to do the job they at least would use the opportunity to catch the ringleaders with whom they had already skirmished at Nanterre. The students in the courtyard therefore marched out of the Sorbonne—and into the assembled police vans, apparently to the surprise of the university authorities, and to the fury of a great mass of students now assembled in the Latin Quarter.

Once the police had carried off the revolutionary leaders and their shock troops for an identity check, ordinary students started battling with the police, as traffic backed up on the left bank. Members of the SNESup, a left-wing teachers union, had been trying to convince UNEF not to boycott exams; as they left the Sorbonne for a break they were pushed around by the police, and so were residents of the Quarter. By evening, 15 years of bad temper and abuse of police authority had united students, staff and local inhabitants against the forces of order for treating them as juvenile delinquents—and against a system which treated all Frenchmen as perpetual minors, while feeding them on a steady diet of smug official self-satisfaction. No one thought the regime or public order were seriously threatened, so people felt free to give vent to their underlying frustrations. Indeed, in the beginning the Events were a tribute to the solidarity of the regime, if a condemnation of its style of government. True to form the Minister of Education dismissed the riots as simply the work of a small number of agitators and of no consequence. He was wrong. Six hundred students were arrested, more or less at random, and 27 were held. The Revolution of May had begun.

But why had the cup overflowed; why did the intervention of the police cause a riot when previously it had always dispersed demonstrators? Was it the mounting frustration of the students; or small organized groups ready for a fight (but it was precisely these that had been arrested); or the example of Germany, as seen in newsreels and on the television; or the sympathy of the neighbourhood and the younger staff; or the obscure belief that if the Vietnamese could lick the U.S., David could always beat Goliath? Or was it the feeling that the authorities always cheated; the contrast between their benevolent attitude to the Vietnam demonstration and the repression of demonstrations on matters closer at home? Or the fury at being treated as children rather than as citizens? Or was it simply that for the first time there were apparently more students than police, and therefore, instead of abandoning their comrades (the typical reaction in previous encounters) the delinquent sub-group united to rescue its own? Whatever the reasons, the students found that they were joined in their flouting of authority by the staff, the neighbourhood, their parents, and a part of the nation. The Gaullist tactic of relying on charismatic plebiscitary authority, of demoting and discrediting *les intermédiaires* had helped create this vacuum of legitimacy. The lack of representative and responsible intermediaries, the disadvantages of government by ante-chamber, the fixation on foreign policy, the price of *grandeur* and of *gloire* now became apparent.

The Prime Minister, one of the few able politicians in the government and its driving force, had left for Iran on Thursday, 2 May to return only on the 11th; the Elysée must have been preoccupied with the forthcoming voyage of the President to Roumania, scheduled for the 14th; more pressing still, Friday's newspapers announced that Americans and North Vietnamese had finally agreed to meet on the 10th—in Paris. With the Prime Minister absent, the Minister of National Education was left to his own devices; the immediate reaction of the Elysée must have been to dismiss the troubles as 'little local difficulties'. Perhaps official circles had allowed themselves to be convinced by the daily refrain of the ORTF, that France was an island of serenity in a world of chaos. In any case, that had to be the impression given to the world, about to descend in force on Paris for the Vietnam 'peace' talks. The Government may have been strengthened in its resolve to face down the unruly students by the hostility to them of Saturday's press; only the *Monde* and *Combat* had any sympathy for the students. The *Aurore* was usually sympathetic only to right-wing troublemakers; the *Figaro* was always afraid of any disorder; the Communist *Humanité* saw the demonstration as the work of the turbulent former members of the old UEC and the trotskyists and anarchists who had shouted down the party's smooth educational expert, Pierre Juquin, when he had attempted to peddle the party line at Nanterre in April. But the press was not representative, for much of the university community had been infuriated by the gratuitous and indiscriminate bullying of the police. Police violence in working class quarters made little impact— the murder of six demonstrators in the Charonne metro station in 1962 by the 'forces of order' had gone unpunished—but breaking middle class heads was a different matter.

Thus began a week of sporadic disorder, which culminated in the great night of the barricades on the 10–11th of May. Cohn-Bendit and his friends were due to appear before the disciplinary committee on Monday the 6th, the same day that the *agrégation* was to begin at the Sorbonne, and that demonstrations in favour of the students were to be held. The Rector, to safeguard his grammar exams, therefore suspended courses in the Sorbonne and the Censier annexe, three weeks before undergraduate exams. Tension always mounted in the spring as exams approached, and with their faculties closed, not only Nanterre but Sorbonne students had time on their hands. The Fouchet reforms made the exams even more crucial for the academic future of the student, but lamentable conditions in the larger faculties hardly gave him a fair chance to survive them; the failure rate was sometimes over 50%; and now even this insufficient provision was temporarily interrupted.

UNEF called for a demonstration in the courtyard of the Sorbonne, Monday at 9 a.m.; the Prefecture refused permission for any demonstration in the Latin Quarter on Monday. The Rector announced that examinations would take place as scheduled; SNESup called for a general faculty strike in favour of the students; the Minister pronounced the strike illegal for want of the required week's notice. Out of the 600 arrested on Friday, 27 were held, 12 charged, 7 given suspended sentences and 4 sent to jail. The students now had a new cry: *Libérez nos camarades*; as the week proceeded, the initial issues were progressively submerged, as each new incident compounded the grievances on both sides, demands and tempers escalated, and a negotiated settlement became increasingly difficult.

On Monday Cohn-Bendit and his friends arrived for their interview with fists raised and singing the Internationale. Crowds grew and a march around Paris developed into violent running battles with the police from tea time until almost midnight. While perhaps 20,000 students chanted *nous sommes un groupuscule* in the streets, on the television (which so far had managed to ignore the whole matter), Peyrefitte explained that police activity was necessary to 'protect the great mass of students against a handful of agitators'. Meanwhile the police were being violently attacked by a section of the crowd, whose excesses were at first condemned by UNEF and SNESup. But as police ripostes became indiscriminate they followed the rule of Lamartine in 1848: 'I am their leader, therefore I must follow them.' By the end of the evening UNEF denounced the police barbarity and swore to support every further demonstration.

Tuesday morning's *Figaro* now called for discussion, and the *Humanité* promised the support of the PCF to the legitimate demands of students and professors. The same morning saw disorder in the Paris lycées; this was a particularly worrying sign, for concentrated round the university quarter were a number of big lycées with large numbers of older pupils; the police would therefore have to cope not only with students but with schoolboys and girls as well. Twenty-year-olds might be counted as fair game, but clubbing 14-year-olds was intolerable; since the police were not over careful about whom they hit in the heat of battle, public sympathy for the government was further at risk. Deputies began to speak out. The Left Federation blamed the government, the Communists called for an amnesty, and the Gaullists denounced fanatics.

But the great student serpentine which wound its way around the capital Tuesday ignored the National Assembly; instead, at 10 p.m. the students moved up the Champs Elysées to the Arc de Triomphe and sang the Internationale (or as much of it as they could remember) shaking their fists over the Tomb of the Unknown Soldier. It was an agreeable way to *épater la bourgeoisie* but unlikely to endear them to war veterans, or masses of perfectly ordinary, patriotic citizens. It was, however, typical of much of the spirit that ran through the Events, reappearing in slogans painted on the walls of the Sorbonne, or unorthodox public behaviour in the occupied university and lycée buildings; a sort of generalized and prolonged *Bal des Quat'z Arts*, the traditional promiscuous rag of the art and architecture students. More ominous were the brutal affrontments with the police late Tuesday night at St Germain des Près before the Café des Deux Magots, 'rendez-vous de l'élite intellectuel': for the student demonstrators were now joined by gangs of youths from the poorer districts.

'The Government has lost control of its Faculties' was the headline in the satirical weekly, the *Canard Enchainé*, which appeared as usual on Wednesday, 8th. Gaullist deputies called for law and order and the Elysée maintained a disdainful silence. But at the new Faculty of Sciences, over the Halle aux Vins, professors known for their sympathy with the students called for the orderly sitting of exams, and UNEF and SNESup declared themselves ready to negotiate with the government on three conditions: that the police were cleared from the Latin Quarter, Nanterre and the Sorbonne reopened, and the arrested students were amnestied and released. In the National Assembly, Peyrefitte adopted a more conciliatory tone, and mentioned the possibility of the Faculties reopening the next day. But the weakness of representative organizations now became vital: pushed on by the rank and file, the president of SNESup, Geismar, threatened that the Sorbonne would be occupied the next day whatever the government decided. Trade unionists participated for the first time in the now regular evening demonstrations and, to the disgust of the extremists, cooled it; there was no further collision with the gendarmerie.

On Thursday, the 9th, students expecting to find the doors of the Sorbonne opened, arrived to find them still shut and guarded; there was a sit-in on the steps of the Sorbonne, and in the evening a mass meeting in the big hall of the *Mutualité*, organized by the JCR and at which various student leaders thundered imprecations. Cohn-Bendit announced the proliferation of political meetings in the university buildings when they were reopened; each group tried to overbid the other in the hope of attracting support, or of forcing the Minister to deal with it. After a visit to the Elysée, Peyrefitte announced at 8 p.m. that the University would remain closed until calm returned. Both sides were playing double or quits. A mammoth demonstration, this time with the full participation of the lycéens was called for the next day.

Friday's parade was to turn into the night of the barricades, 60 of them. After the march, the great bulk of the demonstrators found themselves hemmed in by the riot police in the Place Edmond Rostand, at the junction of the Boulevard St Michel, the Rue Soufflot and the Luxembourg Gardens. While demonstrators and police eyed each other nervously across a no man's land, leaders went off to negotiate with university authorities, who were themselves powerless to accede to the three preliminary conditions (amnesty, reopening, no police). Radio cars of the two commercial stations, Radio Luxembourg (RTL) and Europe No. 1, reported developments minute by minute, and RTL even allowed its microphones to be used for a public conversation between Alain Geismar and vice-rector Chalin. The nation listened on its radios, as did the inhabitants of the district watching from their balconies and windows, and the students in the streets with their transistors, at last the actors and not the objects of History.

The first barricades went up about 9 p.m.; General de Gaulle went to bed at 10 p.m., and no one was willing to give the Prefect of Police the authority he demanded to clear the barricades before they were fully constructed. Some barricades sported the red and black flags and the Internationale; others the tricolour and the Marseillaise, but for the last time during the Events. Early in the morning of the 11th, at 2.17 a.m., the order was finally given to the police and riot squads to storm the barricades. The night of the 10–11th saw the greatest police violence, the greatest enthusiasm among the students, and the greatest sympathy of the population. 'Intelligent, furious, romantic, heroic, impulsive', the students were encouraged by the evident sympathy of the neighbourhood, and exhilarated by the sense that finally they had taken their destiny in their own hands and that this great gesture was being made known to the world through the radio broadcasts to which they were also listening. 'It was extraordinary. After years of lies and bull, an account of the real thing escaping from the transistors. Facts, real facts!...And we were no longer in a ghetto, but in a house of glass. It seemed to me all public life could be changed, if only it [the Events] were talked about.' And another student.

As soon as I heard a transistor I was enormously reassured. They talked about 30 barricades. I jumped for joy and we all shouted 'we're not alone!' We really didn't know how many of us there were. It was through the radio that I heard of the range and number. Behind our barricade we were resolute, but wondered whether it was worth it or not. Myself, I was haunted by a feeling of solitude. We were surrounded. I thought of the Paris Commune, isolated from the rest of France, cut off from everything. I saw my family in the suburbs, falling off to sleep. All those I loved were asleep. All France dead to the world, and we were going to be killed like rats. Because we heard the report of the grenades and we thought it was also gun fire. Anyhow, we didn't really know. And then suddenly a woman came up with a transistor and we heard '30 barricades', and I realized, even maybe if it was foolish, that France was listening in and that if one died, one died with witnesses, linked to the world.

In this delirious atmosphere, wild rumours circulated: tanks were on their way; 10,000 workers were marching from the right bank to join the barricades, with the promise of Revolution. 'The barricade, the street fighting', explained a 22 March militant, 'was the profound desire of these guys; that explains the exaltation that everyone reported. It was joy in the quasi-Neitzschean sense of the word, people were happy to die for it, you see, and I remember for me it was the most beautiful night of my life.' The exhilaration can hardly have been shared by acting Prime Minister Joxe, or Minister of the Interior Fouchet, but in a confused way it was communicated to a large number of perfectly orderly, peaceable citizens, who listened to the radio and worried, for 'they were beating *our* children!' The students were never to be so popular again, but having once started it was difficult to stop.[1]

On Saturday and Sunday the Latin Quarter filled with rubbernecks come to see the desolation they had heard described on the radio, and the various student organizations met with the trades unions. Pompidou flew in Saturday evening from Kabul; after consulting his staff and members of the government he went to the Elysée; at 11.15 p.m. on television he blamed agitators

---

[1] Students quoted in Philippe Labro et al., *Mai/Juin 68 Ce n'est qu'un début* (Paris 1968), pp. 65, 128, 130–1.

but offered an olive branch, promised reforms, pleaded for order, agreed to an amnesty and the opening of the Sorbonne. It was a delayed but intelligent attempt to separate the great bulk of moderate students from the extremists, so that only a minimum of force might prove necessary; but too much blood had already been spilled. It was also the essential gesture if public sympathy was to be snatched from the students, the essential condition for the further use of any force at all against the demonstrators. In this last aim, the Prime Minister's tactics proved successful, but only after a time, and with the (unintentional) help of the students. In any case there was no choice. The police were exhausted by a week of incidents, and demoralized by general public hostility. Any more violence would further damage the government, unless public opinion first turned against the students. But that would take time. For the moment only Gaullists accepted Pompidou's claim that it was all the fault of agitators. It was not an analysis likely to recommend itself to those students who had faced the police, nor householders who had witnessed the battle from their windows, nor anxious parents. Agitators there may have been, but schoolboys and girls had also suffered at the hands of the riot police, the tough CRS. It took another weekend's rioting and a general strike to frighten people out of sympathy with the students and into the arms of the government.

If the immediate public reaction to Pompidou's speech was favourable, the hard-pressed police saw it as a disavowal, and other civil servants too must have wondered if the Prime Minister would support them if they became unpopular in the zealous execution of their unpopular duties. Radical younger workers, at least, took the speech as a confession of weakness. The government had caved in when challenged by a bunch of students, soft-handed sons of the bourgeosie; but was not the government responsible for low wages and unemployment; and were not *workers* the revolutionary chosen class? The unions were ready to move on strictly industrial demands, but the CGT was determined not to allow itself to be used by the students for their purposes; it was the industrial arm of the Communist party, not the plaything of Trotskyite and Maoist '*emmerdeurs*'. The frank hostility of the CGT leaders, and especially the ambivalent feelings of the workers, came as a great shock to the students, who also regarded labour as the anointed revolutionary class and natural allies in their battle against the bourgeoisie. The competition and lack of co-ordination between union and student leaders found its counterpart in the relations between the Matignon (the Prime Minister's office) and the Elysée; not only was there a battle between government and opposition, there were also internecine skirmishes within each camp. But the internal squabble within the opposition was the more damaging.

245

The working class not only shared some of the students' complaints against the system, it also had real and immediate grievances of its own. In 1967 the workers had had to swallow a rise in social security contributions to help pay for the peasants, brought in by a previous extension of the system. These increases were imposed by administrative decree, without discussion in Parliament. Then the rapid modernization of the country had brought some structural unemployment, and workers suspected that the Budget and the Plan had allowed for more of it than necessary as part of the 'stabilization plan'—so that while holding down inflation and reducing tariff barriers in the Common Market, the General could amass his hoard of gold and have his Bomb too. Unemployment was particularly extensive among the young, perhaps as high as a quarter of a million. School leavers with the CAP (Certificat d'aptitude professionnel) found that their training was often irrelevant to the jobs they could find, and that they were often employed on semi-skilled jobs at lower rates rather than in the positions for which they felt their training prepared them.

In the private sector there was unemployment; in the public sector wages were held down by official fiat as part of the stabilization plan; the SMIG, the minimum wage, varied from region to region and had lagged well behind the cost of living. But with weak unions, unemployment and an unfriendly government, possibilities for militant industrial action were restricted. Divided among themselves, in most industries unions were unable effectively to control shop floor procedures. The competition for members (evident also throughout the Events) encouraged an impossible cumulation of demands while making effective concerted action difficult; union bargaining power was thus weakened and employer intransigence encouraged.

The CGT, run by militants of the Liberation generation, continued to talk the language of class war while its daily activity was that of bread and butter unionism. It therefore played a less aggressive role than the CFDT in a series of brief, explosive 'rolling' strikes in the engineering trades, apparently triggered off by younger workers. There was also a more prolonged stoppage in the Lorraine mines and steel mills, and some 24-hour strikes took place in the public services. None of these was very successful, and the government, labour leaders and workers concluded that the unions could mount no real challenge to the stabilization policy. But the extreme left concluded—though not for the first time—that it would have to take over the CGT from its leaders if militant action was to succeed; and the CGT leadership was weakened and its enemies reinforced, by the concurrent crisis in the Communist party. In some plants the Trotskyite *Voix Ouvrière* could appeal to the syndicalist tradition of the working class and to the impatience and insecurity of the young workers. In others JCML students (including *normaliens*) had quit university, taken their CAPs, and gone to agitate and work in the factories, as the narodniki had once gone into the Russian villages. This contact was very restricted, but it meant that at a time when the CGT's ideals and practice were daily growing further apart, the romantic revolutionism of the Latin Quarter was filtering back to the working class, feeding the old indigenous tradition, and so posing a potential threat to union leadership at the shop floor level.

But if anarcho-syndicalism was part of the French working-class tradition, union leaders and organizers had to try and keep their institutions functioning in normal times, despite the hostility of employers, the apathy of workers and the indifference of the government. These spokesmen remembered the savage, vindictive repressions of 1848 and 1871, the catastrophic effects of the abortive rail strike of 1920, of the reaction against the Popular Front in 1938, of the cost of the quasi-political strikes of 1947–8 and 1953 to the unions and their members. Too weak to win or hold concessions on their own, French unions might dream of their ultimate salvation in the revolutionary overthrow of capitalism, but they got immediate results as the consequence of legislation, nationalization, and government pressure on employers during a general strike, as in 1936. Weak in membership and organisation, competing with each other as vigorously as they confronted their employers, they witheringly denounced capital—and then had to treat with it from a position of weakness. Indeed, employers were finding it easier to deal with the CGT, larger and more 'revolutionary' by definition, and therefore safer from attack by its rivals, than with the more vulnerable and often very militant CFDT. It is not surprising that the students and the CGT should have regarded each other with mutual incomprehension. Around 4 a.m., on the morning of the 11th May, as the police 'mopped up' the Latin Quarter, three desperate students are supposed to have telephoned Georges Séguy, president of the CGT, to tell him they could hold out no longer, unless proletarians were sent to help them. 'You don't mobilize the working class at this hour,' Séguy reportedly answered. The story is probably apocryphal, but the states of mind revealed were real enough.

What illusions were left must have been dissipated on Sunday, 12th, when student and union leaders met all day at the Bourse de Travail. The unions now agreed with the students and wanted to move their demonstration, planned for the 14th, to Monday, May 13th, the 10th anniversary of the Algiers coup that had brought down the Fourth Republic. But the CGT objected to Cohn-Bendit marching in the front with the union leaders, and SNESup and UNEF argued that simply militants not leaders ought to lead the parade anyway. Finally there were two combined processions. The CGT, CFDT and FEN (the autonomous teachers' union) called a one-day

247

general strike for the 13th, and organized marches in Paris and the great provincial towns. On the 13th, a great demonstration moved from the Place de la République, in the heart of old working-class Paris, to Denfert-Rochereau, a large strategic road circus south of the university quarter. CGT marshals carefully kept the union contingents from contamination by the students who, for the first time, raised the cry of '*gouvernement populaire*'. Contrary to the wishes of the CGT, Cohn-Bendit moved on to the Champs de Mars, where he held his own meeting; he was later to remark what fun it had been to march with 'the crapulent stalinists'. The official leadership of the CGT and the PCF were to come to hate (and fear?) Cohn-Bendit and his friends, as much as distracted university authorities or blustering Gaullists did.

Other Gaullists picked up the Prime Minister's hints and started to discover a Communist conspiracy behind the Events; the PCF and the CGT were no less treacherous for being cautious. A campaign of much the same nature, emphasizing malign marxist influences in the university, was also begun in the business community, with a paper (later to reappear in the Gaullists' *Dossier du Candidat*) purporting to unmask 'La machine infernale'. Finally, the old Gaullist Resistance networks were quietly reactivated, as they had been in 1961 during the Algiers army putsch. From the Elysée there were unofficial rumblings about the continuing disorders. The first official announcement came on Monday the 13th: General de Gaulle would address the nation on Friday, 24 May, after his return from Roumania. On Tuesday, the 14th, he departed for Bucharest, leaving his Government holding the bag, and the students in possession of the Sorbonne. 'Bliss was it in that dawn to be alive. But to be young was very heaven.'

The occupation of the Sorbonne began after the demonstration of the 13th and was completed the next day. Students, revolutionaries, camp followers, run-away children, idealists, derelicts, delinquents, all moved in to the sanctuary, giving it the air of a medieval monastery immune from the civil authorities and ripe for reform. Happenings in the courtyard amidst the stands of the various grouplets, from the *Action Française* to the most hermetic left-wing sects; marathon teach-ins on everything at once in the big lecture halls; smaller discussions in the seminar rooms on everything from revolutionary warfare to the social function of orgies in the late Roman empire; gangsters in the cellars, fires in the attic, casual sex in the stairwells; serious meetings on university reform, determined plots for workers' risings upstairs and in the Censier annexe; and slogans and posters everywhere; there was a bit of everything at the Sorbonne. Outraged Gaullists denounced the walpurgisnacht; enthusiastic progressives applauded direct participatory democracy in action. There was something in both views. Along with a real desire to discuss, learn and plan one's own future, there were systematic attempts to manipulate the newly freed students. Though the liberated students wouldn't have liked the contrast, the occupied Sorbonne resembled an American nominating convention. In the courtyard there was the ballyhoo, the music, the pretty girls, the propaganda. In the huge amphitheatre the main spokesmen for the different factions harangued enthusiastic audiences, Krivine for the JCR and Cohn-Bendit for the 22 March, while elder statesmen like Sartre, honoured more for their past services than for their present influence, appeared to dignify the proceedings. But the real struggle for power, over personalities and their programmes took place in the committee rooms upstairs between factional representatives, some of them *ad hoc*, all attempting to take over the movement and use it for their own ends. Inside, order was maintained by the official marshals, mostly SNESup assistants, and unofficially by the *katangais*, minor delinquents associated with one of the factions, the comité d'occupation, itself linked with last year's UNEF minority. Outside, demonstrators risked serious clashes with the police. Real power, however, lay outside the reach of the Sorbonne-convention. It was altogether too much like Chicago.

On Tuesday, Pompidou made further concessions to the students in a speech to the Assembly. These were taken as further admissions of weakness by the students, but perhaps the Prime Minister was less interested in their reaction than in that of the rest of the academic community and of the general public. He also made concessions to the police, but in the super-excited atmosphere of the third week of May, no one seemed to notice. The Communists and the Federation tabled a censure motion. Most important, an industrial dispute which had been simmering at the Sud-Aviation plant near Nantes turned into a sit-down strike, and the general manager was welded into the administration building.

On Wednesday the 15th, the sit-in strike jumped from Nantes to the Renault works at Cléon near Rouen and then to Flins and Paris. Students occupied the Odéon and, though disavowed by UNEF, provided a sort of living theatre for all comers. On the 16th Cohn-Bendit, Geismar, and Jacques Sauvageot (vice-president and leader of UNEF and a member of the PSU, the small left socialist party) were interviewed for the first time on television, followed by the Prime Minister denouncing sowers of disorder. Workers downed tools in the engineering industry. On Friday, the 17th, the strike wave spread through the country; although confederal headquarters refused to declare a general strike, the better organized unions began pulling out their big battalions. Peasant organizations, anxious to get in on the act, called their own demonstration for the 24th. It was perhaps just as well that most of the Breton CRS, equally unpopular with local factory and field hands, had been despatched to Paris. For in the Catholic west, an area with serious agricultural problems, the CFDT and peasant organizations, both strong in the region and inspired by the same radical Catholic conscience, tried to establish contact between their respective troops; local leaders of the PSU were also very active in the agitation.

In Paris, the PSU mobilized its academic supporters. Students and teachers had originally been almost exclusively concerned with educational matters, and driven to action mostly by the severity of the police, but as the sit-in strikes spread (finally close to 10,000,000 people came out) they began to believe that if only the CGT and PCF were willing, the government—perhaps even the regime—might be overthrown. They therefore grew more intractable and even refused to negotiate with the legal government. This was a dangerous strategy because it probably misjudged the real nature of the strikes, and certainly ignored the changing effect of the Events on an increasingly anguished public. For most of the strikers, especially the older men in the provinces, were not suddenly applying the thoughts of Chairman Mao; they were following the standard pattern of great labour disputes in France, with the 1936 Popular Front as a model. In 1968 (and in 1953) as in 1936, pent up frustration had exploded in a series of wildcat strikes, which quickly spread, as often as not among the unorganized as among union members; the unions then take command, by calling out their disciplined troops, thus enlarging the action into a general strike; but aware of their inherent weakness, the unions express the general social discontent of the workers in largely industrial terms; the government can then call in the employers and pressure them to accede to union demands; a nervous *patronat* accepts national agreements covering both organized and unorganized men, and these are given official blessing and sometimes the sanction of law; the strike ends with the workers exhausted (they have small strike funds), the employers determined to mount a counter-attack, and the government uncertain for the public has become uneasy.

Miscalculation of public opinion and of its importance was the other great mistake, and one to which students were particularly prone. For in joining professional and political demands, the university rebels moved from an area in which they had maximum public support into an arena where opinion was much more hostile and divided. The combination of these two sets of concerns led to a fatal ambiguity which the government was later to exploit. Moreover, in the inevitable politicization of the movement, all the protesters were identified with the views and judged by the actions of the most extreme or irresponsible elements. Here again, the public risked being alienated from the students; once that occurred the government would find it easier to reestablish order, if necessary by calling on the army. Pompidou had already accused agitators on the 11th, but this tactic was premature until the situation had further degenerated. Then public sympathy for the students would give way to mounting anxiety as public services collapsed, garbage piled high in the streets, transport ground to a halt, banks closed, tinned goods, macaroni, oil and sugar disappeared from the shops, the television stopped transmitting —and the *enragés* claimed street demonstrations were a superior form of democracy and advanced a claim to rule France.

The danger was clearly seen by the PCF and CGT. With mounting irritation they found that they had totally lost the political initiative in the first great mass movement against the regime, and that they risked being involved in operations which they did not control but for which they would be blamed if the movement failed, as they expected it would. But if they were worried by the course of events, they were infuriated by pressure on their left: from students, Maoists, Trotskyites, anarchists, the PSU and the CFDT, who first implicitly and later explicitly challenged their own claim to represent the working class and especially its most advanced and vigorous elements. Since its assumed role as vanguard of the universal class of the future lies at the heart of Communist theology and justifies both the party's organization and its lack of scruple, it became essential to smash these competitors whatever the outcome of the Events. Another Gaullist victory could always be survived, but not such a threat to the fundamental raison d'etre of the Communist movement; the venomous articles in *Humanité* against the student *enragés* were not simply the result of a perfectly rational calculation that the PCF and CGT had more to lose than anyone else from the defeat of an ill-considered revolutionary adventure. The instinctive 'ouvriérisme' (working-class self-sufficiency) of the CGT precluded an understanding with the students from the start. But suspicions turned to hatred when the CGT, which had got a grip on the Events for itself—and the PCF—by calling its own men out and thus extending the strike, saw student radicals nibbling at its base. With millions out, the CGT-PCF's power lay in its industrial bastions in the great factories, and they were not going to share that with anyone. The students were therefore mostly kept strictly away. They naturally responded by turning against the CGT, especially since the CGT and the great bulk of its support—which extends well beyond PCF factory cells— wanted Matignon-style agreements whatever the political issue of the Events, and were reluctant to compromise industrial-social demands with strictly political ones. Unlike the CGT however, the PCF's priorities were strictly political. While the CGT eschewed political slogans, the party cautiously declared its interest in case the situation should prove to be rotten before it was ripe; if there was a collapse, the PCF would be there to take over from its industrial arm in the CGT and claim its inheritance. On the 19th of May, the Communist leader, Waldeck-Rochet, declared that the PCF was ready to assume its responsibilities. Perhaps the prime mistakes of the PCF were first to overestimate and then to underestimate the capacity of the government and the resilience of the President.

A striking example of the government's continuing loss of control was the announcement by ORTF journalists, whose radio cars had been booed because of the network's slavishly pro-government reporting of the Events, that they would refuse further ministerial directives and report the news (at last) in an 'honest, objective and complete' fashion. Perhaps that is what prompted General de Gaulle to cut short his Roumanian junket and return Saturday night rather than Sunday afternoon; 'the immediate advantage of Frenchmen' had suddenly become more pressing than 'the higher interests of France'. The General was welcomed back, by his government, at 11.30 p.m., Saturday the 18th of May.

With the country increasingly paralyzed, a third of the work force already on strike and more coming out every moment, the prefects without instructions, the police tired, angry and demoralized, and the students overtly and the Communists covertly preparing to challenge the government, the President cast himself as Charles X. At the end of the special cabinet meeting on Sunday the 19th, the Minister of Information imperturbably reported that the General's policy was 'la réforme oui, le chienlit non'. 'Le général Chi-En-Li...ou Chaos-Tsé-Tung' was the *Canard*'s comment, and Beaux Arts students promptly turned out a caricature of de Gaulle with the slogan, 'la chienlit, c'est lui'. It was a bon mot disguised as a programme; without a clear lead from the Elysée, the government machine slowed down; those with responsibilities kept their heads low and awaited the censure debate of the 22nd and the presidential address of the 24th. The weekend also saw the corporatist organizations of the liberal professions challenged by their members; it seemed as if the entire elite of the country was having a collective crisis of conscience. The crisis of confidence came later, after de Gaulle's first speech. The Gaullists were already scattering tracts around Paris: 'No to anarchy, no to disorder. Let us defend the Republic!' And in a municipal election in Dijon, the secretary-general of the UDV[e] (the Gaullist party) Robert Poujade, received 49·61% of the vote in a high poll. It was an important sign, but in Paris it went unnoticed by the opponents of the regime. 'The men in power,' declared former premier Pierre Mendès-France, 'have created a revolutionary situation...They can now render only one further service to the country: to get out.'

Tuesday, 21st, school teachers and bank tellers struck, a commando of clerks occupied the offices of the Employers Federation for two hours, and the Assembly began to debate the Federation-PCF censure motion. Professor

René Capitant, left-Gaullist deputy for the Latin Quarter, who had previously announced he could not vote for the government, resigned his seat rather than vote against it; Edgard Pisani, a former Gaullist minister, voted the censure and then resigned. Giscard d'Estaing, leader of the Republican Independents (the right wing of the majority), former Minister of Finance and sworn enemy of the Prime Minister, announced in a brilliantly demagogic speech that his group would not add 'adventure to disorder' and so would not vote the censure, and reaffirmed his loyalty to the President while denouncing his Prime Minister. (Giscard later explained he voted for the government because he expected it to be dismissed by the General.) The Federation and the Communists were still without a completed common programme, and in the debate the Federation gave the impression of a cock boat in the wake of the Communist man-of-war; the Centre was unwilling to leave the Federation alone with the Communists in opposition, and split heavily against the government. Nonetheless, on 22 May the government survived the censure vote by 11 votes, and the Assembly voted the amnesty earlier promised by Pompidou for the students previously convicted; the Prime Minister made another gesture and important material concessions to the police, thus assuaging the serious discontent provoked by his first speech. As if to celebrate its parliamentary victory, the government declared Cohn-Bendit, who was off rabble-rousing in Germany, a prohibited immigrant; the relative calm of the previous few days was immediately shattered by a student demonstration (denounced by the authorities and the CGT) in the Latin Quarter to the chant, 'nous sommes tous les juifs allemands'. On Thursday there were further incidents and the students were pilloried by *l'Humanité* for whom Cohn-Bendit seemed to have become enemy number one. UNEF and SNESup called for a demonstration in his favour on Friday, 24th, the day General de Gaulle was to address his people.

In any presidential system, an address by the head of state in the middle of a crisis is a major event; in the plebiscitary Fifth Republic, and when the orator was General de Gaulle, it acquired a crucial significance. The country was crippled by a general strike; Paris was full of demonstrators; the state machine was dislocated by the successive absences of the Prime Minister and the President, by the administrators' fears of being disavowed by one or the other, and by the disruption of the public services. De Gaulle trotted out his favourite moth-eaten hobby-horse: 'participation'. And the method of consulting the country was as inadequate and inappropriate to the occasion as the substance of the proferred reform. 'Participation' was disliked by both management and labour, but the General no doubt expected to get the votes of the right out of fear, and of the left on vague promises of some sort of undefined workers' control. For participation was to be approved by his favourite constitutional gimmick, a referendum giving him full powers to decide what to put in, how to bake, and how to serve this particular pie in the sky.

The speech was a catastrophic mistake; not only was the referendum unconstitutional, a bad example at a time when the regime needed to appeal to whatever respect for legitimate authority was still left, but conditions were such that the referendum could not possibly take place. On the television, the President looked old, tired and out of touch. As usual, the referendum was also a plebiscite: if the country voted 'no' he threatened to retire, thus adding a crisis of the regime to the other difficulties facing his country. That wildly irresponsible gesture was the last straw. Not only had the old man failed to produce the expected miracle after a wasted fortnight, he had succeeded in making a bad situation much worse. For if the country had exploded it was partially because, while everyone was fed up with the rigidities of French society and the authoritarian manner of French government, no one seriously thought the regime was vulnerable. The General's speech put the regime at risk by proposing an authoritarian, paternalistic solution which nobody wanted and which he was not even in a position to carry through. He dared the French to do without him. With 30,000–50,000 in the streets listening, it was a direct slap in the public's face. Ironically the reaction to this enormous blunder, the mobile riots in Paris, Lyons, Strasbourg and Bordeaux, lost the sympathy of the population for the students and frightened citizens back into the arms of the General and his government. The tone of the radio reports of the disorders changed noticeably during the night of the 24–25th and newspapers like *le Monde* and *Combat* which had been generally sympathetic to the students, were repelled by the gratuitous and almost random violence of that night. The national capacity for sustained civil disorder was finally submerged by the fear and dislike of systematic violence. But before this change in attitude could benefit the government, the President would have to do something to redeem himself. It took a week.

The six days following de Gaulle's broadcast saw the *grande peur* of 1968. With the General's credit lower than ever some ministers (but not the Premier) began to lose their nerve and higher civil servants discreetly disappeared from their offices and suddenly remembered opposition acquaintances they had unaccountably neglected for the past ten years. In the provinces, mayors provided relief for families of the strikers as savings ran low and prefects, left to fend for themselves and with their local gendarmes called to Paris, had sometimes to cope with demonstrations of 10,000 with less than 100 gendarmes to hand. For a few days it was impossible to drive into or out of Le Mans, without paying a toll, proportionate to the value of the car, to an unofficial strike committee. Small plants in small towns had often not been struck until visited by commandos from the larger industrial centres; small communities were shocked when their school teachers, who are important public figures in the villages, struck. Sensible masters arranged to take care of the children anyhow, but where revolutionary virtue forbade child-minding, the teachers became profoundly unpopular. In the west, young workers (or unemployed, nobody knew) requisitioned produce from peasant holdings near the big towns, and in the markets, at their own prices. The CGT put a quick stop to this, but not before the damage was done and the countryside regarded the town workers as the peasants had seen the *partageux* in 1848. In other places the lack of transport or petrol doomed perishable crops. These facts ended any hope of the worker-peasant co-operation. It was just as well for the government; provincial towns had to replace their gendarmes on duty in Paris by cutting the strength of the rural police brigades in half, and calling it to the departmental capitals. The couple of gendarmes who remained in each country district made themselves scarce, on the sensible grounds that they were too weak to control incidents which their presence, in the circumstances, might provoke.

The anguish of ordinary people increased daily at the spectacle of violence, governmental paralysis, and the difficulties of life without post, banks, schools, transport and petrol (the unions kept gas, water and electricity supplies functioning). Meanwhile student leaders became more intransigent and the PCF began to prepare the ground for a change in line should the state somehow fold up instead of fighting back. At 3 p.m. on Saturday, 25th, Pompidou convoked representatives of the employers and the unions to negotiations under his chairmanship at the Ministry of Social Affairs, rue de Grenelle. As in 1936, the *patronat* had been very badly jolted by the occupation of their factories, but were privately reassured by the CGT that it wanted negotiations not revolution. The *patronat* was therefore anxious to move quickly, and so was the CGT which was afraid of losing control if it did not quickly bring home the bacon. Indeed, to protect itself, the CGT warned at the outset that it would not be able to sign any agreement before consulting its rank and file. The government was equally anxious for a rapid result to prevent the situation from degenerating further. Under pressure from it, representatives of the *patronat* agreed, in a marathon negotiation which lasted with only minor interruptions until 7.15 a.m. Monday morning, to a 10% wage increase and to recognition of the union locals as bargaining agents at the shop floor level. But agreement was still pending on the length of the work week, retirement age and strike pay. The government agreed to raise the minimum wage and submit the social security decrees to Parliament (which was required by the Constitution) for a vote (which wasn't so clear).

Pompidou had worked extremely successfully, perhaps too well. Throughout the negotiations Séguy had repeatedly been called to the telephone, from which he would return visibly uneasy. Was it pressure from the Political Bureau of the PCF or, more likely, reports of rank and file discontent? Certainly, the CGT upped the ante during the negotiations: on Sunday it suddenly demanded that salary increases be tied to the cost of living index, so that they would not be eroded by inflation.

The union chiefs accepted the Grenelle agreements in principle, but refused to sign without consulting their members; the CGT sounded relatively satisfied, the CFDT and the FO were more dubious. (In 1936 union representatives had signed the Matignon agreement on the spot.) Séguy went to present the accords to one of the most heavily unionized plants in the Paris area, the great Renault works at Boulogne-Billancourt, where the CGT has been in command since the war and which was its rough barometer of what the workers would take. In 1947 Trotskyite-inspired strikes at Renault against the government's productivity drive, had helped pry the Communists out of the government when the CGT was unable to get the men back to work. The Grenelle protocol was rejected, as a tract circulated before the meeting demanded. Students, Trotskyites, Maoists all claim the credit; there is another report that the PCF cell in the factory had issued it, because the party had decided to let things run a little longer. That morning's *Humanité* carried the headline 'Hundreds of Action Committees for a Peoples' Government'. But no one at Renault was paid the minimum wage and the other concessions by the employers might well not have seemed commensurate with the importance of the strike movement. The workers felt themselves to be in a position of strength and were going to show the bosses, the government—and even, perhaps, the CGT. They thought they could get more (they did, by staying out longer) and this view was encouraged by the competition among the three unions for members. The CGT concentrated on strike pay and the sliding scale; the CFDT noted that the SMIG had been tied to the cost of living too, without really keeping pace with it. The CFDT pushed hard for union representation on the shop floor, with only partial success; the CGT, for political reasons, preferred national negotiations and was afraid of losing control of shop floor branches. The CGT felt it had been sabotaged by FO and CFDT; the *patronat* preferred bickering with the CGT on wages to dealing with the CFDT on union recognition.

Finally, one must remember the weakness of the unions. In most plants they were in a tiny minority, and not in proper control of the strike movement, though even unorganized workers naturally looked to the local CGT factory delegate (when there was one) for guidance. The very lack of effective control casts doubt on the claims of students and the new left that, but for the

CGT, contact between them and the workers would have been forged and a revolution made. Certainly, the CGT was almost pathologically hostile to the students, but by itself, without the passive consent of the unorganized, it could not have kept them out of the plants. But it was true that in the north and the east, where the unions have been longest and most solidly organized and the marxist tradition is most profoundly rooted (Paris and Nantes are anarcho-syndicalist) there was least contact with the students, least effective activity by the groupuscules, and the most systematic industrial action without either demonstrations or clashes with the police.

Whatever the explanation, the accords had been rejected and the General seemed to have shot his bolt. 'In a rebellion, as in a novel, the most difficult part to invent is the end,' noted Tocqueville in 1848. A quiet panic seized the country as the ministries emptied. On the night of that Monday, 27th, UNEF, SNESup, the CFDT and the PSU organized a march to the university stadium (Charléty) at which Mendès-France was present but did not speak. It was boycotted by the PCF and the CGT. The PSU and CFDT hoped to create out of the junction of students, workers and the Comités d'Action Populaires a new movement which, if Mendès would take the plunge, could pick up enough momentum to sweep him to power as the one man who could assume orderly reform. If Mendès could be got to commit himself, the gas and electricity supplies might be cut off and de Gaulle would resign rather than go out ignominiously in civil war. The advantage of a 'constitutional' coup—like the one de Gaulle had mounted against the Fourth Republic in 1958, and for which Mendès had never forgiven him—was that it necessitated only the briefest *vacance de légalité*, the always uncertain gap between the fall of one legitimate authority and its resurrection as a new regime. If de Gaulle resigned as he had threatened to (and he was unable even to hold his referendum much less win it) the Constitution provided that he be temporarily succeeded by the President of Senate, Gaston Monnerville, his bitter enemy since 1962, who would dismiss Pompidou and appoint Mendès. It was true that the Constitution did not give the President the power to dismiss the Premier, and that Pompidou had just won a vote of confidence in the Assembly. But if de Gaulle went, could the majority hold together; and in 1962 had not General de Gaulle replaced Michel Debré with Pompidou without Debré losing a vote in Parliament? Such a rapid and (almost) constitutional transfer of power gave little temptation for the army to intervene; but the threat of the army would keep the PCF from making a Kerensky of Mendès. And so acute was the crisis that Mendès was seen as a saviour not only of the Left, but by a most unlikely collection of allies including the *patronat*, the conservative Centre leaders and even M^e. Isorni, Pétain's lawyer.

But Mendès refused to speak on Monday night and without the PCF the demonstration mustered only 60,000 instead of the 200,000 for which some of the organizers had hoped. Perhaps it was just as well, for there were rumours, cautiously echoed in the press, that some of the most extreme factions were tempted to try and repeat the night of the 24th—this time with firearms—when the police appeared momentarily to have lost control of the capital. The idea of a coup de force was no doubt most gratifying to armchair revolutionaries, who had long dreamed and plotted death and destruction for the bourgeoisie, without ever even being able to elect municipal councillors. Had the wild men had their way and mounted another Commune, they would have provoked immediate massive support for the government, army intervention and a blood bath. It was not counter-revolutionaries who were massacred at the *mur des fédérés* in May 1871.

On Tuesday the 28th, an unsuccessful attempt was made to federate some of the most extreme sects with the Trotskyite and anarchist students. Perhaps this was the CIA-Israeli plot, hawked about by the Gaullist party daily and party functionaries as an explanation of the Events. Negotiations continued in the nationalized sector and agreement was reached with the miners, who refused to go back immediately out of solidarity with other strikers; Peyrefitte's resignation was finally accepted and Pompidou assumed his functions. But SNESup and UNEF were refusing to negotiate with the government. The Conseil d'Etat rightly declared the proposed referendum unconstitutional; it had nothing to do with the 'organization of the public authorities'. Mitterrand, as anxious to contain Mendès-France as he was to displace Pompidou, announced he was a candidate for the presidency of the Republic, and that Mendès might head up the necessary provisional government. The smug, gloating tone of the pronouncement did nothing to improve Mitterrand's always slightly dubious reputation; he was busy counting his resignations before they were announced. More serious, the Communist party moved to outflank its *frères ennemis* in the Federation and the PSU and to torpedo Mendès. At the same time that Waldeck-Rochet denounced the Charléty march, the CGT called for a demonstration the following day in favour of a 'people's government'; that would show where the big battalions were. Finally, in the evening, Cohn-Bendit appeared at the Sorbonne, crossing the frontier despite the ban on his entry. It really did look as if the shadow cabinet was M. Pompidou's rather than M. Mitterrand's.

On Wednesday the 29th ministers arrived at the Elysée for the usual weekly cabinet meeting—to discover that the President had taken French leave, presumably for his country home at Colombey-les-deux-églises. Meanwhile the CGT marched from the Bastille to St-Lazare (not very far from the Elysée) at least a quarter of a million strong. Before what appeared to be a yawning gulf Mendès announced he was ready to form a government supported by the entire left; support came from the CFDT and from the Centre, but not from the CGT or the PCF, flexing their muscles in the streets. So ended the one chance for a peaceful changeover, and with it, the chance of any change. The PSU might dream of calling out the gas and electricity workers, but these were solidly organized in the CGT. Towards the evening, when de Gaulle finally arrived at Colombey, it became clear that he had been to visit the army. But why the mysterious disappearance? Was it because the dramatic gesture was part of his conception of leadership; was it to allow the French to savour the prospect of his resignation? Was it simply to guarantee the loyalty of the army by appealing personally to its leaders and offering them the liberation of ex-general Salan? Or was it because rumours of troop movements were true; that certain officers, perhaps in touch with certain groups of the extreme-right (or Gaullist bully boys) were moving their armoured units towards Paris without orders, and that if the situation got any worse France would be threatened not with a revolutionary soviet but with a junta of colonels whose arrival de Gaulle had both encouraged and forestalled in 1958. It was a sad commentary on 10 years of complacent self-congratulation that France was reduced to the alternatives usually reserved for banana republics. But de Gaulle, whatever his faults, was not a common caudillo.

The President returned to Paris on Thursday, the 30th; at 4.30 he addressed the nation and contemptuously dismissed the opposition as he had once denounced the undisciplined officers in Algiers. He would stay, so would the Prime Minister; the referendum was postponed, the Assembly dissolved and general elections called. Gaullists were told to form action committees to aid the prefects in restoring order, and the prefects were to have plenary police powers. If the revolutionaries tried to impede the elections the government would not hesitate to use whatever measures proved necessary. The message was brutal, short, clear and contemptuous. Shortly after it was finished the President of the National Assembly read to it the presidential decree dissolving the house. Opposition deputies stood to sing the Marseillaise; still slightly worried Gaullist deputies and ministers donned their official tricolour sashes and moved towards the Champs-Elysées. At first, the crowd grew slowly, but soon the Gaullist demonstration, organized earlier but several times postponed, poured out on to the wide avenue. Out came the professional anti-communists, the defeated partisans of *Algérie française*, the extreme right and the frightened denizens of the 16th arrondissement. But out too came hordes of ordinary little people, citizens who wanted change without violence, war veterans, appalled by the disorder they had witnessed and afraid of the anarchy they thought was threatened, those anxious for a return to normal, and for government selected at the polls and not on the pavements, singing the Marseillaise with as much fervour as the students had sung the Internationale. It was the 'rush-hour crowd', that Malraux had once described as the Gaullist electorate.

The change in the atmosphere was immediate and electric. Mitterrand made a pompous statement, but Mendès wisely kept silent. The left had, after all, demanded dissolution and elections. At the Sorbonne, nervous students waited to be stormed by the CRS and the civic action committees. In the provinces the prefects, who during three lonely weeks had patiently negotiated with strikers and provided relief for their families, forcing an often panicky *patronat* to negotiate rather than flee, suddenly found themselves besieged by latter-day heroes anxious for revenge now that it could be had without risk to themselves, and bloodthirsty in direct proportion to their previous lack of civic courage. The prefects and local gendarmerie now restrained the rampaging middle classes as they had earlier held back the strikers. The Ministry of the Interior, which had left them without orders or resources during the crisis, calling their gendarmes and CRS to the capital, now had a new minister, Raymond Marcellin, the conservative boss of Morbihan. Telephone exchanges were cleared and certain prefects at least were encouraged to do the same with some of the big occupied plants in their area. Some had the good sense to hold back.

On Friday the government was reorganized and the *Figaro*, with the franc, recovered from the events of the past few days. The unions backed away from their demands for a change of government and concentrated on industrial demands; only UNEF continued to refuse to recognize the government, and called for a demonstration the next day. But it was Whit weekend, and religiously the French motorist like his English counterpart always makes for the country. The petrol famine was suddenly relieved as the tanker trucks refuelled petrol pumps. Saturday, the students marched, crying 'élections trahison' but this time nobody watched. Everybody who could had left town and the traffic toll was, as usual, horrendous. The new week saw the worst traffic jams in living memory; things were getting back to normal. Gaullists recovered their habitual panglossian self-assurance. Despite the wicked plots and desperate stratagems of the students, the PCF and all their shady friends, the government had never really been in trouble. It had simply allowed things to slide a bit so that people could see what they risked by sympathizing with the insolent and the disorderly. The General's catastrophic first speech was not a mistake either, but an act of policy. It had all been planned as a necesary and salutary—though no doubt painful— lesson to the light-headed and irresponsible French people. '*Puisque ces mystères nous dépassent, feignons d'en être les organisateurs.*'

24 The party of fear: the election of June 1968

by DAVID B. GOLDEY

The Events of May began as a student revolt, but their interest lies in the fact that student demonstrations triggered off a massive general strike and that the combination of the two seemed ready to bring down the impressive façade of the French state. In the heady atmosphere of May, students moved from trying to reform their universities to attempting to revolutionise society; the working class repeated the great sit-in strikes of the Popular Front in 1936; and the state seemed ready to wither away as in May 1958. How then did a movement, which seemed early in May to involve the total rejection of de Gaulle's style of authority and of the substance of his policies produce in the elections at the end of June a massive Gaullist majority, the largest France has ever known?

This remarkable turnabout owed much to the students, who succeeded in their strategy of polarisation more effectively than they knew, and with catastrophic results for their political revolution (though not, perhaps, for their university reforms). Moreover, the factory occupations of 1936 followed the Popular Front victory at the polls, whereas those of May–June 1968 preceded the elections. Finally, neither the reluctant revolutionaries who lead the French Communist party, nor the revolution-happy organisers of the extreme left proved, in the event, to be as expert at subversion as the present Gaullist pillars of law, order and legitimacy had been in 1958, when they saw their main chance and took it.

The Events of May then had three profound effects on the general election of June 1968. The election was itself the key to restoring order in the streets, the legitimacy of the regime and the authority of the General and his government. Secondly, the backwash of the Events formed part of the improvised campaign, contributing to the general sense of insecurity. Thirdly, this continuing intolerable sense of insecurity moved the electorate to adore what it had once burned, and to swing towards the orthodox Gaullists, who emerged from the elections with 294 of the 470 metropolitan seats. The French voted massively for order and a quiet life.

They were to get a surfeit of the former but little of the latter. The new

Minister of the Interior, Raymond Marcellin, did not scruple to use his various police forces; and the police themselves seemed to have felt that the elections gave them license to indulge their nastier instincts. The minister's policy on demonstrations was 'they shall not pass'. But abroad Gaullist *grandeur* was no bar to the Soviet invasion of Czechoslovakia on the night of 20 August. The General chose to regard the invasion as but an eddy in the river of time; and his faithful Foreign Minister, Michel Debré, dismissed it as an 'accident de parcours'; although the executive of the French Communist party expressed 'surprise and reprobation'. For the President had to pretend not to notice that his foreign policy was in ruins; and by his previous dismissal of Pompidou he had sapped his domestic political base. On 10 July de Gaulle replaced his prime minister—who had insisted that elections be held, engineered the Gaullist victory, and emerged from them as the real leader of the party—thus creating a deep malaise in his party, and precipitating the crisis over his own succession. Whatever happens next, the one issue that now counts in French politics is *l'après-gaullisme*—who will succeed the President of the Republic.

But on 30 May all that was clear was that Frenchmen still regarded elections as preferable to civil war and that there was a vast reservoir of fear, fed to overflowing by the Events, which might be channelled towards the Gaullists. Students might protest and march crying 'élections trahison', but the occupied faculties emptied as the vacation period approached. And the three big trade-union federations, the CGT, FO, and CFDT, all quickly turned from political to industrial demands and called for a return to order so that the elections could take place. The Communist party joined the chorus, and even the left-socialist PSU announced it would present candidates.

The elections had to be organised in great haste, for the first ballot was scheduled for 23 June, the second a week later. Candidatures had to be officially registered in the Prefectures by midnight on Sunday, 9 June. But for the first week in June the aftermath of the general strike continued to disrupt communications and other services. The automatic telephone system functioned badly because the circuits had been over-used and not maintained during the strike. In rural areas, operators often did not get back to work immediately, and the lines were old and inadequate in any case. The Post Office strike ended officially only on Thursday, 6 June, the same day the railway workers went back. To add to the confusion, the telephone service had to cope with heavier traffic than normal, a symptom of the generalised anxiety in the community. For the campaign of 1968 (in sharp contrast to the previous election) took place in the most confused and unsettled situation since the war. In 1958 de Gaulle had come to power in May but the elections took place only in November; in Algeria the paratroops loomed in the background, but in France there was no disorder. In 1968 there was less than a month to prepare for the elections, and for the first fortnight in June there were still large numbers of workers on strike, savage battles between strikers and riot police, further demonstrations in the provinces, and one last great night of the barricades, in Paris on the night of 11–12 June. The continuing incidents embarrassed the opposition and served the majority, as did the improvised nature of the elections.

With little more than a week to declare candidatures, the parties could hardly afford the luxury of protracted and complicated negotiations. On Saturday, 1 June, the Communists and the Left Federation led by Mitterrand (Socialists, Radicals and the Convention, an umbrella organisation of political clubs) announced that, as in 1967, they would systematically stand down for each other at the second ballot. Too many Federation members had been elected with Communist support in 1967 for there to be much question of withdrawing from the alliance. But after the 1968 Events, the Centre could not contemplate the slightest contact with the Communists, even at one remove. As in 1967, then, the main non-Communist opposition was divided between Federation and Centre.

The important battle over candidatures went on within the Gaullist camp. In 1967 various tribal chiefs, notably Giscard d'Estaing (former Finance Minister and leader of the Republican Independents (RI), the traditional right wing of the majority) had wanted to treat the first ballot as a popularity contest among the various clans of the Gaullist family; but Pompidou had insisted that from the first ballot only one Gaullist should stand in each seat. At that election Giscard had argued that the modern form of political activity was to burrow from within and influence government activity from inside the majority, by giving Parliament a more active role; immediately after the elections he was humiliated by the government taking decree powers to carry out social and financial reforms without reference to Parliament. The Giscardiens had been forced to vote for the government without having any very noticeable influence on policy; from his position as president of the Assembly's Finance Commission, Giscard could do little more than maintain his contacts within the bureaucracy and use their leaks to embarrass the government. He also attempted to set up his own organisation in the country in the guise of 'clubs' (the modern French substitute for old-fashioned political parties). In May he affirmed his loyalty to the President while delivering a backhanded attack on the prime minister. By June 1968 the stakes had escalated, for the succession seemed no further away than 1972, at the very latest.

Giscard therefore sought a means to impose his policies and himself on the next government by attempting to establish his faction as the indispensable but potentially independent component of the majority; but to do this he had to break the unity of candidature imposed by Pompidou in 1967. Giscard therefore announced that RI candidates would stand on the first ballot against official Gaullists (rebaptised Union pour le Défense de la République—UDR) in seats held by the opposition. Pompidou retaliated by planting a UDR candidate against Michel Poniatowski (Giscard's right-hand man); the prime minister may have decided not to go further because he felt confident of detaching at least half of Giscard's deputies from him should the need arise. Certainly, the RI ministers showed no taste for insurgency, and the new Minister of the Interior although officially RI was known to be totally independent of his ostensible leader.

As a further counter-weight to the RI, the prime minister also enlisted his political enemies, the left Gaullists. He made certain they were given winnable seats, for however much the left Gaullists disliked Pompidou, they detested Giscard even more. Moreover, had not the General committed himself publicly, once again, to their dreams of participation? Professor René Capitant, who had called the prime minister a snake and refused to vote on the censure motion of 22 May, was rewarded with the Ministry of Justice in the new pre-election goverment (he was the President's minister, he explained). The prime minister thus remained in firm control of the vast bulk of his party, and although the 1967 symmetry of candidatures was not quite preserved in 1968, it was close enough. And in 1968, as at the previous election, it was the Centre that paid the price of party discipline to its left and right.

Briefly wooed by the Gaullists (and Giscardiens), the Centre-PDM (*Progrès et démocratie moderne*) looked longingly to the Federation. But although the majority of its deputies had voted the censure motion it did not have enough votes in the country to offer the Federation, and the Gaullists were unwilling to offer it very much. The UDR would have an alliance only on its own terms, and these precluded any real Centre influence on policy; on these terms the PDM could not accept. Deprived of allies, the Centre was also affected by the lack of communications. More a collection of rural notables with a parliamentary co-operative than the other national parties, the speed with which candidatures had to be announced and the failure of the provincial telephone exchanges made it difficult to make the necessary contacts, promise effective support and iron out local rivalries in good time. In any case, private polls showed that the Centre on its own stood very little chance. The party therefore decided to concentrate its resources (short in men but sufficient in money) in seats where it might come ahead on the first ballot, and particularly in the 7th and 16th arrondissements in Paris, where its candidates were Bertrand Motte and General Stehlin.

Because of these difficulties, PDM fielded a third fewer candidates than in 1967, with only 267 nominees in 1968. The left-socialist PSU, at the other end of the party spectrum from the PDM, made up for its small size and lack of money by the enthusiasm and activity of its militants and tripled its candidatures: 316 in place of 107 in 1967. Among them were Pierre Mendès-France who had privately resigned from the party, but postponed the public announcement until after the election; he had the nomination of the Federation as well. The PSU also nominated a whole bevy of former leaders of UNEF, the students' union. The affluent society, denounced by the party's student supporters, meant that militants had automobiles to replace the disrupted train and telephone services.

The Federation ran 429 candidates, 17 more than in 1967, of whom 195 were Socialists, 59 Radicals, 77 (at least) Convention, and 98 Federation 'without prefix or suffix'. The Communists had their habitual first ballot quota of 470, one candidate for every constituency. The UDR, which could presumably count on the services of the state machine to get its messages through to the provinces, stood directly in 462 seats. Of the eight seats contested in 1967 but not in 1968, four were held by centrist deputies who had refused to vote the censure (MM. René Pleven, Poudevigne, Fouchier and the duc de Montesquiou) and three by independent and RI candidates who benefited from UDR 'support'; Giscard ran with neither the UDR coupon nor a UDR competitor in his Puy-de-Dôme fief. Included in the 462 were 40 of the 43 RI sitting members: aside from Giscard, one RI member retired, Poniatowski had a feeble UDR put in against him late in the day by an angry Pompidou, and the UDR sitting member in Vendée had an RI opponent. There were 45 more RI standing against UDR candidates in opposition seats; all in all Giscard nominated 118 supporters—more than enough to guarantee him television time.

There were two other vaguely centrist groups, whose major effort was concentrated on collecting candidates before the election rather than votes at it; for any party with more than 75 candidates qualified for campaign time on the ORTF, the state radio–television network, still half on strike for much of the election. *Technique et Démocratie*, in favour of democracy and progress as its name indicated, passed the magical threshold with 79 candidates, mostly in the Paris area; all but nine of its candidates were eliminated after the first ballot for winning less than 10 per cent of the register (about 12 per cent of the vote). Edgard Pisani, ex-prefect and former minister who had resigned over the decree powers in 1967 and voted the censure motion of 22 May 1968, organized the *Mouvement pour la Réforme*, with only 28 candidates. Pisani attracted some attention in Paris but little interest in his own constituency; he got over 10 per cent of the electorate, but 23 of his candidates did not and were eliminated. The extreme right had only 17 candidates of whom 10 fell below the 10 per cent minimum. Frightened by the spectre of red revolution and split by the promised release of ex-General Salan, former leader of the OAS, its leaders reserved their venom for each other. Tixier-Vignancour, presidential candidate in 1965 and Salan's lawyer, came out for the UDR, causing a scandal in his splinter party, the ARL. Georges Bidault, former chief of the CNR, political front of the OAS, returned from exile to organize a 'Movement for Justice and Liberty', but no one paid the slightest attention.

Hardly less serious, but infinitely more diverting, was the traditional individualist candidate in the Latin Quarter; the representative of the *Club des Egaux*, he had stood in 1962, and after a brief respite in 1967 was again seeking election—perhaps because he had not used up all his 1962 posters.[1] His programme was no more coherent than it had been eight years before, and the government had severely undermined its main plank by legalising contraception. But he made a laudable effort to bring himself up to date by abandoning the occupation of poet for that of an unemployed electrician. The Events of the previous month, however, had been too traumatic, and the number of crackpot candidates was small. Of the total of 2,267 candidates (77 more than in 1967), over three-quarters were nominees of the five national parties.

The official television campaign was scheduled to open on Wednesday 12 June, but as usual General de Gaulle got in first, out of season; on the evening of the 7th he was interviewed by Michel Droit, editor of the *Figaro Littéraire*. The President presented his standard planetary overview of the problems of technical civilisation and the crisis of progress in France, once more dangled the panacea of participation, and made it clear in passing that he had no intention whatsoever of allowing the ORTF to lapse into impartiality. The hour-long monologue was occasionally interrupted by polite requests for further enlightenment from the deferential interviewer, who clearly felt on familiar ground. For the total effect was very much like that of the typical article in his weekly: elegant in expression, pretentious in form, empty in content. Its favourable reception showed that the ravages of the *classe de philo* in the lycées were not confined to utopian students, but also infected more conservative sections of society. The General surfaced once again on the ORTF, this time after the close of the official television campaign, on Saturday the 29th, when no one could answer back. His speech was ostensibly non-partisan, in defence of the regime, but its message was clear enough: vote UDR. It had no perceptible effect.

The real burden of the UDR's campaign on television was borne by

[1] For details see my article in *Political Studies*, vol. 11, no. 3 (October 1963), p. 297. In 1968, he got one vote.

Pompidou, who again revealed himself to be a most accomplished television performer, dominated the whole campaign, and emerged from it as the effective and acknowledged leader of the vast horde of new Gaullist deputies. Pompidou savaged the PDM only slightly less brutally than he attacked the Communists, and he countered Giscard's efforts with the call for a 'strong and coherent majority'. The other party leaders did well with the medium and Mitterrand partially redeemed the damage done to his reputation by the Events, but Pompidou kept the initiative. There were also the usual debates and interviews on the independent stations, Europe No. 1 and Radio Luxembourg. On 11 June on Europe No. 1, Capitant declared in favour of workers' co-operatives in every plant. The employers' association, the CNPF, protested vigorously, but were hardly in a position to oppose the government, whose police might be required to remove striking workers from their factories.

Edmond de Rothschild came out openly in favour of the PDM position; if the PDM lacked candidates—and voters—it was not short of funds. The Centre's view was ably expounded by Jacques Duhamel, its parliamentary leader. The party was at once European and Atlantic. The confrontations of May had shown the dangers of dividing France into two hostile blocs, the very danger the Centre had warned against in 1967. It was an argument with some resonance; a poll in the middle of the campaign showed that twice as many respondents as in 1967 wanted a UDR–PDM majority, and a third fewer favoured a straight UDR majority. But given the pattern of candidatures, the only way for Centre supporters to vote for stability was to support the UDR. Duhamel's argument had a certain appeal to sections of the technical and professional middle classes, Lecanuet's clientele in the 1965 presidential election. But most people were more worried than thoughtful.

Not only Centre voters had been shaken loose from their party allegiances by the Events. As the campaign progressed, Federation candidates became aware of how upset their own people were. The Federation was hurt by the discredit surrounding Mitterrand who had, at the end of May, seemed more anxious to forestall Mendès and grab the presidency for himself, than to restore order. The electoral pact with the Communists, vital to return any number of Federation deputies, was now anathema to centre electors whose votes the Federation had so successfully garnered in 1967. Without breaking discipline, some leaders began making conciliatory noises to the Centre, notably Gaston Defferre, Socialist mayor of Marseilles. The Federation's key arguments were that the Events showed the incapacity of the Government; that nothing like it had ever happened when they had been in power; and therefore what was needed was not more of the same, but a change. Otherwise it might all start up again in the autumn. The Federation offered firm and stable government, but one responsive to the needs of the electorate.

Second-ballot partners of the Federation, the Communists modestly disclaimed any desire to take power by themselves; they were quite happy to offer stability and reforms in alliance with the Federation. The PCF favoured democracy and order, were indignant that the Gaullists accused them of fomenting revolution, and attacked the General's domestic, though not his foreign policy. The Communists' great rally at the Porte de Versailles (an arena too big for anyone but the PCF or the UDR) was marked by a waving tricolour and the singing of the Marseillaise. But the Communists also felt a chill wind blowing up from the electorate. Their candidate in the 6th arrondissement, scene of repeated bloody conflicts with the police in May, urged her electors to 'Vote usefully. To vote usefully is to reconcile one's heart with the circumstances. Vote Communist!'

The Communists were ready to counter attacks from the right. But for the first time since its foundation in 1920 attacks from the extreme left seemed seriously to challenge the party's claim to be the vanguard and incarnation of the working class, and thus to threaten its whole history, organisation and role. Faced with this attack, *Humanité* lashed out at the *gauchistes*, and some Communist speakers, like René Andrieu (editor of the paper) at a big meeting at the Paris Law Faculty, shouted, purple-faced, that they alone were the anointed representatives of the working class, no one else could presume to be, and therefore only the PCF was entitled to say what the workers really wanted. The sharpest Communist criticisms were reserved for the extreme left—and the PSU. The PSU answered in kind, and the dog-fight did neither side much good.

No party in the campaign supported the students or offered an apologia for the May Events, except the PSU; even its secretary-general, Michel Rocard, was quick to point out on television that it had never called for violence and blamed all of that on the police. But the PSU, with over 300 candidates, was trying to play the role of constitutional political party without losing contact with its revolutionary student constituency. The big PSU rally in the *Mutualité* (the big convention hall in the university district) provided a platform for the banned left-wing organisations, and a defiant revolutionary atmosphere for a predominantly (but by no means exclusively) student audience. The PSU's foreign policy consisted of support for the North Vietnamese, who returned the compliment by inviting the PSU leaders to visit them before the first ballot. But although the peace negotiations were proceeding in Paris, Vietnam as an issue had been totally submerged by domestic French concerns.

For interlaced with and dominating the official campaign was the unfinished business of May. Although the first week in June saw a return to work in essential services, in other sectors the pattern was very spotty. Some provincial plants went back to work directly after the 30th, others actually came out on strike for the first time. There were arguments about who should organise the return-to-work ballots, employers or unions, for the results of the vote and the balance of power in the factory might depend on it. In some plants a minority of militants prevented an earlier return to work; picket lines were not crossed, but revenge could be had by voting UDR. The Government may have hoped to play on the divisions among workers, and the fatigue of their families, by sending in the CRS to clear out the Renault factory at Flins, near Paris (on the 5th), and the Peugeot works at Sochaux near Montbéliard. Students joined with workers to try and reoccupy the Flins factory, and there was a running battle through the surrounding woods. The students who flocked to Flins were dispersed by the CRS and denounced by *Humanité*. Over the weekend a schoolboy was drowned in the Seine, perhaps pushed in by, more likely fleeing from, the rampaging riot squad. At Sochaux there was a pitched battle between the strikebreaking police and workers, with two strikers shot dead; police cars going through Montbéliard were booed and stoned by furious crowds and only the good sense of the Socialist mayor, M. Boulloche (once a Gaullist minister), saved the government from having more blood on its hands. A CFDT–CGT threat to call another general strike unless CRS were evacuated from factories also helped convince the authorities to withdraw the police. Further incidents were avoided because sensible prefects and commandants de gendarmerie had declined to storm occupied factories, some of which (like the Renault works at Le Mans) had been turned into fortified camps by the strikers. After Flins and Sochaux, the government backed away from direct strikebreaking; it was clearly no way to win working-class votes. But the students were another matter.

Although much of the heart went out of the student movement with the speech and demonstration of 30 May, the faculties were still occupied, despite departures due to fatigue, disillusionment, or the approaching vacations. And there were more—and better—student posters in the 5th and 6th arrondissements than official party ones. The government had banned further street demonstrations during the election campaign, but on the 10th there was sporadic rioting in the Latin Quarter when the drowning of the schoolboy at Melun became known. UNEF called a demonstration for the evening of the 11th, which was promptly forbidden by the authorities. The night of 11–12 June saw the last barricades, 72 of them, attacks on five police stations, 1,500 people arrested for questioning, and the great barricade on the rue des SS-Pères by the new Faculty of Medicine, left there in the morning to remind Parisians of how they had felt at the end of May. Concierges who earlier had seen only police brutality now reported only the atrocities of urban guerrillas. The fear of subversion greatly modified the normal French hostility to their police. The *Humanité* had its own axe to grind against the *groupuscules*, but it was not far wrong when it commented with its habitual measure that 'the Gaullist authorities have found precious auxiliaries among certain leftist groups who play at the Revolution as Marie Antoinette played at being a shepherdess'.

The independent radio stations, more circumspect in their reporting since the 30th, were sparse in their coverage of the last night of the barricades; there was less popular support for this demonstration than for any previous one. Left-wing candidates in Paris complained that each new barricade cost them 500 votes. The government took the occasion, on the 12th and 13th, to dissolve 12 Trotskyite, Maoist and anarchist organisations, student and industrial, under the 1936 act directed against the fascist leagues; the fascist league, *Occident*, was left to continue its raids on university buildings, and outlawed only in the autumn. Georges Bidault had already returned, and the next few days saw the return of two former officers involved in the OAS terror, Colonel Lacheroy and Captain Sergent, who announced to a press conference at the Hilton, 'I've come to participate too.' A week before the first ballot, ex-General Salan, former head of the OAS, was released from prison and pardoned. '"Thank you, Cohn-Bendit" signed: Salan', read the little box by the masthead of the *Canard Enchaîné*.

Students continued to drain away from the faculties, whose remaining occupants increasingly feared a police takeover, perhaps on the pretext of an *Occident* attack, perhaps because some buildings were coming to resemble pestholes. On 13 June, SNESup *assistants* threatened to abandon the Sorbonne unless the katangais (minor toughs who were supposed to help keep order) were expelled, the building was cleaned and a semblance of order restored. The katangais departed, some of them for the Odéon, where they were flushed out when the police evacuated the theatre the next day; hardly any students were left in it, a fact which certainly had not escaped the notice of the authorities. On Sunday the 16th the Sorbonne itself was evacuated by the police on a trumped-up incident, and an attempted demonstration quickly dispersed. At Orleans, an *Occident* commando, with the help of bully boys from the Gaullist Comité pour la Défense de la République and perhaps even of some policemen out of uniform, attacked the university campus. The revolutionaries had succeeded so well in their aim of polarization that, after the riots of the 11th–12th, the clearing of university buildings was electorally profitable.

The last week of the campaign saw a further return to work; Renault settled though Citroën and Peugeot remained out. On Friday the 21st, Malraux explained to a large Gaullist rally at the Porte de Versailles that the French Events really represented a crisis of western civilisation, thus at once flattering their nationalism and exculpating the government from any responsibility. Other Gaullists sought targets closer to home, concentrating their fire on subversives and leaving western civilisation to fend for itself, at least until after the elections. Their campaign theme was simple and effective: defence of the Republic and the liberty of its citizens from anarchy and the Communist menace. Little anonymous stickers with red and black flags and the slogan 'Never Again!' were everywhere but especially over Communist and PSU posters. The UDR demanded the greatest majority ever, since only strong government could prevent a recurrence of the troubles, and the Centre was assaulted for playing into the hands of the Left.

Political meetings seemed to attract as many people as ever, their tone was not noticeably different, but they were often noisier than usual because of systematic barracking by certain groups of students. In Grenoble, Mendès and Jeanneney had to call off a debate because of the uproar; the disorder hurt Mendès more than his opponent, whatever the intentions of the claque. The usual battle of posters raged, at least in Paris, largely between the PSU, 'Worker power, peasant power, student power, power to the people: PSU', and the UDR, 'Union for the Defence of the Republic' with a photograph of de Gaulle in a red and blue V. Rival groups of illegal bill-stickers engaged in more than the usual number of battles, shots were fired, and one young Communist was shot dead in Arras; Gaullist thugs carried guns, a gratuitous precaution since only they could count on police protection.

All this contributed to the general climate of unease and unhappiness. The persistence of one of the agreeable features of the Events, those casual conversations among strangers, and the constant use of the telephone were obvious expressions of an undefined but generalised anxiety. Compulsively ready to talk about life, art, and especially the Events, but strangely un-enthusiastic and unwilling to talk about the elections, voters seemed to be still reacting to the Events rather than the campaign. Only two IFOP polls were published before the election, on the 20th and 22nd. The first showed only the UDR and PSU improving on their 1967 performance; all the other parties had lost support. In the second poll the trend continued in favour of the UDR and PSU, the Communists and Federation continued downwards, and the Centre position improved slightly. The poll (previously cited) which showed voters preferring a UDR–PDM majority, also showed a third fewer respon-dents than in 1967 preferred a Federation–Communist victory.

For what the *grande peur* of 1968 had done was to revive the old nineteenth-century division on the French Revolution between the 'party of order' and the 'party of movement', expressed in contemporary France in terms of hostility to or acceptance of the French Communist party. The party had been helped to emerge from its ghetto by destalinization in Russia, General de Gaulle's foreign policy and the need of the Federation for Communist votes to elect Socialist deputies. Memories of Hungary, of the insurrectionary strikes of 1947 and the 'Ridgeway-la-peste' riots of 1952 were dimming. The electoral opportunism of the party had in no way diminished, but its ideological aggressivity had—except against the Maoists. The party committed itself to coming to power legally, though it hedged on whether it would voluntarily leave office; the vast majority of its own voters were anxious for the party to enter a government, most of them hoped in alliance with the Federation.[1] By 1966 only 7 per cent of the electorate thought of the PCF as 'the party that wants revolution'; only 1 per cent of the party's own supporters thought of it in these terms, and they (and most others) felt the party had become younger, more dynamic and independent, closer to the preoccupations of Frenchmen and more open. It was also perceived as 'less faithful to its principles', but this too appeared to count in its favour, for only $1\frac{1}{2}$ per cent of those who rejected the PCF did so because it was not revolutionary enough. The percentage of those who thought the party played a generally useful role rose from under 40 per cent in 1964 to just over 50 per cent two years later.[2]

But there remained a lingering fear of the party. It was increasingly acceptable as a partner in government again—but not at the Ministries of the Interior, Foreign Affairs or National Defence. The Federation could win seats that the Communists lost to the UDR, and ordinary, non-political people, especially women, still suspected the Communists as zealots who politicised everything, creating unnecessary difficulties and family quarrels. This latent fear was revived during the Events, despite the very discreet behaviour of the party—by its call for a 'gouvernement populaire' and by the unhappily familiar tone of the stalinist attacks on the students and later the PSU. When a Paris poll was taken on 27 May, over a third thought worse of the party while a quarter thought better of it than at the beginning of the Events. In the provinces, where hostility to the students had been the predominant emotion from the beginning, the change was probably even more striking. Suspicion of the party was particularly strong among older electors, and the 1968 register was the oldest in fifty years.

Of the troubled citizens who made their way to the polling stations on Sunday, 23 June, 36 per cent were over 55, 19 per cent over sixty-five, and only $8\frac{1}{2}$ per cent under 25. The election, precipitated by the actions of the young was to be decided by the oldest electorate since World War I. The

[1] See the IFOP poll in *Le Nouvel Observateur*, no. 171 (21–27 February 1968), pp. 6–7.
[2] See 'Les Français, la politique et le parti Communiste', *Cahiers du Communisme*, no. 12 (1967), pp. 53–74; and no. 1 (1968), pp. 22–48.

TABLE 15. *Five general elections, 1956–1968*

Dates	Comm.	Other Left	PDM	Gaullist	Extreme Right	Do not vote	Register
			Votes (millions) at first ballot				
1956	5·5	6·5[b]	5·4	0·9	2·9	4·9	26·8
1958	3·9	4·5	7·8	3·6	0·7	6·2	27·2
1962	4·0	4·1	3·1	6·9	0·2	8·6	27·5
1965		7·7[a]	4·2[a]	10·5[a]	1·3[a]	4·3[a]	28·4
1967	5·0	4·7	3·0	8·5	0·2	5·4	28·3
1968	4·4	4·5	2·7	10·1	0·03	5·6	28·2
		Votes (millions) in seats fought at the second ballot					
1958	3·8	3·3	6·1	5·2	0·2	.	.
1962	3·2	3·4	2·0	6·4	.	.	.
1967	4·0	4·7	1·3	8·0	.	.	.
1968	3·0	3·1	1·2	7·0	.	.	.
			Seats			Total	
1956	145	162[b]	166	16	55	544	
1958	10	65	203	187	.	465	
1962	41	106	64	249	.	465	
1967	72	120	27	234	.	470	
1968	33	57	26	346	.	470	

[a] For presidential candidates.
[b] Includes right-wing Radicals: 1 million votes, 32 deputies.

government had considered reopening the rolls, which would have allowed the 420,000 who had turned 21 since the end of February to put themselves on the register, but it was probably relieved when the Conseil d'Etat ruled against the decree on a legal formality. There was only a month in which to revise the electoral lists, a feat accomplished by the inefficient old Fourth Republic at the end of 1955, but apparently beyond the capacity of the dynamic Fifth. In spite of governmental threats there were half a dozen unofficial elections open to those between 18 and 21, in which the PSU did remarkably well—coming in second place, well behind the UDR.

Turnout was less than 1 per cent below 1967; since the lists and the electorate were both old, there was probably no increase at all in the real number who did not vote. Spoiled and blank ballots were very slightly fewer, so valid votes cast were 78·58 per cent (against 79·11 per cent in 1967). There was probably a slightly greater turnover in the electorate than these figures indicated. Local citizens, who regularly staff the polling stations, reported in Paris, the west and the centre, that some habitual voters had stayed at home but were compensated for by others who rarely voted. In Marseilles, where candidates regularly visit the cafés and bars to meet their supporters, Gaston

Defferre found that he and his Socialist colleagues were being avoided by some of their traditional friends, presumably unwilling to accept a drink without promising a vote. Turnout fell more than average in seats fought by Centre candidates in 1967 but not in 1968, and (on the second ballot) where PDM and Federation candidates withdrew in 1968. And every party (except the PSU because it had doubled its candidatures) lost votes while the Gaullists gained.[1]

The election of 1968, therefore, saw a continuation of the process begun with the referendums of 1958, 1961 and 1962 and the elections succeeding them: first the detachment of voters of the old parties from their former allegiances, and then the progressive transfer of their votes from de Gaulle to his party. The year 1962 marked a watershed in this process of detachment, for at over 31 per cent abstentions were higher than at any election since 1881, while the Communist party emerged from purdah as an acceptable ally. By 1967 the Communists had recovered over half the $1\frac{1}{2}$ million votes they had lost in 1958, and the Gaullist party had come within striking distance (20 per cent short) of the General's first ballot total in the presidental election of 1965. But in 1968 the Communists again lost most of their previous gains, while the Gaullists finally overtook their great patron. A comparison of the percentage of the electorate supporting the major parties in 1967 and 1968 will show the magnitude of the transfer (Table 16).

TABLE 16. *Change in party shares of the electorate, 1967–1968 (first ballots)[a]*

	Communist	PSU	Federation	PDM	Gaullist
Percentage ...	− 2·0	− 2·5	− 3·0	+ 1·0	+ 8·5

[a] Columns do not add across because minor parties are omitted.

Centre losses are greater than appear because the party ran a third fewer candidates in 1968, standing where it was strongest and therefore winning a higher average vote per constituency fought. The enormous losses suffered by the Centre can better be judged by comparing the percentage of the electorate voting in the few seats contested by the four major formations over the whole period from 1958. A third of the 1958 Centre vote has moved to the UDR and the Gaullists have increased their vote over 1958 by more than 50 per cent (two-thirds from Centre defectors, most of the rest probably from new voters). For comparing 1962 with 1968, while everyone except the Centre profited a bit from a higher poll, the Gaullists gained most from the

---

[1] The author would like to express his warmest thanks to Mr Philip Williams, who did a large number of the calculations and collaborated on most of the rest on which the following analysis is based, and for general psephological aid, succour and comfort.

TABLE 17. *Party shares of the electorate 1958–1968. Change in comparable seats (first ballots)*

Gaullists vs:	No. seats	Turnout (%)	Comm. (%)	Fed. (%)	PDM (%)	Gaull. (%)
4-cornered fights, 1958–68:						
1958 Comm. Fed. PDM	8	77·1	11	19·5	24	22
1958–62 Comm. Fed. PDM	,,	−8	=	−3	−11	+6
1962–8 Comm. Fed. PDM	,,	+12	+1·5	+2	+2·5	+6
Total 1958–68 Comm. Fed. PDM	,,	+4	+1·5	−1	−8·5	+12
4 and 3-cornered fights, 1962–8:						
1962–8 Comm. Fed. PDM	19	+15	+1	+3	+1	+8
Comm. Fed.	8	+11	=	=		+10
1967–8 Comm. Fed. PDM	43	=	−1·8	−1·4	−2·3	+ 5
Comm. Fed.	10	=	−4·5	−4·0		+ 6·5
Comm. PDM '67/Fed. '68	7	−2·5	−3·4			+19
Comm. Fed.; PDM '67 only	24	−1·0	−1·0	+0·3		+10

increased turnout. The party has prospered at the expense of conservative Radicals in Champagne, Burgundy and the Rhône valley and along the Atlantic Coast; at the expense of the Catholic Centre in Brittany, Savoy and the industrial north; and from Right and Left along the Mediterranean littoral. From 1962 to 1968 there are significant Gaullist losses only in Meurthe-et-Moselle, where the party is still paying the price for the President's ill-judged and unsuccessful attempt to requisition miners in the strike of 1963.

But the memories of most voters went no further back than the Events of May. In comparable seats fought by the major parties in 1967 and 1968 the Gaullist vote increased at everyone's expense, most from the Centre, least from the Federation. Where PDM dropped out in 1968 turnout was down, and the Gaullist share of the electorate doubled, while the Federation vote remained unchanged, suggesting most PDM supporters went to the Gaullists and perhaps a fifth to the Federation. Where there was no Centre candidate at either election, Centrists who had voted Left in 1967 now voted Gaullist; where a Federation candidate replaced a Centre one in 1968, the Gaullists gained over half the 1967 Centre vote, and the Federation supporters who had voted Communist now had their own candidate to return to.

The Communist share of the vote was down in 86 departments (out of 95), by less than 4 per cent in 72 of these, and by more than that in the remaining 14.[1] The big losses (nowhere above 8 per cent) were concentrated in the east and west, Burgundy and Champagne, and Dordogne, Lot, and Pyrénées-

[1] See F. Goguel, 'Les élections législatives des 23 et 30 juin 1968', *Revue Française de Science Politique*, XVIII, no. 5 (October 1968).

Orientales. The party gained slightly in Indre, Cher, Nièvre, Allier, Lot-et-Garonne and Alpes-Maritimes at the expense of the Federation, whose losses exceeded Communist gains. Around Paris, and in certain industrial areas like Longwy, Montbéliard, Melun (Flins), Elbeuf (Cléon), St Nazaire and Nantes the PSU took Communist votes.[1] In Paris the PSU took Federation votes (there were not many left to be had) and came in ahead of it in most of the conurbation's constituencies. But in general the left-Socialists had little reason to rejoice; in the 96 seats contested in 1967 and 1968 their vote was slightly down. As in 1967, the pattern of the Federation vote was rather variable. It lost under 4 per cent of the vote in 38 departments, including Paris and region, but it also gained votes from the Centre.[2]

But the Centre suffered most at the hands of the majority. It lost over 40 per cent of its 1967 vote in the east, the south-east and the Massif Central. The UDR share of the vote was down only in Côtes-du-Nord and Deux-Sèvres, where MM. Pleven and Fouchier were standing without Gaullist opposition, and in Jura (Duhamel's department) and Hautes-Pyrénées, where there were especially strong PDM candidates. The Gaullists got their highest percentage of the vote in their traditional strongholds: the east, the west and the Massif Central. More strikingly, they made some of their biggest gains (from 12 to 20 per cent) in traditional left-wing strongholds of the centre and south.[3] The party thus accentuated the progress it had made in 1967 in rural, left-wing and backward France.

Of the 470 metropolitan seats, 154 were decided on the first ballot, the highest number ever won on the single-member, double-ballot majority system. Communists won six; the Gaullists took the lion's share with 142 seats (including 28 RI); the UDR supported M. Hunault in Loire-Atlantique and opposed neither Giscard (RI) nor the four PDM deputies re-elected on the first round. The first ballot nicely symbolised the victory of the 'party of order'. Robert Poujade, secretary-general of the UDR, increased his share of the vote by two-thirds, the Prime Minister by a third to capture 80 per cent of the poll, and the Minister of the Interior with $81\frac{1}{2}$ per cent of the vote, the biggest majority in all of France.

The 154 first-round victors defeated 509 other candidates, and 668 more were eliminated by the 10 per cent rule, among them only two UDR, but

---

[1] See A. Lancelot, 'Les élections des 23 et 30 juin 1968', *Projet*, no. 28 (September–October 1968).

[2] The Federation lost from 4 to 8 per cent in the old Radical bastions of Provence (except Var), Normandy, Burgundy, and Champagne, and in Socialist Haute-Vienne and Tarn; and 8–12 per cent in the Socialist fief of Aude, Radical Charente and Indre. It gained from the Centre slightly along the Atlantic coast, in the east and in the Massif Central; more heavily (from 4 to 8 per cent) in Poitou, Mayenne, and Lozère. The Centre took Federation votes in Franche-Comté, Dauphiné, and Aude, Haute-Vienne, Calvados and Eure-et-Loir.

[3] Indre, Creuse, Dordogne, Tarn, Hérault.

151 of the 267 PDM, 52 Communists, 74 Federation and most of the PSU (in the eight departments of Paris and region the only PSU candidate to qualify for the second ballot was its secretary-general, Michel Rocard, who stood down for a Communist). The Federation, PSU and Communists withdrew for the best-placed Left candidate; this left three PSU (including Mendès) to fight the second round, 134 Federation and 160 Communist candidates. In 1967 the Communists led in 13 seats where they nevertheless withdrew in favour of the Federation; this time they made only three such gifts—to MM. Estier, Dayan (both close to Mitterrand) and Malvy. Together the Left stood in 297 seats; the UDR had 296 candidates, and RI about 15 more. PDM had come in first place in only 18 seats; the Federation would withdraw for it only where its candidates had voted censure motions in the past and promised to do so in the future; and the UDR stood down for it only if a Communist or other Left candidate might slip by, though Pompidou withdrew the UDR candidate standing against Duhamel, as a gesture likely to help the UDR nationally. Among the Centre casualties was the party's 1965 presidential nominee, Jean Lecanuet. The Centre was left with 68 candidates at the second ballot.

Of the 316 seats to be decided at the second ballot, one (Vendée 3) had only one, UDR, candidate; half the electorate turned out, 30,672 to vote for him, 6,273 to spoil their ballots. There were 269 duels (85 per cent of the contests) in which the UDR fought 107 Communists, 3 PSU, 121 Federation, and 14 PDM; the RI opposed 3 Communists, 4 Federation, and 3 PDM; and 6 PDM stood against Communists. Of the 46 three-cornered battles, over two-thirds were between Communists, PDM and UDR. Taken with the Gaullist success on the first ballot, this pattern of candidatures meant that the UDR (without the Giscardiens) might win a clear majority of seats (244) in the new Assembly—if the electorate did not change its mind between ballots. For in 1967, pollsters and official spokesmen had assumed that Right and Centre voters would swing to the Gaullists; instead many anti-Gaullists had voted for the Left. In 1967 the Ministry of the Interior had made its usual ingenious arrangement of the statistics to minimise the strength of the opposition; in 1968 the operation was performed in order to diminish the apparent strength of the majority.

Michel Debré might declare on RTL: 'Je ne sais pas ce que c'est un gouvernement qui n'est pas autoritaire. Ce n'est pas un gouvernement.' But Pompidou was determined that no mistake of his should frighten away the 'party of funk'. He therefore emphasised the need for a coherent majority, described the first ballot result as a 'national' victory, and again invited the Giscardiens and the Centre to come aboard for the great work ahead. Surveys gave the Gaullists between 285 and 260-odd seats—15–20 seats on either side of a UDR majority, which put all the heat on the voters, and helped Pompidou in his campaign.

On Monday the 24th Citroën returned to work, leaving only a few thousand workers still out in the Paris area; Dunkirk steel and Lyons engineering works were the last large remaining strikes unsettled. Early in the morning of the 27th the Beaux-Arts were taken by the police; new posters, however, continued to appear under the imprint of the student press. Science Po., as befitted an institution which prepares most of the future servants of the French state, evacuated itself—to the strains of the Internationale. Nearby, the fortress-like new Faculty of Medicine remained in student hands, offering films of social significance and a meeting on Literature and Revolution. Built in the fascist style favoured for public buildings all over Europe in the 1930s it was near impregnable to assault, and its vast expanse of bare stone wall at ground level was covered with posters. Students still hawked *Action* and the *Enragé*, the most successful revolutionary journals, in the streets of the Left Bank; and at the Censier annexe of the Sorbonne, joint staff–student committees and general meetings struggled to complete their proposed restructuring of the university and of the syllabuses, before they too were cleared out by the police. But the processes of direct participatory democracy were better suited to discussion than decision, and in the bigger general meetings speakers were rarely brief and often not to the point. The Comités d'action still issued communiqués and revolutionaries tried to sound defiant, more to keep their spirits up than because they believed it. But there was enough for the Minister of Interior to resurrect the red peril for the second ballot, and for the prime minister to denounce the plot against the Republic. On Saturday the 29th, the eve of poll, an 18-year-old Communist was shot dead in Arras by a CDR commando, 500 students demonstrated in the Latin Quarter, and de Gaulle appealed for unity.

The second ballot amplified the trend of the first and gave the UDR its majority: it gained 95 seats to give it 282 (plus 14 overseas)—a comfortable margin in the 487 strong Assembly (470 French plus 17 overseas). The Republican Independents gained 21 seats for a total of 64, 58 elected with the UDR coupon. The Centre was reduced to 26 seats; the Federation lost 61 to return 57 members, the Communists 39 to return 33; and all the PSU candidates were beaten, Mendès by 132 votes. All the candidates of the Left had observed their alliance; unlike 1967 when five Federation nominees had refused to stand down for Communists and were expelled from their party for their trouble, no one broke discipline in 1968. Instead it was the Left's electorate that backed away from the Communist alliance, as it had in 1962. And this time Centre and Right voters overcame their anti-Gaullist sentiments for the sake of voting against disorder—often the work of their own children in Paris. In the capital and around it the majority took 58 of the 78 seats; only one UDR sitting member lost, to General Stehlin (PDM), in the 16th. In the 5th, René Capitant had the biggest majority in the capital, 63 per cent, and the lowest turnout, 64 per cent; turnout in the 6th was under 69 per cent. These two arrondissements had borne the brunt of the student agitation and police battles. Perhaps residents found it difficult to choose between barricades and tear gas. Indeed, abstentions were quite unusually higher in Paris (at 28 per cent) and region than average.

In the 316 seats fought at both ballots, participation was down slightly between the two ballots, from 80 to 78 per cent and spoiled ballots increased from 1·3 to 2·2 per cent. Total Gaullist gains exceeded the losses of Centre and Right, so that some of the UDR gain was due to Left voters and some, no doubt, to differential abstention. Between the ballots the Left (Communist–Federation–PSU) lost 2 per cent of its vote, and half a million voters; in 1967 it had increased its percentage of the poll and maintained its vote. In the 160 seats contested by the Communists on the second ballot the party fell $9\frac{1}{2}$ per cent short of the total Left vote on the first ballot; the Federation $2\frac{1}{2}$ per cent in its 134 contests. In five constituencies the Communists fell short of their own first ballot total. Communist voters also appear to have broken discipline by refusing to vote for several right-wing Socialists and Radicals, notably Robert Lacoste, Max Lejeune and Georges Bonnet.

The indiscipline of Left voters, the general disinclination to vote Communist, and the collapse of the Centre on the second ballot can also be seen by comparing the percentage of a party's candidates who win on the second ballot with an average poll on the first, with those who lose after first coming in striking distance of victory. The percentage of Gaullist candidates who won their seats after polling 10–30 per cent on the first ballot rose six times from 1967 to 1968, while the number of Communists with 30–50 per cent on the first ballot who were beaten on the second increased by more than half (Table 18).

Gaullists could collect Left votes where the Centre could not. Comparing 1967–8 Centre–Communist with Gaullist–Communist duels, it seemed that some Communists (or anti-conservative Federation voters looking for a home) preferred to abstain or even vote UDR rather than cast a ballot for their hereditary enemies on the right. In Communist–Gaullist straight fights the entire Communist loss appears to transfer to the UDR in the provincial seats, but in Paris defectors tended to stay home rather than vote UDR; in Montbéliard the intervention of the CRS cost the Gaullists votes, for in these circumstances order was represented by the Socialist mayor and deputy, M. Boulloche. Working-class Communist support seemed to hold relatively well in industrial seats, but Gaullists took seats from the Com-

TABLE 18. *Party fortunes: surprises, 1967 and 1968 (second ballots)*

	Comm.	PSU	Fed.	PDM	Gaull.
% who *win* with 10–30% (as % such candidates)					
1967	$1\frac{1}{2}$	$6\frac{1}{2}$	$11\frac{1}{2}$	2	$3\frac{1}{2}$
1968	0·3	—	6	2	20
% who *lose* with 30–50%					
1967	33	—	12	37	42
1968	58	(100)	41	49	26

munists in the industrial north and east, and Le Mans, and also in Berry, Nivernais, the Mediterranean coast and rural Haute-Vienne. The Federation also lost seats to the majority in the north, and the Mediterranean, but also in the Rhône valley, in Burgundy and Champagne, Brittany, the basin of the Eure and Loir, and in its great traditional strongholds of the south-west, where it had been threatened once before, by Pierre Poujade. In 7 of the 26 departments where the Poujadists took over $12\frac{1}{2}$ per cent of the vote in 1956, the Gaullists increased their share of the electorate by over 12 per cent, and by 8 to 12 per cent in another 11; and a small number of ex-Poujadists were returned as UDR members. Poujade himself had been acquired by the government before the election of 1967; still on retainer, he visited the prime minister before the election and called on his friends to vote Gaullist.

Not only small shopkeepers but small farmers heard the call. Edgar Faure, the Minister of Agriculture, who had brought peasant voters back to the majority in 1967, had successfully maintained contact with the agricultural organisations during the Events. In the 200 most rural constituencies in France (those with no town over 30,000) the UDR increased its share of the vote by 25·8 per cent compared to its national average of 14·3 per cent, polling over 80 per cent in 20 of them. Seventy-nine UDR candidates were returned from these seats on the first ballot (37 in 1967). Over half the Gaullist first ballot victories were thus won in rural seats, and 40 per cent of all the rural seats went to the majority on the first round. The Minister of Agriculture was returned in his own bailiwick with three-quarters of the vote. The trend of 1967 is therefore much amplified, and the UDR now represents backward as much as modern France. Some internal cohesion may be the price of this electoral success; and for a party already heavily dependent on older age-groups for its support, a shift in its internal balance away from active France may have deleterious effects on the UDR's future capacity to appeal to the rising, numerous, and increasingly urban generation.

But in 1968 not only the peasantry (who feel no party cares sufficiently for their problems) were dramatically rallied to the regime by their fear of the *partageux*; and anxiety was felt far beyond rural areas. A Paris survey taken on 27 May showed that public confidence had increased in the trade unions (including the CGT) but had turned against the students and all the political parties (including the Communists). Over half the sample viewed the future with foreboding, but while their trust in the President and his party had been badly shaken, the prime minister's standing had actually increased. After the General's second speech, confidence partially returned, but 40 per cent were still worried. After the election, all the faculties were cleared by the police, ending any hope of 'people's summer universities' desired by some of the revolutionary students at least. There were incidents at the Avignon Festival, and in Paris around Bastille Day, but the police were very much in command of the situation. The usual lemming-like departure for the holidays began, but vacation areas complained of fewer people spending less money. As Paris emptied the deputies returned for a special session, determined to maintain order, but not quite sure how.

The new enlarged majority looked to the prime minister, first of all for present leadership, and then as living proof that Gaullism had a future after the departure of its founder. The prime minister had increasingly extended his control over the government before the Events; during them he had emerged as its effective head. Pompidou had dominated the campaign and the electoral victory of the UDR was also a political triumph for him. He was rumoured to be sceptical of some of the General's ventures in foreign affairs, but if he remained in office, his position as designated successor to the President would be confirmed. And then, who would bother with the General? The biggest electoral victory in French history was an answer to the revolutionary Left, but it did not represent an increase in the president's popularity. That fell sharply in May, and continued downwards in June when Pompidou's popularity was rising fast. By the end of the month he was within seven points of de Gaulle, and it looked as if for the first time a prime minister might overtake the President in the polls. On 19 July Pompidou was sacked.

25 Gaullism without de Gaulle? The 1969 referendum and presidential election

The crisis of 1968 succeeded in shattering, not the Fifth Republic, but the already crumbling prestige of its founder. The student revolutionaries in the end ensured the overwhelming electoral triumph of the previously declining Gaullist party. But the mass movement had demonstrated the discontent of ordinary people with de Gaulle's concentration on France and neglect of Frenchmen, and their repudiation of his style of government. The final victory of the regime owed far more to the prime minister than to the President of the Republic.

Within three weeks the premier was relegated to 'the reserve of the Republic' like his predecessor Michel Debré six years earlier, and replaced by the colourless Maurice Couve de Murville. Pompidou continued to comport himself as the natural successor; de Gaulle countered by announcing that he would serve his full term, till 1972. But the affection and confidence of his subjects had been further shaken by the November currency crisis, and so he refurbished his familiar instrument for rallying friends and defeating enemies, and called a referendum for the following spring. As usual, two different questions were to be linked together. The creation of stronger (though still financially feeble) regional authorities responded to the new vogue for 'participation' in government, and sugared the pill for de Gaulle's long-cherished Second Chamber reform.

The Senate had remained, as in previous republics, an upper house elected by and mainly composed of mayors and local councillors with a strong rural and small-town bias. Because of the conservatism of its usually elderly members, because the areas of Gaullist strength were under-represented in it, and because it reflected the outlook of the local politicians against whom de Gaulle had so often waged war, it had been throughout the Fifth Republic an opposition stronghold. Now the President proposed to transform its composition, associating with the elected spokesmen of the new regions a large professional, corporatist element. The local politicians feared that behind the reconstruction of the Second Chamber which represented them in Paris there loomed an impending reform of the municipal authorities on which their power was based.

Thus by attacking the Senate de Gaulle incurred the hostility of the whole political class, local as well as national, apart from his loyal followers in the UDR: even their Conservative allies, led by Valéry Giscard d'Estaing, chose this opportunity to defect to the opposition. By linking the unpopular Senate reform to the popular regional proposals, and flatly refusing to allow two separate answers, the General ensured that the struggle would be a hard one—so that if he won, the victory would have real significance. In September 1963 he had said, 'It is essential for [me] to understand the needs of the French people, to know what the French people want. I am conscious of having discerned this for the last quarter of a century. Since I still have the strength, I am determined to continue.' Now, seven years after his last referendum, three and a half years after his inglorious re-election, he needed reassurance. If he won his reign would continue; if not he had found his honourable exit. For despite his announcement about 1972, he threatened once again to retire if defeated, plunging the country into unknown dangers.

He lost. The old appeal was no longer compelling. The double question recalled the old tricks; the demand for personal confidence on a subsidiary matter of policy seemed quite unnecessary; the implied threat ('me or chaos') was both resented and disbelieved. For France had discovered in May 1968 that de Gaulle and chaos were not incompatible, while Pompidou, the real victor in June, was available in the 'reserve of the Republic'. Indeed, his availability so handicapped the OUI campaign that strong pressure was put on him to decline to stand if de Gaulle resigned; it failed, and some Gaullists consequently regarded Pompidou as one of the two men most responsible for their eventual defeat. The other was Alain Poher, the new President of the Senate, a political unknown who had unexpectedly been chosen in October 1968 to succeed Gaston Monnerville, *persona non grata* at the Elysée for violently denouncing de Gaulle's unconstitutional conduct six years earlier. Poher's election had thus been a gesture of appeasement to the Gaullists, but when they launched their attack on the Senate he emerged as its most active and effective defender.

On 27 April 1969 de Gaulle suffered his first defeat for 11 years when, in a poll of over 80 per cent, 53 per cent voted 'No'. The Gaullist vote declined everywhere and only 24 departments out of 95 gave a majority of their votes to the President; 18 were in the once overwhelmingly Gaullist north-west and north-east, still faithful—except for one mining area—but now by far narrower majorities. The General departed without fuss and soon afterwards left France for an obscure Irish hotel. In accordance with a constitutional provision which the referendum would have altered, Poher, as President of the Senate, became acting President of the Republic. René Capitant, a Left Gaullist minister, resigned from the government. There were no riots and no demonstrations. De Gaulle had gone. Poher, not Pompidou, had come. Chaos had not.

With the General's departure, the unexpected opportunity of revenge on the Fifth Republic galvanised the politicians of the Fourth into activity. Their hopes rested on the sudden boom in Poher's popularity. He had become widely appreciated in the referendum campaign as a reasonable, reassuring, moderate man: no glamour, but safety first. After eleven years of de Gaulle, the 'higher interests of France' had had a good run and most people wanted more attention paid to the 'immediate advantage of Frenchmen'. In Poher, therefore, the Centre politicians saw a champion who could perhaps restore their shattered political fortunes. But to defeat Pompidou— the only serious Gaullist contender—it would be necessary to unite the entire opposition at the second round. A Left candidate could not do so—he would drive Centre voters into the Gaullist camp. A strong Centre candidate might —but if there was a single Left contender at the first ballot he would push Poher into third place and eliminate him from the race. Only left-wing disunity on the first round could offer a chance of defeating the Gaullists at the second.

As usual, therefore, the crucial decision rested with the Socialist Party. For several years it had promoted unity of the Left, and at that very moment it was about to hold the inaugural conference of a new party in which it was hoping at last to absorb most of the scattered Socialist groups and clubs to its Left. Open support for a Centre candidate would split the old Socialists and alienate the new. Yet the Soviet invasion of Czechoslovakia had revived all the old suspicions against the Communist Party, while the natural candidate of a united Left, François Mitterrand, had discredited himself by his conduct in May 1968. Guy Mollet therefore hoped that the Socialist Party would put forward a weak candidate (or none at all) on the first round, so that Poher, given a comfortable lead over his rivals within the opposition, could gather in all their votes at the second. But Gaston Defferre rashly assumed that he could revive in 1969 the presidential bid which had been foiled in 1965. He announced his own candidature and had it narrowly approved at the party conference, against the opposition of both Mollet's friends and Mitterrand's, and then found himself the spokesman of a hopelessly divided party competing at once against passionate Communist hostility and a strong Centre rival—and, as the opinion polls pitilessly showed, failing catastrophically against both.

Hoping to crush the badly situated Socialist candidate, and determined to retrieve their voters who were already drifting towards Poher, the Communists put forward the best man to rally their own forces, Jacques Duclos (perhaps the most effective of all the candidates), and mobilised their full strength for his campaign. Michel Rocard, the general secretary of the PSU, and Alain Krivine, a Trotskyite student leader, hoped to harness the enthusiasm of the May rebels; both propagated their ideas effectively on the capitalist State television (though at workers' meetings Krivine was howled down by the Communists). Beside these four candidates of the Left there also stood a millionaire businessman of conservative views, Louis Ducatel. Defferre and Rocard—the only candidates who seriously discussed policy issues—both publicly offered to withdraw in favour of Pierre Mendès-France, despite his previously stated unwillingness to stand in the presidential election. But a Communist leader, Georges Marchais, at once violently denounced the former premier. Defferre then announced that Mendès-France would be his prime minister; thereafter they campaigned together. It was far too late, for Defferre's ship, under-financed and with only a skeleton crew, was already hopelessly waterlogged when the new pilot came aboard.

On the Right, Pompidou began his campaign with confidence, backed by all the Gaullist notables and even his old rival Giscard. But though he undertook an exhausting provincial tour, his 40 per cent support in the earliest opinion polls remained unchanged throughout the following four weeks. Meanwhile, the almost unknown Poher was advancing rapidly; by mid-May the polls put him only 4 per cent behind Pompidou for the first ballot, and 12 per cent ahead for the second. (Pompidou protested at the publication of second-ballot polls, which were then stopped.) At this low point the Gaullists were very worried men; yet even then they were cheered by the support of 12 out of 33 Centre deputies (including three well-known leaders: Jacques Duhamel, Joseph Fontanet and René Pleven) to outweigh Poher's allies of the anti-Gaullist extreme Right (Jacques Soustelle, Georges Bidault, Jacques Isorni—and J. L. Tixier-Vignancour, who switched to Pompidou at the second ballot).

Poher's strength fell away as fast as it had come. As acting president he was reluctant to campaign vigorously, and limited himself to television appearances which did him little good; until his final effective and aggressive broadcast on the last Friday, he was moderate, reassuring and non-committal. His appeal suffered from a fatal contradiction. He promised a quiet life without the constant crises in which the General had revelled. Yet could he form a government backed by the overwhelmingly Gaullist National Assembly, or would he have to dissolve, plunging the country into a general election from which no coherent majority might emerge? The Left, through Mitterrand, warned that they would not switch to Poher on the second ballot unless he promised to dissolve; but to do so would forfeit conservative support to Pompidou, who naturally stressed his rival's dilemma throughout his campaign. Poher pledged that he would seek to govern with the existing Assembly and would dissolve only if the Gaullist majority made that course impossible. To preserve his image as a guarantor of stability he abandoned his reputation as the architect of change.

Pompidou faced a similar difficulty. As the opposition gathered strength he began emphasising the need for new policies over the whole gamut of political topics from Israel to agriculture, from the role of Parliament to Britain's entry into the Common Market. But this seemed a cowardly repudiation of his old leader, and his rivals asked insistently why he had not made these changes in his six years as prime minister. Later in the campaign, with Poher slipping in the opinion polls, Pompidou's tone hardened and he became notably more enthusiastic about the General's policies.

The results were to justify his reviving confidence. In an 80 per cent poll, 7 per cent below that of 1965, Pompidou exceeded the pollsters' predictions and held the same vote as General de Gaulle three and a half years before: 44 per cent. Both were strongest among women and old people. Pompidou did worse than the General in the industrial north and north-east, but substantially better in the conservative west and especially in the poor and backward areas of the centre and south-west, where Gaullist promises of favours from Paris were building up the party's strength. Poher had only 23½ per cent, little more than Lecanuet, Tixier and Marcilhacy in 1965: he too did notably well in the south-west, where the declining Left suffered severely, and in the north-east where the Gaullists were still paying for the miners' strike in 1963. Duclos with 21½ per cent ran close behind him, confounding expectations that the Communist Party would collapse in the presidential elections. It was instead the non-Communist Left which collapsed, its derisory vote splitting 5 per cent for Defferre, 3½ per cent for Rocard; for by the time Poher had begun to slip, Defferre was no longer credible as a serious candidate and Duclos reaped the benefit. The total Left vote was equal to Mitterrand's in 1965 and 14 per cent worse than in the catastrophic election of 1968.

Poher declined to withdraw, despite the discouragement of his supporters, and at the second ballot Pompidou was comfortably elected. In one of the Fifth Republic's lowest turnouts he had 42 per cent of the votes cast; most Communists obediently stayed at home. The Gaullists survived de Gaulle with a safe majority in the Assembly and a new leader in the Elysée, who spoke of adjusting past policies in order to gain support in the Centre. No longer inspired by or even appreciative of the General, Frenchmen still prized the stable government his regime had brought them and still suspected that the politicians of the past would undermine it. The Gaullist party promised that stability, under the firm rule of the Right. But had France, as May 1968 perhaps suggested, exchanged frequent but minor cabinet crises for occasional but catastrophic crises of the system?

TABLE 19. *The Presidential election of 1969*

1965 (first ballot)			Thousands		% of vote		% of electorate	
	Thousands		1st	2nd	1st	2nd	1st	2nd
	28,235	Registered	28,776	28,761				
	4,233	Not voting	6,275	8,907				
	244	Spoiled	290	1,295				
	23,758	Voted	22,211	18,559				
De Gaulle	10,387	Pompidou	9,763	10,688	44·0	57·6	33·9	37·2
Mitterrand	7,659	Poher	5,202	7,871	23·4	42·4	18·1	27·4
Lecanuet	3,767	Duclos	4,782		21·5		16·6	
Tixier	1,254	Defferre	1,128		5·1		3·9	
Marcilhacy	413	Rocard	814		3·7		2·8	
Barbu	278	Ducatel	285		1·3		1·0	
		Krivine	236		1·1		0·8	

With the Centre and the non-Communist Left as divided as ever by their feuds, and the Communist party solid on its base but incapable of expansion, there was—after eleven years of Gaullist constitution-building—no alternative government. The glacial pace of Communist liberalisation and the parochial vision of other opposition leaders bore much responsibility for that state of affairs. But so did the short views and petty partisanship of most of the Gaullist chieftains, and the General's own contempt for the health of organisations and institutions which, in the long run, are indispensable to democratic politics.

TABLE 20. *Party Fortunes and Surprises, 1958–1968*

	Comm.	PSU	Soc. (Fed.)	Rad., etc.	MRP (Centre)	CNI	Gaull.	V Rep.
Party fortunes: deputies elected on first ballot								
1958								
Candidates	461		421	149	214	241	343	
Winners	1		2	—	7	16	7	
1962								
Candidates	463		330	128	189	204	400	30
Winners	9		1	4	14	6	46	12
1967								
Candidates	470	107	411		389		470	
Winners	8	—	1		1		50	
1968								
Candidates	470	316	429		267		462	48
Winners	6	—	—		4		142	—
Party fortunes: poll on first ballot (% of all party's candidates)								
1958								
High (30–50 %)	10		13	7	14	24	27	
Average (10–30 %)	73		59	51	53	61	62	
Low (under 10 %)	17		28	42	29	8	9	
1962								
High	16½		14	21	14	19½	52	23
Average	68		55	54	39	48	36	20
Low	14		31	22	39	30	0½	—
1967								
High	19	2	22		14		63	
Average	70	28	68		55		25	
Low	10	70	10		31		0·2	
1968								
High	14	1	17		13		52	14
Average	70	6	52		63		15	51
Low	15	93	31		23		—	34
Party fortunes: surprises on second ballot								
% who *win* with average poll (as % of such candidates)								
1958	—		3	5	19	23	42	
1962	2½		15½	13	11	5	13	17
1967	1½	6½	11½		2		3½	
1968	0·3	—	6		2		20	6
% who *lose* with high poll								
1958	79		44	20	48	12	8	
1962	66		17	19	28	44	19	—
1967	33	—	12		37		42	
1968	58	(100)	41		49		26	45

NOTES

Party labels. 'V Rep.' 1962 were allies (mostly deputies) from other parties having UNR endorsement; in 1968, those Republican Independents (Giscardiens) who were competing with a UDR candidate. 'Gaull.' includes all candidates having the official Gaullist endorsement except V Rep. 1962. Other parties strictly defined.

Section 1 of the Table gives each party's total *number* of candidates and the *number* winning on the first ballot, i.e. polling over 50 % of the vote. Section 2 shows the *percentage* of each party's candidates who on the first ballot scored a high, average or low poll (respectively 30–50, 10–30 or under 10 % of the vote). Section 3 shows first the *percentage* of surprise winners, i.e. the percentage of each party's candidates with an average first-ballot poll who won at the second ballot; then the *percentage* of surprise losers, i.e. percentage of candidates with a high first-ballot poll who lost at the second. The former measures discrimination in favour of a party, the latter discrimination against it. (Nobody won from a low poll.)

Overseas seats are excluded. The 1958 figures were calculated by Dr B. D. Graham.

TABLE 21. *Results in selected constituencies, 1951–1968*

In 1951 and 1956 members were chosen in large constituencies (usually departments) by P.R. modified by a premium for party alliances. The 1951 figure is the vote in the *department* divided by the number of constituencies which it comprised in 1958. The 1956 figure gives votes actually cast within the area later forming the 1958 constituencies. (Naturally sitting members chose to stand in their best areas.) From 1958, to win on the *first* ballot a candidate needed a majority of all votes cast; on the second, more votes than any rival. Votes cast for members elected are italicized.

(a) Same candidate as last election.   P Poujadist.
(b) Sitting member.   R Radical.
(c) Both (a) and (b).   RR Right Radical.
(d) Votes of more than one candidate combined.   L Left.
  ER Extreme Right.

	1951	1956	1958		1962		1967		1968	
AISNE I (LAON), NORTHERN FRANCE — 1958 El. 52,704 / El. 52,485										
Comm.	(14,800)	(c)12,229	7,914	—	(a)7,405	—	8,772	12,237	(a)9,429	15,507
Soc, Fed.	(7,100)	(c)10,791	(c)8,945	15,076	(a)9,273	18,530	6,230	—	5,912	—
Rad, etc.	(1,250)	(d)4,619	—	—	—	—	—	—	—	—
MRP	(3,850)	3,247	—	—	—	—	—	—	—	—
Cons.	(4,300)	3,972	13,202	24,694	(a)7,861	—	11,286	13,790	[a]7,513	—
Gaull.	(8,500)	3,496	9,980	—	13,390	21,081	(c)17,429	18,366	(c)20,609	25,285
Other Rt	P(3,700)	P3,199	—	—	—	—	—	—	—	—

Cons. incl. MRP 1951; same Cons. 1958, 1962, 1968. Gaullists win a Left seat.

	1951	1956	1958		1962		1967		1968	
AUBE 2 (INCL. PART TROYES)—DECHRISTIANIZED CHAMPAGNE — 1958 El. 48,594 / El. 51,181										
Comm.	(9,500)	(c)11,251	(c)8,116	11,326	7,096	11,511	8,551	—	(a)6,079	—
Soc, Fed.	(6,500)	(c)5,984	6,816	—	5,154	—	[a]11,149	22,157	(a)11,480	18,447
Rad.	(2,200)	3,206	—	—	—	—	—	—	—	—
MRP	—	1,016	—	—	—	—	—	—	—	—
Cons.	(11,000)	(c)8,814	15,252	22,201	(a)9,889	11,588	—	—	—	—
Gaull.	(6,550)	1,608	5,977	—	8,961	10,868	[a]16,300	18,880	17,996	22,436
Other	(700)	P6,332	—	—	—	—	—	—	—	—

Gaull. 1958 was unofficial; Cons. 1958, 1962 ran as Gaull. 1967. Same Soc. 1958, 1967; both local mayors.

	1951	1956	1958		1962		1967		1968	
BOUCHES-DU-RHÔNE 3 (PART MARSEILLES) — 1958 El. 61,080 / El. 58,047										
Comm.	(14,100)	(c)15,164	9,883	10,762	(a)9,156	—	(a)11,149	—	9,420	—
Soc, Fed.	(7,200)	(c)11,088	10,441	13,193	10,676	20,584	(c)13,469	23,222	(c)11,495	19,611
Other Lt	(500)	R3,676	(a)4,963 R	—	—	—	(d)1,269	—	1,138 PSU	—
Cons., MRP	(4,000)	(d)8,113	6,963	14,353	(c)6,313	—	2,195	—	—	—
Gaull.	(9,200)	—	5,803	3,465	(a)8,395	14,547	9,995	15,201	(a)16,101	19,025
Other Rt	(1,250)	P4,886	(d)2,841	—	—	—	(d)2,053	—	(a)994	—

Gaull. 1951 was Cons. 1956; Gaull. 1958 was unofficial; Defferre (mayor) was Soc. except 1958.

	1951	1956	1958		1962		1967		1968	
CANTAL 2 (ST FLOUR)—CATHOLIC CENTRE — 1958 El. 56,286 / El. 52,291										
Comm.	(7,000)	(a)6,237	4,007	4,021	(a)3,868	5,981	(a)4,198	—	(a)7,847	—
Soc, Fed.	(8,900)	6,696	4,127	—	2,608	—	1,963	—	—	—
Rt Rad.	(5,900)	(a)7,089	—	—	—	—	—	—	—	—
MRP	(3,700)	2,207	9,150	—	4,631	—	2,584	—	—	—
Cons.	(13,200)	(c)10,884	(c)11,199	13,111	5,849	8,483	6,598 (unoff.)	—	—	—
Gaull.	(2,600)	—	9,182	21,698	(b)13,318	19,492	25,388	—	(a)30,129	—
Other	—	P6,463	—	—	—	—	345 ER	—	—	—

Gaull. dep. Sagette 1958, 1962 became Pompidou's second 1967. Other parties crumble.

	1951	1956	1958		1962		1967		1968	
CORRÈZE 2 (BRIVE)—DECHRISTIANIZED CENTRE — 1958 El. 60,608 / El. 61,552										
Comm.	(18,100)	(c)16,100	12,576	14,805	(a)12,669	21,471	10,996	—	(a)9,538	—
Soc.	—	(c)5,652	5,247	—	—	—	—	—	—	—
Rad.	(19,850)	(c)11,088	7,032	9,222	6,319	—	—	—	—	—
Other Lt	—	RR2,940	—	—	[a]6,713	—	15,215	27,396	(b)15,860	—
Cons., MRP	—	7,077	(d)8,014	—	4,876	—	—	—	—	—
Gaull.	(6,500)	—	10,769	23,748	11,266	22,169	(c)25,096	26,979	26,455	—
Other	—	P2,940	3,062	—	—	—	—	—	—	—

'Other Left' 1956 was Right-wing Rad.; 1962 was the Rad. of 1958. Note Communist decline.

	1951	1956	1958		1962		1967		1968	
HÉRAULT 3 (SÈTE)—MEDITERRANEAN PORT — 1958 El. 59,165 / El. 63,495										
Comm.	(13,900)	(a)16,316	12,239	13,676	(a)13,581	—	17,209	27,396	(c)16,177	22,636
Soc, Fed.	(7,800)	(c)8,360	(c)12,284	15,244	(a)11,313	24,281	11,806	—	(a)10,824	—
Rad, etc.	(4,700)	(c)2,352	—	—	—	—	—	—	—	—
MRP	(4,150)	(c)4,220	6,325	—	—	—	4,988	—	—	—
Cons.	(5,200)	2,110	—	—	3,026	1,216	—	—	—	—
Gaull.	(4,250)	—	7,643	16,905	(a)12,042	16,836	10,828	20,062	(a)21,920	26,176
Extr. Rt	—	P8,633	2,744	—	—	—	1,429	—	—	—
Other	(2,100)	(d)3,313 L	—	—	—	—	[a]2,139	—	—	—

Moch was Soc. till 1962. Other: Left RC 1951, also Left Rad. 1956 (Rad. was Right); in 1967, the ex-Gaull. member.

	1951	1956	1958		1962		1967		1968	

1958 El. 55,503 MAYENNE I (LAVAL)—CATHOLIC WEST El. 56,806

	1951	1956	1958		1962		1967		1968	
Comm.	(3,400)	4,621	3,608	—	3,989	—	(a) 5,044	—	(a) 4,188	—
Soc. Fed.	(4,300)	4,950	(c) 6,174	—	(a) 6,424	—	8,193	9,960	6,758	—
Rad.	(4,300)	4,037	—	—	—	—	—	—	—	—
MRP	(16,300)	(c) 14,437	(c) 25,333	—	[b] 25,635	—	(c) 16,310	15,154	9,238	—
Gaull.	(11,650)	(c) [8,175]	—	—	—	—	16,884	19,630	(b) 25,549	—
Other Rt	—	P 7,412	8,414	—	—	—	—	—	—	—
Other Lt	(280)	988	—	—	—	—	—	—	—	—

Ex-Gaull. stood 1956 as Cons.; MRP minister (R. Buron) replaced 1958 by his second who lost 1967; MRP crumbles.

1958 El. 49,850 NIÈVRE 3 (CHÂTEAU-CHINON)—EAST CENTRAL El. 45,575

	1951	1956	1958		1962		1967		1968	
Comm.	(11,400)	9,112	6,178	—	5,007	—	3,840	—	(a) 4,464	—
Soc.	(6,500)	(c) 7,785	8,774	10,483	(a) 7,068	—	—	—	—	—
UDSR	(6,800)	(c) 10,096	(c) 7,768	12,219	(a) 10,385	21,703	(c) 20,392	—	(c) 15,776	20,208
Cons.	—	3,930	12,940	15,318	3,480	—	—	—	—	—
Gaull.	(11,650)	(c) 3,093	—	—	5,800	10,510	12,008	—	15,698	17,326
Other	MRP (2,400)	(d) 5,192P	—	—	—	—	—	—	—	—

Two Cons. lists 1951, one allied with Gaull., one with Mitterrand (UDSR, later Fed. candidate).

1958 El. 55,187 PAS-DE-CALAIS I (ARRAS)—NORTHERN INDUSTRIAL El. 61,507

	1951	1956	1958		1962		1967		1968	
Comm.	(15,400)	(c) 14,581	11,143	8,285	(a) 11,362	—	(a) 13,816	—	(a) 11,956	—
Soc. Fed.	(10,800)	(c) 14,905	(c) 17,524	20,561	(c) 12,944	24,375	(c) 16,447	29,618	(c) 13,698	27,058
MRP	(5,350)	(c) 7,551	10,116	17,993	(a) 5,960	—	4,723	—	3,887	—
Gaull.	(7,100)	(c) [6,070]	—	—	14,233	21,810	17,883	22,259	(a) 20,869	24,796
Other	(d) (3,500)	P 4,661	(d) 7,280	—	—	—	—	—	1,533 PSU	

Ex-Gaull. stood 1956 as Cons. Other 1951 were two Cons., one pro-Mollet (as 1958 ?). Gaulls. endorse Mollet 1958.

1958 El. 66,108 HAUTES-PYRÉNÉES I (INCL. PART TARBES)—SOUTH-WEST El. 67,799

	1951	1956	1958		1962		1967		1968	
Comm.	(10,300)	(a) 11,770	7,809	7,512	7,874	—	9,712	—	(a) 8,323	—
Soc.	(5,400)	9,486	5,007	—	—	—	—	—	—	—
Rad. Fed.	(13,100)	(c) 17,161	(c) 18,282	21,629	(c) 19,845	30,283	(c) 21,392	33,196	(c) 17,367	26,340
MRP	(2,100)	3,351	6,420	—	(a) 2,911	—	5,539	—	12,627	25,486
Cons.	(12,700)	(c) 8,232	[P 573]	—	—	—	—	—	—	—
Gaull.	(3,450)		7,993	16,419	10,493	13,677	14,336	17,808	[a] 12,835	—

Billères (Catholic leader of Rad. party) losing ground. Same Gaull. 1962, 1968.

1958 El. 67,247 HAUT-RHIN I (COLMAR)—ALSACE El. 69,001

	1951	1956	1958		1962		1967		1968	
Comm.	(4,300)	5,028	2,872	2,159	(a) 2,604	—	3,889	—	(a) 2,995	—
Soc. Fed.	(7,350)	(c) 9,289	7,180	3,885	4,182	—	[a] 4,762	—	3,565	—
Rad.	(1,000)	5,447	—	—	—	—	—	—	—	—
MRP	(14,300)	(c) 23,453	(b) 22,676	20,135	9,614	—	16,536	—	14,603	—
Cons.	(1,550)		—	—	—	—	—	—	—	—
Gaull.	(17,500)	(c) 8,275	18,135	26,419	(c) 30,844	—	(c) 28,520	—	(c) 31,321	—

Gaullists not MRP gain from decline of Left and higher turnout. Same Soc. 1951, 1956, 1967.

1958 El. 65,714 SEINE 5 (PARIS, VIIe ARRONDISSEMENT)—LEFT BANK El. 52,022

	1951	1956	1958		1962		1967		1968	
Comm.	(10,200)	7,079	4,576	5,638	4,242	4,836	3,585	—	2,734	—
Soc. Fed.	(3,650)	(c) 3,770	3,731	—	2,546	—	4,118	—	1,669	—
Rad.	(2,800)	(c) 8,681	—	—	—	—	—	—	—	—
MRP	(3,450)	(c) 3,738	3,502	—	—	—	—	—	—	—
Cons.	(3,300)	[c] 21,014	(c) 24,968	37,934	(c) 15,121	16,111	(a) 16,049	19,761	14,327	18,067
Gaull.	(10,100)	1,619	9,893	—	17,621	21,152	17,983	19,526	17,790	18,816
Extr. Rt		P 3,144	—	—	—	—	—	—	—	—
Other Rt	(d) (4,000)	(d) 2,118	3,541	—	1,150	—	396	—	879	—
Other Lt	(840)	1,913	—	—	—	—	768 (Barbu)		568	—

Frédéric-Dupont, Cons. 1946–67, stood as Gaull. 1951; beat Couve de Murville 1967. Barbu stood for President 1965.

1958 El. 61,558 SEINE-ST DENIS 3 (AUBERVILLIERS)—PARIS SUBURBS El. 65,265

	1951	1956	1958		1962		1967		1968	
Comm.	(18,750)	(c) 27,564	[b] 23,233	25,409	(c) 28,278	—	(c) 31,601	—	(c) 27,036	—
Soc. Fed.	(4,000)	(c) 4,255	5,146	—	—	—	4,389	—	2,289	—
Rad.	—	4,639	—	—	—	—	—	—	—	—
MRP	(2,700)	(c) 2,999	6,511	—	3,345	—	2,554	—	4,300	—
Cons.	—	2,478	—	—	—	—	—	—	—	—
Gaull.	(12,650)	(c) 2,018	11,456	22,903	12,419	—	15,226	—	16,264	—
Extr. Rt	—	(d) 3,136	981	—	—	—	1,239	—	—	—
Other Rt	(d) (3,450)	1,752	1,183	—	—	—	—	—	—	—
Other Lt	(1,000)	1,956	—	—	—	—	—	—	2,274 PSU	

Waldeck Rochet, now Comm. leader, brought from provinces to this safe seat 1958.

TABLE 22. *Eight referendums and nine general elections, 1945–1969*

These results follow François Goguel's classification of the parties and their alliances. They are taken, in somewhat simplified version, from his tables in F. Goguel and A. Grosser, *La Politique en France* (Colin, 1964), pp. 269–77 and in the *Revue française de science politique*, vol. 17, no. 3 (June 1967), pp. 436–7 and vol. 18, no. 5 (October 1968), p. 840. (A few missing figures for 1967 and 1968 have been added by the author.) The figures are internally consistent, but differ slightly from my own classification in the earlier tables owing to different treatment of various minor groups such as dissident Gaullists or right-wing ex-Radicals; also the *seats* figure in this table includes overseas members who joined the main parties.

EIGHT REFERENDUMS

	Yes	No	Spoiled	Not voting
(1 a) 21 October 1945. (For a new constitution; Radicals *opposed*.)				
	17,957,868	670,672	1,025,744	4,968,578
% electorate	72·9	2·7	4·1	20·1
% votes cast	96·4	3·6		
(1 b) 21 October 1945. (For limiting the powers of the new Assembly; Communists and Radicals *opposed*.)				
	12,317,882	6,271,512	1,064,890	Same
	50·0	25·4	4·3	
	66·3	33·7		
(2) 5 May 1946. (For the first draft constitution, *proposed* by Communists and Socialists.)				
	9,109,771	10,272,586	513,054	4,761,717
	36·9	41·6	2·0	19·3
	47·0	53·0		
(3) 13 October 1946. (For the constitution of the IVth Republic; Comm., Soc., MRP *for*; de Gaulle *against*.)				
	9,002,287	7,790,856	336,502	7,775,893
	36·0	31·2	1·2	31·2
	53·5	46·5		
(4) 28 September 1958. (For the constitution of the Vth Republic; Communists and Radicals *opposed*.)				
	17,665,790	4,624,511	303,559	4,006,614
	66·4	17·3	1·1	15·1
	79·2	20·7		
(5) 8 January 1961. (For self-determination and provisional government of Algeria; Comms., Rads., some Right *opposed*.)				
	15,200,073	4,996,474	594,699	6,393,162
	55·9	18·3	2·1	23·5
	75·2	24·7		
(6) 8 April 1962. (For the Algerian independence treaty and powers to implement it; Extreme Right *opposed*.)				
	17,508,607	1,795,061	1,098,238	6,589,837
	64·8	6·6	4·0	24·4
	90·6	9·3		
(7) 28 October 1962. (For the direct election of the President; only Gaullists *for*.)				
	12,809,363	7,932,695	559,758	6,280,297
	46·4	28·7	2·0	22·7
	61·7	38·2		
(8) 27 April 1969. (For regional and second chamber reform; few but Gaullists *for*.)				
	10,512,469	11,945,149	635,678	5,562,396
	36·7	41·7	2·2	19·4
	46·8	53·2		

NINE GENERAL ELECTIONS

	Votes	% of electorate	% of votes	Seats
Communists and allies				
21 Oct. 1945	5,024,174	20·4	26·2	159
2 June 1946	5,145,325	20·8	25·9	153
10 Nov. 1946	5,430,593	21·6	28·2	182
17 June 1951	5,056,605	20·6	26·9	103
2 Jan. 1956	5,514,403	20·6	25·9	150
23 Nov. 1958	3,907,763	14·3	19·2	10
18 Nov. 1962	3,992,431	14·4	21·7	41
5 Mar. 1967	5,029,808	17·7	22·5	73
23 June 1968	4,435,357	15·75	20·0	34
Extreme Left				
23 Nov. 1958 (UFD)	261,738	0·9	1·2	—
18 Nov. 1962	449,743	1·6	2·4	—
5 Mar. 1967 (PSU)	506,592	1·8	2·3	4
23 June 1968 (PSU)	874,212	3·1	3·9	—

	Votes	% of electorate	% of votes	Seats
		Socialists		
21 Oct. 1945	4,491,152	18·2	23·4	146
2 June 1946	4,187,747	16·9	21·1	128
10 Nov. 1946	3,433,901	13·7	17·8	102
17 June 1951	2,744,842	11·1	14·6	107
2 Jan. 1956	3,247,431	12·1	15·2	94
23 Nov. 1958	3,193,786	11·7	15·7	44
18 Nov. 1962	2,319,662	8·4	12·6	66
5 Mar. 1967 (Fed.)	4,207,166	14·9	18·8	116
23 June 1968 (Fed.)	3,654,003	13·0	16·5	57
		Radicals and allies		
21 Oct. 1945	2,018,665	8·1	10·5	71
2 June 1946	2,299,963	9·3	11·6	52
10 Nov. 1946	2,136,152	8·5	11·1	69
17 June 1951	1,887,583	7·6	10·0	90
2 Jan. 1956 (Lt)	2,389,163⎫	9·3	11·3⎫	77
2 Jan. 1956 (Rt)	838,321⎭	3·1	3·9⎭	14
23 Nov. 1958	1,503,787	5·5	7·3	33
18 Nov. 1962	1,384,498	5·0	7·5	39
5 Mar. 1967 (in. Fed.)				
23 June 1968 (in Fed.)				
		MRP		
21 Oct. 1945	4,580,222	18·6	23·9	150
2 June 1946	5,589,213	22·6	28·2	166
10 Nov. 1946	4,988,609	19·9	25·9	173
17 June 1951	2,369,778	9·8	12·6	95
2 Jan. 1956	2,366,321	8·8	11·1	83
23 Nov. 1958	2,273,281	8·3	11·1	56
18 Nov. 1962	1,635,452	5·9	8·9	55*
5 Mar. 1967 (CD)	3,017,447	10·7	13·5	42*
23 June 1968 (CD)	2,700,864	8·2	12·2	27*
		Gaullists		
10 Nov. 1946	585,430	2·3	3·0	
17 June 1951	4,058,336	16·5	21·6	121
2 Jan. 1956	1,094,908	4·0	5·1	21
23 Nov. 1958	4,165,453	15·2	20·4	212
18 Nov. 1962	6,645,495	24·0	36·3	268
5 Mar. 1967	8,558,056	30·1	38·2	244
23 June 1968	10,201,024	36·1	46·0	358

(*Includes* new allies, esp. Republican Independents who had 35 seats in 1962, 44 in 1967 and 64 in 1968. In 1968 some of their candidates opposed the official Gaullist; the dissidents polled 537,419—included above.)

		Conservatives		
21 Oct. 1945	3,001,063	12·1	15·6	53
2 June 1946	2,538,167	10·2	12·8	67
10 Nov. 1946	2,487,313	9·9	12·9	67
17 June 1951	2,369,778	9·8	12·6	96
2 Jan. 1956	3,259,782	12·1	15·3	95
23 Nov. 1958	4,502,449	16·5	22·1	118
18 Nov. 1962	1,742,523	6·3	9·6	— (with MRP)
5 Mar. 1967 (in CD)				
23 June 1968 (in CD)				
		Extreme Right		
2 Jan. 1956 (Pouj.)	2,483,813⎫	9·2	11·6⎫	
2 Jan. 1956 (E.R.)	260,749⎭	0·9	1·2⎭	52
23 Nov. 1958	533,651	1·9	2·6	
18 Nov. 1962	159,682	0·5	0·8	
5 Mar. 1967	194,776	0·7	0·9	
		Not voting		Total seats
21 Oct. 1945	4,965,259	20·1		586
2 June 1946	4,481,749	18·1		586
10 Nov. 1946	5,504,913	21·9		618
17 June 1951	4,859,869	19·8		627
2 Jan. 1956	4,602,942	17·2		596
23 Nov. 1958	6,241,694	22·9		552
18 Nov. 1962	8,603,286	31·3		482
5 Mar. 1967	5,404,687	19·1		487
23 June 1968	5,631,892	20·0		487

* Including Conservatives.

Map 1. Income (1951) and agriculture (1954)

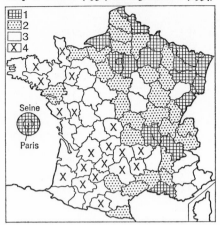

1. Income per head above national average.
2. Income above 85% of national average.
3. Income below 85% of national average.
4. Over 50% in agriculture (nat. av. 27%).

Rural France is poor.
For industry see no. 21.

Map 2. Catholicism and anticlericalism

1. Over 30% children in private (Church) primary schools, 1959.
2. Most adults attend Mass.
3. Minority of adults attend Mass.
4. Over 70% of voters petition against private schools bill, 1960.

Compare anticlericals with nos. 8 and 11.

Map 3. Electoral Turnout 1946–65

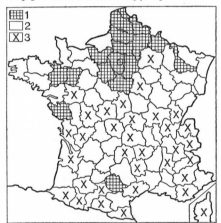

1. Always above national average.
2. Sometimes above national average.
3. Never above national average.
    (1st ballot 1958, 1962; both ballots 1965).

Workers and Catholics vote most, mountaineers least.

Map 4. Right and Left in III Republic

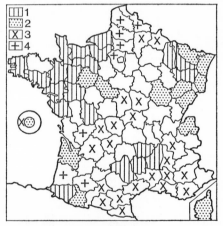

1. On Right since before 1900.
2. On Right since before 1940.
3. On Left since before 1900.
4. On Left since before 1940.

Compare nos. 8–12 (Left), 5–7, 13–20 (Right).

SOCIAL AND HISTORICAL BACKGROUND

Religion is an older and still stronger influence on voting than is occupation.

For names of departments see map 21, p. 301. The systems of shading on the political maps (5–20) differ sharply from one another. Changes in the political situation are indicated by changes in the shadings rather than by the appearance of the maps.

Map 5. Conservatives and MRP in IV Republic

1. Cons. over 20% 1951, 1956.
2. Cons. over 20% only 1956.
3. MRP over 20% 1951, 1956.
4. MRP over 20% only 1956.

MRP stronger in the most Catholic areas.

Map 6. 'Centre' and allies in V Republic

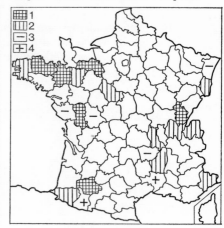

1. Over 25% 1967 and 1968.
2. Over 20% 1967 and 1968.
3. Over 20% 1967 only.
4. Over 20% 1968 only.

General decline, some recruitment from Rads.

Map 9. Socialists and Radicals in IV Republic

1. Soc. over 20% 1951, 1956.
2. Soc. over 20% only 1956.
3. Rad. over 20% 1951, 1956.
4. Rad. over 20% only 1956.

Rads. include all factions and allies. Both mainly rural.

Map 10. Left Federation in V Republic

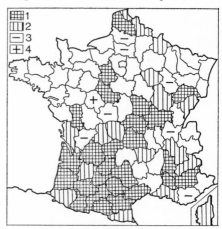

1. Over 25% 1967 and 1968 (incl. PSU).
2. Over 20% 1967 and 1968 (excl. PSU).
3. Over 20% 1967 only (excl. PSU).
4. Over 20% 1968 only (excl. PSU).

Weaker in industrial north *and* decline in traditional south.

OPPOSITION PARTIES

(*a*) All percentages of the vote (on the first ballot, except no. 11).
(*b*) Some departments had two or three constituencies in the IVth Republic; Seine and Seine-et-Oise split up in 1967–8.

Map 7. 'Centre' and extreme Right in presidential election (1965)

Map 8. The Opposition 1961–1962–1965

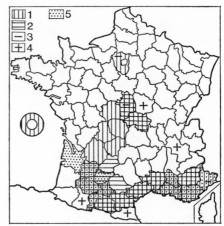

1. Lecanuet over 25% 5 Dec. 1965.
2. Lecanuet 20–25% 5 Dec. 1965.
3. Tixier over 7½% 5 Dec. 1965.
4. Poujadists over 15% 2 Jan. 1956.

Poujadists not a right-wing vote.

1. Over 30% NON 8 Jan. 1961 (self-determination).
2. Over 50% NON 28 Oct. 1962 (direct election).
3. In group 1 or 2 but for de Gaulle 19 Dec. 1965.
4. Not group 1 or 2 but for Mitterrand 19 Dec. 1965.
5. Over 12½% NON 8 Apr. 1962 (Algerian independence).

Compare Tixier's vote 1965 (no. 7) to NONS 8 Apr. 1962.

Map 11. Mitterrand for President (1965).

Map 12. Communists (1951–68)

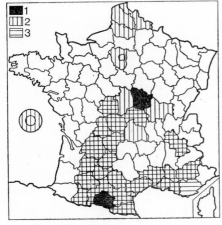

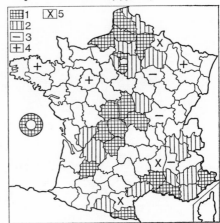

1. 50% 5 and 19 Dec.
2. 35% 5 Dec.
3. 50% 19 Dec.

See nos. 10 and 12; note weakness in industrial north.

1. Over 25% in IV and V Reps.
2. Over 25% in IV, 20% 1968.
3. Over 25% in IV, under 20% 1968.
4. Under 25% in IV, over 20% 1968.
5. Sometimes 25% in IV; over 20% 1968.

Note strength in rural centre and south.

OPPOSITION PARTIES

(c) Compare nos. 1 (wealth), 2 (religion), 4 (history), 21 (industry).

Map 13. Oui à de Gaulle (21 Oct. 1945 and 28 Sept. 1958)

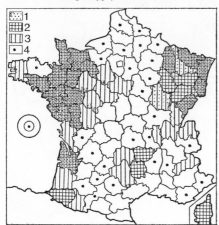

1. Over 70% 1945.
2. Over 85% 1958.
3. 80–85% 1958.
4. 75–80% 1958.

Two constitutional referenda; in both, Comms. and many Rads. opposed de Gaulle.

Map 14. Oui à de Gaulle (8 Jan. 1961 and 28 Oct. 1962)

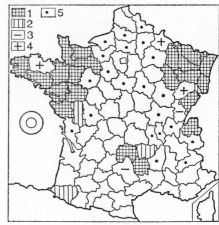

1. Over 80% 1961, over 70% 1962.
2. Over 80% 1961, 65–70% 1962.
3. Over 80% 1961, 60–65% 1962.
4. Under 80% 1961, over 65% 1962.
5. Under 80% 1961, over 60% 1962.

Comms., Rads., Right opposed 1961; also Socs., MRP, Cons. 1962.

Map 17. Gaullists 1951, 1958 (and Poujade)

1. Gaullists 25% on 17 June 1951.
2. Poujadists 20% on 2 Jan. 1956.
3. Gaullists 20% on 23 Nov. 1958.

Small overlap with Poujade (cf. no. 7). Strong in the north.

Map 18. Gaullists 1958 and 1962

1. 30% on 23 Nov. 1958.
2. 30% on 18 Nov. 1962.
3. 20% on 18 Nov. 1962 (& H-Alpes, Lozère).

Gaullists here *exclude* deputies who joined the party later.

DE GAULLE AND THE GAULLISTS

(a) Note the diminishing gap between de Gaulle's declining personal vote and his party's growing strength. The gap looks on this page less than it is because the shadings differ sharply between top and bottom maps.

Map 15. De Gaulle for President (1965).   Map 16. De Gaulle defeated (1969).

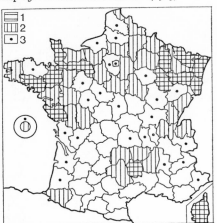

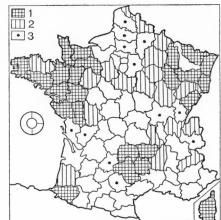

1. 50% on 5 Dec. 1965.
2. 55% on 19 Dec. 1965.
3. 50% on 19 Dec. 1965.

1. 50% Oui 27 Apr. 1969.
2. 46·8% Oui 27 Apr. 1969.
3. 45% Oui 27 Apr. 1969.

Note that shadings are comparable to nos. 19 and 20 but *differ* sharply from nos. 13 and 14.

Map 19. Gaullists 1967   Map 20. Gaullists 1968.

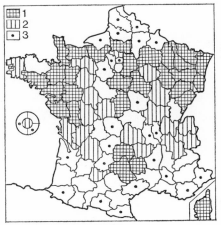

1. 50% on 5 Mar. 1967.
2. 40% on 5 Mar. 1967.
3. 30% on 5 Mar. 1967.

1. 50% on 23 June 1968.
2. 45% on 23 June 1968.
3. 40% on 23 June 1968.

Note that the shadings are comparable to nos. 15 and 16 but *differ* sharply from nos. 17 and 18.

DE GAULLE AND THE GAULLISTS

(*b*) All percentages of the vote on the first ballot.
(*c*) Some departments split, see p. 296, note (*b*).
(*d*) Compare nos. 1 (wealth), 2 (religion), 4 (history), 21 (industry).

Map 21. Distribution of industry 1954 (working population)

Map 21. Distribution of industry 1954 (working population)

Legend:

- ▦ Industry and transport over 50%
- ▥ Industry and transport over 40% nat.av.41%
- ◪ Intermediate
- □ Agriculture over 40% nat.av. 27·5%

Index

French names are indexed according to French practice: Bas-Rhin and Haut-Rhin under R, de Gaulle under G, Le Pen under L, Mendès-France under M. Organisations are indexed under their initials, grouped at the start of the first letter; thus DCF is the first entry under D. For their full titles see list on p. xiii.

Index

Decazeville, 135, 200
Defferre, Gaston, 95, 103, 106, 108, 117, 120, 157–8, 161–73, 182–9, 193, 207–8, 217 and n, 225, 231, 267, 274, 284–7, 290
Delbecque, Léon, 103, 104 and n, 108, 111–12
Democratic Party (US), 67, 69, 169; Advisory council of, 69
Denfert-Rochereau, 248
Dépêche du Midi, La, 46, 96, 120, 135, 194
Depreux, Edouard, 15, 151
Deux-Sèvres, 276
Dien Bien Phu, 5, 50 n, 61
Dieppe, 40 n
Diethelm, André, 28
Dijon, 77, 78, 81, 199, 252
Dixiecrats, 70
Dogan, Mattei, 82, 84
Dôle, 46
Donnybrook Fair, 65
Dordogne, 17 n, 78, 275, 276 n
Dorey, Henri, 21
Dorgères, Henri, 39, 55 n, 80
Dossier du Candidat, 212, 248
Douai, 217
Dreyfus affair, 75
Droit, Michel, 266
Drôme, 57 n
Dubedout, Hubert, 184–5
Ducatel, Louis, 285, 287
Duchet, Roger, 16, 51, 78, 90, 105–6, 110–11, 117
Duclos, Jacques, 46, 49, 95, 108, 284, 286–7
Duhamel, Jacques, 267, 276, 277, 285
Dunkirk, 278

EDC, 5, 52, 61
Economic development, 222–4; — policies, 4, 5, 30
Eden, Sir Anthony, 72
Edmond Rostand, Place, 243
Ehrmann, Professor H. W., 77 n, 80–4
Elbeuf, 276
Election alliances, 39–41, 50–76, 90–1, 116–18, 141, 162, 178, 182, 186–9, 208, 263–7; campaigns, 39–49, 51–2, 96–9, 118–21, 189–95, 209–12, 222–4; law, 10, 11 and n, 12, 15, 17 and n, 19, 50, 58 and n, 101–3, 177–8, 180–2, 205 and n, 216; *see also* Municipal elections, Presidential elections
Elysée, 107, 184, 228–9, 237, 240, 242–8
Employers, *see* CNPF
Encounter, 236 n
Enragé, L', 278
Epernay, 46
Est républicain, L', 49, 55, 203
Estier, Claude, 277
Eu, 40 n

Eure, 60, 199, 280
Eure-et-Loir, 276 n
Europe, —an, 24, 25 n, 37, 52, 136, 138, 168, 186, 188, 193, 196, 213; — Army, 5–6, 52, 62, *see also* EDC; — Coal and Steel Community, 4, 5; — Movement, 55, 188; — Union, 5, 55, 91, 192
Europe No. 1, *see* Radio
'European Liberal Party', 187
Evian agreement, 128–30, 135, 137
Evreux, 180
Express, L', 48–50, 53, 54 n, 56, 57 n, 60 and n, 165–6, 194

FEN, 247
FER, 232, 239
FGDS, 207–21, 224, 243, 249, 252–3, 258, 263–8, 272, 274–8 n
FLN, 6, 7 n, 88, 98–9, 101, 113–18, 122–3, 126, 128, 137, 158–60
FNSEA, 79, 194
FO, 121, 161, 229–30, 256, 262
Fanon, Frantz, 235
Faure, Edgar, 8, 18 n, 20, 29 n, 32, 39, 45, 46, 49, 50–8, 69, 72, 89, 108, 154, 206, 217, 235, 280
Faure, Maurice, 168, 188, 193, 199, 207–8, 217
Fauvet, Jacques, 77 n, 79, 82 n, 83
Fécamp, 40 n
Fifth Republic, 38 n, 87, 91, 100, 102, 104, 107, 114, 127, 136–9, 146, 159, 160, 166–71, 177, 180, 186, 204, 213, 229, 253, 273, 282, 284; Fifth Republicans (political coalition), 141, 206, 208, 220–1, 289
Figaro, Le, 49, 194, 240, 242, 260; — *littéraire*, 266
Fischer, John, 65 n, 70, 71, 72
Flandin, P. E., 16, 22, 31
Flins, 249, 269, 276
Fontanet, Joseph, 285
Fouchet, Christian, 229, 241, 244
Fouchier, Jacques, 265, 276
Fourth Republic, 4, 7, 8, 21 n, 26, 33, 64–76, 94, 95, 100, 102, 104, 108, 129, 133, 139, 140, 146, 159, 160, 166–7, 177, 182, 194, 213, 273, 284; fall of, 84, 87–95, 126, 157, 257, 273
France, regions of; *see* Votes
France-Avenir, 195
France-Référendum, 97, 118, 195
France-Soir, 49, 97, 118, 194
Franche-Comté, 276 n
Frédéric-Dupont, Edouard, 210, 291
Freemasons, 46 n, 83, 173, 183
French, P., 35 n
French Community, 99, 129; — Union, 32, 55, 91
Fréville, Henri, 180
Frey, Roger, 108, 180, 182, 195

306

Index

Index

Index